Deconstructing Archetype Theory

I0131062

This important book offers a critical and timely reassessment of one of the cornerstones of analytical psychology, Jung's concept of archetypes.

Exploring not only Jung's original writings but also the range of interpretations used by Jungian scholars today, the book argues that Jung's conceptualization of archetype theory is not a single coherent theory; rather, it is four different theories which must be understood separately. Roesler goes onto deconstruct these four ideas: the biological, the anthropological, the transcendental and the psychological in context with contemporary insights from each of these disciplines. A thorough analysis of the state of knowledge in the respective disciplines (i.e., biology, anthropology, religious and mythological studies) makes clear that the claims archetype theory makes in these fields have no support and should be given up. *Deconstructing Archetype Theory* concludes by arguing that a universal process of psychological transformation is the only part of archetype theory which should be maintained, as it provides a map for psychotherapy.

Rigorous and insightful, this is a book that will fascinate scholars and practitioners of analytical psychology, as well as anyone with an interest in Jung's original work.

Prof. Dr. Dipl.-Psych. Christian Roesler (1967) is Professor of Clinical Psychology at the Catholic University in Freiburg/D, Lecturer of Analytical Psychology at the University of Basel/CH and Associate Professor of Psychotherapy Sciences at the Sigmund Freud University/Austria. He is a Jungian psychoanalyst in private practice in Freiburg and member of the faculty of the C.G. Jung institutes in Stuttgart and Zürich. He has specializations in work with couples and families, applying interpretive research methods. He has research and publications on analytical psychology and contemporary sciences, couple counselling, postmodern identity construction, narrative research and media psychology.

Deconstructing Archetype Theory

A Critical Analysis of Jungian Ideas

Christian Roesler

Routledge
Taylor & Francis Group

LONDON AND NEW YORK

Designed cover image: Sandsun as rendered the owner on Getty Images

First published 2024
by Routledge
4 Park Square, Milton Park, Abingdon, Oxon OX14 4RN

and by Routledge
605 Third Avenue, New York, NY 10158

Routledge is an imprint of the Taylor & Francis Group, an informa business

British Library Cataloguing-in-Publication Data
A catalogue record for this book is available from the British Library

Library of Congress Cataloging-in-Publication Data
Names: Roesler, Christian, 1967– author.
Title: Deconstructing archetype theory : a critical analysis of Jungian ideas / Christian Roesler.
Description: Abingdon, Oxon ; New York, NY : Routledge, 2023.
Identifiers: LCCN 2023008615 (print) | LCCN 2023008616 (ebook) | ISBN 9781032390505 (hardback) | ISBN 9781032390499 (paperback) | ISBN 9781003348191 (ebook)
Subjects: LCSH: Jung, C. G. (Carl Gustav), 1875–1961. | Jungian psychology.
Classification: LCC BF173.A25 R64 2023 (print) | LCC BF173.A25 (ebook) | DDC 150.19/54—dc23/eng/20230510
LC record available at https://lccn.loc.gov/2023008615
LC ebook record available at https://lccn.loc.gov/2023008616

ISBN: 978-1-032-39050-5 (hbk)
ISBN: 978-1-032-39049-9 (pbk)
ISBN: 978-1-003-34819-1 (ebk)

DOI: 10.4324/9781003348191

Typeset in Times New Roman
by Apex CoVantage, LLC

Contents

Chapter 1

Introduction

If we go back to Jung's original formulations of the archetype, we do not find a consistent definition. So today, we first have to ask the question: To what does the term archetype refer?

Even though the concept of the archetype has to be considered as central to AP, from the beginning, there has been controversy around its theoretical and empirical foundations. Jung always made great efforts to show that his conceptualization of the archetype was firmly based in biology (e.g., Jung, CW 18, para. 1228).[1] There have been many attempts to formulate new theoretical foundations for arguing for universal archetypes, but no fully satisfying theoretical conceptualization is at hand. As a consequence, there is no consensus on how archetypes are defined in contemporary AP. I agree with Mills, who states:

> Jung failed to make this clear. And Post-Jungian schools including contemporary Jungian movements have still not answered this most elemental question. As a result, there is no clarity or consensus among the profession. The term archetype is thrown about and employed, I suggest, without proper understanding or analysis of its essential features. . . . The most basic theoretical tenet of the founding father of the movement is repeatedly drawn into question within postclassical, reformed, and contemporary perspectives to the degree that there is no unified consensus on what defines or constitutes an archetype. This opens up the field to criticism – to be labeled an esoteric scholarly specialty, insular self-interest group, Gnostic guild, even a mystic cult. Jungianism needs to rehabilitate its image, arguably to modernize its appeal to other academic and clinical disciplines.
>
> (Mills 2018, p. 1)

As the concept of archetypes, together with the concept of a collective unconscious, can be called the core concept of AP, which distinguishes it from other schools of psychotherapy and psychoanalysis, the confusion about the definition is an intolerable situation. There is a strong need to redefine and reconceptualize archetype theory so that AP can make use of a generally accepted theory, which is in accordance with contemporary insights in other disciplines, namely, biology, genetics, psychology, anthropology, cultural studies and the neurosciences.

DOI: 10.4324/9781003348191-1

Despite these inconsistencies, we find, beginning with Jung and continuing throughout the practice of AP, a typical use of the concept, which is based on an understanding of archetypes as universal patterns producing meaning and guiding development. This is the basis for the practice of Jungian psychotherapy which counts on the fact that, through a special relationship like the analytical one, archetypes will constellate and will guide the process of therapeutic development and that these archetypes can be found in every human being. Seen from this point of view, the defining element of universality becomes the most central for the archetype concept, and it becomes clear why Jung made enormous theoretical efforts to secure this element and why he relied on biological explanations to do so. Now for more than two decades, this biological explanation of how archetypes come about has been seriously called into question, and Jung's viewpoints of innatism and preformationism have been demonstrated to be refuted. This results in the situation that even recent approaches cannot satisfactorily explain the universality of such complex archetypes. Yet the theory and practice of AP are based on the belief that the whole set of universal archetypes can be found, at least as a potential, in every human being. This creates a serious situation; the theoretical foundations for the practice of AP have collapsed. Not enough with that, it seems to me that large parts of the community do not even care about this situation or have only limited awareness of it.

In my opinion, AP is currently being confronted by the problem of being founded on a concept for which the original explanatory theory has evaporated. The question to be answered is this: How do these patterns that we call archetypal, and on which we base much of our theory as well as our clinical practice, come about? And what actually are they, how can they be defined, what do they contain, what are their effects, etc.?

Some schools of Jungian therapy might say that the concept of archetypes in the aforementioned sense is not so fundamental to the practice of AP and that there are many Jungians who do not even use the concept anymore. That may be so but would then raise the question of what differentiates these practices from other schools of psychodynamic psychotherapy.

Some schools, such as archetypal psychology, for example, might not even see a problem here. Interestingly, an argument based on a transcendental definition of archetypes would give a coherent explanation for the existence of even very complex archetypes if the basic assumption is accepted that there are more factors influencing reality than just the causal factors of classical physics, or, to be more precise, of the deterministic model of sciences. It would mean accepting the view that the archetypes influencing the analytical process come from a transcendental sphere and would place Jungian therapy in the field of religious practices, which I must admit makes a lot of sense (see Roesler & Reefschläger 2022). Nevertheless, there is an ongoing debate among Jungians attempting to solve the problem formulated earlier in a way that would allow us to preserve the concept of archetypes while maintaining a place for it in the field of normal science.

For Jung, his theory was not to just a theory but a strong belief based on his personal inner experience, which could not only explain individual psychological development but became something like a "Welterklärungstheorie" (world explanation), which could explain the similarities and differences of peoples and cultures, yes, even the development of mankind. As a consequence, the conceptualization of archetype theory he presented contains far-reaching statements and claims regarding matters in anthropology, prehistory/palaeoanthropology, religion, comparative mythology, etc., which, as I will demonstrate, are based on highly problematic theories established in the 19th century which were incorporated into AP and are still continued today. It seems as if in the decades since Jung, there has been no updating of these ideas and theories inherent in archetype theory in relation to the development and contemporary state-of-the-art of disciplines, like anthropology, comparative mythology, comparative religion, prehistoric studies, etc. Sometimes it appears as if AP had totally lost contact to these disciplines so important for the ideas contained in archetype theory. This neglect results in a widespread ignorance of the developments in the respective disciplines, which amounts, lastly, to a certain arrogance, as if other sciences had nothing to do with AP or could easily be ignored. In so far, the discomfort stated by Trevi (1992), although it may sound harsh, still provides a correct picture of the situation of AP:

The discomfort I am talking about can assume various forms: that of an uneasiness with some unsolved contradictions in AP itself; that of a refusal of the constant turning into ontology of the origin of the metaphorical language of AP; that of a refusal of the typical ahistorical suspension typical of AP that never established any fruitful exchange with those problems of the philosophical, anthropological, and methodological thought which during the same years had appeared and established themselves; that of the suspicion caused by the divorce that AP continuously maintains towards those empirical observations coming from other fields of psychological research, or that, on the contrary, of the repudiation of it's all too easy syncretistic way of uncritically accepting everything, thus destroying the essential character of AP; that of the doubt about the distance between its theoretical hypothesis and their practical applications; that of a diffidence about a field which has never consistently faced a radical, or even pitiless, rethinking of its foundations; that of a nausea for the careless, superficial and uncritical use of the comparative method in the de-metaphorization of the images of fantasy or of dreams without any care for historical or cultural differentiation: that of the suspicion for all too easy a recourse to the therapeutic practice, or to a recourse to experiences either purely emotional, or of a dangerously parapsychological nature and thus banally suggestive; the discomfort, finally, of a repugnancy for a linguistic and hence theoretical carelessness in most of the scientific production which goes under the name of AP.

(Trevi 1992, p. 356)

As a result, AP has lost contact to the wider field of academic sciences relevant for its topics and is caught in a state of isolation. It is also interesting to note that this state of affairs has been criticized as early as the 1970s, and even many of the points that will be presented in this investigation have been made for decades, seemingly without much effect on the larger community. It seems to me that this is due to a certain attitude which started with Jung but has continued since then in the Jungian community.

Of course, for many developers of scientific theories, their ideas are supported by strong beliefs, but in Jung, this is heightened to an extreme. Even though he points out the fact of the "personal equation", I want to argue here that in his own case, he was not able to consider that and to distance himself, at least from time to time, from his own ideas; to at least try to take a neutral stance, what in academia is called scientific scepticism; and to discuss it openly – in the sense of being open for criticism and for corrections. It became a creed, and consequently, when he presented his ideas to the public, it came close to a preaching. This has to do with the fact that Jung's ideas and concepts were so closely linked with his own experience. For him, it was a kind of truth, and thus, he was not interested in finding evidence for his theories or was unwilling to accept criticism.

My hypothesis is that in his time, and still today, followers are drawn to his ideas because there is a certain need to have a belief in such a "holistic" creed. There is no doubt that there has been a lot of publication activity on these problems, especially in Jungian scientific journals, and many of the points I am making here have already been discussed, e.g.:

> Jungian analysts cannot get around the "Jung cult" argument started off by Richard Noll (1994) simply by attacking its author. . . . there is sometimes an excessive deference shown in Jungian groups to analysts in general, and to senior analysts in particular, a deference which it is quite often hard to justify in terms of the productivity and output of those individuals. . . . This means that something has got attached to seniority, chronological seniority, as much as professional seniority, which urgently needs critique.
>
> (Samuels 1998, p. 17)

Yet my impression (e.g., from teaching at training institutes and in the Router Program of the IAAP) is that outside of more academic circles in the Jungian community concerned with science and research, there is still a strong tendency to idealize Jung and to cling to very classical positions in AP and to a conservative reading of Jung's works. It seems to me that the differentiated state-of-the-art in critical publications has not had a strong reach into the Jungian community. It seems to me to be even worse: there seems to be an attitude of superiority, which can be found in Jung as well as in many of his followers today, in the sense that their model of how the psyche develops and how psychotherapy works is ultimate, as if they were in possession of the truth about the psyche. This has led to reification and ontologizing of concepts which originally were just a personal experience of Jung's. This attitude of superiority has also led to a tendency to isolate themselves against insights, findings and ideas from other disciplines.[2]

From my point of view, AP as a scientific theory as well as the theoretical culture within the Jungian community are in a bad state: even after more than 100 years, there is no consensus about even the definition of the core concept of AP, the archetypes, and the debate about this concept refers frequently to completely outdated theories and concepts from psychology and elsewhere. Again, this has been pointed out by Jungian scholars for many years:

> We run the risk of working with increasingly outdated and inaccurate models of the human mind if we avoid subjecting them to the rigour of scientific scepticism, for fear that the numinous or spiritual will be destroyed by the scientific advances in understanding the way the mind actually works.
>
> (Knox 2001, p. 616)

There is general agreement that Jung's works are full of contradictions, and a lot has already been written about that:

> Jung repeatedly insisted that he did not have a theoretical system of his own. In so far, as he claimed that his ideas were not theoretical abstractions but founded on his own direct clinical experience, he did not feel compelled to present them as a neat system with their own logical coherence, which would enable his readers to access them easily. This close relationship between Jung's theory and practice could account for the fact that his writings are accepted as lucid and indeed inspirational by some and as incomprehensible by others.
>
> (Papadopoulos 1992a, p. XIV)

As this author points out, Jung, on the one hand, relied heavily on his own inner experience in formulating his psychological ideas and concepts, while on the other hand, he was desperately trying to avoid being seen as a philosopher, as he wanted to be regarded a scientist. Consequently, many of his ideas and concepts are presented by him in the fashion of nomothetic statements, as empirically grounded insights, if not truths. There is no doubt that Jung was innovative in how he introduced introspection into the forming of a psychological theory, but his repeated claims that his findings should be regarded as hard empirical facts frequently leads into aporia. My impression is that this tendency, to be not aware of the inherent tensions and contradictions in AP, continues up to the present day. Many Jungian authors, when confronted with this problem, argue that this was a conscious and deliberate strategy by Jung and indeed ingenious and that his paradoxical statements should be seen as a new form of doing psychology. From my point of view, this is a glorification of Jung's inability to clarify basic epistemological and scientific standpoints. What I am trying to point out in the following is that there is confusion on Jung's side, that this is not a systematical strategy in Jung's writing but a failure to see the limitations of his own thinking and that the eternal glorification of Jung in the sense that he was deliberately – and indeed ingeniously – paradoxical has to be regarded as a defensive strategy in the Jungian community. I would argue that this attitude in Jung as well as in the community is at the root of the still ongoing and severe theoretical problems that we have today in AP, the lack of a consensual definition of archetypes, a resistance against considering theoretical developments and insights in relevant disciplines and against a testing of the theory in the sense of research. My hypothesis is that at the core of all this is a certain attitude, which again can be connected with Jung's personality but which continues in Post-Jungian developments up to the present day. This style of doing science in Jung formed attitudes and a certain mindset in the community of Jungians. This attitude includes (a) the belief that in the development of the person, everything comes out of the individual, which (b) leads to the consequence that there is, in Jung as well as in AP today, the lack of a coherent theory of interpersonal relationships and their impact on development and especially how this relates to archetype theory, which has consequences for clinical work. This attitude includes (c) a lack of willingness or even resistance against testing one's own theories (because they are regarded as an inner truth) by confronting them with insights from other disciplines, which (d) has as a consequence that the method of gaining insight as well as the resulting theories become unscientific. As a consequence, it is, at least from my point of view, no wonder that Jungian psychology has been more or less ignored by academical psychology, which is often interpreted by Jungians as bad will, whereas to me as a scientist, it makes, at least partly, a lot of sense. This state of affairs is in direct opposition to the strategy proposed by the IAAP to reconnect AP with academia, manifested, for example, in a series of joint conferences with universities all over the world.

My intention here is not to focus on Jung as a person. As any other human being, he was subject to inner contradictions, conflicts, ambivalences and blind spots. These aspects are only relevant in so far as they have an impact on the forming of theory in AP in his time, with consequences up to the present day. This has to be made the subject of discussion even more because of the aforementioned tendencies to idealize Jung as a person. This can be seen, for example, in the fact that we are, in comparison to Freudian psychoanalysis, still more occupied with Jung as a person than with his theory. It is actually not customary in Jungian circles to speak about Jungian psychology as a scientific theory. However, it would be important to see Jung's work as a compilation of scientific concepts and ideas which can, in general, be criticized. This means we have to differentiate between the person and his assumed intentions on the one side and theoretical elements, schemas and figures of thought that can objectively be found in Jung's works. There has in fact been an extensive discussion in recent years about the foundation of Jung's thinking and his concepts, but it seems to me that the reach of these discussions in the international Jungian community should not be overestimated. I can say at least for the German-speaking countries that publications on Jungian concepts do not often take into account contemporary insights in relevant disciplines, and teaching at the institutes is often restricted to very classical positions without any reference to recent developments; and from my experiences with teaching in other countries, I have often had the impression that the situation there is even worse.

The problematic state of affairs in AP culminates in archetype theory. The present book is based on an investigation into archetype theory, aiming at reformulating the theory, which was financed by the IAAP and conducted by the author in cooperation with the Institute of Applied Research at Catholic University Freiburg. As a first step, a survey was conducted with experts in the field of archetype theory, asking them to provide answers to a number of questions regarding the definition of the concept, explanatory theories of how archetypes come about, whether they are seen to be universal, etc. The results demonstrate that the lack of a consensual definition in the community is confirmed; a variety of different definitions and explanations of archetypes was presented which are, at least partly, incompatible (Roesler 2022).[3]

This lack of a consensual definition for the concept of archetype presents a major problem within AP. Henceforth, I will not attempt to provide the said definition here. In my book *C. G. Jung's Archetype Concept* (Roesler 2021), I have summarized what could be called the classical or mainstream position in Jungian psychology. Although I have pointed to some contradictions and problems in Jung's works concerning the archetype in that earlier publication, it focusses on the development of the concept in the mainstream of Jungian psychology as well as on the applications. In the following, I will refer to this earlier book when pointing to definitions, concepts and examples from the classical viewpoint.

In contrast to this earlier work, in the present investigation, Jung's ideas regarding the archetype were traced throughout his works in the sense of a historical and critical analysis (in the tradition of what Michel Foucault has called discourse analysis). The aim is to reconstruct the lines of thought that are inherent in Jung's theories around the term archetype. This analysis will be based on Jung's own statements in the complete works as well as in other publications (e.g., *Memories, Dreams, Reflections*). I will demonstrate that these lines of thought are continued in the mainstream of AP to the present day. Following this theoretical reconstruction – which is in some sense also a deconstruction – the background of Jung's thoughts will be illustrated by referring to influential theories and authors that were of importance for the development of Jung's thoughts.

In this context, it might be interesting for Jungian readers to know that starting in 2012, a team of researchers at Vienna University is now compiling a historical-critical Sigmund Freud Edition, which has already produced some insights in how some of the central concepts of Freud's psychoanalysis came about (Diercks & Skale 2021). This historical-critical method was first applied to the works of Nietzsche, starting in the 1960s, whereby Colli and Montinari edited the complete works of Nietzsche (1967ff.) together with a critical commentary. This was then followed by the critical commentary edited by the Heidelberg Academy of Sciences in 2012. The same method was applied to the critical edition of the works of Heidegger. I think such a historical-critical investigation into the works of Jung, which would include a critical commentary on how the texts came about, what were the influences, etc., is highly needed. The investigation presented here attempts to provide such an analysis with a special focus on archetype theory, but of course, there may be much more to be said about this central element of Jung's thought.

Following the reconstruction of Jung's thoughts and ideas around the concept of archetypes in his works, the criticism which has been directed to this theory and the problems inherent in the concept are summarized, bringing together critics from inside as well as from outside of AP.

As a major conclusion from this analysis, I will demonstrate that inherent in Jung's theory of archetypes are actually four different theories, which in Jung's writings are confused with each other, and this confusion can serve as an explanation for many of the problems outlined previously. So as a step towards clarification of the concept, I recommend to differentiate these four theories from each other, as they are dealing with separate fields of knowledge. Jung attempted throughout his life to bind these four theories together into one coherent theoretical account, which, as I will point out, is impossible and is the reason behind the problematic state of archetype theory we are confronted with today.

These theories in Jung make statements and claims referring to the fields of biology, anthropology, history of religion, palaeoanthropology and comparative mythology. So in the following chapters, I will deal with these disciplines in detail. I will try to summarize the state of the debate in the respective discipline and confront it with Jung's statements and claims in his theory of archetypes. At the end of each chapter, I will summarize the conclusions resulting from this confrontation. In general, it can be concluded that large parts of classic archetype theory have to be regarded as refuted, as they are not in line with the insights and findings in the respective disciplines.

In the final chapter, I will point out what will remain of archetype theory as well as directions for future research in AP.

Notes

1 Jung is quoted throughout this text by referring to the *Collected Works*' volume and paragraph, e.g., CW 7, 460.
2 In a new German publication (Loomans 2020), this attitude of superiority, of being in possession of the truth, is investigated by comparing Jung's psychology and Karlfried Graf Dürckheim's initiatic therapy.
3 The complete report contains detailed data and findings as well as supplementary material.

Chapter 2

Definitions of "archetype" in AP

In this chapter, I will provide an overview of definitions of the concept of archetype, as they were presented in AP in the last decades. The aim is to demonstrate that there is a lack of consensus regarding the definition of this most central concept, which parallels the results of the survey.

Historically, there is a strong tradition in AP that authors follow Jung's argumentation in that they view archetypes as being rooted in biology. Namely, that they are instincts or patterns of behaviour – a viewpoint which is often linked with the notion that archetypes are genetically transferred. An outstanding protagonist of this viewpoint is certainly Anthony Stevens, who linked Jung's theories around the archetype with his concept of evolutionary psychiatry:

> Archetypes are understood as neuro-psychic units, which are formed through natural selection and which are responsible for the determination of behavioural characteristics as well as for the typical human emotions and cognitive experiences.
>
> (Stevens & Price 1996, p. 6)

Gordon (1985) provides a comprehensive account of this viewpoint while fully adopting Jung's biological viewpoint, albeit pointing out the confusion that Jung created through his casual use of terms:

> There is frequently a confusion between the first three mental functions – archetype, image and symbol – and Jung himself has often been guilty of encouraging such confusion, at least as far as his casual use of these terms is concerned. . . . Thus, when he wrestled with the concept of the archetypes he described them as psychosomatic entities whose physical expression is instinctual action, reaction and behaviour, while their mental expression is in the form of images. . . . It seems that he already then (1938) recognized the considerable kinship between his thoughts about instincts and archetypes and the ethologists' concepts of the pattern of behaviour and of the innate release mechanism (IRM), concepts which link the biological to the psychological functions. . . . They seem to exist as potential

DOI: 10.4324/9781003348191-2

images which then programme the organism to respond in a certain manner when it encounters an object or situation that matches this potential image.

(p. 120)

Humbert (1988) gives a sketch of the interesting idea that Jung was hinting at an idea which was not yet available to Jung's time – the concept of information – while, at the same time, adopting Jung's view that archetypes are innate:

> The role Jung attributed to archetypes is perfectly intelligible, if one uses the concept of information theory: (1) archetypes condition, orient, and support the formation of the individual psyche according to a plan that is inherent to them; (2) whenever the psyche is disturbed, archetypes intervene by considering information received either from the psyche itself or from the environment; (3) archetypes ensure an exchange of information between the psyche and its surroundings. Let me add that for Jung, and he was not hesitant on this point, the archetypes are inscribed in the body in the same way that all organs of information are inscribed in living matter. This implies, among other things, that archetypes are genetically transmitted.
>
> (p. 101)

I would also like to add a definition provided by Michael Fordham, which does not really depart from Jung's notions but expands the archetype concept to the development of the child:

> By conceiving archetypes as dynamic structures closely related to drives, expressed in impulses originating in neurophysiological structures and biochemical changes, the theory of archetypes brings body and psyche together and makes Jung's thesis as to their bipolarity particularly meaningful: the archetypes are unconscious entities having two poles, the one expressing itself in instinctual impulses and drives, the other in spiritual forms. In contrast to the instinctual drives, which are relatively fixed and few in number, the spiritual component has wide and flexible application. Transferring this idea to childhood and starting from the spiritual components, the theory of archetypes means that a predisposition exists in the child to develop archaic ideas, feelings and fantasies without their being implanted in him or without his introjecting them.
>
> (Fordham 1976, p. 5)

In *Jung Lexicon*, Daryl Sharp (1991) provides a definition, which closely follows and includes all the relevant ideas in Jung's works. Nancy Krieger's (2019) highly comprehensive account of the different definitions, as well as her attempt to create some order, is a more recent example of an author who closely follows Jung's classical definitions. While the previously quoted definitions are more than 30 years old, this is also a good example for the tendency of uncritically adopting Jung's different definitions and argumentations around the archetype concept in contemporary publications. In comparison, the definition provided by Patricia Berry in 2021, accessible on the website of the IAAP (https://iaap.org/archetype-2/), is much more careful in the claims made.

The aforementioned definitions attempt to defend Jung's statements and viewpoints. In my first book (Roesler 2021), I have attempted to provide a comprehensive overview of this classical position in archetype theory and its developments in the debate in AP. In contrast to this, a Post-Jungian definition, provided by Andrew Samuels (1990), gives the following account:

> Archetypal theory has also been rethought. A radical change has taken place in what we require of an image before we call it archetypal. Archetypal images no longer have to be large, impressive, or decorous; **what is archetype is to be found in the eye of the beholder and not in a particular image itself** (highlighted by C.R.). We can set aside preconceived schemes or hierarchies of archetypes; the archetype of experience is a state of mind. . . . We do not have to get hung up on the question of transpersonal, invisible, unknowable, noumenal, skeletal, crystalline, hypothetical so-called structures, held to be somehow deeper than ordinary human experience and imagery.
>
> (Samuels 1990, p. 295)

In contrast, George Hogenson (2009) attempted to not depart too far from Jung's original definitions and preserve a certain link to biology, as well as the behavioural sciences; he thus proposed understanding the archetype as an "elementary action pattern" (Hogenson 2009, p. 325). Hogenson played an important role in the development of the emergentist position in archetype theory (see chapter "Biology, genetics and inheritance").

Jungian scholar Pietikainen (1998) suggested a radical departure from the discussion about innateness and proposed that, with the help of Cassirer's approach, archetypes could be understood as "culturally determined functionary forms, organizing and structuring certain aspects of man's cultural activity" (Pietikainen 1998, p. 325).

Van Meurs (1990) provides an overview of the use of the term archetype in literary criticism and mentions the following interesting definition:

> Northrop Frye acknowledged the influence of Jung on his theory of literary myths, and he borrowed the term archetype from him. But symbols, myths, and archetypes are for Frye strictly literary concepts. He means by an archetype a typical or recurring image. . . . The symbol which connects one poem with another and thereby helps to unify and integrate our literary experience.
>
> (p. 243)

A perspective from object relations theory: Lambert (summarized in Papadopoulos 1992, Vol. 2, p. 197)

> accepts the archetype as a predisposed potential in the psyche to expect that real objects when presented to the individual can be experienced in accordance with certain forms, patterns, or images to be found in the average expectable

environment. This average expectable environment is the term used by object relations theorists to account for the context of relationships with real objects.

To get an overview of the definitions that are currently circulating in AP, a systematic survey was conducted as part of the research project. In this survey, experts from Jungian psychology, who have published on archetype theory, were asked to provide short texts defining the term archetype. These definitions are grouped around recurrent themes or concepts in archetype theory (see research report for details, Roesler 2021): Definitions

- which generally argue that archetypes are very basic, typical patterns, predispositions and capabilities common to all men/universal; often, there is a reference to cross-cultural similarities in art, religion, ritual and social practices provided as "evidence", or to the concept of anthropological universals
- which are closely linked with biological argumentations and/or ethology/behavioural biology, preserving the definition of archetypes as instincts/pattern of behaviour, as innate, as genetically transmitted, etc.
- of the kind: archetypes are contentless forms which shape human perception into definite images and ideas but also behavioural patterns
- which include the last conceptualization but that add a viewpoint of dynamic systems theory, stressing the aspect of self-organization of the psyche, as well as the interaction of individual and environmental factors
- which argue with highly formal (e.g., mathematical or probabilistic) characteristics; in some cases, they refer to ideas in the context of the Pauli-Jung-dialogue:
- philosophical conceptualizations: archetypes are formal categories given a priori that provide the basis for human perception and action; often, these definitions make references to Aristotelian metaphysics, Kantian categories or Platonian ideas
- transcendental conceptualizations in the broadest sense
- a category of argumentations which strongly emphasize the limitations to know anything about archetypes, stress the quality of unknowing, etc.

There is one general conclusion that can be drawn from the analysis of the contributions from the Jungian experts: there is definitely no consensus on how the term archetype should be defined, but there is a great variety of viewpoints, which represents a large scope of differing and, in some ways, also incompatible epistemological viewpoints. Another general finding is that they all take up or point to lines of thoughts or figures of argumentation, which can already be found in Jung. Therefore, in the next step, the analysis will turn to Jung's original texts and how he defines or theorizes around the concept of archetype.

Chapter 3

The theory of archetypes in Jung's works

In 1912, Jung published *Wandlungen und Symbole der Libido* (later revised as *Symbols of Transformation*, CW 5), in which he investigates the fantasies of a young woman and, for the first time, describes these based on what he later named as archetypal patterns. This was also the point at which he clearly departed from Freud's psychoanalysis and started to form his own AP. It is shown here how basic the concept of archetype is in AP. In this publication, Jung examines the parallels between the fantasy images of a young woman and mythological themes, for example, the myth of the hero. His first usage of the term archetype appeared in 1919:

> In this deep level we find the a priori, innate forms of intuition, namely the archetypes of perception and cognition, which are the necessary a priori determiners of all mental processes.
>
> (Jung 1919, in CW 9/1)[1]

Before that, and synonymously throughout his works, Jung also uses the term pre-image, primeval or primordial image; other terms used by Jung are "symbolic formulae" and "structural dominants".

In the "Definitions" from 1921, Jung refers to the term archetype under the heading image (CW 6, pp. 759–773), which means a fantasy image, the product of unconscious fantasy activity. These fantasy images have an archaic character.

> On a primitive level, that means in the mentality of the primitive the inner image projects easily as a vision or a hallucination, without being pathological.
>
> (CW 6, 759)

This image is a concentrated expression of the total psychological situation not only of unconscious contents but also of those that are momentarily constellated. The constellation comes about through the activity of the unconscious itself, which is stimulated by the current situation of consciousness. Archaic images have a

DOI: 10.4324/9781003348191-3

striking similarity with mythological motifs, which are, therefore, named collective unconscious.

> The primeval image, which I also called archetype, is always collective, which means it is at least shared by whole peoples or epochs. Probably the main mythological motifs are common for all races and times; so I was able to identify a series of motifs of Greek mythology in the dreams and fantasies of mentally insane thoroughbred negroes. From a causal viewpoint of natural sciences one can understand the primeval image as a mnestic engram (Semon) which has formed through compression of countless, similar experiences. In this sense it is the precipitate and therefore a typical basic form of a certain, always repeated psychological experiencing. . . . In this perspective it is the psychical expression of a specific physiological-anatomical heritage, a very predisposition.
>
> (CW 6, 760)

Jung expands that the form of these psychological images cannot merely be the result of the observation of processes in nature (e.g., the rising and setting of the sun and moon). This could not, he argues, explain the allegorical/symbolical use of these images. On the other hand, as in the quote earlier, he illuminates that he sees the archetypes as being formed by experiences of early humans repeated again and again, by typical experiences of humanity. However, according to Jung, these are not experiences in the outside world but more in the inner world of the psyche, which may be only activated by external events. Therefore, the archetypes provide a picture of the inner world of humans and not of their environment.

Furthermore, Jung argues for a biological and hereditary basis of the archetypes. We will see that in Jung's works, there are different lines of argumentation concerning this biological basis; one is the idea that the interindividual and intercultural similarity of archetypal patterns come about through the common similar brain structure shared by all humans:

> We therefore have to assume that the given structure of the brain is not only an effect of natural conditions . . . The given form/structure of the organism is therefore a product on the one hand of external conditions and on the other hand of the inherent specifications of the living itself.
>
> (CW 6, 761)

The primeval image is, therefore, the precondition on which observations in nature and their perceptions receive their order. The primeval image is also the precondition for ideas: the image in its appearance as a symbol takes over the task to connect undifferentiated perceptions and psychological states with feelings/emotion. It is, therefore, a mediator.

> The primeval image . . . is a living organism, gifted with the power of generation, because the primeval image is an inherited organization of

psychological energy, a fixed system, which is not only expression, but also precondition of the processing of energy. It characterizes on the one hand the way, in which the energetic process since primeval times has taken place again and again in the same manner, on the other hand it enables also again and again the lawful process, by enabling the apprehension or psychological perception of situations in a way, so that life can continue. It is therefore the necessary counterpart to the instinct, which is appropriate action, but also a meaningful and appropriate apprehension of the relevant situation. This apprehension of the given situation is secured through the a priori existent image.

(CW 6, 761)

What can already be clearly deduced from this early text is the outline of the concept and the central elements of Jung's theories around the concept of archetypes. I would even argue that the main elements of the concept were present in Jung's thought well before that. They can be found in *Symbols of Transformation* and were then confirmed through his own experiences during his crisis after the break with Freud. These elements are the following:

- the a priori nature of archetypes, which means that they are given to the human mind before there are any experiences
- they are fully unconscious and were never conscious, so they were never an element of conscious experiencing (in strong contrast to Freud's conception, who assumed that unconscious material consists mainly of formerly conscious experiences which then were repressed, with the exception of the so-called primal fantasies)
- they are organizers of perception and behind the formation of ideas and psychic images (CW 8, 403)
- they appear first and of all as images
- they are collective, so they are similar over all times, epochs and peoples
- they link modern humans with archaic humans in prehistory and with the history of nature in general
- they channel emotion and psychic energy
- they have a biological basis and are, somehow, parallel to instincts in animals

The archetype is pure, unvitiated nature, and it is nature that causes man to utter words and perform actions whose meaning is unconscious to him, so unconscious that he no longer gives it a thought. [. . .] In view of the findings of modern psychology it cannot be doubted that there are preconscious archetypes which were never conscious and can be established only indirectly through their effects upon the conscious contents. There is in my opinion no tenable argument against the hypothesis that all the psychic functions which today seem conscious to us were once unconscious and yet worked as if they were conscious.

We could also say that all the psychic phenomena to be found in man were already present in the natural unconscious state.

(CW 8, 412)

This quote adds two more elements to the basic features of Jung's archetype concept: Jung assumes that the primary state of the psyche is unconscious, which means that during development, consciousness develops from a general primary state of unconsciousness. On the other hand, there is the idea that this collective unconscious, which contains the archetypes, has a certain direction, aim or even intention (see next section on process).

Universality

The perhaps most important characteristic of Jung's concept of the archetypes is their universality, which means that they are shared by all humans, regardless the time and place (CW 9/I, 273). This thought is highly important for Jung's argumentation in that they can reappear spontaneously in every individual at any given time, namely, in the case of psychopathology. Following this, it is highly important for his concept of the psychotherapeutic process because this is based on the assumption that the process is guided by archetypes. Jung counts on the existence and availability of all the archetypes in every human being. The universality aspect is also significant concerning Jung's explanation for similarities in cultural habits, mythologies and religious ideas.

> [there exists a] psychic system of a collective, universal, and impersonal nature which is identical in all individuals. This collective unconscious does not develop individually but is inherited. It consists of pre-existent forms, the archetypes, which can only become conscious secondarily and which give definite form to certain psychic contents.

(CW 9/I, 90)

Archetypes are archaic and link modern humans to prehistory and archaic humans

Basic to Jung's concept is the idea that archetypes have developed in the prehistory of humans, hence, their archaic character (**arche**-type). They are a heritage that has come upon us modern humans from earlier times (CW 7, 104).

> the unalterable structure of a psychic world.

(CW 9/1.451)

In some sense, they are our archaic nature and link us to our ancestors in prehistory.

> Over the whole of this psychic realm there reign certain motifs, certain typical figures which we can follow far back into history, and even into prehistory.

They seem to me to be built into the very structure of man's unconscious, for in no other way can I explain why it is that they occur universally and in identical form.

(CW 16, 254)

Just as the body has an anatomical prehistory of millions of years, so also does the psychic system. And just as the human body today represents in each of its parts the result of this evolution, and everywhere still shows traces of its earlier stages – so the same may be said of the psyche.

(CW 9/I, 348)

These archaic patterns are thought of by Jung to be closer to nature. Respectively, the presence of archetypes, the collective unconscious that we all have access to, enables modern humans to lead a more wholesome life.

It throws a bridge between present-day consciousness, always in danger of losing its roots, and the natural, unconscious, instinctive wholeness of primeval times.

(CW 9/1, 293; see also the term "archaism" in CW 6, 754)

There exists the idea in Jung that the archetypes have formed over thousands of years in prehistory as **a precipitation of experiences** of early man. They are "residues, or engrams" (CW 7, 158); therefore, arche-**type** ("A typos [imprint]", CW 18, 80).

Where do these archetypes or primeval images come from. It seems to me that their development can not be explained other than that we assume, they are precipitates of continually repeated experiences of mankind. . . . The archetype is a preparedness to reproduce again and again the same or similar mythic ideas. It seems therefore, as if what is impregnated into the unconscious, is solely the subjective fantasy stimulated through the physical process.

(CW 7, 109; see also quote earlier p. 12, CW 6, 760;
Jung & Meyer-Grass 2008, p. 162)

There are as many archetypes as there are typical situations in life. Endless repetition has engraved these experiences into our psychic constitution.

(CW 9/I, 98)

A biological conception: Innateness and instinct

It has already become clear that the innateness idea of archetypes is central to Jung. In the first publication in which he used the term "archetype" (Jung 1919), Jung explicitly speaks of the archetype as "the a priori *innate* forms of intuition" (italics added). Almost in every instance, where Jung defines or describes the term archetype, he points to his conviction that they are innate. To be more precise, Jung assumes that archetypes are similar to instincts; they form our instinctual nature. Jung equalizes his archetypes with the term pattern of behaviour from ethology, which he also uses synonymously with the term instinct. In Jung, the archetype is an innate pattern of perception and behaviour, which influences human perception and action and shapes it into similar forms.

In his text "Instinct and the unconscious", Jung (1919, CW 8) expands the idea that there is a close connection between the concepts of archetype and that of instinct in more detail:

> He argues that instincts are typical forms of behaviour. Wherever there are similarly repeated forms of reaction this can be described as an instinct (273). Whereas the instincts in humans motivate them to specific human behaviours, the archetypes force the perception of the outside world into specific human images and concepts; in this sense the archetypes are regulators or determinants of human perception (177). It should be noted that there is a difference in Jung's theories of instinct and archetype, albeit a close correlation. Later, as we will see, Jung synonymously uses the terms instinct/pattern of behaviour and archetype. In his paper from 1919 Jung summarizes, that in the same way as every human has instincts, as do they also all have primeval images/archetypes. The collective unconscious is the sum of all their instincts and their correlates, the archetypes (281).

> this term does not relate to an inherited experience, but rather presuppositions of experience, an inherited mode of mental functioning, corresponding to inherent ways in which the chicken hatches an egg, the bird builds its nest, a certain type of wasp strings the motor ganglion of a grub, and eels find their way to Bermuda and so on . . . in other words, it is a pattern of behaviour [English term in the original German version]. This aspect of the archetype, the completely biological aspect, is the only object of scientific psychology.
>   (Jung, CW 18, 1228; similarly, CW 8, 404; CW5, 158; CW 9/I, 136)

An important implication of this perspective is the viewpoint that humans are not born as a tabula rasa/blank slate, an assumption that was very dominant in Jung's time during the newly arising behaviourism. As a consequence to this belief, there exists the important idea by Jung of a preformation of the psyche:

> Man possesses many things which he has never acquired but has inherited from his ancestors. He is not born as a tabula rasa, he is nearly born unconscious. But he brings with him systems that are organized and ready to function in a specifically human way, and these he owes to millions of years of human development. . . . Man brings with him at birth the ground plan of his nature, and not only of his individual nature but of his collective nature. These inherited systems correspond to the human situations that had existed since primeval times;

youth and old age, birth and death, sons and daughters, fathers and mothers, mating, and so on. Only the individual consciously experiences these things for the first time, but not the body system and the unconscious.

(CW 4, 728; see also CW 8, p. 435; CW 5, 224)

The meaning of the archetype

Jung uses somewhat mysterious descriptions or definitions about the relations between instinct and archetype and how they manifest themselves in the psyche (e.g., the image represents the meaning of the instinct, and the archetype is the self-depiction of the instincts in the psyche) (CW 8, 277).

Instinct and the archaic mode meet in the biological conception of the "pattern of behaviour". They are, in fact, no amorphous instincts, as every instinct bears in itself the pattern of its situation. Always it fulfils an image, and the image has fixed qualities. . . . Such an image is an a priori type. It is inborn . . . prior to any activity, for there can be no activity at all unless an instinct of corresponding pattern initiates and makes it possible. This scheme holds true of all instincts and is found in identical form in all individuals of the same species. The same is true also of man: he has in him these a priori instinct types which provide the occasion and the pattern for his activities, in so far as he functions instinctively. As a biological being he has no choice but to act in a specifically human way and fulfil his pattern of behaviour. This sets narrow limits to his possible range of volition, the more narrow the more primitive he is, and the more his consciousness Is dependent upon the instinctual sphere. . . . They are not just relics or vestiges of earlier modes of functioning; they are the ever present and biologically necessary regulators of the instinctual sphere, whose range of action covers the whole realm of the psyche and only loses its absoluteness when limited by the relative freedom of the will. We may say that the image represents the meaning of the instinct.

(CW 8, 398)

the archetypes are the unconscious images of the instincts themselves, . . . they are patterns of instinctual behaviour.

(CW 9/I, 91)

Jung's pupil Jolande Jacobi (1986) provides an attempt of explanation in her over-view of Jungian psychology:

The archetypal image could be described as self-depiction of the instincts in the psyche, as a picture turned to a mental process, as a basic pattern of human behaviour. An Aristotelian would say: the archetypes are images formed from the experience of real fathers and mothers. A Platonian would say: the archetypes have first become fathers and mothers because they are pre-images, the prototypes of phenomena. The archetypes are formed a priori for the individual, originating from the collective unconscious and therefore excluded from a sense of individual becoming or fading away.

(p. 51)

As I understand Jung here, he tries to put forward the following idea: the instincts in animals are activated by typical signals or situations (inborn release mechanism/IRM in ethology) and can be seen as an appropriate reaction to this situation, an adaptation to the requirements set by the environment – which is a very Darwinian form of argument. Parallel to these instincts in animals, he sees the archetypes in humans as a system which prepares the person for an appropriate reaction to a certain situation in their environment. It is, in some sense, an adaptive, wholesome form of behaviour in harmony with nature; and nature can be understood here both as environmental requirements as well as the requirements of man's own psyche. And instead of the inborn release mechanism of ethology, Jung assumed that the parallel in the archetype is an image, as for example, in the following quote:

These inherited systems correspond to the human situations that have existed since primeval times. I have called this congenital and pre-existent instinctual model, or pattern of behaviour, the archetype.

(CW 4, p. 728)

See also von Franz: "The form and the meaning of instincts are represented in the images produced by the archetypes" (von Franz 1980, p. 81).

Therefore, archetypes are and appear primarily as **images** (CW 8, 440). Jung originally even used the term image instead of archetype (e.g., "Definitions", CW 6). The idea outlined earlier that the archetype activates a preformatted behaviour pattern as an adaptation to certain typical situations (which humans have been confronted with again and again since prehistory) relates to the **idea of a release mechanism** by which Jung again attempts to parallel the archetype with the concept of pattern of behaviour:

In any situation of panic, whether external or internal, the archetypes intervene and allow a man to react in an instinctively adapted way, just as if he had always known the situation: he reacts in the way mankind has always reacted.

(CW 18, p. 368)

The term image is intended to express not only the form of the activity taking place, but the typical situation in which the activity is released.

(CW 9/I, p. 152; see also CW 10, p. 547)

Identical brain structure

When reasoning about the question of how the biological basis of these archetypal patterns can be specified, Jung often argues with the **identical brain structure** that is shared by all humans:

> They are inherited with the brain structure – indeed, they are its psychic aspect.
>
> (CW 10, p. 53; also, CW 6, 748; CW 7, 109)

Untouched by experience and never been conscious before

Jung describes "the collective unconscious" as psychic contents that have "**never been in consciousness, and therefore have never been individually acquired**, but owe their existence exclusively to heredity" (CW 9/I, 88).

This describes the meaning of the term **a priori**, which Jung uses repeatedly to characterize the archetypes. In general, it means that archetypes are present before there is any personal experience which could shape the mind. In that sense, archetypes are untouched by experience, they also do not change through experience and most importantly, they are first and foremost unconscious and have never been conscious before (CW 9/I, 265).

> The collective unconscious is a part of the psyche which can be negatively distinguished from the personal unconscious by the fact that it does not, like the latter, owe its existence to personal experience and consequently is not a personal acquisition.
>
> (CW 9.1, 88)

> were there before any invention was thought of. They represent the unalterable structure of a psychic world.
>
> (CW 9/1, 451)

> absolute unconscious which has nothing to do with our personal experience. This absolute unconscious would then be a psychic activity which goes on independently of the conscious mind and is not dependent even on the upper layers of the unconscious, untouched – and perhaps untouchable – by personal experience.
>
> (CW 8, p. 311)

But, in point of fact, typical mythologems were observed among individuals to whom all knowledge of this kind was absolutely out of the question, and where direct derivation from religious ideas that might have been known to them, or from popular figures of speech, was impossible. Such conclusions forced us to assume that we must be dealing with **autochthonous revivals** independent of all tradition, and, consequently, that myth forming structural elements must be present in the unconscious psyche.

(CW 9/I, p. 259)

[unconscious phantasies] of an impersonal character, which cannot be reduced to experiences in the individual's past and thus cannot be explained as something individually acquired. These fantasy-images undoubtedly have their closest analogues in mythological types. We must therefore assume that they correspond to certain collective (and not personal) structural elements of the human psyche in general, and, like the morphological elements of the human body, are inherited. Although tradition and transmission by migration certainly play a part, there are . . . very many cases that cannot be accounted for in this way and drive us to the hypothesis of "**autochthonous revival**".

(CW 9/I, 262)

Autochthonous revival

The **idea of autochthonous revival of archetypal elements** is absolutely crucial for Jung's psychology ("they can rearise spontaneously, at any time, at any place, and without any outside influence", CW 9/I, 153) since his psychotherapeutic method is based on his conviction that these elements are reactivated in the form of images within the clients' mind in the course of the psychotherapeutic process.

I therefore took up a dream-image or an association of the patient's, and, with this as a point of departure, set him the task of elaborating or developing his theme by giving free rein to his fantasy. This, according to individual taste and talent, could be done in any number of ways, dramatic, dialectic, visual, acoustic, or in the form of dancing, painting, drawing, or modelling. The result of this technique was a vast number of complicated designs whose diversity puzzled me for years, until I was able to recognize that in this method I was witnessing the spontaneous manifestation of an unconscious process which was merely assisted by the technical abilitiy of the patient, and to which I later gave the name "individuation process".

(CW 8, 400)

On the other hand, Jung finds evidence for the workings – the autochthonous revival – of archetypal patterns in the **creative productions of his patients**:

The chaotic assortment of images that at first confronted me reduced itself in the course of the work to certain well-defined themes and formal elements, which repeated themselves in identical or analogous form with the most varied individuals. I mention, as the most salient characteristics, chaotic multiplicity and order; duality; the opposition of light and dark, upper and lower, right and left; the union of opposites in a third; the quaternity (square, cross); rotation (circle, sphere); and finally the centring process and a radial arrangement that usually followed some quaternary system. . . . The centring process is, in my experience, the never-to-be-surpassed climax of the whole development, and is characterized as such by the fact that it brings with it the greatest possible therapeutic effect. . . . I can only say that there is probably no motif in any known mythology that does not at some time appear in these configurations. If there was any conscious knowledge of mythological motifs worth mentioning in my patients, it is left far behind by the ingenuities of creative fantasy. In general, my patients had only a minimal knowledge of mythology.

(CW 8, 401)

Archetypes and psychopathology

The concept of archetypes developed resulting from Jung's psychiatric experience with psychotic patients and their fantasies in the "Burghölzli" hospital. He experienced cases where psychotic patients developed fantasies, which were parallel to motifs from ancient mythology. The most important case in this respect is the so-called "solar phallus man", a patient at "Burghölzli" who told Jung about a phallus coming out of the sun which produces the wind. Jung was extremely surprised by this since he had just translated an ancient Egyptian text which included the same image (speaking about the solar phallus man):

> This observation is not an isolated case: it was manifestly not a question of inherited ideas, but of an inborn disposition to produce parallel images, or rather of identical psychic structure as common to all men, which I later called the archetypes of the collective unconscious. They correspond to the concept of the pattern of behaviour in biology.
>
> (CW5, 158)

> The archetype does not proceed from physical facts, but describes how the psyche experiences the physical fact, and in so doing the psyche often behaves so autocratically that it denies tangible reality or makes statements that fly in the face of it.
>
> (CW 9/1, 260)

Later, he assumed that behind the psychopathology in psychosis and schizophrenia was a breakthrough of the collective unconscious, which appears as "archaic drives in combination with mythological images" (CW 8, graph 281). So an important idea is that archetypes shape the fantasies, even the symptoms in psychopathological disorders, especially in psychosis and in all forms of paranoia. Archetype theory originally was an attempt to explain the imagery of psychosis, based on Jung's and Bleuler's innovative approach to the treatment of schizophrenia, namely, to assume that there is meaning behind these fantasies, and for therapeutic purposes, it is important to get access to an understanding of these ideas and images. But not only in psychosis do the archetypes act as an explanatory model. Jung also assumes that archetypes underlie and form the basis of personal complexes:

> The conscious then comes under the influence of unconscious <u>instinctual</u> impulses and contents. These are as a rule complexes whose ultimate basis is the archetype, the "instinctual pattern".
>
> (CW 8, para. 856)

> Because of its instinctual nature, the archetype underlies the feeling-toned complexes and shares their autonomy.
>
> (CW 10 para. 847)

In general, Jung's explanatory theory of psychopathology using the archetype concept is based on the idea that the psychological disorders, especially the psychotic disorders, have to do with a lack of differentiation of consciousness from the collective unconscious, respectively, archetypal forces. If consciousness is not capable of separating from the collective unconscious/archetypal powers, it is somehow overrun, and fantasy production is dominated by archetypal patterns. The need to separate from and differentiate from the archetypes is not just a matter in psychopathology; it applies to all human development.

Primitivism/archaism

In the following, the view on the general process of human development will be further examined. Individual development is linked, according to Jung, to the idea that the problem of differentiation of consciousness from the collective unconscious can also be found on the level of the development of humanity from prehistoric times – a concept termed the homology of phylogeny and ontogeny (for details, see chapter "Anthropology"). To be specific, there is the idea of a primitive or developmentally early state of mind in which consciousness cannot differentiate between the productions of the person's own inner world and experiences in the outer physical world. Jung calls this "identity", a term which must be differentiated from the contemporary psychological term identity, in the sense of a self-concept. To Jung, the meaning is more or less the same as fusion, in the sense of an absence of differentiation. In this state of mind, the person cannot reflect upon his or her inner world; there is no observer position regarding the inner world. Jung goes as far as claiming that this primitive state of mind is generally to be found in what he calls primitive peoples, as well as in certain psychopathological states of mind in modern humans, namely, when projections of unconscious content appear. These two are equated in Jung's theory. For these states, he makes use of Levy-Bruhl's

(1912) concept of "participation mystique", which he quotes over 50 times in his works (e.g., CW9/I, 226).

> Our mentality is still so primitive that only certain functions and areas have outgrown the primary mystic identity with the object. Primitive man has a minimum of self-awareness combined with a maximum of attachment to the object; hence the object can exercise a direct magical compulsion upon him. All primitive magic and religion are based on these magical attachments, which simply consist in the projections of unconscious contents into the object. Self-awareness gradually developed out of this initial state of identity . . . Although the men of antiquity no longer believed that they were red cockatoos or brothers to the crocodile, they were still enveloped in magical fantasies. In this respect, it was not until the Age of Enlightenment that any essential advance was made.
>
> (CW 8, 516)

> The definiteness and directedness of the conscious mind are qualities that have been acquired relatively late in the history of the human race and are for instance largely lacking among primitives today. These qualities are often impaired in the neurotic patient, who differs from the normal person in that his threshold of consciousness gets shifted more easily; in other words, the partition between conscious and unconscious is much more permeable. The psychotic, on the other hand, is under the direct influence of the unconscious.
>
> (CW 8, 134)

> The archetype is pure, unvitiated nature, and it is nature that causes man to utter words and perform actions whose meaning is unconscious to him, so unconscious that he no longer gives it a thought. . . . all unconscious functioning has the automatic character of an instinct, and that the instincts are always coming into collision or, because of their compulsiveness, pursuing their courses unaltered by any influence even under conditions that may positively endanger the life of the individual. As against this, consciousness enables him to adapt in an orderly way and to check the instincts, and consequently it cannot be dispensed with. Man's capacity for consciousness alone makes him man.
>
> (CW 8, 412; also, CW 9/1, 293; CW 6, 770)

Although Jung stresses the point that he sees the archetypes as rooted in the biology of humans, meaning human behaviour is strongly directed by instinctual patterns or energies, the central topic of his psychology is the question of how humans can develop out of these limitations and become free to make their own choices and live a conscious life. This is, as Jung sees it, the major aim of the individuation process as well as of psychotherapy/analysis: to become conscious of the unconscious and of archetypal factors influencing the personality, thus liberating the mind from solely being something natural. Therefore, Jung calls analysis and individuation an "opus contra naturam".

> In the psychic sphere, as we have seen, the will influences the function. It does this by virtue of the fact that it is itself a form of energy and has the power to overcome another form. . . . But at the (permitting such an expression) upper limit of the psyche, where the function breaks free from its original goal, the instincts lose their influence as movers of the will.
>
> (CW 8, 379; similarly, CW 8, 386)

In this sense, Jung agrees with Freud that where there was unconsciousness, there shall be consciousness.

Cross-cultural similarities in patterns, myths, rites and religious beliefs

Strongly connected with the idea outlined earlier, of a primitive state of mind which is undifferentiated from the archetypes/collective unconscious, there is the idea that the archetypes are behind cross-cultural similarities in patterns, beliefs, mythological motifs, etc., as they can be found in anthropology – at least Jung claims that there are such similarities (e.g., CW 5, 419). This is due to an "inherited tendency of the human mind to form representations of mythological motifs" (CW 8, 523; see previous section, CW 6, 760, and "autochthonous revival", CW 9/I, 160 and 259–262).

> Mythological research calls them "motifs"; in the psychology of primitives they correspond to Lévy-Bruhl's concept of "representations collectives", and in the field of comparative religion they have been defined by Hubert and Mauss as "categories of the imagination".
>
> (CW 9/1, 89; also, CW 8, 402; CW 18, 80)

> The archetype is a preparedness to reproduce again and again the same or similar mythic ideas.
>
> (CW 7, p. 109)

Archetypes are connected to emotionality

For Jung, the term archetype is strongly connected with the term image; archetypes appear primarily as images. However, as he points out, these images are not abstract but loaded with emotions, which gives them their energy to influence human fantasy production and behaviour (CW 18, 257; CW 9/II, 34; CW 9/I, 4). In this context, he also uses the term "numinous" to describe the strong emotional impact archetypes can have on a person, meaning both fascinating and intimidating (tremendum et fascinosum). It could be said that archetypes are channels for emotions or psychic energy in general, which give the energy a certain shape and direction.

> It would be an unpardonable sin of omission were one to overlook the feeling-value of the archetype. This is extremely important both theoretically and therapeutically. As a numinous factor, the archetype determines the nature of the configurational process and the course it will follow, with seeming fore-knowledge, or as though it were already in possession of the goal to be circumscribed by the centring process.
>
> (CW 8, 411)

> if the image is charged with numinosity, that is, with psychic energy, then it becomes dynamic and will produce consequences.
>
> (CW 18/1, 589)

Archetypes as psychic organs

In this regard, archetypes can also be seen as psychic organs (CW 11, 845), which means they are part psyches which have their own life and energy, yes, even a certain amount of intentionality (CW 9/I, 271).

> They are as well feeling as they are thought; yes, they have even their own, independent life, somehow like that of partial souls.
>
> (CW 7, 104)

> a self activating organism.
>
> (CW 6, 754)

> Archetypes were, and still are, living psychic forces that demand to be taken seriously, and they have a strange way of making sure of their effect. Always they were bringers of protection and salvation, and their violation has as its consequence the "perils of the soul" known to us from the psychology of primitives. Moreover, they are the unfailing causes of neurotic and even psychotic disorders, behaving exactly like neglected or maltreated physical organs or organic functional systems.
>
> (CW 9/1, 266)

Archetypes and religion

As archetypes activate strong emotions and are connected with experiencing the feeling of (what Jung calls by referring to Rudolf Otto) numinosity and thus have "determining effects upon the conscious mind" (CW 9/I, 451), they are closely linked to religious feelings and beliefs. They are even thought to be behind the development of religion itself, as in the last quote earlier, which implies that the gods who are worshipped are the archetypes themselves. In "Definitions" (CW 7, 108), Jung provides as an example the idea of energy and how it influences the concept of magic in religions. Specifically, as Jung argues, the "primitives" had an idea of primitive energetics, the general idea of a magical force. At the core of this effect, which produces religious feelings as well as in effect religion itself, is the fact that archetypes transmit meaning, which is a central term in Jung's psychology. The archetypes are important for psychic life since they connect the person to a sense of meaning in life (CW 8, 415). This idea is connected in Jung with the concept of psychic wholeness as the goal of the individuation process.

> There is a mystical aura about its numinosity, and it has a corresponding effect upon the emotions. It mobilizes philosophical and religious convictions in the very people who deemed themselves miles above any such fits of weakness. Often it drives with unexampled passion and remorseless logic towards its goal and draws the subject under its spell, from which despite the most desperate resistance he is unable, and finally no longer even willing, to break free, because the experience brings with it a depth and fullness of meaning that was unthinkable before.
>
> (CW 8, 405)

> The essential content of all mythologies and all religions and all isms is archetypal.
>
> (CW 8, 406)

> Archetypes are complexes of experience that come upon us like fate, and their effects are felt in our most personal life.
>
> (CW 9/1, 62)

As an example:

> Rebirth is an affirmation that must be counted among the primordial affirmations of mankind. These primordial affirmations are based on what I call archetypes. In view of the fact that all affirmations relating to the sphere of the suprasensual are, in the last analysis, invariably determined by archetypes, it is not surprising that a concurrence of affirmation concerning rebirth can be found among the most widely differing peoples.
>
> (CW 9/1, 207)

The archetype even has an *a priori* knowledge of its aim which comes close to supernatural forces: "that the archetypes have about them a certain effulgence or quasi-consciousness, and that numinosity entails luminosity" (CW 8, 388; see also CW 8, 411; CW 9/I, 68). In these definitions, archetypes are regarded as independent, purposeful entities, similar to spirits or gods. This idea is as important to Jung's psychology, as it is mysterious. It implies that in a person, there is an additional consciousness, wisdom or intentionality besides ego consciousness, which knows well before there is any conscious self-reflection the aim of the person's development. This leads to the process idea at the core of archetype theory (see next section).

The archetype as such: Structure/form without content

As a consequence to critique coming mainly from biologists that his biological conception of the archetypes was not based on contemporary insights in biology (see Chapter 5), Jung introduced a further differentiation in 1947 between the archetype as such and its concrete manifestations. Jung points out that the archetype is devoid of content. Only a general structure is represented, which organizes content or information (CW 9/I, 6 and 155; CW 7, 101). It could also be called a general attractor. To illustrate this aspect, Jung uses the structure of a crystal:

> Their form is comparable with the lattice system of crystal, some of which pre-forms in certain ways the structure of the crystal in the mother liquor (the archetype per se), without itself having a material existence. This existence appears first in the manner of the shooting of ions and molecules. The lattice system determines simply the biometric structure, but not the concrete form of the individual crystal . . . and just as the archetype possess . . . an invariable central meaning, which constantly only in principle and not in a concrete form, determines how it appears.
>
> (Jung, CW 9/1, 95)

> The archetypal representations (images and ideas) mediated to us by the unconscious should not be confused with the archetype as such. They are very barren right structures which all point back to one essentially irrepresentable basic form. . . . We must, however, constantly bear in mind that what we mean by archetype is in itself irrepresentable, but has effects which make visualizations of it possible, namely, the archetypal images and ideas.
>
> (CW 8, 417)

> There are as many archetypes as there are typical situations in life. Endless repetition has engraved these experiences into our psychic constitution, not in the form of images filled with content, but at first only as forms without content, representing merely the possibility of a certain type of perception and action.
>
> (CW 9/I, 98)

Based on the differentiation between the archetype as such and its manifestations, it becomes clearer that archetypes are factors which organize experience, perception and also inner processes into definite forms. The conscious experience is unconsciously informed by archetypes; they "give definite forms to the contents that have already been acquired" (CW 15, 81). In the last end, the archetype itself is indescribable:

> The intellectual judgement always seeks, naturally, to assess their uniqueness and thus get past the essence, because above all the only thing about their nature which can be assessed, is their ambiguity, their almost immeasurable wealth of meaning, which each clear formulation makes impossible.
>
> (Jung, CW 9/1, 80)

References to philosophy

In contrast to his assumptions about mythological motifs and religious beliefs being archetypal, Jung makes references to philosophy by assuming that archetypes are basic categories of human thought, reason and perception. Here, Jung draws on a tradition of German philosophy – a line of thought, which has always assumed that there are *a priori* categories of perception, that the human mind contains universal forms which shape human perception and reasoning.

> From these references it should be clear enough that my idea of the archetype – literally a pre-existent form – does not stand alone but is something that is recognized and named in other fields of knowledge.
>
> (CW 9/1, 90)

Jung is clearly influenced by Kant's philosophy, which also emphasizes that time, space and causality are a priori forms of apperception ahead of any actual experience. Jung says explicitly that archetypes are "similar to the **Kantian categories**" (CW 10, 10; also, CW 9/I, 160); they are "categories analogous to the logical categories which are always and everywhere present as the basic postulates of reason . . . Categories of the imagination" (CW 11, pp. 517–518).

Jung, on the other hand, is an outspoken Platonian and equals his concept of archetypes with **Plato's ideas** in several of his writings. He says they are positioned in no real place but in a transcendental sphere: "the eternal ideas are primordial images, which are stored in an otherworldly place as transcendent forms" (CW 9/1, 68; also, CW 8, 388). The true archetype is not accessible by consciousness but is of a transcendental nature and even has an *a priori* knowledge of its aim.

> Archetype is an explanatory paraphrase of the Platonic εἶδος. . . . we are dealing with archaic or – I would say – primordial types, that is, with universal images that have existed since the remotest times.
>
> (CW 9/1, 5)

As a numinous factor, the archetype determines the nature of the configurational process and the course it will follow, with seeming fore-knowledge, or as though it were already in possession of the goal to be circumscribed by the centering process.

(CW 8, 411)

The ideas or respective archetypes precede and thus first produce the experience of reality. Jolande Jacobi (1986) makes this even more clear:

> An Aristotelian would say: the archetypes are images formed from the experience of real fathers and mothers. A Platonian would say: the archetypes have first become fathers and mothers because they are pre-images, the prototypes of phenomena. The archetypes are formed a priori for the individual, originating from the collective unconscious and therefore excluded from a sense of individual becoming or fading away.
>
> (Jacobi 1986, p. 51; see also Hopcke 1989, p. 13)

The transcendental concept

So it becomes clear that there is also a transcendental conceptualization of archetype to be found in Jung's works. In his paper *On the Nature of the Psyche* (CW 8), Jung deals with the ambiguity of his archetype concept in the sense that it has a material, if not biological, base and, on the other hand, is located on a transcendental sphere. The solution he finds is that archetypes in general have an inherent structure of opposites. For the archetype in general, this means that on one end of the polarity, the archetype is characterized by matter/body/instinct, whereas on the other end of the polarity, it is characterized by spirit (CW 8, 406). In so far, it cannot be clearly stated that the archetype is psychic (CW 8, 439); Jung, therefore, coins the term psychoid to describe this structure of opposites inherent in the archetype. To elucidate this concept, he uses the spectrum of light as a metaphor, with one end characterized by violet, the other by infrared (CW 8, 414). This also implies that every archetype contains a wholeness regarding its specific theme or content.

> all archetypes spontaneously develop favourable and unfavourable, light and dark, good and bad effects.
>
> (CW 9/2, 423)

> The natural archetypal symbolism, describing a totality that includes light and dark.
>
> (CW 9/2, 427)

The process idea: Individuation

These reflections result in Jung's idea that there is an inherent dynamism in the archetypes, respectively, in the collective unconscious, which can be described as a process with a certain aim. The archetypes represent a totality or an image of wholeness of the personality. Their influence on the person can most generally be characterized as initiating a process of development of the personality towards integration and greater wholeness. This process results in a synthesis of consciousness and the unconscious (CW 9/I, 297) as a solution for the tension between the two.

> I use the expression Individuation in the sense of that process which generates a psychological individual, which means a separate, indivisible, and whole individual.
>
> (Jung, CW 9/1, 490)

> the principle that the archetype, because of its power to unite opposites, mediates between the unconscious substratum and the conscious mind. It throws a bridge between present-day consciousness, always in danger of losing its roots, and the natural, unconscious, instinctive wholeness of primeval times.
>
> (CW 9/1, 293)

> the archetype as an image of instinct is a spiritual goal toward which the whole nature of man strives; it is . . . the prize which the hero wrests from the fight with the dragon.
>
> (CW 8, 415)

> (This is a reference to the hero myth, which Jung regards as an archetypal image for the individuation process and its stages.)

Jung argues that he found the general structure of this process by investigating the images produced by his patients:

> I therefore took up a dream-image or an association of the patient's, and, with this as a point of departure, set him the task of elaborating or developing his theme by giving free rein to his fantasy. This, according to individual taste and talent, could be done in any number of ways, dramatic, dialectic, visual, acoustic, or in the form of dancing, painting, drawing, or modelling. The result of this technique was a vast number of complicated designs whose diversity puzzled me for years, until I was able to recognize that in this method I was witnessing the spontaneous manifestation of an unconscious process which was merely assisted by the technical ability of the patient, and to which I later gave the name "individuation process".
>
> (CW 8, 400; see also CW 8, 401 on p. 19 and CW 8, 411 on p. 25)

In this last quote, Jung specifies the process as centring. Here, the archetype of the Self must be introduced because in Jung's view, this archetype represents the transcendent centre of the process and of the personality. In the centre of the psyche, which Jung describes as the Self, an archetypal structure can be assumed. This

Self would be a kind of structure which expresses wholeness as well as individual uniqueness. As the Self is centre of the person as well as its totality simultaneously, it is a paradoxical description which Jung nevertheless consciously makes. The concept of the Self discussed here is a very clear example that Jung conceptualized archetypes as transcendent.

The quote is interesting in the sense that it implies the idea that there is something like a consciousness, an intention or a higher wisdom contained in the unconscious, which has the aim to move the personality towards wholeness.

[The Self] is at once external and inside, totally ourselves and also unrecognisable to us, a virtual middle point of mysterious constitution [. . .] The beginnings of our whole spiritual life seem to spring inextricably from this point. Our highest and ultimate goals seem to come out of it. It is a paradox that is nevertheless inevitable.

(CW 7, 260)

The Self, moreover, is an archetype that invariably expresses a situation within which the ego is contained. Therefore, like every archetype, the Self cannot be localized in an individual ego-consciousness, but acts like a circumambient atmosphere to which no definite limits can be set, either in space or in time.

(CW 9/2, 257)

Over the course of a person's life, movement comes from the Self, confronting the person with a number of archetypal stages.

For years I have been observing and investigating the products of the unconscious in the widest sense of the word, namely dreams, fantasies, visions, and delusions of the insane. I have not been able to avoid recognizing certain regularities, that is, types. There are types of situations and types of figures that repeat themselves frequently and have a corresponding meaning. I therefore employ the term "motif" to designate these repetitions. Thus there are not only typical dreams but typical motifs in dreams. . . . [These] can be arranged under a series of archetypes, the chief of them being . . . the shadow, the wise old man, the child (including the child hero), the mother ("Primordial Mother" and "Earth Mother") as a supraordinate personality ("daemonic" because supraordinate), and her counterpart the maiden, and lastly the anima in man and the animus in woman.

(CW 9/I, 309)

The process of transformation in psychotherapy

It could be said that Jung's major interest in establishing his psychology was to create something signifying a map of said process (summarized in CW 7). Therefore, Jung referred to alchemy, the study of religions and mythology. The idea is that the archetypes, which shape the process, are also expressed in the form of mythologi-cal motifs and narratives in the myths and fairy tales of peoples of the world (CW 9/I, 260). If the map of this process and its stages were available, elements of the process could be detected in material provided by patients in analyses (e.g., in dreams) (e.g., 9/II, 208).

> By way of introduction, I described those concepts and archetypes which mani-fest themselves in the course of any psychological treatment that penetrates at all deeply. The first of these is the shadow, that hidden, repressed, for the most part inferior and guilt-laden personality whose ultimate ramifications reach back into the realm of our animal ancestors and so compromise the whole historical aspect of the unconscious.
>
> (CW 9/2, 422)

Jung's main interest in establishing his psychology was to provide a detailed description of the process he called individuation and of the distinct stages of this process, which are equivalent to specific archetypes. This being also the reason for his intense inquiry on alchemy, as he found that the alchemists had attempted to describe such a process of transformation of the psyche in metaphors of chemical substances and their transformations:

> These various terms also have found their way into many a description of the individuation process: nigredo, for the dark night of the soul, when an individual confronts the shadow with it; separatio, for the moment of emotional and spir-itual discrimination; mortification or putrefactio, for the stage at which the old neurotic ways of being are cast off; dissolutio, for the initial disorientation after the old self is discarded.
>
> (Hopcke 1989, p. 165; see also Edinger 1985)

In general, it can be said that in Jung's idea of the individuation process, the arche-types form a sequence, most clearly described in "The relations between the ego and the unconscious" (CW 7): whereas initially, the ego identifies with the persona, in the transformation process, it must deal with its counterpart, the shadow. If this is accomplished, the ego meets the anima/animus and must establish a relationship to the unconscious/to the soul. On the further road, the ego will meet the wise old man and the great mother (the Mana personalities), which surround the archetype of the Self. The divine child often appears at moments where transformational pro-cesses take place because it symbolizes the new hope for the future. The trickster is a helpful figure, sometimes accomplishing tasks through tricks and twists, which the ego cannot overcome. The coniunctio is closely related to the realization of the Self, which is symbolized in mandala-like figures or symbolisms of wholeness, completion, etc.

Another model for the individuation process is provided by the mythological pattern of the journey of the hero, again, a sequence of stages. A systematic account of this sequence is, however, missing in Jung's works. Nevertheless, the general idea that the myth of the hero is behind transformational processes in the psyche can be found in *Symbols of Transformation* (CW 5), as well as in other pieces scattered throughout the *Collected Works*. The idea was later thoroughly elaborated by Joseph Campbell (1971) in his *The Hero with a Thousand Faces*. Attributes/elements in the hero's story: the divine birth; the descent into the underworld; heroic actions he must undertake, such as battles with dreaded monsters or dangerous tasks to be performed; the presence of helpful companions; the motif of defeat; death; and rebirth.

On the other hand, Jung characterizes the process more formally as a centring process, as in the previous quote (CW 8, 401).

A number of publications by Jung deal with exemplifying this process with case material (*Dream Symbols of the Individuation Process*, CW 12; *The Empiricism of the Individuation Process*, CW 9/1; *The Psychology of Transference*, CW 16).

In my overview of classical archetype theory (Roesler 2021), I have provided a summary of those papers in which Jung concerned himself extensively with the central archetypes (to be found in CW 9): shadow, anima and animus, Self, the great mother, father, puer/the divine child, Kore/the maiden, hero, wise old man, trickster, coniunctio, mandalas and rebirth; it also contains a detailed description of the clinical applications of this process model.

A widespread use of archetypes in AP is making an association between an image, pattern or symbol within the dream of a client to a fairy tale or other mythological story. This is then utilised as informative material for the further process of the therapy. The general idea, put more technically, is that the unconscious of the client makes a connection to a broader archetypal pattern, which is spelt out in the mythological story in symbolical form and *which contains additional information (in respect to the conscious information that client and therapist have)* that is helpful for the therapeutic process. In this sense, archetypes are transporters of information which foster psychological development, information which comes from beyond and has – by definition – never been conscious. The Jungian therapist relies on the belief that the whole of archetypal information is potentially accessible to any of his/her clients via the (collective) unconscious and can be activated in the suitable circumstance. This means that a concept of *universal* archetypes is necessary for AP since we count on the existence of all archetypes in every one of our clients. If we could not count on this, we would be unable to work as we do.

This aspect of archetypes as universal patterns is at the core of what Jung meant by the term archetype. It is at the core of AP and its clinical practice.

It is important to note that the classical archetypes described in detail by Jung are all part of the stages of the individuation process. This stands in contrast to, for example, a Kantian category of perception, which is also described as archetypal. There is another contradiction in that Jung characterizes the archetype as form without content, whereas concepts like the anima are described in long texts and with detailed characteristics (e.g., CW 17, 338), which cannot be called contentless. There has also been an extensive debate in AP about Jung's characterization of the psychological male and female being heavily influenced by his patriarchal views, which are not at all "eternal" (see Roesler 2021 for a discussion).

Note

1   Some of the quotes from Jung's *Collected Works* in this chapter are repeated under different headings, as they may exemplify different elements of Jung's theory of archetypes.

Chapter 4

Problems and criticism

In this section, I will attempt to point out problems that are inherent to Jung's conceptualizations and also to contemporary ones. These are inconsistencies, contradictions, aporia and similar. By inherent problems, I mean the kind of problems that are obvious to the critical reader, without testing the assumptions of archetype theory against insights and findings from neighbouring disciplines. I will also highlight the criticism that was formulated in the development of AP – and also from outside – to the present day, following these principles:

> A science which hesitates to forget its founders is lost.
>
> (Whitehead 1916, p. 413)

> How does depth psychology develop a psychological theory that is itself self-conscious? In other words, how does it develop a theory capable of consciously carrying an awareness of its own figural aspects and implicit assumptions, that is, its own unconsciousness?
>
> (Kugler 1990, p. 317)

Structure without content?

A major problem lies in Jung's conception of the archetype as such: Jung argues that the archetype exists only as structure without content. It is difficult to imagine even a single mental concept which carries no content since, as Knox argues, even a pattern or an organizing structure can never be entirely without representational content and the archetypal forms to which Jung refers imply symbolic meanings and, therefore, mental content (Knox 2003, p. 33). Of course, it is understandable what Jung tries to convey that there are similarities in the structure or patterns that archetypes produce but that the contents can vary (e.g., from culture to culture). But this argument creates the problem of how this contentless structure of the archetype as such can be conceptualized, how it is stored in the brain/genome/biological outfit of humans, etc. In addition, the concept of the archetype as such, a

DOI: 10.4324/9781003348191-4

form free of content, was hardly maintained by Jung. Instead, numerous examples of archetypes are determined very clearly by their content (for example, the archetype of the hero myth). Hopcke (1989) attempts to defend Jung's viewpoint while, at the same time, acknowledging the confusion that is created by Jung's definitions.

I believe that the problem can be clarified when instead of the terms structure and content, the term information is used and an information theory approach is applied. Even though Jung attempts to differentiate between content and structure, from an information theory point of view, content as well as structure must be regarded as containing information, in so far as they are viewed as being specific. It then, however, becomes clear that also the archetype as such contains information; otherwise, it would not be specific, and all archetypes would be the same, which is not the case ("the archetype possesses . . . an invariable central meaning, which constantly only in principle and not in a concrete form, determines how it appears" [CW 9/1, 95]). No mental content or structure can be imagined without being specified. If the archetypes would not contain specifications, they would all be the same, and no distinction between, for example, the anima and the wise old man would be possible. Seen from this point of view, it becomes clear that also the archetype as such contains information. This automatically creates the problem of where this information is stored.

Humbert (1988) took up the idea to apply the concept of information theory to Jung's theories around archetypes. However, this leads to the assumption that archetypes are genetically transmitted. In more recent publications, the problematic inherent in this kind of argumentation is pointed out clearly: "Jung jumps from the collective unconscious immediately to archetypes without spelling out exactly how archetypal images form from the so-called archetype-as-such or 'form without content', and unfortunately, he only confuses the issue with muddled metaphysical speculations involving Kant" (Goodwyn 2020a, p. 920).

The relationship of stability and change in archetypes

"The archetypes are the imperishable elements of the unconscious, but they change their shape continually" (CW 9/1, 301).

The relationship of stability and change in archetypes is not clear. If one adds the idea that archetypes have developed as a "precipitate of endlessly repeated experiences", this would imply that archetypes can change through differences in the environmental conditions of human life, including cultural changes.

There is a certain tension between Jung's general assumption that the archetypes have come to exist from early prehistoric times and have not changed, although the conditions of life for humans in modern times are enormously different compared to conditions during the Stone Age – what he uses as an argument for explaining archaic behaviours or ideas in modern humans. On the other hand, he believes that "endless repetition" and "countless, similar experiences" (CW 6, 760) have inscribed these archetypal patterns into the biological outfit of humans. This implies that there has been a time when experiences and environmental conditions shaped the archetypes and inscribed them into the genetic makeup of humans. But as far as Jung can be understood, this is not the case anymore today; today, archetypes are stable. So there is a certain contradiction between stability and change in his conception of archetypes. This produces the question of why the archetypes have not changed in the last millennia since the evolution of civilization.

The cultural versus the biological, the personal versus the collective

Another dissonance can be found in Jung's theories concerning the relation between the individual and the universal in the archetype, as for example, in the following quote:

> The psyche of the child in its preconscious state is . . . already preformed in a recognizably <u>individual</u> way, and is moreover equipped with all specifically human instincts, as well as with the a priori foundations of the higher functions.
> (Jung 1989, p. 348)

Especially the archetype of the Self is conceptualized as containing the most individual, the uniqueness of the person and, at the same time, being a universal structure. A similar kind of confusion concerns the relationship of the cultural versus the biological, which leads to such contradictory statements as the following (from the survey):

> While the archetype as a structure is vital, representations of the archetype are only typical for the species or individual. We may detect an archetypal woman, man, child, enemy, or experience the archetypally American, French, Japanese, feminine, masculine, human, unhuman etc . . . These definitions can be experienced as stigmatising or old-fashioned, but the fact remains, they all represent a real or imagined attitude towards life, and provide us with the information of what is typical, or archetypal, for just that way of living.

The "this-is-all-the-same" error

In connection with the discordancy regarding the relationship of the personal and the universal, a pattern of arguments can be observed in Jung as well as in Jungian publications to the present day, which I would name the "this-is-all-the-same" error. By this, I mean a pattern of hypotheses which identifies certain similarities or analogies between cultural habits or beliefs, mythological narratives or dream elements, etc. Behind these observed similarities, an archetype is immediately identified, without consideration of any apparent differences or differentiations and possible alternative explanations (there is an example with a detailed discussion concerning the concept of shamanism in the chapter on religion).

Angela Connolly (2018) has discussed this problem at length and draws a critical conclusion:

> The difficulty in analogy, therefore, is finding enough similarity to warrant giving a common name to disparate items while acknowledging their significant variations. Analogies should not be confused with establishing identity or isomorphism. This, however, is exactly what Jung did when he conflated images taken from very different cultural and historical contexts . . . Conflating images in this way lead Jung to believe that while the content of images varies, the underlying form can be reduced to a limited number of uniform and internal patterns.
>
> (Connolly 2018, p. 72)

An unlimited number of archetypes?

Another problem is the specific number of archetypes which exist.

> There are as many archetypes as there are typical situations in life.
>
> (CW 9/I, 98)

Jung does not provide much specification of what he means by typical situations in life. Furthermore, the majority of typical situations that humans experience are culturally shaped.

> above all the only thing about their nature which can be assessed, is their ambiguity, their almost immeasurable wealth of meaning, which each clear formulation makes impossible.
>
> (Jung, CW 9/1, § 80)

Together with the second quote, it becomes very difficult to clearly define what an archetype is and what it contains. This stands in strong contrast to the actual descriptions that Jung provided about several archetypes – namely, anima and animus, the great mother, the wise old man, rebirth, the divine child to name just a few. It cannot be denied that, according to these descriptions, archetypes are specific. So in a broader sense, the problem of the number of archetypes relates to what could be called the catalogue of archetypes. There is no consensus at hand which elements this catalogue of archetypes should contain, only the "classic" archetypes which Jung described, abstract categories of perception and "all the typical situations in human life". But from which epoch, prehistory, classical antiquity?

The use of the term archetype in AP can itself be described as inflationary – e.g., in the *A Critical Dictionary of Jungian Analysis* (Samuels et al. 1986, p. 44): "The number of archetypes is theoretically unlimited".

Different levels of complexity

Archetypes are images while also having an emotional aspect. They may also be thoughts, ideas or beliefs. These are different psychic elements and, from a developmental point of view, differ enormously in their level of complexity. On the one hand, Jung describes the archetype of centring, which describes the process he could observe in his patients in psychiatry and which is pictured in mandala-like images. On the other hand, Jung calls the myth of the hero an archetype, which is a complex narrative with several different stages. These two concepts are on highly different levels of complexity. The one can be defined as an abstract form or shape. The other is a complex narrative.

The impact of archetypes: Determination, (in) formation, structuring, ordering?

Another question concerns the impact archetypes have on the psyche and the development of the personality. There is a surprisingly large number of experts in the survey who still argue that archetypes **determine** psychic experiencing and behaviour, even the life of the individual (and so does Jung in many quotes). At the other end of this scope, the general assumption can be found that archetypes are nothing more than basic categories for human perception and action.

The epistemological status of archetypes

A major problem is the broad variety of definitions and conceptualizations to be found in Jung's works, which are, at least partly, epistemologically incompatible. It is not possible to argue that the archetype is a genetically transmitted pattern of behaviour and, at the same time, to state that archetypes have their place in a transcendental sphere and are principally in themselves not knowable. This problem is heightened by the fact that, as far as can be seen in Jung's writings, he was not able to reflect on these incompatibilities and inconsistencies.

Other Jungian authors have pointed out these contradictions regarding the archetypes (e.g., Knox 2003; Hogenson 2004; Pietikainen 1998). In analysing Jung's writings on archetypes, several different conceptualizations or explanatory concepts can be found, which partly contradict each other. Knox previously outlined "four models that repeatedly emerge in the debate about archetypes", identifying these as biological entities, organizing mental frameworks of an abstract nature, core meanings containing representational content and eternal metaphysical entities (Knox 2003, p. 24). In my earlier work on archetypes (Roesler 2012a, 2021), I have given a list of four conceptualizations of archetypes that overlap with but also differ from Knox, thus underlining the confusing variability involved in Jung's discussion of his core concept: a biological conceptualization, a statistical definition (referring to the finding of interindividually similar core complexes in his association studies), a cultural concept and a transcendental conceptualization.

When we look at these different approaches, all presented together in Jung's works, it becomes obvious that they contradict each other. A concept that is thought to be transcendental and having no place in this world cannot be at the same time a biological entity and part of the genetic code (see also Knox 2003). Jung mixes up theories that are categorically on different levels and not compatible. There is no consistent epistemology of archetypes in Jung and, in my view, still missing in AP. Even more problematic is that Jung never discusses these inconsistencies and contradictions in his theory so that it must be assumed that he was unaware of them. His concept of the archetype as such, which he formulated in 1947 to solve these problems, is no real solution (see previous section).

Jung jumps from one epistemological position to the other (Neher 1996). Kugler (1990) reviews the different positions that can be found in Jung, on the basis of the development of epistemology from modernism to postmodernism. A first position that Jung takes is in line with the modernist approach, which was also basic for Freud's approach and that of early psychoanalysis. In this sense, there is an objective meaning to elements or events in the inner world (e.g., a dream). In psychoanalysis, there is the idea of a "correct" interpretation. But Jung goes even further than that by mentioning: "We may say that the image represents the meaning of the instinct" (CW 8, 398). The same can be found in Jung's direct followers: "The form and the meaning of instincts are represented in the images produced by the archetypes" (von Franz 1980, p. 81). These statements imply that the meaning which the archetype has for the individual is a feature directly attached to the archetype itself. That is, it exists in itself and is independent from the experiencing individual and not, as a humanistic viewpoint would imply, as a result of interpretation. For Jung, the meaning of the archetype is already pre-existent and has been forever eternal; therefore, it is an "arche" (from old) type. By referring to this viewpoint, Kugler points out:

> The process of factoring time into a phenomenological understanding has disclosed that the ultimate grounds of Western knowledge all lapse into a temporal regress or progress. For example, Freud and the modernists attempted to explain the meaning of the text through authorial intention; Jung and the structuralists later tried to account for meaning and interpretation through unconscious psychic structures. These solutions are not solutions at all, because they do not account for the "authority of the author" or the "structurality of structure". These accounts simply posit the author or structure as existing in time prior to the emergence of the text, psyche, or system of thought.
>
> (Kugler 1990, pp. 314–315)

Consequently, it is necessary for Jung to argue that archetypes were formed millennia back in prehistoric times.

Kugler criticizes this view from a postmodernist viewpoint and reveals the fallacies and inconsistencies of this empirical approach by Jung, which is a form of naïve realism:

> The movement from structuralism to poststructuralism is a shift from seeing the text as a closed entity with definite, decipherable meanings to seeing the text as irreducibly plural, oscillating between literal and figural significance that can never be fixed to a single centre, essence, or meaning. . . . For we have come to realize that language of any sort – be it literary, philosophical, clinical, or scientific – does not allow for a transparent view to the so-called empirical world. . . . The modernist fantasy of an objective hermeneutic imagined the reader's subjectivity to be a transparent focus of the lens through which a detached consciousness viewed the content of a stable text. This empiricist idea continued through the structuralist tradition, except that the focus of the detached observer shifted from the content of the text to its structure. . . . The modernist-structuralist idea of a detached observer is being replaced by the idea of an intersubjectivity in which the images in the text interfuse with and alter the lens of the viewer reading the text. We not only read texts, but we read the world through texts. And it is precisely this realization that has undermined our epistemological confidence in the authority of our transcendental signifiers. . . . Postmodernism with its intense focus on the problematics of self-reflection, textuality, and the process of psychic representation has revealed that these unquestionable absolutes are not the eternal, archetypal structures we once thought them to be, but are rather temporal and linguistic by products resulting from a representational theory of language.
>
> (Kugler 1990, pp. 315–316)

When Jung says, "Between intellectus and res there is still anima, and this esse in anima makes the whole ontological argument superfluous" (CW 6, 66), he does not only present himself as a thoroughly essentialist thinker, who attributes a privileged ontological position to anima/soul, he also openly denies that there is any sort of epistemological problem at all. This does not solve the inherent problems; it demonstrates that he was not aware of them. The majority of his statements about archetype have an essentialist character, which is additionally often disguised as an empiricist attitude (e.g., when he argues that the archetype is a pattern of behaviour, that it is innate, etc.) (see also: "I firmly believe . . . that psyche is an ousia [essence]", letter to Victor White 1949, Jung 1973, p. 540). Of course, I understand that when Jung speaks of the "objective psyche", he tries to convey the idea that the inner world has its own reality and is not identical with ego or consciousness. Nevertheless, he gets entangled in epistemological inconsistencies and contradictions. However, many descriptions and definitions which Jung gives for the archetype have the shape of nomothetic statements, as if the archetype concept was something of a natural law or an empirical fact, as can be found in the natural sciences.

> Despite their opacity, archetypes are empirically well-documented hypotheses whose empirical derivation is based on anthropology, art and cultural studies, sociological and psychological findings. Their character of reality is not concrete or even material but rather connected to the inner and at the same time collective soul, they are founded in "psychic fact".
>
> (CW 11, 553)

This results in a strongly positivistic character of Jung's statements and concepts, even though Jung (and a considerable part of contemporary Jungians) sees himself in opposition to what is characterized as "positivistic science", respectively materialism – one more contradiction inherent in Jungian psychology that is often not reflected upon.

Reification and ontologization

Because of this attitude, the concept of archetypes, together with that of the collective unconscious, has become ontologized and reified so that parts of the Jungian community deal with it as if it were an external reality as opposed to a theoretical concept, which attempts to explain and describe certain psychological phenomena.[1]

Warren Colman (2016) writes about his experience with Jungians from the classical school while giving lectures in Zürich:

> I was surprised to discover that my audience seemed relatively unconcerned by this question [where do symbols come from?]. They seemed more or less to take the existence of archetypes for granted.
>
> My impression was that . . . archetypes are not so much a hypothesis as a living reality that provides orientation and meaning for the practice of psychotherapy and living in general.
>
> (pp. 2–3)

In referring to the feminine principle, the anima, Samuels takes a comparable viewpoint:

> It is assumed that there is something eternal about femininity and, hence, about women; that women therefore display certain essential transcultural and historical characteristics; and that these can be described in psychological terms. . . . What is omitted is the ongoing role of the prevailing culture in the construction of the feminine, and the confusion develops between what is claimed to be eternal and what is currently observed to be the case. It is here that the dead weight of the heritage of archetypal theory is felt, but as the mirror image of Jung's

problem. He assumed that there is something eternal about women and, hence, about femininity.

(Samuels 1990, p. 296)

There is even what has been called "vulgar Jungianism – the mechanical and reductivist allegorical rewriting of a text according to the master code of the archetypes" (Barnaby & D'Acierno 1990, p. XXI), or what Andrew Samuels (1998) has called Jungian fundamentalism:

> Jungian fundamentalism stresses Jung the man and his prophetic and even, it is sometimes claimed, divinely inspired words. But what gets particularly stressed is how Jung lived. Sometimes this is called "the Jungian way". . . . It is a worldview that tends to ignore everything else that is going on in psychotherapy generally, or in the worlds of ideas, politics, the arts or religion.
>
> (pp. 21–22)

Miller (1990) puts it ironically:

> In Jungian psychological orthopraxy, we know that cats in men's dreams mean anima, that eggs in women's dreams mean fecundity, and so on. . . . Today Christian literalism and Jungian fundamentalism are symbolic. They have become a knowing.
>
> (p. 328)

Phenomenology

In strong contrast to such positions, Jung argues: "Psychology cannot establish any metaphysical truths, nor does it try to. It is concerned solely with the phenomenology of the psyche" (CW 18, 742). In fact, Jung took a phenomenological viewpoint by basing his idea of an autonomous process in the psyche on his observations of psychiatric patients and their creative productions (e.g., see previous section, CW 8, 401). Unfortunately, Jung never published this material from his time at Burghölzli nor is it accessible for further research. In the few instances when Jung dealt with empirical material intensively (e.g., in *Symbols of Transformation*, CW 5; the *Vision Seminars* and *Dream Symbols of the Individuation Process*, CW 15), no systematic method of interpretation is identifiable. In contrast, Jung is notorious in the humanities for the lack of a systematic interpretation method (Trevi 1992; Barnaby & D'Acierno 1990).

This is highly irritating, as Jung uses the term phenomenology again and again but without any reference to the science and methodology termed phenomenology, established by Edmund Husserl, who built on the works of Franz Brentano. This approach had developed a detailed methodology for the interpretation of psychic contents, which was accessible by the early 1920s. Again, Jung does not refer to or make use of such an elaborated methodology. He probably did not even know about this scientific approach so important for the discussion between psychology and philosophy during his lifetime. It is interesting that phenomenology criticized what they called "Psychologismus" (psychologism), a position which does not differentiate between the act of thinking or perception and the object which is perceived or thought about – a position which is very close, if not similar, to what Jung proposes throughout his works by stating that there are objects which only exist in the psyche but have an existence of their own, what he calls the "objective psyche".

Jung's interpretation method

There is a continuous contradiction throughout his works: Jung's insistence on the scientific (even empirical) nature of AP, on the one side, and his actual work process (exegesis of texts), which is highly hermeneutic and influenced by the humanities. After leaving the university psychiatry in Zürich, Jung stopped conducting empirical research – which conforms with natural science – and continued researching texts from religious studies, mythology, alchemy, etc. He did not realize at any point that the psychology he was forming was applied humanities/cultural studies. As a medical doctor, he was not educated in this kind of research. Jung never attempted to acquire methods for this type of research, as for example, systematic hermeneutic methods, theological exegesis or social science methodology (e.g., the methodology of constructing ideal types by Max Weber), even though all of these methods were already available in his time. In my opinion, this contradiction is still an unresolved problem in AP to this day. The majority of Jungian publications belong to the field of hermeneutic interpretations or applications of methods taken from, for example, anthropology, whereas the claim is still that AP is biologically founded – at least the relation of the two "worlds" in the foundation of AP is still unclear.

The lack of an adequate scientific system and methodology results in confusion in many of Jung's publications. Jung compiles the material and references in an extremely associative and unsystematic manner; there are no alternative interpretations considered. Statements just are the way he sees them. This makes many of his books extremely hard to read (e.g., *Symbols of Transformation*, CW 5), which has, therefore, been criticized by many authors:

In the midst of her fantasies Miss Miller imagines a city of dreams. This provokes Jung to a discourse about cities in old cultures and mythologies. Then he states that cities and women have a relation to the land; which makes him think about the movement of the sun over motherly waters; which again reminds him of Frobenius' concept of the nekyia; this stimulates Jung to think of Noah's journey, but he adds that traveling is an expression of a wish for rebirth; this starts a discussion about the book of revelations; etc.

(Homans 1979, p. 66)

The author clearly shows that in this work, Jung has produced a report of his own fantasies rather than a systematic interpretation of myths and symbols.

With reference to Jung's anthropological statements, Belmonte (1990) summarizes the critique concerning Jung's unwillingness to consider the insights and findings as well as the methodological premises of other disciplines:

> The exile of Jung to a place far beyond the borders of admissible argument in academic anthropology must be seen in the light of . . . Jung's own failure to invent and refine a terminology that would do justice to the novelty of his ideas. Nor did Jung ever clarify . . . the evolutionary premises of his psychology. . . . He uncritically accepted an instinctual and Lamarckian ground for the evolution of mind and embraced Haeckel's notion of ontogeny recapitulating phylogeny in the embryo as a fair description of the growth of the individual psyche. Like Konrad Lorenz and Edward Wilson, Jung was a sociobiological structuralist for whom the terms of mental life were at once transpersonal and preformed.
>
> (Belmonte 1990, p. 48)

Transcendentalism

In contrast to his empiricist self-understanding, Jung's argumentation is often openly transcendental. Apart from that, there is a constant confusion of transcendental and scientific argumentations, especially due to what is called the Pauli-Jung-dialogue and their attempt to redefine the archetype by making use of concepts from quantum physics. This has been the object of massive critique from several disciplines. Also, contemporary Jungian authors (Burda 2019) clearly point out that Jung is permanently switching between the – contradicting – epistemological positions of realism and constructivism, between premodern thought in the line with Renaissance theories of cosmological unity on the one side and the separation of esse et essentia (entity per se and appearance) in the Kantian tradition on the other.

Finally, there is the position of what could be called unknowing: "The concept of the unconscious posits nothing, it designates only my unknowing" (in a letter to Max Frischknecht 1943; Jung 1973).

Jung's scientific method and way of "doing science"

Problematic is that Jung sees reality primarily as the inner psychic reality – the relation of personal and objective is unclear. Therefore, he equates his own inner psychic experience with empirically proven facts. For Jung, his theory may be a successful attempt to embed his experiences (during his so-called confrontation with the unconscious), which are put down in the *Red Book* into a coherent theoretical background of explanation. Surprisingly, a question that is almost never asked in AP – with a few exceptions (e.g., Saban 2019) – is whether these concepts of the individuation process are relevant for other people. Maybe these experiences of so-called archetypal figures are solely Jung's personal experience and do not apply for anyone else. Saban (2019) points out that Jung, like Freud, himself never had a formal training analysis. Ergo, it can be assumed that his way of introspection might be subject to faults. There is a tendency in Jung, as well as in his direct successors, to give much more emphasis to the inner world and its demands than to the outside reality – which could be a result of a neurotic development (Kirsch 2004). Connected with this problem is another attitude of Jung's to systematically choose an archetypal explanation instead of making use of biographical information as an explanation. An example is provided by Neher (1996) discussing Jung's famous dream of God's turd falling on the Basel Cathedral:

> At this point, it should be noted that Jung was the son of a clergyman, with whom he had serious personal conflicts. Knowing that, does it not seem possible that this fantasy could be explained in terms of Jung's own life experiences? To me, it seems eminently possible. Thus the mystery, for me, is Jung's seeming inability or unwillingness to acknowledge this possibility. We will see the same theme, of downgrading the personal element in his own – and other people's – experience. . . . To summarize, it is clear that Jung's own experiences provided him with the initial motivation to develop a theory of unconscious content that arises not from our own life histories but from a nonpersonal source, which he eventually called the collective unconscious. But, after examining the experiences of his that he emphasized in his writings, we have seen that his claim that they cannot be explained in terms of his own life history is far from convincing.
>
> (pp. 72–74)

Usually, in the development of a scientific theory, one would expect the following: Jung has a personal experience. Based on this experience, he develops a hypothesis about structures of the psyche and processes of psychological change. He then publishes this hypothesis and puts it up for discussion. This would be followed by a systematic collection of evidence, in the sense of proving and disproving the hypothesis, from relevant research and scientific findings. This, precisely, does not occur for Jung and his theories. Rather, for Jung, after 1916, his theory was interpreted as proven and had absolute validity. After that, he solely presented material that would fit into his preconceived concept and even this sporadically. This tradition, not to search systematically and open-mindedly for evidence speaking for or against the concepts and disregarding relevant findings of neighbouring disciplines, begins with Jung and continues within AP until today (Jones 2014).

One example from Jung regarding ethnological research: Jung repeatedly mentions the existence of human universals, customs, ideas or rituals that can be found in every culture, tribe or nation. But he never systematically studies the field of research in anthropology, which was already available to his time. In Volume 9 of the *Collected Works*, which contains his publications on the archetype concept, there are several hundred citations, mainly from religious studies, but only a few ethnological researchers (Eliade, Mauss, Paul Radin, Baldwin Spencer, James Stevenson, Winthius), and even these are only mentioned in footnotes. Jung quotes Levy-Bruhl (1921) more than 60 times in his works, referring mainly to the concept of participation mystique; but Levy-Bruhl is an anthropologically orientated philosopher in the tradition of 19th century science, instead of an empirically oriented anthropologist. The most important researchers and theorists of his time – Marcel Mauss and Bronislaw Malinowski – Jung mentions only once. This means he knew of their works but chose nevertheless not to include them. This is surprising, especially in the case of Malinowski (1924), because he conducted research about the occurrence of the Oedipus complex in different cultures of the world, which should have been of interest for Jung. Claude Levi-Strauss (1949) is not mentioned at all, even though he created an alternative theory to Jung's archetype theory and began to publish these ideas in the 1940s.

This is the case still today. I have never experienced Jungian publications referring to ethnographic data samples like the *Ethnographic Atlas* (Murdock 1967a, 1967b), the *Standard Ethnographic Sample* (Naroll 1965; Naroll & Sipes 1973) or the *Standard Cross Cultural Sample* (Murdock & White 1969) (see chapter "Anthropology"); there even is a scientific journal called *Cross-Cultural Research*. All of these could provide empirically based answers to the question whether there are cultural similarities and to what extent these exist. Jung only claims that certain traditions and patterns are universal without providing evidence in detail. In fact, overviews of empirical research in ethnology show that there are only very few universals, and these do not support Jung's idea of archetypes (Brown 1991). It is not similarity that characterizes the ideas and practices of peoples but diversity and variation (see chapter "Anthropology" for more details).

The same sort of critique has been put forward from experts in literary criticism. Jung attempted to apply his method to literary works (e.g., James Joyce's *Ulysses*, CW 15).

This paper, however, can hardly be called an analysis of the novel, as Jung frankly says that the book bores and irritates him, the only beauty of it being that it perfectly expresses the futility and squalor of modern life.

(van Meurs 1990, p. 239)

Another example concerns of what Jung calls **"Autochthonous revival"**: For to argue that archetypes have **"never been in consciousness, and therefore have never been individually acquired"** (CW 9/I, 88), Jung also had to rule out for all his cases that there had been any prior contact to the image or idea by the person producing the archetypal image; this also implies to rule out cryptomnesia respectively all kinds of subliminal/unconscious acquisition of certain motives, images, patterns or stories. This is, of course, hard to accomplish, if not impossible.

"In particular, demonstrating – on a case-by-case basis – that a proposed archetype could not have derived from personal or common cultural experience, and therefore must be genetic in origin, is exceedingly difficult, if not impossible" (Neher 1996, p. 86). But Jung does not seem concerned with this problem nor does he conduct any attempts to provide evidence for his assumption. We even know today that the first case by which Jung presented his archetype concept, the Miss Miller in Volume 5 of the *Collected Works*, was not a pseudonym but a well-known performing artist whose specialty was dressing up as a member of an exotic ethnic group and reciting the respective poetry so that she was well acquainted with everything Jung connected with the collective unconscious. So there is no speaking of an autochthonous revival here, and the whole case seems to be flawed (Samuels 1998, p. 18).

In sum, Jung does not make the effort of systematically inspecting empirical material for testing his theories. He selects contents that prove his arguments and ignores the need for providing support for his ideas. This approach is continued by his followers. One example: Erich Neumann's (1949/1966) famous work *Ursprungsgeschichte des Bewusstseins* (*The Origins and History of Consciousness*), in which he expands Jung's theory about the parallels between mythology and the development of consciousness. Norbert Bischof (1996), a professor of psychology at the University of Zürich, was one of the few academic psychologists who recognized Jung's psychology and attempted to test it empirically. He demonstrated that Neumann selectively used mythologies in his publication which would verify his theory and systematically excluded other material. Bischof included the material that had been excluded by Neumann in his analysis and reached a very different conclusion about the relationship of mythology and psychological development. I have never seen a reference to this critique by Bischof in Jungian publications on Neumann, which – from my point of view – is another striking example for the continuation of an attitude of theoretical isolation in AP up to the present day.

A dynamic systems theory point of view

Jung makes the mistake of believing that if there are similar patterns found inter-individually in beliefs and practices of different cultures, there must be a template inside each person. By this, he means information inscribed in a biological or genetical way, which then produces the observed similarities. This way of arguing is not necessary. Seen from the perspective of dynamic systems theory, it can generally be said that the formation of systematic patterns is a feature of nature itself, especially of living systems. The ocean produces systematic patterns of waves, weather phenomena follow systematic patterns, individuals and groups develop routines to solve problems that come up repeatedly, families develop systematic patterns of rules and habits, etc. From the viewpoint of general systems theory, it is a natural characteristic of physical as well as organic systems that they produce systematic structures by way of self-similar patterns. The view, which is inherent in Jung, that there must be a template somewhere stored in the person – in the genes, brain structure or biological makeup – which is then expressed in repetitive structures is a common fallacy. It is not necessary to assume an inherent or innate pre-configuration to be able to explain the development of similar structures in the lives of humans, in the structures of society, etc.

> It is my contention that what Jung termed archetype is actually a biosocial manifestation of a widespread natural phenomenon, originally identified by Claude Shannon as a self-healing code. Had Jung formulated his theory of the archetypal synapse connecting mind, myth, and culture now, he would have undoubtedly adopted a perspective based on cybernetic as opposed to linear notions of causality in that position and a symbolic process with in its total semiotic context and dominant media environment. Once this step is taken, a great deal of the crass reductionism that moores Jung's psychology melts away and his most valuable intuitions become available for reconsideration.
>
> (Belmonte 1990, p. 47)

George Hogenson proposed that the archetype could be understood as an "iterative moment in the self-organization of the symbolic world" (Hogenson 2004, p. 279). McDowell stressed that the archetype was a pre-existing principle of organization of the personality (McDowell 2001).

In the 1920s, the Berlin School of Gestalt Psychology (Metzger 1954) identified a quality of the cognitive structure as the capacity of creating a good "Gestalt". This means a stable configuration of perceptions, which are, therefore, ubiquitous. This Gestalt principle was also empirically supported (Stadler & Kruse 1990). The factor that produced the similarity was called convergence. It is the same principle that makes the bodies of fish and whales so similar even though the two species differ biologically. The similarities develop because the qualities are the best adaptation to the same conditions.

Saunders and Skar (2001) have adapted this theory for AP. They argue that when Jung speaks of the archetype as form without content, he really means a process, not a form, which produces similar patterns. Accordingly, psychological archetypes are the product of processes of self-organization by the brain. Saunders and Skar suggested that the archetype was an emergent structure which derived from the self-organizing properties of the brain (Saunders & Skar 2001). Dynamic systems theory in its application to cognitive psychology claims that once the brain has developed a pattern of perception and interpretation, subsequent information is processed on the basis of these existing patterns. This explains why different information is processed into similar psychological concepts. This is a quality of self-organizing systems. It also provides an alternative explanation for archetypes and would also solve the problem of the "archetype as such":

> When we employ a dynamical systems view of development, we no longer need the archetype-as-such to explain the formation of complexes. In fact we could do without it altogether and still have the same basic psychological system that Jung proposed.
>
> (Skar 2004, p. 247)

To a certain extent, the systemic idea of self-organization can already be found in Jung when he speaks of the psyche being a self-regulating entity. It also becomes clear that this idea is in opposition to the essentialism being found throughout Jung's works, as pointed out earlier – another inherent contradiction.

As later highlighted (see next section), there is an overlap to the viewpoint of the functionalist school of anthropology, specifically, that similarities between peoples of the world are a result of the fact that human communities have a set of shared problems which must be solved (e.g., to avoid incestuous relationships producing offspring with a high risk of genetic defects). Since these problems are interculturally similar, the discovered solutions are comparable – such a systemic perspective can explain the observation of interindividual and intercultural similarities.

Associated with this viewpoint is the insight that some forms or patterns in the environment of humans or, simply speaking, in the world have a certain objective meaning, and to grasp and incorporate that meaning is simply unavoidable during life. As an example, I would present the circle resp. the globe/sphere. There is a line of argumentation, in Jung as well as in some authors from the survey, that these forms can only be grasped because there is an innate preformed pattern or template. This line of thought, especially in connection with the example of the sun, is irritating, in so far as during human life, there is no way of avoiding recognizing there are perfect circles/globes to be observed in nature (e.g., the sun, the moon, the wave pattern if a stone is dropped into water, blossoms and fruits, etc.). (There are many more examples provided by Neher [1996, p. 79].) The classical Jungian argumentation assumes that we as humans were not able to recognize this if we did not have an inborn template. Apart from the fact that this is a misconception about how human perception develops (bottom-up instead of top-down; see chapter "Biology, genetics and inheritance"), it is also highly implausible that nature would use the limited space for information in the genome to prepare the development of a perception which can be acquired just by using input from the environment.

> Further, when it comes to humanlike archetypes, such as the wise old man, it is even easier to imagine that they would be part and parcel of the experience of any culture in any historical, prehistoric, period.
>
> (Neher 1996, p. 79)

It is different if Jung (and some of his followers) would argue that the circle is a biologically preformatted symbol of perfection, completeness, wholeness, etc. One could go against this view by pointing to the fact that the circle is, mathematically or geometrically speaking, a perfect form in itself and can also be defined as such mathematically. It is no wonder that humans have used the circle for symbolizing perfection, completeness, wholeness, etc. (see also the discussion of Goodwyn's arguments in the chapter "Biology, genetics and inheritance").

A history of criticism

It is interesting to find out that many of the problems identified in classical archetype theory in the previous account have been pointed out quite early in the development of AP, as for example:

> The archetypal image is postulated to be the end result of the interaction between the innate archetype per se and the environment. . . . We saw that the archetypal theory does not attempt to specify precisely how these two factors interrelate to produce the archetypal image. Thus, in the absence of any archetypal laws specifying how these two factors interact to produce the archetypal images, the question arises as to how the innateness of the archetype per se is to be established. For if we are not in fact able to separate these two factors through some type of isolation experiment, it might well seem that the claim that the archetypes are innate, rather than acquired as a result of experiences individual development, would be on very weak ground. Moreover, if we cannot substantiate the innate nature of the archetype per se, then the theory as a whole will lack a credible basis. . . . Jung argues, then, that the archetypal images are due to innate factors primarily on the basis of paradigm cases in which it can be reasonably acertained that the persons involved have had no previous exposure to the sort of motifs that appear in the dreams of visions (e.g. the Solar Phallus case; C.R.). . . . Naturally in most cases of the alleged archetypal manifestations, this degree of control will not be possible. For when individuals report that they cannot trace a specific image to something they have acquired through learning, they must be either lying or mistaken. In the latter's case the possibility of cryptomnesia must always be kept in mind.
>
> (Shelburne 1988, pp. 66–67)

Therefore, Michael Fordham has claimed:

> The truly gigantic and fundamental nature of Jung's labors, however, could never blind us to our own capacity to work out in more detail, or to apply in new spheres, those concepts which can and need to be subjected to scrutiny, constructive criticism, and elaboration.
>
> (Fordham 1955, p. 4)

Consequently, Fordham was the first direct follower of Jung's who attempted to reformulate classical archetype theory by adding his concept of the deintegration reintegration process (for details, see Roesler 2021).

As the results of the survey demonstrated, there is still no consensus about the definition, the conceptualizations still refer to outdated theories and concepts and there is still a widespread neglect of the epistemological and other problems inherent in them. In the history of criticism, there is general agreement that Jung's works are full of contradictions, and much has already been written about it:

> Jung repeatedly insisted that he did not have a theoretical system of his own. In so far as he claimed that his ideas were not theoretical abstractions but founded on his own direct clinical experience, he did not feel compelled to present them as a neat system with their own logical coherence, which would enable his readers to access them easily. This close relationship between Jung's theory and practice could account for the fact that his writings are accepted as lucid and indeed inspirational by some and as incomprehensible by others.
>
> (Papadopoulos 1992a, p. XIV)

As this author points out, Jung, on the one hand, relied heavily upon his own inner experience by formulating his psychological ideas and concepts. On the other hand, he was desperately trying to avoid being seen as a philosopher, as he wanted to be regarded a scientist. Consequently, many of his ideas and concepts are presented by him as nomothetic statements, as empirically grounded insights, if not truths (e.g., the anima is said to be an objective fact). There is no doubt that Jung was innovative in his way of introducing introspection into forming a psychological theory. However, his repeated claims that his findings should be regarded as hard empirical facts frequently lead to aporia. Jung tends to shift between these positions, and the main problem is that he was not aware of this contradiction:

> On the one hand he admired immensely Plato's depth of insights and scope of vision and made extensive references to the platonic opus in his own writing; however, on the other hand he was concerned not to be branded as an idealist philosopher (or any kind of philosopher for that matter) when he was eagerly attempting to establish himself as an empirical psychologist with in a strictly scientific paradigm. Jung's own references to this issue are varied. At times he accepted archetypes and forms as synonymous and analogous and at other times he emphasized his claim that Plato's forms were metaphysical and transcendental whereas his own archetypes were empirical facts. His position is epitomized in a letter in 1943 when he wrote "If I posited the archetypes. . . . I would not be a scientist but a Platonist". This claim demonstrates that he was not in a position to investigate this issue objectively; one cannot underestimate Jung's fear of being branded a philosopher when he was desperate in wishing to be recognized as a scientist.
>
> (Papadopoulos 1992, p. 4)

My impression is that the tendency of being unaware of the inherent tensions and contradictions in AP is present to this day. Many Jungian authors, when confronted with this problem, argue that it was a conscious and deliberate strategy by Jung and indeed ingenious that his paradoxical statements should be seen as a new form of conducting psychology.

A good example for this attitude is Claire Douglas's article on the historical context of AP in *The Cambridge Companion to Jung* (Young-Eisendrath & Dawson 1997), where she states:

> The strains of positivism and romanticism warred in Jung's education and training but also produced a dialectical synthesis in which Jung could use the most advanced methods of reason and scientific accuracy to establish the reality of the irrational (another interesting ontologization; CR). It was Jung's romantic genius, and number two character, that allowed him to understand that humans, himself included, could be at one and the same time Western, modern, secular, civilized and sane – but also primitive, archaic, mythical and mad.
>
> (p. 20)

From my point of view, this is a glorification of Jung's inability to clarify basic epistemological and scientific standpoints. I wish to point out that there is confusion on Jung's side. It is not a systematic strategy in Jung's writing but a failure to see the limitations of his own thinking. That the eternal glorification of Jung, by arguing that he was deliberately – and indeed ingeniously – paradoxical, must be regarded as a defensive strategy in the Jungian community. I would argue that this attitude in Jung, as well as in the community, is at the root of the ongoing and severe theoretical problems present in today's AP (e.g., the lack of a consensual definition of archetypes, a resistance against theoretical developments and insights in relevant disciplines and against a testing of the theory in the sense of research).

Papadopoulos (1992), in his compilation of criticism of Jung's theory, summarizes several critiques, which mainly refer to Jung's use of philosophers and especially his distinction of reality and fantasy:

> Prof. de Voogd reaches the conclusion that Jung understood and used the Kantian epistemology in an incorrect way and mainly to back his own claim for being scientific and thus respectable. She claims that Jung's Kantianism was therefore both self-contradictory and self-defeating. She asks how it was possible for Jung to rely on Kant so completely and for so long when his colleagues in other disciplines had no difficulty recognizing Kant's limitations. The answer perhaps lies in the firmness of distinction which Kant drew between the transcendent metaphysics of his predecessors and the new Kantian epistemology he introduced which relied on causality and objectivity. This neat alienation between what is scientific and what is not scientific can easily be deduced from Kant and indeed it was used by many authors subsequently in order to establish such clear-cut criteria. It is these criteria that Jung also wished to rely upon. However,

on closer examination, de Voogd demonstrates that Jung himself moved further along the Kantian dichotomy when he introduced the reality of fantasy. Quoting from Jung that the psyche creates reality every day, the only expression I can use for this activity is fantasy, she argues that such an ontology requires a descriptive model that puts metaphor before concept. This is so because Jung not only recognizes fantasy but even puts it ahead of fact. Therefore, such fantasies lead us to the root metaphors at work in the given context, the metaphors in terms of which we fashion our notions and concepts.

(Papadopoulos 1992a, pp. 5–6)

Wolfgang Giegerich took issue with the way in which Barbara Eckman asserted Jung's Hegelianism by pointing out that the theories of the psychoid archetypes as well as of synchronicity are theories of an ontic, factual reality. . . . However, as he points out, this kind of knowledge refers to that which is absolved (freed) from the difference between the absolute and the empirical, the infinite and the finite. His argument is that Jung was unable to grasp either this distinction or its implications. However, paradoxically, both his psychology as well as his theory and practice of psychotherapy incorporate this principle which, regrettably and yet understandably, he himself was unable to apply to his own logic. This state of affairs . . . left Jung attached to a pre-Kantian mode of thinking in so far as he insisted on the empiricism and objectivity of his work. This very logic of Jung's, anchored in the ontic level, prevented him not only from appreciating his affinity with Hegel but also from healing the dissociation between his own psychology and logic.

(pp. 6–7)

The critical points previously are brought together astutely in Trevi's (1992) critique of Jung, quoted at the beginning of the introductory chapter. According to Trevi, there are two different tendencies present in Jung. The first is to build a coherent and systematic view of psychic life. The second is to move away from this systematic plot which gives space to an essentially experiential content, breaking up the theoretical frame.

In particular in Jung's text it is easy to find the affirmation of psychology as a natural science and the negation of it as a science for the constitutive aporia of psychology itself: the inescapable presence of the observer in the object that is observed, and so the inevitable reciprocal shift of psychology as a science into a psychology as an original attitude of the observer. . . . The same jump of Jung from the phenomenology of subjective psychic life to a claimed objective psyche, which should be unmovable and atemporal under the headlong historical variations of subjectivity and culture, constitutes itself as an attempt to draw from a somehow unattackable and coherent system.

(p. 359)

Besides this strenuously critical methodological position, sentences of the so-called objective science (i.e. naturalistic) of the psyche appear in the rhapsodic disorder which is characteristic of Jung. It does not matter that Jung, who also tries to unmask the naturalistic nature of psychological research from which he comes, continuously falls in the circle of the same naturalism.

(p. 363)

He points out that Jung desperately strived for seeking a superior point of view above all these contradictions. Finally, Jung failed to succeed in reaching that point, and thus, his psychology remains full of contradictions and aporia. He concludes, while at the same time aiming to constitute his psychology as a science, with the nomothetic ideal of the natural sciences. He gives up categorizing his psychology to be a science, reducing it to the experience of the understanding of the psychic process. In the end, Jung's psychology takes on the character of a symbolic or metaphorical language, a hermeneutic endeavour. I will return to this viewpoint in my final chapter on the core of archetype theory.

Other authors (e.g., Tresan 1996) have already accused Jung of an inappropriate reductionism in his attempts to find a biological foundation for archetypes.

In line with many authors mentioned earlier, I assume that behind Jung's decade-long effort to force his archetype concept into a biological conception is the need to defend his theory against suspicions of not being scientific. Jung (as well as Freud) received his academical training as a medical doctor, a natural scientist. He made it very clear that he always saw himself as such and psychology as a natural science, for example, as stated in a seminar at the University of Basel in 1939: "Psychologie ist sozusagen die jüngste der **Naturwissenschaften** und steht erst am Anfang ihrer Entwicklung" ("Psychology is, so to say, the young-est of the **natural sciences** and is only at its beginning"; transl. C.R.). This atti-tude is also evident in Jung's attempt to align his theory of psychic energy with the laws of thermodynamics (e.g., when referring to the law of entropy, which is basic for Jung's theory of the balance of psychic energy). Ironically, these are now considered as being refuted, which astoundingly, to my knowledge, has not been received in AP, as it would have led to a change in the very concept of energetics. There are many other cases in which Jung made use of concepts from physics for his own psychology (e.g., he attempts to explain the exchange of energy between consciousness and the unconscious as a system of communicating tubes). It can be summarized that Jung attempted to bestow upon his psychology the shape of a natural science. Firstly, because this was the way he was trained to observe con-sequential to his academic background and, secondly, because he (unconsciously) needed this as a defensive strategy against not being seen as a real scientist (e.g., CW 9/1, 90).

Habermas (1968) accused Freudian psychoanalysis as "scientistic self-misunderstanding". The same applies, in my opinion, to AP. Indeed, all psychol-ogy is concerned with meaning and, as such, with structures of meaning. Jung had clearly indicated this, with an emphasis on the centrality of "meaning". This cannot be thought of as natural science but rather leads to the necessity of an interpretative mind.

Even more important, in my view, is what Jung did throughout most of his life: making psychological interpretations of texts, dreams and fantasies. His practical approach to psychology was hermeneutical. So here we find Jung in line with a long tradition of hermeneutics, interpretation and cultural theory, even though his own self-understanding was that of a natural scientist. Whereas in practice, his psychology deals with culture, meaning and interpretation and, therefore, belongs to the humanities – something of an "applied humanity". The German psychoanalyst Alfred Lorenzer (1973) attempted to reinterpret psychoanalysis on the basis of social sciences and accused Freud and his psychoanalysis of "Geschichts und Gesellschaftsblindheit" – a blindness towards historical and societal conditions and viewpoints, which, from my viewpoint, also applies to Jung. A comparison with the historical development in Freudian psychoanalysis is informative here. As far as I can see, in the second half of the 20th century, the Freudian tradition successfully rid itself of Freud's outdated conception of drives, which has a lot of similarities with Jung's biologistic conception of archetype theory. In my opinion, such a development is yet to take place within AP.

Criticism from outside of AP

In fields of scholarship and research, Jung's ideas are well-known (e.g., in anthropology, comparative mythology, comparative religion, etc.). Hence, there has also been criticism on Jung's ideas about archetypes from scholars of these fields, who are not analytical psychologists or psychoanalysts. Andrew Neher (1996), for example, has conducted a thorough and detailed investigation of archetype theory, from an epistemological viewpoint as well as from the viewpoint of relevant disciplines. He also explicitly criticizes Jung's way of doing science and theorizing which makes it impossible to clarify whether earlier positions were changed: "The reason is that he rarely repudiated his earlier positions, so that, in most cases, it is difficult to tell whether a later position is intended to replace, or merely supplement, an earlier one" (p. 64). He summarizes the results of his investigation as follows:

> From this analysis, it appears that Jung's theoretical assumption – of universal, transpersonal archetypes – led him astray. Thus he prematurely dismissed the role of personal experience on the one hand, and universal cultural experience on the other, in his examples. This allowed him, having rejected competing theories, to offer his transpersonal theory as the only viable explanation for the similarities in expressions of the unconscious that he cited. As we have seen, however, it is difficult, if not impossible, to eliminate these alternative explanations. Thus Jung's efforts to verify his transpersonal theory must be seen as provocative perhaps but hardly convincing.

(p. 80)

Referring to the similarities found in mythologies from all over the world, the anthropologist Michael Witzel argues:

> More importantly, if the Jungian explanation by archetypes were correct, we would expect that individual archetypes would indeed turn up in all parts of the globe. This, however, is debatable: not all of the supposed archetypes do indeed turn up worldwide. While we may grant that the human psyche has a universal biological substrate in the cortex that may produce similar images worldwide, it is, however, unclear how far this actually underlies local manifestations in myth, art, ritual, or certain stereotypes of behaviour and how far such similarities can be explained by a monolateral metatheory such as that of Jung. At any rate, archetypes do not result directly in elaborate structural details and certainly not in long sequences of such tales, the storyline.
>
> (Witzel 2012, p. 13)

Even more basic is the critique formulated by Levi-Strauss (1970) in his structural approach to anthropology. Interestingly, both Jung and Levi-Strauss attempted to find answers to the same question, namely, how the apparent similarities in mythologies of different ethnicities can be explained – a fact which has seemingly not been dealt with in AP, except by Gras (1981). Levi-Strauss points to a specific mistake made by Jung throughout his works in that he assumes a biologically founded link between a myth or mythological image and its meaning.

> Some of the more recent interpretations of mythological thought originated from the same kind of misconception under which those early linguists were labouring. Let us consider, for instance, Jung's idea that a given mythological pattern, the so-called archetype, possesses a certain meaning. This is comparable to the long-supported error that a sound may possess a certain affinity with a meaning.
>
> (Levi-Strauss 1970, p. 204)

The German scholar and theoretician of psychotherapy integration, Hilarion Petzold et al. (2014), who in his extensive works dealt explicitly with Jung and his archetype theory, takes a critical viewpoint on Jung's argumentation:

> Jung assumed a collective unconscious of the human race, but it has to be assumed that these are rather cultural area determined, interiorised collectivities in the sense of Moscovici's social psychological conception of collective mental representations, that is conscious, pre-conscious and unconscious mentalizations, which can serve as an alternative for the explanation of myth building structural elements, what Jung called archetypes.
>
> (pp. 439–440; transl. C.R.).

Petzold is clear about the fact that these can only be transmitted by socialization and culturalization from one generation to another. He then points out what Jung conceptualizes as archetypal similarities can indeed have rather different connotations depending on different environments and cultural contexts. So, for example, water in the Sahara Desert has a very different connotation from what it receives in England as a nation of seafarers. Another example are the symbolic connotations of the sun, which, as he points out, in the cool North is female, whereas in the hot South, it is male. On the other hand, where there are similarities, for example, the moon being considered as female, it is not necessary to explain them only by reference to universal archetypes:

> This may be because of the rough correspondences of the phases of the moon to the menstrual cycle of women . . . It is not difficult to see that this common symbolism, acquired through experience and not genetically, could account for the perception.

> (Neher 1996, p. 75)

Referring to the works on mythology, in which Jung cooperated with Kerenyi, he argues, similarly to Witzel, that the assumed similarities in mythological motifs cannot be found in detailed research. In general, he accuses Jung of neglecting social, environmental and political contexts of mythologies, religious beliefs and social practices.

Jung dealing with criticism: A lesson from the history of the Zürich Psychological Club

How did Jung deal with criticism that was directed against his theory? The Zürich Psychological Club, which became Jung's main forum very early on to introduce his theories, can serve as an example. At the beginning, real debate between the members would take place, which later developed into a sole forum for Jung's point of view. This development was caused, to a large extent, by Jung's inability to accept and handle criticism. This can even be seen in the arrangement of the room: wooden chairs for the audience; in the first row, a big leather armchair for Jung with two more leather armchairs, one on each side, for Emma and Toni Wolff. When Jung disliked a speaker, he talked loudly to Toni Wolff during that lecture. When Hans Trüb (chairman at the time) asked him to respect the lecturers, he lashed out in rage and avoided the club for more than two years. Then Toni Wolff became chairwoman and made sure that only admirers and enthusiastic supporters of Jung remained in the forum, who formed a resonance space for him (interestingly enough, he derogatorily called them the "11,000 virgins") (Bair 2003; Healy 2017).

In the beginning, there were few members who could defy Jung theoretically, which he tried to shout down with the strength of his voice, for example, Alphonse Maeder and Hans Schmid.

Hans Schmid, beyond all criticism a lifelong friend of Jung's, criticized him explicitly because of his way of dealing with relationships. He observed that Jung would always be sarcastic when the subject of romantic relationships was brought up and reproached him for lacking in sensitivity concerning the needs and feelings of others (Healy 2017, p. 178). The following is an interesting comment about Jung's style of debating and his position within the club by Schmid:

> In a tower at the Obersee you . . . have adopted the heritage of Nietzsche, a father to no one, a friend to no one, completely self-sufficient, fulfilled by yourself. Across the way, here and there, live a few other male and female introverts, each in his own tower, loving humanity in those "farthest away" thus protecting themselves from the devilish love of their "neighbours".
>
> (Bair 2003, p. 283).

There is even more to this story: Schmid once invited the philosopher Martin Buber to speak at the club, and Jung attempted to keep the other members from participating in the lecture (Bair 2003). This, of course, has to do with the opposing viewpoints Jung and Buber had on relationships, Jung emphasizing development as coming out of the individual, whereas Buber is well known for his philosophy of dialogue, emphasizing "Das Ich wird am Du" ("The ego develops in the dialogue with Thou"). Jung openly disliked Buber, as can be seen in his "Answer to Martin Buber" (CW 18/II; the topic of Jung's attitude to relationships will be expanded in the last chapter).

The same thing happened at the Eranos conferences. In the beginning, there were a few participants who countered Jung's views (e.g., the biologist Adolf Portmann, who criticized the biological foundation of Jung's archetype theory). Instead of accepting the criticism, Jung talked badly about Portmann behind his back (Shamdasani 2003). The organizer of the conference then stopped inviting such critics so that Jung and his psychology were not questioned anymore (Healy 2017).

Bair (2003) puts it like this: Jung welcomed the new as long as it came from him. He was not afraid of changing or specifying his position or admitting that he had been wrong but only if he was the one to state it first. He would allow a dialogue and divergence but only if he had the last word. There were people who dared to question his authority and had creative additions or new insight into his method. He simply broke off relations with those people. The other group of people was composed of the ones who were willing to sit at his feet, listen to his word and carry it on exactly the way he said it. Many of these later became authors of Jungian literature and are being most quoted in the history of AP and concerning the biography of Jung. The only exception is Wolfgang Pauli, from whom he accepted corrections simply because he was not educated in quantum physics.

From this, the following picture of Jung is present: it seems as if his theory was, for him, the truth at a very early point in time. He was not interested in verifying his theories scientifically or putting them up for discussion. During his career, he continuously isolated himself and put up a hard shell that from a certain point on, nobody, and no facts, could penetrate. What he himself may have called introversion seems to be a sort of theoretical isolation, which I think still can be seen in AP today.

As an example, I will again refer to Norbert Bischof. I tried to research whether there was ever an exchange of any kind between Norbert Bischof, Professor of Psychology at the University of Zürich and the Zürich Jung-Institute, which were so close to each other. I could only discover that Bischof held a lecture at the Jung-Institute once. However, this event did not have any lasting impact on the Jungian literature or theory. Another example, already mentioned earlier, is the work of Hilarion Petzold, who is the founder of integrative therapy and an expert of analytical literature. He refers to Jung in many of his publications while, at the same time, criticizing him. Nowhere in the Jungian literature can a reference be found to this critique by Petzold.

Is archetype theory a belief system?

Neher (1996) points out the crucial question:

> If Jung's theory of archetypes and the collective unconscious is as flawed as it seems, we are faced with the question raised previously: why does it hold so much appeal – for Jung, for Jungian's, and for many others since Jung's time?
>
> (pp. 82–83)

I would like to coin the following hypothesis: for Jung, his theory was not merely a theory but a strong belief based on his personal inner experience. It could not only explain individual psychological development but became something of a "Welterklärungstheorie" (world explanation). This could explain the similarities and differences of peoples and cultures, even the development of mankind. Of course, for many developers of scientific theories, ideas are supported by strong beliefs, but in Jung, this is heightened to an extreme. Although he points out the fact of the "personal equation", I wish to mention that in his own case, he was not able to consider this and to distance himself from his own ideas. He was unable to take a neutral stance, what is called scientific scepticism in academia, and to discuss it openly – in the sense of being open for criticism and for corrections. It became a creed, and consequently, when presenting his ideas to the public, it turned into somewhat of a preaching. A reason being that Jung's ideas and concepts were so closely linked with his own experience. For him, this was a kind of truth; thus, he did not concern himself with finding evidence for his theories and was unwilling to accept criticism.

My next hypothesis is that in his time and still today, followers are drawn to his ideas because there is a certain need to have a belief in such a "holistic" creed. This has already been observed by others:

> Much of the responsibility for the uncritical acceptance of Jung's theory, however, must be borne by his disciples, who have tended to view his ideas as gospel rather than as tentative hypotheses that require ongoing testing and development. . . . Whatever the reasons, the unfortunate consequence is that the theory of archetypes continues to flourish, and even make new inroads, unchecked by reason and thoughtful scrutiny.
>
> (Neher 1996, p. 63)

Neher argues, by quoting Jung's argument, that the idea of archetypes has a healing effect, as one realizes that individual pain and bitterness unites all humanity: "Granted, this perspective may sometimes be soothing, but the danger is it may also encourage people to discount the personal implications – of the dream, for example – when these need to be recognized to resolve a personal issue" (p. 83). I think this dangerous misinterpretation of the idea of archetypes has manifested many times in the history of AP (see also the discussion in the final chapter).

There is no doubt that much has been published on said problems in Jungian literature, and many of the points I am making here have already been discussed. Nevertheless, my impression is that outside academic circles, there is still a strong tendency to idealize Jung and cling to very classical positions in AP and to a conservative reading of his works in the Jungian community. It seems that the differentiated state-of-the-art in critical publications has not had a strong reach into the Jungian community. Rather worse is the impression: there seems to be an attitude of superiority, which can be found in Jung as well as in many of his followers today, in the sense that their model of how the psyche develops and how psychotherapy works is ultimate, as if they were in possession of the truth about the psyche. This has led to an objectification and ontologizing of concepts which originally were just a personal experience of Jung. This attitude of superiority has also led to a tendency of isolation against insights, findings and ideas from other disciplines.

Conclusion: Not one but several theories

It was pointed out that there are not only different epistemological approaches to be found in Jung's archetype theory but there are also different lines of thought which run through his theorizing around archetypes. Consequentially, not only Jung's writings but also the general state in AP concerning archetype theory is characterized by confusion and a lack of a consensual definition. As a consequence, if some author attempts to provide proof for the existence of archetypes, it is not clear what is meant by this term and which of the many definitions is applied in the respective context.

Resulting from the analysis of different statements and the definitions of Jung as well as the community and as an attempt to present a solution to this problematic situation, which puts into question the core of AP, I would like to propose the idea that in Jung – and in the debate around archetype theory in AP – we find not one coherent theory but several distinct theories. These must be differentiated and separated from each other. The following figure provides an overview of four distinct theories that can be found concerning archetypes. They should be seen as an attempt to organize different lines of thought into distinct categories, creating a theoretical order:

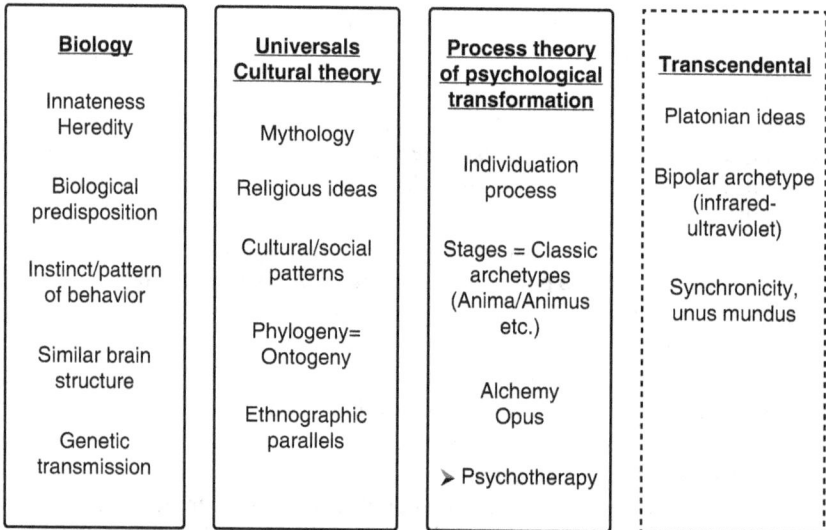

Biology	**Universals Cultural theory**	**Process theory of psychological transformation**	**Transcendental**
Innateness Heredity	Mythology		Platonian ideas
Biological predisposition	Religious ideas	Individuation process	Bipolar archetype (infrared-ultraviolet)
Instinct/pattern of behavior	Cultural/social patterns	Stages = Classic archetypes (Anima/Animus etc.)	Synchronicity, unus mundus
Similar brain structure	Phylogeny= Ontogeny		
Genetic transmission	Ethnographic parallels	Alchemy Opus	
		➤ Psychotherapy	

Figure 4.1 Four different theories inherent to archetype theory

Theory 1: A theory of biologically preformatted (genetically transmitted) mental capacities

According to this theory, humans are not a blank slate at birth. Due to their biological makeup, their genome and the similarity of their brain structure, etc., certain preformed features are innate. These can take the shape of instinctual behaviours/ patterns of behaviour, preformatted categories that direct and form perception and patterns which govern the formation of images, ideas, etc. These features or patterns are thought to be transmitted from one generation to the other by way of genetic code. They are considered to have the character of archaic behaviour and can appear primarily in regressive states of consciousness, especially in psychopathology (e.g., in psychoses). This is a biological theory embedded in the natural sciences and has strong connections to the medical disciplines, human genetics, neurosciences and ethology/behavioural biology. Concepts from evolutionary theory are included, whereby humans are viewed as the product of a long line of evolutionary development, this being the reason why humans demonstrate archaic behaviour that can also be linked to our animal ancestors. Another associated idea is that there exists a "natural" way of living for humans, a way of life appropriate according to the background of our evolutionary history and development, in other words, a form of living which is "close to our nature" respectively, fulfilling the needs implanted in our biological makeup. This theory contains the idea that we can learn about this way of human life by looking back into the history of mankind.

Theory 2: An anthropological theory of human universals

This theory belongs to the field of anthropology and deals with the assumption of human universals that can be found in peoples from all over the world and from different epochs. The focus lies on similarities that are said to be found cross-culturally in social rules and patterns, cultural habits and symbols/images, religious beliefs and ideas, mythological motifs and narratives, etc. Information is drawn from ethnological and archaeological findings from indigenous or prehistoric human societies and cultures. This theory entails an idea characterized as the homology of phylogeny and ontogeny, meaning that the psychological development of the individual recapitulates the evolutionary and cultural development of mankind. Included in this idea is the assumption of a scale of different levels concerning developmental maturity from archaic/primitive to developed/civilized, which can accordingly be applied to individual as well as cultural and societal development.

Theory 3: A process theory of psychological transformation (in psychotherapy)

This theory is concerned with describing transformational processes, which can be observed in psychotherapy as well as in other forms of transformational phases in human life. Such transformational processes can also be observed in the sense of decomposition or regression and in certain cases and phases of psychopathology, namely, in the course of a psychotic development which produces a succession of certain typical ideas and images. The general idea of this theory is a force within the human organism/psyche, which is behind this process of psychological transformation and has the aim of greater integration of the personality, respectively, wholeness. This is synonymous with psychological healing and sanity. It includes the idea that the integration of the totality of a person, often called wholeness, is preformatted in the psyche/unconscious. This also includes the uniqueness in the sense of the individuality of a person. The second idea of this theory is the assumption that there is a general form or shape of the transformational process towards integration and healing, which is applicable to all human beings and can, if explicated, be used as a map for the psychotherapeutic process. The general assumption exists in archetype theory that models for this universal map of transformational processes in the psyche can be found in symbolic form in certain cultural and religious traditions, namely, alchemy, mystic traditions in different religions (e.g., gnosis, yoga, the Buddhist path etc.), religious scriptures (e.g., the Gospel, the *Tibetan Book of the Dead*, etc.), as well as mythologies and fairy tales. One of Jung's major aims in forming his psychology was to create an universal map of the transformational process, so as to be applied in the practice of psychotherapy. The archetypes, which Jung provides a detailed description of and which I have called the "classical archetypes" (anima/animus, the shadow, the wise old man, the great mother, the Self, the trickster, the journey of the hero, etc.), were conceptualized as being stages of this process. This demonstrates that the archetype concept is important for Jung's psychology, especially because it is the explanatory concept behind the conceptualization of the process. It is assumed that the process and its stages are preformatted in the psyche of every individual, throughout the world, during every epoch. Training in Jungian institutes is concerned mainly with creating a deep understanding of this transformational process, and research and publication activity in the Jungian world contributes to establishing a map of this process. I would go as far as stating this theory is the core of AP. In the following, I will, therefore, refer to this theory as the core theory. This idea is a unique contribution of Jung's to the development of psychotherapy theory. As far as I understand, he was the first to present this idea, which in turn had a strong impact on the formation of other psychotherapy schools, namely, the humanistic and transpersonal approaches. It should be noted, however, that there are different versions of the transformational process. This ranges from an idea of a centring process to a highly detailed map with a large number of stages, as for example, described in the journey of the hero.

These first three theories could be subsumed under so-called "normal science", meaning the theoretical concepts, statements and assumptions are subject of specialized disciplines in the field of sciences (e.g., biology, anthropology, etc). These disciplines can provide footing for the aforementioned concepts, or better yet, the theories summarized earlier can be tested against contemporary insights and empirical evidence provided by these disciplines. The confrontation with contemporary insight and state-of-the-art disciplines will be conducted in the following chapters for each of the aforementioned part theories separately. As I have pointed out earlier in the section on criticism, in theories around the archetype concept in AP, nomothetic statements have frequently been made, which can be tested in this sense.

The fourth and last theory inherent in the archetype concept is, in contrast to the first three, not part of the field of normal science. It can, therefore, not be tested in the aforementioned sense and will not be dealt with further in this report.

Theory 4: A transcendental theory of a unity reality

This theory attempts to transcend the usual limits of normal science, the so-called deterministic model, and bridge the gap between mind and matter by making use of ideas and concepts from quantum physics. These ideas were mainly developed in the Pauli-Jung-dialogue, a conversation which Jung conducted over decades with the physicist and Nobel laureate Wolfgang Pauli (Gieser 2005). A product of this conversation is the concept of synchronicity and the idea of unus mundus, a potential reality in which mind and matter are still united. This is a conceptualization comparable to ideas of quantum physics. Even before this dialogue, Jung introduced philosophical and transcendental concepts into his archetype theory, namely, Platonian ideas and Kantian categories – metaphysical concepts in the broadest sense. These ideas depart clearly from normal sciences, are highly speculative and present one of the main reasons why Jung has been accused of esoteric thinking and mysticism. It is a quasi-religious concept, yes, even connected with premodern forms of thinking and speculation (e.g., medieval cosmologies), although it attempts to connect these speculative ideas with concepts from modern physics. It can be regarded as another one of Jung's attempts to give the archetype concept a foundation in the natural sciences. Because of their speculative character, these ideas cannot be grounded in empirical observations. Nevertheless, they did have a strong impact on the development of concepts in parapsychology and contemporary consciousness studies, where they have been developed further (for detailed accounts and overviews of these developments, see Roesler 2014, 2018a; Atmanspacher & Fuchs 2014; Atmanspacher et al. 2002; Walach et al. 2011; Cambray 2009). These ideas also had a strong influence on the development of transpersonal psychologies, psychotherapies and spiritually integrated therapies (Roesler & Reefschläger 2022). In this regard, these speculations resulted in being very fruitful for different academic fields.

Due to the earlier analyses of different definitions to be found in AP for the term archetype and based on the history of criticism, it can be summarized that there is a high degree of confusion in the term archetype. My conclusion from this analysis is the following: this lack of consensus and clarity in the debate around archetypes is a product of Jung's (and others') attempt to combine the four aforementioned theories at all costs. I would even go as far as stating that Jung was fixated on the idea of weaving these different lines of thought and scientific traditions together into one coherent concept – **which has failed because it is fundamentally impossible**. This attempt has resulted in a big mess of contradictions, aporia, highly speculative ideas in the disguise of nomothetic statements, problematic assumptions about the nature of humans, etc. Enormous damage to the reputation of AP within the scientific field was caused, in some sense, justly, as there is no way of healing this theoretical disaster while maintaining Jung's original concept. The only fit solution I see is to take apart the different theoretical elements, as described earlier, to review them for compliance with the contemporary, state-of-the-art knowledge and with the relevant disciplines to see what remains. This will be carried out in the following chapters. Previous practices, often found in Jungian publications, drew out a singular theoretical concept or empirical finding from a scientific theory or discipline and used it as "evidence" that Jung was initially correct. Again, this attitude has been criticized before:

> A Jungian writer knows a lot about some obscure tribe, or one particular fairytale, or one particular mythologem, or subatomic physics, and appears, in the Jungian world, to be a big authority on it. But when you actually go out and find academics who are into fairytales, or that particular tribe, or that particular myth, or mythology in general, or physics, what they have to say about the level of the sort of knowledge and sophistication shown by the Jungian is rather damning.
>
> (Samuels 1998, p. 29)

In contrast to this, the current review will apply the following methodology: the different lines of thought and theories will be confronted with mainstream knowledge as they developed in the respective disciplines. If necessary, historical developments will be traced for explaining earlier misconceptions, as well as how they were overcome. In the course of this confrontation of archetype theory with contemporary knowledge, a description of the historical predecessors and influential ideas, theories and traditions, which impacted Jung's theory, are included. At the end of each chapter, a conclusion will be drawn regarding the validity of archetype theory.

Note

1 A recent example: in the IAAP newssheet of October 2021 (#18), a research project is presented, with the aim of investigating dreams dealing with the COVID pandemic; the following are the research questions:

What is happening within the collective psyche during this time of turmoil? This question remains at the heart of the study . . . the primary hypothesis:

During times of historic turmoil, apocalyptic imagery may emerge within dreams as Jung himself analyzed during the outbreak of World War 1. Our focus remains on the collective expression of the unconscious, the objective psyche during such times.

Here, the idea of a collective psyche, respectively, "the objective psyche", is ontologized, without any awareness of the hypothetical, if not to say speculative, character of this concept; it is dealt with as a given. Such a use of theoretical concepts has to be regarded as unscientific; in such a research design, it is unclear whether individual dreams are an expression of the hypothesized collective unconscious or not, how this shows in the data, whether this is then seen as proof of an objective psyche, etc. At the same time, Jungians want their theory to be seen as a scientific theory and are surprised when the scientific community regards it as mystical or esoteric, which is no wonder when being confronted with such an understanding of science as presented in the previous quote.

Chapter 5

Biology, genetics and inheritance

In this chapter, the first of the four theories outlined earlier will be discussed, which is the biological line of argumentation, and will be examined with contemporary insights and the state-of-the-art in the respective disciplines. These are behavioural biology, human genetics, evolutionary theory, evolutionary psychology and biological anthropology in general.

Innateness

For Jung, his psychology was certainly a natural science, and thus, biology was a part of it.

> Although psychology rightly claims autonomy in its own special field of research, it must recognize a far-reaching correspondence between its facts and the data of biology.
>
> (CW 8, p. 232)

Jung was obviously convinced that archetypes are genetically imprinted and transmitted from one generation to the next via biological pathways. Jon Mills (2018) gives an overview where Jung refers to this biological argumentation in his works. In this context, Jung argues that the archetype is identical with, or at least similar to, instincts and explicitly equalizes it with the term pattern of behaviour from behavioural biology. He also believes that typical life situations and experiences, which have been endlessly repeated in the history of mankind, have been imprinted into the biological outfit of humans. Jung does not use the term explicitly, but what he tries to convey here in contemporary terms means that these experiences have changed the genome. Archetypes in this conceptualization are thus genetically imprinted (therefore, arche-*types*), innate and the same or like instincts and patterns of behaviour. This view has been repeated again and again in the history of AP. Until recently and even today, there is still a considerable number of Jungians who closely follow Jung's biological conception of archetypes (e.g., McCully 1971; Gordon 1985; Humbert 1988; Krieger 2019; to a certain extent, also Goodwyn 2020a, 2020b). Such ideas are not a matter of the past. It was also found to

DOI: 10.4324/9781003348191-5

be a widespread pattern of argumentation in the survey conducted for this study. The general idea that archetypes and instincts are closely related and that instincts are a considerable factor in human psychology is transmitted even in very recent publications which draw on contemporary neuroscientific findings (Alcaro et al. 2017; see next section).

For many years, the most important protagonist of the biological approach to archetypes was Anthony Stevens (1983, 2003). In his conceptualization, archetypes are genetically encoded and transmitted, and this is the explanation for their universality. Stevens argues that there is a continuum of behaviours, ranging from those which are environmentally stable and those which are environmentally labile. Stevens claims that Jung conceived of the archetypal plea of the phylogenetic psyche as determining and coordinating the basic patterns of human life in a way which was characteristic for all members of the species. He proceeds to argue that unconscious images can also be part of the blueprint on which behavioural systems are based and concludes that from a biological standpoint, the archetype is an ancient genetically determined releaser or inhibitor which directly influences our behaviour. He exemplifies this argument with focus on attachment theory and attachment behaviour which he sees as a striking example of biologically based, genetically determined behaviour patterns (see next section for a detailed discussion of the findings of attachment research and contemporary viewpoints in attachment theory).

Another proponent of the biological inheritance paradigm is John R. Haule (2004, 2011). He argues that there is a considerable synthesis between modern genetics, the Darwinian paradigm in general and Jung's ideas about the archetype. "Jung dreamt the dream of the biological and human sciences at the time before a synthesis of these disciplines was possible" (Haule 2004, p. 150) and stresses the point that "Jung never gave up on this Darwinian intuition" (p. 151).

No account of the human condition can be taken seriously if it ignores the 5 million years of natural selection that have made us what we are. . . . These were to be archetypal realities, passed on through DNA, and expressed in distinctive neuronal tracts in the brain. They would include customs and laws regarding property, incest, marriage, kinship, and social status; myths and legends; beliefs about the supernatural; gambling, adultery, homicide, schizophrenia, and the therapies to deal with them. Jung said pretty much the same things 80 years ago.
(p. 154)

Haule then argues with what he calls the "language archetype", meaning the innate capacity for language acquisition (see next section).

The course of the debate in AP

Interestingly, the state of the debate in AP has moved far beyond these reductionistic and biologistic conceptualizations and for quite a long time now. The limitations of the biological argumentation were already put forth by George Hogenson in his debate with Anthony Stevens at the IAAP International Congress in 2001 (Stevens et al. 2003; for an overview, see Hogenson 2019). It could be said that after this debate, together with a publication by Hogenson (2001, see also 2003) from the same year, it was quite clear that a position such as that of Stevens, which could be characterized as a naïve innatism and biological reductionism, could no longer be sustained:

> one would have to say that the archetypes of the collective unconscious do not exist, in the sense that they cannot be said to be some place. They are not *in* the genome. . . . one must look at the complete context within which we attribute their existence to a set of interacting phenomena.
>
> (Hogenson 2003, p. 19)

Already around that time, there was a huge amount of evidence from biology, genetics, developmental psychology, etc., which speaks clearly against the biological assumption. First of all, there is consensus in behavioural biology that humans do not have instincts (see next section for a detailed discussion). There are some basic reflexes in new-born infants, but these are quickly lost and replaced by mental patterns stemming from experience. Understanding the human genome led to the insight that symbolic information cannot be genetically encoded. Also, even if there are genetically preformed mental patterns, they are subject to strong influence from the environment via epigenetic processes. The key concept of contemporary theories of human development, therefore, is gene-environment interaction. A detailed analysis of these contemporary insights and their implications for archetype theory was already presented by Jean Knox (2003). Later, she again stressed the following point:

> The fact that animals demonstrate patterns of automatic motor action, . . . is mistakenly used by Jungians as the basis for arguing archetypes are also an inherited pattern of mental representation, imagery and thought, apparently part of our genetic make-up. . . . Automatic behaviour patterns can be under significant genetic influence . . . mental imagery and thought are the result of much more complex interactions between brain, mind and environment, in which genetic "hard-wiring" plays virtually no part.
>
> (Knox 2009b, p. 311)

There is a strong consensus of experts dealing with archetype theory in the last two decades that Jung's assumption of a biological/genetical transmission of archetypes can no longer be supported; this consensus was reflected in a number of papers published in the last 20 years (for an overview, see Roesler 2012a; Merchant 2019).

In contrast to this clarification in the expert literature, the state of the debate seems to have only little or even no impact on the teaching of archetype theory in Jungian training institutes. I am part of the faculty in a number of Jungian training institutes, and it seems to me that training candidates are often taught about archetypes as if nothing had happened since Jung's days. The same applies to many Jungian publications, which still apply an undifferentiated biological approach to archetype theory almost identical with that of Jung's late years.

Already in 2003, Jean Knox pointed to this problem, stating that often extremely outdated concepts are used in Jungian psychology, especially when it comes to archetypes. Such an ignorance of contemporary insights and debates, of course, creates a massive problem when AP attempts to find a place in academic psychology today. Merchant (2009) even suggested that the use of the term archetype itself should be questioned:

> If contemporary neuroscience does ultimately reveal that the archetype-as-such is not innate as originally conceived, then the question arises – is the word "archetype" itself too suffused with innatism and preformationism meanings to prevent confusion? . . . (For) if we think, act and clinically practise as if archetypes are *a priori*, innate psychic structures which determine psychological life when this is not the case, then we could become irrelevant to the broader psychotherapeutic community.
>
> (Merchant 2009, p. 355)

Consequently, authors such as Hogenson, Knox and Merchant developed what today is called the emergentist position (see also Cambray 2002), which attempts to integrate the contemporary state-of-the-art in genetics, developmental psychology and neurosciences with archetype theory, which will be discussed in detail later. However, as a first step, the question whether there are instincts/patterns of behaviour in humans will be discussed.

Are archetypes instincts/patterns of behaviour?

Primarily, it has to be said that the parallel Jung made between archetypes in humans and instincts in animals is not supported. Norbert Bischof, Professor of Psychology at Zürich University and Ethologist trained in the school of Konrad Lorenz, published a very differentiated and sophisticated study of Jung's theory in the light of modern developmental psychology and ethology (Bischof 1996). He points out very clearly that there can be no parallel between instinctive patterns in animals (e.g., how birds build their nest) on the one hand and complex symbolic structures like mythological stories or rituals in human beings on the other. In ethology/behavioural biology (Bischof 2020), an instinct/pattern of behaviour is a technical term and, as such, is clearly defined having three components:

1. a trigger mechanism, which means that there is a specific stimulus in the environment which can be detected by the individual, which then
2. activates a drive, which leads to
3. an inherited coordinated action pattern

There is no such thing in human beings (Bischof 2020). Human infants have no inherited action programs but only certain reflexes, which, in some cases, can only be shown in the first days of life and then quickly vanish. The innervation of the extremities in human beings is highly unspecific and only develops into specific action patterns by instruction and/or trial and error.

In contrast to these findings, Jung sees himself and all humans in general as objects to archetypal powers with no possibility to resist the unfolding of those powers, as they are thought to have instinctual power.[1] In the concept of the individuation process, this is even highlighted as the sense of life – to fulfill the potential which is (biologically) rooted in the person. There is the idea of a certain inevitability in the unfolding of archetypal powers, which has implications for Jung's view on human relationships. Bischof (1996) examined in detail the analogy archetype – inborn release mechanism (IRM) using the "child schema" from ethology (Eibl-Eibesfeldt 1987) and the archetype of the (divine) child (Jung, CW 9/1) to test whether parallels can be drawn between ethology and psychology. The so-called "child schema" consists of the idea that for most animal species, the head of the young animals is bigger in relation to the body and the face is compacter, therefore, meaning a squat nose or that the eyes, nose and mouth are closer together, etc. This form presents a trigger for the adult individual that inhibits aggression and activates caregiving behaviour among other reactions. Bischof contrasts Jung's explanations on the child archetype, in particular, the pictorial representations in which the child appears. His conclusion:

> These two patterns of interpretation are poles apart. . . . For the ethological concept the central point of interest is evidently the physiognomic appearance of the child form. There are very definite formal characteristics which must fit like a key in a lock of the perceptual filter which should trigger the nurturing behaviour.
>
> (Bischof 1996, p. 121f)

Such a key-in-the-lock-principle does not exist in humans, and the same applies to the nurturing behaviour which should be triggered. Concerning nurturing behaviour, a meta-analysis of cross-cultural studies showed that there is no universal pattern of nurturing behaviours in human beings (Ahnert 2010).

For the pictorial representations, which Jung researched as manifestations of the child archetype, the child carried a symbolic meaning which is transmitted through the spatial symbolism:

> The child is a carrier of meaning who is not at all interested in how he looks, but rather only that he is in the middle of the image and that he is enclosed on all sides by a protective, uterine shell. It is easy to imagine that a diamond in a chest, a pearl in a mussel, a precious elixir in a retort evokes similar images and therefore these pictures are also named by Jung as possible alternatives.
>
> (Bischof 1997, p. 122)

The problem is, therefore, that Jung places two entities in parallel which lie on categorically different levels. On the one hand is an instinctive pattern of behaviour, almost on the level of a reflex, and on the other hand is a more or less complex symbolic structure of meaning. Precisely, this issue runs throughout Jung's whole biological argument on archetypes. Bird behaviour patterns cannot be equated with complex, meaningful patterns, such as rituals or mythological stories in humans.

On the other hand, according to Bischof, it seems quite plausible that in contrast to instincts, there are actually certain categories of perception and logic which are biologically predetermined in human beings. These categories organize perception and behaviour in certain directions. Bischof (2020) gives a number of examples: the distinction of figure and background, truth and appearance, main and minor matter/Substantia et Accidentia, causality and the concept of identity in the sense that something remains the same over time and situations. Infants, for example, can identify whether a moving object is a living organism or not at the age of only a few months (see next section for a detailed discussion of innate mental capacities).

Unfortunately, this differentiated work by Bischof never received attention in AP, as has happened to a number of important scientific findings.

Instincts, drives and the human condition

The question whether humans have instincts, or drives, and if so, to what extent they influence human behaviour, has haunted anthropology for centuries. In philosophical anthropology, this state of affairs has been characterized with the term "Hiatus" (Arnold Gehlen), which means that there is a gap between the human drives or impetus on the one side and its aims on the other. Human drive is unspecific; therefore, the gap enables humans to inhibit behaviour and to place reflection and culturally transmitted aims in the gap. This Hiatus also leads to the fact that human motivations tend to differentiate, expand and destabilize and, therefore, need cultural regulation. Examples for such secondary motivations are the need for admiration or competitiveness, as well as the awareness of one's own mortality and, based on this, transcendent motivations.[2]

The "primacy of images"

Much of the same as was said earlier also applies to Jung's use of the term image and his idea that images are primary. Instead, as ethology clearly states, human infants are born without any preformed images. They do not even have the neural capacities for constructing visual representations and store them in the brain before the age of at least six months. A proponent of a modified biological approach to archetypes, such as Goodwyn (2020a), clearly states: "We do not inherit images, although culturally-specific, learned content can be utilized in the construction of archetypal images" (p. 924). Nevertheless, even in current publications, Jungian authors continue to argue with the primacy of images in total neglect of the respective scientific knowledge. A current example: in a recent German textbook on the work with symbols in Jungian psychology (Dorst 2015), Jung's assumption that images are primary in the psyche is repeated, without any reference to current brain research, which clearly shows that until the age of 4–6 months, there are no image representations possible because of the immaturity of the neural system. The first psychic representations are embodiments, not images. The latter point was taken up by Angela Connolly:

> The problem is evident in that Jung conceived of the image as something purely internal, springing entirely from the unconscious. . . . The result of this outlook was that Jung failed to adequately take into consideration the role of the body and the wider material environment in the creation of meaningful images.
>
> (Connolly 2018, p. 73)

Mark Solms (2016) points to the fact that in the limbic system or other innate brain structures, no images are stored. Images, as in dreams, for example, are secondary products involving preconscious or even conscious processes. This means that there are no primary images; in other words, there are no images that are totally unconscious and no images that have never been conscious before that were not conceived based on experience.

Colman (2016) argues very much in a similar way:

> I want to argue that any kind of formal structure is secondary to the process whereby archetypal images are created through the activity of symbolic imagination. That is, symbolic imagination is not shaped by pre-existing psychic forms so much as being the means by which it is possible to conceive of such forms in the first place. Ontologically, the image is primary and the abstract forms were present for the levels of symbolic thought being constituted by rather than being constitutive of symbolic imagination.
>
> (Colman 2016, p. 16)

The "similarity-of-brain-structure" argument

Another line of argument to be found in Jung as well as in recent publications in AP (and in the survey as well) is to assume that all humans share the same brain structure. The proponents of a biological foundation of archetypes argue that the similarities in social patterns, religious ideas, etc., which are thought to be archetypal, come about through this general similarity of the brain structure in all human beings (e.g., Stevens 2003; Haule 2011).

For a long time, this viewpoint has been shared by brain researchers, who investigated large samples and identified regions of the brain which were thought to be the locations of certain processes or capacities. In the last years, however, there has been a shift in brain research based on more detailed investigations of interindividual differences in neurologic performance as well as functional brain structure. A group of researchers from University College London (Foulkes & Blakemore

2018) took the considerable effort to investigate individual differences in the maturation of the brain in adolescents and young adults and found considerable differences in the time frame of the maturation of different parts of the brain. They argued that the formation of the functional structure of the brain is not only genetically preformatted but is also subject to influences from the environment and the social network of family and friends. These findings were supported by results of researchers from Columbia University in New York (Noble et al. 2015), who could demonstrate the differences being closely correlated with the socioeconomic status of the parents: the higher the status, the larger was the cortical surface in many brain regions at the same age. These differences also resulted in higher competencies in speech, reading, social cognition and other fields of intellectual performance. These findings have received further support from other recent studies of neuroscientific researchers (Seghier & Price 2018). So generally speaking, those parts of the brain which are evolutionary later developments are to a much greater extent subject to environmental influences (e.g., in the sense of education) than was previously assumed. This is, again, a striking example for how misleading research can be when it starts from pre-conceptualized theories and convictions of preformationism, in this case, the unquestioned prejudice that human brains are similar by nature.

In the same line, Verhoeven (2011) argues that there is no need, as cognitive theorists in anthropology, to assume a biological foundation of religious representations because these are only categories good to think with and are, therefore, persistent components of human minds.

> The neurophysiologist Diamond, . . . found that enriched or impoverished environments respectively had positive and negative effects on brain growth throughout the life of rats. Very probably this holds for humans as well.
>
> (p. 121)

Genetics

Jung argues that archetypes can be located in the genetic makeup of human beings. This very general assumption has been repeated again and again in AP in the past as well as in recent publications, as well as in the survey. Therefore, in the following, the state-of-the-art in genetics, with a special focus on human genetics, will be summarized. Very generally speaking, instincts/patterns of behaviour in animals (e.g., the pattern of how the weaver bird builds its nest) is certainly genetically imprinted and transmitted from one generation to the other, which means that no learning, instruction or experience is necessary for the birds to perform this pattern. A complex mythological concept (i.e., cognitive content) simply cannot be genetically coded. First, genes encode only the construction of certain proteins which in turn entails certain biological processes – not symbolic information. Second, the space to store such complex information in the genome simply does not exist; the existing genes (be it 24,000 or even 100,000) would never be sufficient to achieve the coding of that which is conceptualized as archetypes in Jung's theory. We need to keep in mind that the biological/genetic hypothesis of archetypes has to explain how such complex symbolic structures, as for example, the myth of the hero (which is a narrative structure), the anima with all her attributes, etc., come about in the human mind.

Human geneticists are very clear in their assertion that genes cannot serve as carriers of complex symbolic information. Only subcortical structures arise through genetic control in early human development. Symbolic information, however, needs networks in the neocortex that only form during development, well beyond the first year of life (Knox 2003). This means that archetypes, in the sense of complex symbolic structures (e.g., the myth of the hero), fundamentally cannot be genetically coded, and the existing innate mental structures are so rudimental, or only orientated around sensory perception, that they are miles away from these complex symbolic patterns.

There have already been all kinds of attempts by Jung and others after him to rescue the biologic and genetic concept of archetypes. Jung was also to some extent conscious of the problem that symbolic information cannot be genetically coded. He made a distinction, therefore, from 1947 between the archetype as such, which is only a core and empty of content, and the concrete archetypal image, where there is indeed culturally different content (see previous section for the problems connected with the concept of the archetype as such).

Jung's assertion of a genetically invested complex archetype is based on the fragmented knowledge of genetics in his time. The actual way in which genes function, as we know today, is clearly distinct from the notion which Jung assumes as a basis and which also appears in many current arguments. This outdated idea has been called the blueprint model (Knox 2003) and is synonymous with genetic determinism: the genetic code provides a blueprint in that the whole construction of a human being and also their brain is predetermined, and this blueprint is only read and implemented in early development.

In contrast to this outdated model, and based on contemporary insights in the workings of genes, even a proponent of an evolutionary genetical approach to archetype theory as Goodwyn (2020a) states:

> Genetics can tell us about the effects of the absence or presence of a particular protein, or it can tell us about biomarkers for various mental illnesses, but for more specific questions about psychic contents, genes are not very useful because the processes involved are just far too complex. It is a long and labyrinthine journey from gene to psyche (even ignoring the difficulties of the mind-body problem), with ultra-complex details we can barely track and the danger of cross category errors (like asking how genes can encode symbols) looming around every corner. Genes modify each other, and still other genes modify those genes that modify other genes.

(pp. 2–3)

Epigenetics

It has been found, in recent years, that there are different mechanisms by which genes interact with their environment. Biological and genetic structures can be even changed by social and mental influences during development (Meaney 2010; Cassidy & Shaver 2018).

> We have learned that genes are not only instruments of inheritance in evolution but also targets of molecular signals originating both within the organism and in the environment outside it. These signals regulate development. Rapid progress in understanding these molecular genetic mechanisms has revealed an unexpected potential for plasticity, which can enable relatively few evolutionarily conserved cellular processes to be linked together by differential gene expression into a variety of adaptive patterns that respond to environmental changes, as well as to genetic mutations. The resulting plasticity allows a variety of developmental pathways, evident in both behavior and physiology, to be generated from the same genome.
>
> (Polan & Hofer 2018, p. 118)

It seems that there are sensitive periods for the development of certain capacities and competencies, such as language acquisition (Spelke 2010) or the development of a secure attachment. Again, this demonstrates that the genetic makeup is only responsible for preparing the human infant and child to be especially sensitive for environmental stimuli, namely, caregiver behaviour and interaction, but it does not shape or preform it.

These mechanisms of gene-environment interaction are called epigenetics and have been described in detail in my earlier publication on archetypes (Roesler 2021, pp. 92–105). The most interesting thing is the new insight that gene expression can be altered through early experiences within the uterus and in the first months of life. An example would be the modification of the reaction to stress (Bauer 2006; Meaney 2010). Maternal care in the first months of life leads to various neurobiochemical intermediate steps to remove the methyl groups from the gene switch of the glucocorticoid receptor gene, which means that the gene is permanently accessible for reading. This causes a permanently lower level of stress hormones (e.g., cortisol) and thus represents a permanent buffer against stress.

Based on these early investigations by Michael Meaney (2010), the processes around the establishment of stress-coping mechanisms on the biological level are now very well investigated (for an overview, see Roth 2019). In addition to the aforementioned processes, in which the quality and intensity of maternal care modulates the development of the regulating mechanisms for stress hormones, it was found that also the prenatal levels of stress in the pregnant mother-to-be have an influence on the development of the stress-axis in the embryo. After birth, stressful events for the child as well as for the mother (e.g., a conflictual separation of the parents) can have comparable effects and results in long-lasting changes on a biological level (e.g., in the density of receptors for certain hormones, e.g., oxytocin). In effect, the general capability for stress regulation and coping as well as the self-soothing system are permanently changed. Thus, it can be concluded that psychosocial experiences (e.g., the extent of maternal care) have far-reaching and long-lasting effects on the biological level.

This last observation plays on the famous debate of "Nurture or Nature" which has essentially dominated the discussion in numerous sciences, for example, in developmental psychology, throughout the 20th century. Regarding this debate, it can be said that this question, namely, of whether or not a biological system or environmental factors are prevalent in the formation of mental features, has basically been answered through the knowledge of epigenetics – both are correct. The interesting question here is actually this: How does the interaction between the two variables work?

Gene-environment interaction

Bakermans-Kranenburg and van Ijzendoorn (2018) give a comprehensive account of the insights of contemporary research into epigenetics and the mechanisms of gene-environment interaction. These insights contrast strongly with earlier conceptions, where it is assumed that the genetic makeup of every individual is invariable, originating from conception and remaining basically the same across the lifespan. However, it was found that even monozygotic twins with identical DNA structures may grow apart in gene expression because of changes in the epigenome that influences the expression of genes. It was discovered that three-year-old twin peers had about 1,000 gene differences, whereas when the two have reached 50 years of age, the differences account to more than 5,000 differently expressed genes.

The authors provide summaries of empirical studies supporting this viewpoint: the brains of deceased young males from a suicide brain bank with and without a history of abuse were examined and compared to a matched group of victims of fatal accidents. They found that through methylation of the GR, gene expression (which is crucial in the down regulation of the levels of cortisol) in the brains of the suicide victims was decreased but only when they had experienced child abuse. These specific epigenetic alterations have also been found as a result of child maltreatment or structural neglect in orphanages and in adolescent children whose mothers were exposed to intimate partner violence during pregnancy.

So genetic research has now identified different gene variants which accompany mental features but nevertheless also integrate with environmental influences. Small variances in the "depression gene" (5-HTTLPR), for example, increase the risk of depression – although only in conjunction with adverse childhood experiences. Similar results to those mentioned earlier were found for the 5-HTTLPR gene and its variants which have been associated with depression:

> Carriers of the long variant of 5-HTTLPR showed more unresolved loss or trauma but only when demethylation was observed. Thus, the potentially

protective effects of the long variant seem to be mitigated by the effects of methylation suppressing the activity of this variant. . . . What this study shows, however, is that genetic effects on attachment might be hidden behind interactions with epigenetic changes, which in turn might be critically dependent on environmental input, such as abusive or neglectful parenting.

(Bakermans-Kranenburg & van Ijzendoorn 2018, p. 163)

Belsky and Pluess (2009) coined the term "differential susceptibility" for this.

Taken together, these results mean one thing first and foremost: even when humans are without a doubt constructed with genetic information, the experiences, especially those in the early stages of development and predominantly experiences in relationships with caregivers, essentially play a role in which genetic information can be read and indeed how and when they are read (gene expression) (Marcus 2004, p. 98). Experiences ultimately cause a very different formation of the same genetic predispositions, and certain genes can generally be activated based on certain experiences. The key word of modern developmental theory is, therefore, no longer "blueprint" but rather, "interaction". The debate of "Nurture or Nature" has, therefore, become obsolete.

A particularly important implication concerns the universality of archetypes. Jung thought the archetypes to be present in the same way for all people and that this would only be guaranteed when the archetypes are genetically rooted. Present-day genetics calls this into question. Even if something is genetically predisposed, it in no way means that it also leads to the same characteristic in all gene carriers. As has been shown, this depends to a high degree on environmental influences, with the consequence that the statement "the same gene is present in multiple people" means hardly anything. This also means the argument that archetypes arise from the same construction of the human brain becomes obsolete because this similarity is in no way a given (see also previous section). If people have different experiences over the course of their lives, then they ultimately also have different brains due to the experiences having an impact on the structure of the brain. In addition, there exists the insight in the high sensitivity of biological development to context conditions. Even the smallest influences can, in the course of development, trigger massive changes so that, even by optimal control of gene and environmental conditions, practically no predictions about the formation of features are possible.

This clashes primarily with one of Jung's conceptions, which implicitly pervades his entire work. He contests that the individuality and the mental idiosyncrasy of a person are somehow innate, preformed and independent from external influences. Archetype theory is only the most prominent form of this underlying conception (see also Roesler 2021). This over-emphasis of the autonomy of the individual and the interior is surely, to use Jung's own words, his "personal equation". Jung has made an enormous contribution to the rehabilitation of the inner world and the imagination, of introversion and individual development in the psychology of our rather extraverted culture. This orientation had the downside, in my opinion, however, that it neglected, for the most part, the significance for development of interpersonal relationships. Moreover, it can be said that the current insights of epigenetics only strengthen the significance of the environmental conditions and, in particular, those of early relationships with caregivers, namely, that the same genotype, dependent on the environmental conditions and here above all experiences in close relationships, leads to completely different formations not only in the mental but also in terms of physical biology. The consequences for the role relationships play in development and in psychotherapy will be discussed in the chapter "The core theory".

Temperament

Jung, with his ideas about typology, can be counted to those scholars who strongly argue for interindividual differences in temperament. Now the interesting insight in recent studies regarding temperament differences is that psychological qualities associated with temperament, in contrast to earlier conceptions that they form stable personality orientations which are not influenced by environmental differences, are the basis for brain plasticity and for flexibility in reaction to changes in the environment.

> These kinds of results offer compelling evidence that variations in human action, cognition, and emotion have a material basis, and that the central nervous system participates in these functions in a complex, transactional manner. Moreover, results of these studies support the notion that virtually every physical/physiological structure associated with temperamental variability has multiple functions in both development and adaptation, and that these functions may become reorganized as the environments to which the child must adjust change over ontogenetic time. Finally, the studies highlight the interactive nature of these underlying material participation in behavior, cognition, and emotion, in so far as the effects of temperament and their underlying structures are often mediated and/or moderated by aspects of the physical and social environments.
>
> (Vaughn & Bost 2018, p. 205)

For a number of years now, neurobiologists and neuropsychiatrists have been searching for genes or gene combinations which are responsible for the outbreak of psychological disorders and psychiatric diseases. This movement was strongly backed by pharmaceutical industries in the hope to find drugs which could heal psychiatric disorders. After more than two decades of this kind of research, the results are more than disappointing. It becomes even more clear that even very complex combinations of genes account for just very small percentages of the variance, that is, for the influences behind the outbreak of psychological illnesses (Plomin et al. 2013). So for example, more than 1,000 genes and their combinations have been associated with depression, but even in the largest samples and when all of these gene variants are taken into account, they can explain not more than 2–4%

perception and action, and species typical forms of interpretation, embedded in the typically human environment of symbolic, narrative interaction will be seen to give rise to the immense beauty and complexity of the great myths of our species.

(Hogenson 2001, pp. 607–608)

The most elaborated formulation of this approach is Jean Knox's (2003) book *Archetype, Attachment, Analysis*. Here, she sees development starting from genetically fixed mechanisms, but these are only predispositions for development which need certain cues from the environment to unfold.

Innate mechanisms focus the infant's attention onto features in the environment which are crucial to the infant's survival. . . . Innate mechanisms are activated by environmental cues, interacting with them and organizing them, leading to the formation of primitive spatial and conceptual representations (image schemas or archetypes). These form the foundation on which later, more complex representations can be built.

(Knox 2001, S. 631)

This approach clearly accepts the role of environment and socialization on the formation of archetypes. I understand Merchant to be referring to this point when he says:

The crucial point is that such imagery would be arising out of mind brain structures which are themselves derived from early preverbal developmental experience and not from innate archetypes. The ramifications are substantial, for the very existence of archetypes as Jung conceived them is called into question.

(Merchant 2009, p. 342)

Merchant (2012) has excellently summarised the implications of these insights for the theory of archetypes, as well as the current state of the debate between proponents of a fully biological grounding of archetypes, versus supporters of an interactionist viewpoint. Interestingly, Merchant comes to the realization in this recent work through reviewing Jung's own case studies, with which he sought to prove the genetic predisposition of archetypes that all of these classic case studies can well be explained without the stringent assumption of biologically inherited archetypes (see Roesler 2021 for a detailed discussion of the emergentist position). Knox writes about these basic schemata:

[I]t is a mental Gestalt which develops out of bodily experience and forms the basis for abstract meanings, both in the physical and in the world of imagination and metaphor. . . . These image schemas are early developmental mental structures which organize experience while themselves remaining without content and beyond the realm of conscious awareness.

(Knox 2004, p. 69)

Critique of the emergentist position

Now Knox claims that the emerging archetypal structures are universal because the environmental conditions in this early stage of development are the same:

> these image schemas . . . are not innate, but already reflect a considerable degree of learning. The pattern of learning is nearly identical for all children because certain key features of the environment that the child's attention is focused on remain constant across all cultures.
>
> (Knox 2003, pp. 61–62)

However, the emergence approach to archetypes is not satisfying given the theoretical problem we have to solve. Saying that archetypes are emergent properties does not really explain how these properties come into existence in any detail; the concept remains too vague as for example, in the quote from Hogenson earlier. As long as nobody can draw a detailed explanatory line of development from a basic human pattern to something as complex as "the myth of the hero" and still prove that this development takes place in every human being in the same way, then this approach remains unconvincing.

Do we not have to assume that there are more differences than similarities in the development of children, given that research cannot find even basic similarities in strategies of childrearing across cultures (Ahnert 2010)? As Knox (2009b) has emphasized, the innate predispositions need environmental cues to be activated. This complex interaction is reached by a minimum of genetic information but presupposes the existence of a caregiver who reacts to the infant in a highly specific way, a point that remains implicit at this stage of Knox's argument. If the caregiver, for example, is permanently drunk and does not recognize the signals sent by the infant, no developmental sequence will start and the genetic information has no effect. Developments like this can be found, for example, in the case of the aforementioned glucocorticoid-receptor-gene, where a lack of motherly care actually leads to a personality with a much lesser protection against stress. This again falsifies the argument that archetypes were based in the universal similarity of the brain's structure (e.g., Stevens 2003). In fact, people have different brains depending on the (early) experiences they had. Even something as basic as "containment" is not, as we know, experienced reliably by every individual.

Secondly, although Knox can certainly draw a detailed line of development from genetic information to image schemas, it nevertheless seems to me that the end products of this development (i.e., image schemas) are still on such a primitive and basic level that a huge gap remains between these primitive schemas and the concepts Jung is talking of.

In my view, the emergence model is no real solution to the problem of how to explain the universality of complex symbolic archetypes. There are too many variables on the developmental path that could disturb the process of acquisition, at least to the extent that there would be major differences in the archetypes thus acquired – so they would not be universal anymore.

As I tried to show earlier by referring to epigenetics, even similar genetic information does not necessarily produce similar developments. We have also seen that the early developmental processes and their achievements can easily be disturbed to the extent that certain developments do not happen at all. Even the structure of the brain is not similar from person to person because its development is so strongly influenced by early experiences (e.g., a person with an early traumatization has a different brain from that of a person without) (Bauer 2002).

I must, therefore, conclude that also the theoretical explanation for universal psychological archetypes provided by the emergentists is no solution to the general problem. At least, however, this position makes clear that we should give up the assumption of a genetical transmission of complex symbolic archetypes, for everything we know about genetics today speaks against this. We also must accept that there certainly are major influences on the formation of archetypes from socialization and enculturation.

Gene-environment co-action and self-generated learning

In an attempt to clarify the still unclear relation between genome and developmental influences, which could not be clarified in the emergentist position, Goodwyn (2020a, 2020b) presents the concept of gene-environment co-action. Because the crucial question still being: "Just how do genome and environment combine to causally contribute to the development of the collective unconscious (meaning the unconscious contents that are universal by virtue of our species' inheritance) and its archetypes, if at all?" (Goodwyn 2020a, p. 914). Merchant (2009, 2020) has pointed out and summarized the earlier critique of the lack of clarification in the emergentist position. For instance, Maloney (1999) stated that "There are neither genetic effects without environments, nor are there environmental effects without genes. There is only a complex interplay that creates an emergent regularity, the features of which have yet to be fully described" (pp. 105–106). Similarly, Hogenson (Stevens et al. 2003) makes a parallel point in that "The crucial question in a discussion of biology and psyche is not whether the two domains are linked, but how they are linked'" (p. 368).

The concept of gene-environment co-action, as presented by Goodwyn (2020a), emphasizes the reciprocal influence of gene activity on the biological side and behavioural as well as social and cultural influences on the other side. The concept emphasizes that there are genetic starting points, which in a certain sense are made for specific environmental input.

> The important thing to remember, though, is that *the genome* decides which kind of environmental input is relevant or not (by sending out specific environmental variable-detecting gene products), and the *genome* decides the circumstances required to seek out such input. . . . The point is that the mere presence of "environmental input" does not automatically imply "not innate". It depends on how such input is used.
>
> (Goodwyn 2020a, p. 916; same citation for the following quotes)

He then provides a number of examples:

- language acquisition capacity, upon which we *learn* a specific language
- mental rotation capacity
- ability to imagine and dream three-dimensional environments
- theory of mind
- capacity for mood
- basic emotional systems that underlie anger, fear, resource seeking, attachment and sex (these are largely intact even at birth)
- facial and body expressions of basic emotions

He then points out that not all learned contents are the result of *locally observed or culturally taught* contents that are unique to the individual's personal history. Some learning is self-directed and universal and would occur in *any* environment.

> For example, learning to walk is obviously a genomically directed process . . . but it involves trial-and-error type learning. This learning, however, has nothing to do with culture, observation, or imitation. It's self-organizing development strongly influenced by the genome.
>
> (p. 921)

Goodwyn arrives at the following definition of archetype:

> Thus, an **archetypal element** is defined as *a universally self-organizing, emotionally significant, embodied symbolic association.* They arise in everyone as a result of species-typical gene-environment co-action that does not require learning in the above sense. Any learning involved in the construction of these is purely self-directed learning that will be immediately obvious to any normally developing member of species *Homo sapiens.*
>
> (p. 926)

Goodwyn then provides a list of examples: Cold = social isolation, Heat/ Fire = intense emotion, Light and dark = states of knowledge and safety, The Centre = the "important" part, Water = the hostile unknown or the mysterious, Size/ Up = power, Symmetry = conceptual harmony, Round shape = wholeness.

Critique of Goodwyn's position

I have already pointed out earlier that such associations as Goodwyn provides as examples for archetypal elements can come about reliably through experience in the life of humans, and there is no need to assume any biologically preformed pattern of association. Goodwyn argues that similar mental structures are the result of self-directed learning, but he oversees the possibility that these similarities come about through experiences with comparable conditions in the world outside. It is not necessary to have a preformed category of above and below because there is no way of getting around the experience of gravity. It is also not necessary to have a preformed pattern for a circle, as there are perfect circles in nature (e.g., the sun, the moon, etc.), and as I have pointed out earlier, the circle is in itself (objectively/mathematically) a perfect shape, so it is no wonder that it was associated with perfection and completeness in different cultures. There is no doubt that such developmental processes as Goodwyn describes exist and that they can explain a considerable amount of learning processes in humans. We will also see later, when contemporary theories of innate mental capacities are discussed, that several of the elements that Goodwyn describes are, in fact, part of the biological makeup of humans. Nevertheless, this approach cannot explain how such complex symbolic structures as the anima, the wise old man or the journey of the hero should come about. It is very clear that the examples Goodwyn provides are far away from such complex structures (see also debate in *Journal of Analytical Psychology*, 2023, issue 1). It is interesting that this author provides as evidence for the existence of such genetically preformed processes the example of a bacteria – which is certainly quite different from higher mental structures in the human mind:

> To that end we will look at the classic didactic case of the *lac* operon of the organism E. Coli.
>
> (Goodwyn 2020a, p. 915)

John Merchant (2020), in his response to Goodwyn's argument, stresses the point that the emphasis on the genome in gene-environment co-action is problematic, if not dangerous.

> no doubt because his focus is more on the genetic background rather than any environmental foreground.
>
> (p. 132)

So in sum, Merchant realizes that Goodwyn does not fall into simplistic and naïve assumptions about preformationism, which, as he notes, are widespread among Jungians today, but he criticizes the over-emphasis on the biological/genetic side of the interaction and neglecting the influence of environmental input and development.

> Critically, once developmentally produced mind/brain (image schema) structures are in place, they have the capacity to generate psychological life. Imagery can then appear as if it is innately derived when that is not the case.
>
> (p. 133)

He then quotes Lickliter (2017, p. 88):

> Although much research in evolutionary biology continues to focus on identifying genes for phenotypic innovations, there is a growing trend among

researchers toward exploring gene function and regulation in the context of changing internal and external environmental conditions. Fundamental to this approach is the recognition that although genes are essential to development, heredity, and evolution, they are <u>not causally privileged</u>, but, rather, are part of the individual's entire developmental system. I argue that evolutionary explanation cannot be complete without developmental explanation because it is the process of development that generates the phenotypic variation on which natural selection can act.

What may be even more important is the fact that, although Goodwyn puts an emphasis on the biological side, he implicitly introduces an important role of experience. This definition departs clearly from Jung's original conceptualization in the sense that archetypes are no longer preformed before any personal experience. The same applies to the aforementioned emergentist position:

> Archetypes play (a key role) in psychic functioning and (are) a crucial source of symbolic imagery, but at the same time (are) emergent structures resulting from a developmental interaction between genes and the environment that is unique for each person.
>
> (Knox 2003, p. 8)

This results in a big shift in contemporary conceptualizations of archetypes, which attribute a major role to (early life) experience in the coming about of archetypes. This is a major contrast to classic archetype theory.

Jung, evolutionary thought and Darwinian theory

Even though Jung argues in a very evolutionist way, it seems that he did not fully understand Darwin's theory (1859, 1871), in so far as Darwinian theory – with its modern reconceptualizations (Huxley 1948; Pigliucci 2010) – clearly points out that the only driving mechanisms of evolution are mutation and selection. Jung hardly quotes Darwin (twice in the CW), although the whole biological line of thought in his archetype theory is based on an evolutionary approach to human development. It seems that Jung had only a very vague idea of evolutionary theory and was not greatly interested in it.

Jung argues that archetypes are the result of precipitations of experiences of early humans repeated again and again. This is in strong contrast to the insights of modern evolutionary theory, which has found out that the only mechanisms at work in changing the genome are mutation and subsequently selection. There is no way how experiences can change the genetic code, the so-called Weissmann-Barrier (Huxley 1948): all the epigenetic changes that have accumulated over an individual's life course are extinguished in the genome of the germ cells. The way of argumentation that can be found in Jung is called Lamarckism, an early evolutionary theory by Jean Baptiste Lamarck that was refuted by Darwinian theory, but even Lamarck is not quoted by Jung. Jung's argumentation led to a confrontation at the Eranos conference in Ascona in 1948 with the biologist Adolf Portmann, who pointed out to Jung that his argumentation was not in line with contemporary insights in evolutionary biology (Shamdasani 2003). As a consequence, Jung introduced the concept of the archetype as such, but this did not provide a solution to the problem, as pointed out earlier. Additionally, "Although Lamarck's theory was clearly outdated long before he died, as far as I know Jung never repudiated his Lamarckian orientation" (Neher 1996, p. 66).

This attitude towards evolutionary theory that becomes visible in Jung tells us that apart from not really understanding evolutionary theory, Jung was also not interested in these biological concepts. Apart from not correctly quoting and not making use of evolutionary theories, Jung seemingly never updated his knowledge about the theoretical developments in evolution theory. For example, he would have been able to read Huxley's modern synthesis of Darwinian theory, which was first published in 1942. He would also have been able to learn about the discovery of the DNA code by Osvald Avery and colleagues in 1944 and the consequences for the understanding of evolutionary developments, if he had been interested. He also used the technical term pattern of behaviour and introduced it into his archetype theory in the late 1940s when he came across the first publications on ethology (e.g., by Konrad Lorenz 1941, 1965; Nico Tinbergen 1951) but again without quoting these publications. Even in the whole chapter with the title "Pattern of behaviour and archetype", published in 1947 (CW 8, paras. 397–420), the only reference to biology provided is a German translation from 1909 of Conway Lloyd Morgan's *Animal Life and Intelligence* of 1890. Paradoxically, Morgan, in his model of ethology, emphasizes the point that the evolution of consciousness cannot be explained by biological measures alone; he also takes the viewpoint that in ethology, only observable behaviour should be regarded as a proper scientific description and was thus a precursor of behaviourism. This again demonstrates how careless, yes, sloppy, Jung's approach was to scientific knowledge and its use in his theories.

It seems to me that he used these concepts from natural sciences merely as a defensive strategy to create the impression that his archetype theory was a real scientific theory and part of the natural sciences and thus to impregnate it against critique (see also Trevi 1992; Papadopoulos 1992). Paradoxically, the biological part of archetype theory has become the most controversial and the most questionable.

Andrew Neher (1996) in his detailed analysis of the scientific base of Jung's archetype theory points out some more problems connected with evolutionary theory, referring to Jung's argument that archetypes arise from endlessly repeated typical experiences of early humans:

Because archetypes evolve from continuously repeated experiences of humanity and because of these experiences necessarily vary somewhat from culture to culture, we should expect that the corresponding archetypes will also be varied. This expectation is reinforced by the long time period involved since the disposal of human populations around the world. There has been plenty of time, in other words, for distinctive archetypes to evolve. This reasoning, of course, is directly contrary to Jung's belief that we all inherit identical archetypes.

(pp. 67–68)

He then refers to Jung's conviction that ether (a concept from antiquity) was a universal archetype:

In fact, because archetypal images, as in the case of the ether theory, do not necessarily bear any relationship to external reality, this implies that there are a large number of archetypes that can lead us down wrong paths and thus, instead of enhancing fitness, will actually reduce it. It is obviously difficult to conceive how such archetypes could evolve.

(p. 69)

Another major problem in Jung's theory is what Neher (1996) calls the decline in the importance of inherited traits:

the fact that our conceptual experience is largely independent of our genetic heritage makes it possible for us, more than any other species, to conceptualize totally new ways of dealing with the world. The concepts that proved useful, of course, become part of our cultural heritage, which we then acquire through our experience, not through our genes. As far as I know, there is no body of evidence, other than that offered by Jung and Jungians, that we inherit an extensive collection of unconscious conceptual content, such as the theory of archetypes proposes. . . . The analysis above demonstrates that although Jung's theory of archetypes draws upon notions of evolution and genetics, he did not base his arguments on well-established principles in these disciplines.

(pp. 70–71)

If one looks into contemporary conceptualizations of evolutionary theory (e.g. Machalek & Martin 2004), it quickly becomes clear that contemporary views have departed strongly from the original Darwinian conceptions. A very interesting finding for a discussion of archetype theory was reported by the anthropologist Henry Harpending (Weiss 2018). He could demonstrate that the mutation rate of the human genome changed over the course of the development of Homo sapiens consequential to cultural developments. So, for example, the mutation rate changed 40,000 years ago when Homo sapiens began to inhabit Europe, and it accelerated again by a factor of 100 around 5,000 years ago because of the introduction of agriculture and the accompanying massive changes in the way of life (the so-called Neolithic Revolution, see chapter "Prehistory"). This demonstrates that evolutionary processes interact with environmental changes and especially with cultural factors so that the species can adapt to changes in life conditions more quickly. It can, in fact, be argued that Homo sapiens, by developing culture and civilization, changed their own biological evolution.

An overview of the insights on contemporary evolutionary psychology[3]

Following the publication of the first account of evolution theory by Darwin, the ideas and principles were applied to human development and also human psychology as an attempt to explain the specificity of certain human behaviours. This line of thought has developed into what is today's evolutionary psychology (the account in the next section follows the overview by Buss 2015). It is obvious that Jung was very much influenced by these ideas, which had an enormous impact on the shape he gave his theory of archetypes. The founders of the biological discipline of behavioural biology or ethology, Niko Tinbergen (1951) and Konrad Lorenz (1941), started to publish in the 1930s. The issues these ethologists were interested in were the following:

1. the immediate influences on behaviour
2. the developmental influences on behaviour
3. the function of behaviour, or the adaptive purpose it fulfills
4. the evolutionary or phylogenetic origins of behaviour

They also coined and investigated the terms instinct and pattern of behaviour (Tinbergen 1951); fixed action patterns are the stereotypic behavioural sequences an animal follows after being triggered by a well-defined stimulus. They found that once a fixed action patterns is triggered, the animal performs it to its completion. This concept can be found again in Jung's idea that once an archetype is activated, it forces the individual to fulfill its whole pattern. This demonstrates how much Jung was influenced by this way of biological thinking. Another example can be found in Lorenz (almost the same language which is later used by Jung):

> Our cognitive and perceptual categories, given to us prior to individual experience, are adapted to the environment for the same reason that the horse is suited for the planes before the horse is born, and the fin of the fish is adapted for water before the fish hatches from its egg.
>
> (Lorenz 1941, p. 99; transl. by Eibl-Eibesfeldt)

A climax of the development of evolutionary psychology was reached with the theory of sociobiology (Wilson 1975, 2012). In this theory, far-ranging explanations were given for human behaviour stemming from genetic imprints, but from the beginning, there was strong criticism against these assumptions:

> Despite Wilson's grand claims for the new synthesis that would explain human nature, he had little empirical evidence on humans to support his views. The bulk of the scientific evidence came from nonhuman animals, many far removed genetically from humans. Most social scientists could not see what fruit flies had to do with people.
>
> (Buss 2015, p. 16)

Contemporary accounts in evolutionary psychology take a more careful stance and do not fall into the traps of such far-reaching explanations. And even proponents of an evolutionary psychology/sociobiology approach to human behaviour stress the point that cultural diversity is extremely pronounced in our species (Chapais 2017). Some basics about evolutionary psychology (for details see Buss 2015):

> **Human behaviour is not genetically determined!** Human behaviour cannot occur without two ingredients: evolved adaptations and environmental input that triggers the development and activation of these adaptations. So notions of genetic determinism – behavior is caused by genes without input or influence from the environment – are simply false. They are in no way implied by evolutionary theory or by evolutionary psychology.
>
> (p. 17)

It is a misunderstanding to imply that when evolutionary theory states some human behaviours are influenced by evolutionary developments, they are impervious to change. In contrast, knowledge of our evolved social psychological adaptations, along with the social inputs that activate them, gives us power to alter this social behaviour if we desire to do that.

> Evolved psychological adaptations along with the social inputs that they were designed to be responsive to, far from dooming us to an unchangeable fate, can have the liberating effect of paving the way for changing behavior.
>
> (Buss 2015, p. 17)

So what is standard knowledge about evolutionary influenced human behaviours in contemporary evolutionary psychology? In general, evolutionarily shaped behaviours are usually directed to solve specific problems and are, therefore, adaptive. The next mentioned insights are the product of systematic testing of evolutionary hypotheses, relying on comparisons of different species, of people in different cultures, of people's physiological reactions and brain images, of people with different genes, of males and females within a species and of different individuals and comparing the same individuals in different contexts. It also draws on archaeological record, comparisons with contemporary hunter gatherer societies, observer reports, laboratory experiments, etc.

Humans live in groups and have social hierarchies; it is highly important for humans to be and stay member of the social group. Being outcast is one of the great fears of humans. Being member of the group includes the problem of getting ahead because resources increase as one rises in the hierarchy, and therefore, there is competition and the fear of losing status in the group. The evolutionary reasons behind this tendency to live in groups is the need to hunt large game under Stone Age conditions, which is only possible in groups with cooperation.

Therefore, a genetically based tendency in humans can be found for cooperation and altruism. There are different forms of altruism, but it seems that selective altruism is supported, which is based on the importance of kinship as a predictor of helping behaviour. Kin classification systems seem to be based on a universal grammar that includes genealogical distance, social rank and group membership resemblance. Also, humans seem to have the biological ability to recognize kinship by association, odour and facial resemblance. The need to cooperate also explains why humans form families, which is very rare in the animal world and found only among roughly 3% of all mammals. Another quality which belongs to the category of cooperation and altruism is the unique human quality to form long-lasting friendships.

As a consequence of living in groups with up to 150 members (the assumed largest size of human groups under Stone Age conditions), humans have to deal with typical problems of social conflicts which have to be regulated. It is assumed in evolutionary psychology that this is the reason for the development of morale, including the development of emotions like shame and embarrassment. But more importantly, it serves as an explanation for the development of the large human brain and its high intellectual capabilities. Reason being the social problems involved in living in complex social groups create the need for complex social abilities, such as forming coalitions, punishing cheaters, detecting deception and negotiating and changing complex social hierarchies. The development of theory of mind/mentalization capacity is another product, as it allows for predicting others' behaviour.

Evolutionary formed habits or behaviour tendencies serve to protect humans against dangers. Therefore, the most common human phobias across all cultures occur towards snakes, spiders, heights, darkness and strange men and not other cues, as for example, rabbits.

Regarding places to live, humans have evolved preferences for landscapes rich in resources and places where one can see without being seen – the so-called savanna hypothesis.

Evolutionary psychology has dealt a lot with sexual behaviour, mating strategies and the respective differences between men and women (de Sousa 2015; Penke & Asendorpf 2008). The findings speak for certain tendencies in women: they seem to prefer men with resources, high status and qualities that make them able to produce resources for their family and offspring, but women also look for signs of commitment, for which love is a signal. So in general, women look for resources, commitment and protection; therefore, they also look for signs of good health in men, and these qualities signal that the man will be a good provider and a good father.

Men, on the other hand, seem to look for signals of high fertility, or reproductive value, in women, therefore, looking for cues of youth and health (e.g., clear skin, full lips, symmetrical features, facial femininity, etc.), which together make what usually is seen as female attractiveness. Also, in many countries, men value virginity in potential brides, but this preference seems to not be universal, as from an evolutionary point of view, sexual fidelity would be a more important quality.

One of the largest differences between men and women in regard to sexuality is the difference in the desire for sexual variety. It has often been argued that the main interest of men would be to spread their sperm, whereas women have a high interest in selecting a long-term partner and testing his qualities before having sex, as their "investment" is much higher. But this argumentation neglects the fact that under Stone Age conditions, a woman alone would not be able to raise children or to even secure their survival, so for both sexes, the most effective strategy, from an evolutionary point of view, would be to cooperate in the care for the offspring. This is in effect empirically supported and explains the cross-cultural support for long-term heterosexual relationships which are also sanctioned by marriage – which is a close to 100% universal.

Beyond the selection strategies reported earlier, there seem to be only small (and only statistical) differences between the sexes, in contrast to widespread assumptions. Even in the tendency to infidelity, it was found that there are, if at all, only very small differences between the sexes (Conley 2011). Also, many of the alleged differences between men and women – women are more talkative, have a higher capacity for empathy, etc. – could not be empirically found (Mehl et al. 2007; Meyer 2015). In general, there are no significant differences between men and women in social behaviours (Hyde 2005). Contemporary anthropologists even assume that in prehistoric hunter gatherer societies, women also were hunters and warriors, as can be found in 32 indigenous hunter gatherer societies still existing today (Hill 2011).

In her overview of the neuroscientific research on brain differences between the sexes, Rippon (2019) demonstrates that if there are any differences, they are only small. If a single brain is investigated, it is not possible to tell whether it is male or female. There are mass differences, but it is not clear what that means, if it has consequences for the functionality of the brain and if so, what kind they are. In general, it can be said that the differences between individuals, also within one sex, are larger than between the sexes. The author points out that in the historical beginnings of this kind of comparative research, there was a certain intention to provide scientific evidence for the inferiority of women, which then could serve as a legitimization for the role of women in society. These findings have, of course, far-reaching implications for archetype theory, namely, for the concepts of anima and animus. They are practically refuting Jung's assumptions in this field.

Since evolutionary psychology assumes that genetically inherited behaviour tendencies aim at solving certain problems and tasks, it was also found that there are universal cognitive abilities in humans: the general abilities to learn, imitate, calculate means-ends relationships and infer causality, compute similarity, form concepts, remember things and compute representativeness. Humans also have a tendency to make inferences in the sense of forming patterns and structures which serve to reduce complexity. There is also the so-called hyperactive agency detection device, which leads us to infer that unseen forces are human agents, which is seen as a reason for the development of religion (Buss 2015).

Innate mental patterns/abilities

We know today that there actually are innate mental patterns: research on emotions has proved that there are basic emotions that we find in every human infant and which can also be decoded by humans from all cultures (Ekman 1994; Ekman et al. 1987); there are innate mental systems for language acquisition (Sotirova-Kohli 2018); and there are primitive perception and behavioural programs, for example, face recognition (Knox 2003). There is also evidence from experimental studies that humans all over the world have certain universal connections between colours and emotions, so for example, pink with love, green with satisfaction, white with relief, etc., but there are also a considerable number of colours for which only culture-specific meanings are attributed.

These are important findings since they show that Jung was right and the behaviourists of his time were wrong in their assumption that the human infant is a tabula rasa or blank slate. There is no doubt that the tabula rasa hypothesis has to be refuted (Pinker 2002). But are these innate mental capacities the same as archetypes, or do they provide evidence that classic archetype theory is right? Even a proponent of such a view of innate mental structures such as Lieberman points out:

> Imitation is probably the most important mechanism for the transmission of human culture. There is no need to postulate a special purpose innate fork use brain mechanism to account for the way that children learn to use forks. . . . Imitation and a desire to be like others clearly can account for most of the short-term changes in human culture, and perhaps for most of its major achievements.
> (Liebermann 1993, p. 142)

So it is necessary to have a closer look and go into the details with these findings.

Which qualities are really innate?

There are a number of human qualities and mental capacities which apparently are rooted in the biological basis and seem to be genetically imprinted (Liebermann 1993). This is the language acquisition device, certain patterns in thought (e.g., hierarchical categorization systems) (Izard et al. 2009), imitation and selfless behaviour in the sense that humans tend to cooperate, at least with close relatives. Humans have innate brain mechanisms that facilitate and structure the acquisition of language. This is connected with a critical or sensitive period in life, covering mainly early childhood until the age of about eight years.

Affects/Emotions: Starting already in the 19th century, there was a debate about innate affects or emotions. Darwin (1872) proposed joy, surprise, interest, fear, distress, anger, contempt and shame. The Jungian author Louis Stewart (1987) created a list very similar to Darwin's (anger, sadness, fear, shame, enjoyment, love, surprise and disgust) which he linked to instinctive, life-preserving responses. Following Darwin, in 1908, William McDougall published his well-known work *An Introduction to Social Psychology* in which he focused on the influence of instincts on human personality. This work was known to Jung, and he certainly referred to these thoughts, even though McDougall himself was quite sceptical about the extent of the influence of instincts on human behaviour. He coined the term primary emotion but rejected the idea that there was anything like a religious instinct and various other debatable higher order effective cognitive processes. He included only seven behaviourally well-defined emotional instincts, which he labelled flight, repulsion, curiosity, pugnacity, self-abasement, self-assertion and parental instinct.

Affective Neuroscience: On the background of this historical development of research and theorizing about basic emotions or instinctual patterns given to human beings, the theory of Jaak Panksepp (1998, 2011) has received the greatest attention in the field of the neurosciences and psychology. The theory is extremely well empirically founded. The mainstream in neurosciences agrees with the basic tenets of this approach, which has been called neuroaffective theory or theory of basic emotional systems. Panksepp (1998) identified seven "basic affective systems": SEEKING (expectancy), FEAR (anxiety), RAGE (anger), LUST (sexual excitement), CARE (nurturance), PANIC/GRIEF (sadness) and PLAY (social joy). These basic emotion systems are inherited; they work on a subcortical, that is, automatic, level; they closely connect the activation of certain emotions with trigger stimuli (such as being attacked by a carnivore); and the emotions then activate fixed behaviour patterns (such as flight or freeze). These basic emotion systems form closed neurological and biochemical circuits in the brain, they are hardwired and work with specific neurotransmitters and hormones and they are, therefore, not to be influenced by experience or learning processes. It has to be noted that these basic emotion systems are only activated in existential situations, such as life-threatening events, and they then switch off the functioning of higher order mental processes, as for example, those located in the prefrontal cortex. Once activated, they are very difficult to be modulated or influenced by the person. These basic emotion systems are, in a certain sense, lifesavers since they circle around existential needs and situations. In the course of psychological development of the person, it is only possible to raise the threshold for the activation of these basic systems. For example, a person can raise the threshold for the activation of existential fear and flight impulses.

It is also important to note that in the human brain, bottom-up and top-down processes are differentiated which are connected via regulatory systems. Neuropsychological systems, such as Panksepp's basic systems, are called bottom-up processes in cognitive neurosciences. In humans, they are regulated and modulated by top-down mechanisms (e.g., controlled by the prefrontal cortex) up to the point that they can be totally inhibited. These regulatory mechanisms are fully dependent on one's individual history of experiences, first of all, in primary caregiver relationships.

It also has to be noted that the findings around these basic emotion systems clearly show that in contrast to Jung's thoughts, the genetic information does not directly activate behaviour patterns, but it activates an affect/emotion, which is consciously experienced and then initiates actions. So there is no direct path from genes to behaviour, at least when it comes to the basic emotion systems discussed here, but the path goes from genes via emotions to behaviour. So even if affective neuroscience has found genetically fixated patterns, they do not directly encode behaviour but only emotions. The fixated patterns also do not react to trigger stim-uli, as instinctual behaviour in animals does – for example, birds feed their young automatically when they are confronted with their wide-open mouths and certain acoustic signals. They do not reflect on whether they want to feed them or whether they are their own offspring or not, etc. This is the reason why the cuckoo can lay his egg in the nest of other birds and can rely on the fixated pattern which will cause the bird parents to feed this foreign chick. In contrast to such an instinctual pattern, the basic emotion systems described here in humans create existential needs which are activated via emotions and lead to typical behaviour directed mostly towards the caregivers.

These insights of affective neuroscience have well been confirmed by a number of leading neuroscientists such as Damasio (2010) and Le Doux (2012) and also by the neuropsychoanalyst Mark Solms (2015, 2016), who has also contributed significantly to a better understanding of psychoanalytic concepts in the light of neuroscientific research, namely, the relationship between consciousness and the unconscious. The findings of affective neuroscience had the interesting result that the development of consciousness had to be thoroughly reconceptualized:

It became increasingly clear, . . . that most primary affects, at least in raw uncon-ditioned form . . . are neurologically constituted at the level of subcortical brain regions, and not cortical ones. It became equally clear that the mechanisms for affect were largely confluent with those for consciousness as a whole. This applies to all mammals, including humans. . . . It is here, we have suggested, where affective consciousness – the core valenced states of mind – first emerged as a unified emotional behavioural and affective evaluative process in evolution. This contrasts with traditional wisdom – actually prejudice – that the subcortical ream in isolation is unconscious. That is conventional, but in our opinion not consistent with the evidence.

(Panksepp et al. 2017, pp. 188–189)

This has an interesting consequence that, contrary to Jung, consciousness is devel-opmentally primary, not the unconscious. So the general idea of Jung's, which is constitutive for his whole psychological theory and also the theory of archetypes, that the unconscious is primary and consciousness slowly develops out of "an ocean of unconscious" has to be refuted on the background of these neuroscientific findings.

It is very important to note that the basic emotion systems are not influenced by psychological development over the course of life and that they do not provide the foundation for higher order processes. In contrast, these secondary processes develop independently from the primary basic emotion systems and are definitely not inherited (Panksepp et al. 2017). So if one wanted to argue that Panksepp's neuroaffective systems are a modern conception of what Jung called archetypes (e.g., Alcaro et al. 2017), this parallel has to be regarded as illegitimate. The basic emotion systems are neither connected with images or narratives nor do they form connections with higher order processes, such as cultural expressions, as has been argued by Jung regarding archetypes:

> The reason that led me to conjecture a localization of a physiological basis for this archetype [the Self] in the brainstem was the psychological fact that besides being specifically characterized by the ordering and orienting role, its uniting properties are predominantly affective.
>
> (Jung, CW 3, para. 582; similarly, CW 9/I, 348)

Also, the basic emotion systems form very primitive behaviour patterns, which are very clearly defined (e.g., flight or freeze) and thus have nothing to do with what Jung described as archetypes. In animal experiments, it is actually possible to sever the connection between the cortex and neocortical higher functions – in the sense of learned behaviours – from the subcortical structures, and the animal will still be able to survive based on its basic emotion systems. These experiments, though horrible, clearly demonstrate that there is no connection between inherited (instinctual) behaviour patterns and the higher cortical structures which develop during psychological development. And this makes sense, from an evolutionary point of view, as these basic emotion systems and inherited behaviour patterns have evolved because they secure the survival of the animal/person, and therefore, to remain unchanged, by experience and by reflection. They have developed into fixated patterns and are transmitted genetically in this fixated form because they are emergency programs on which the survival relies.

> In this context, it is again important to consider that much of the massive neocortical expansions since human divergence from greater apes was substantially controlled by a single gene variant, ARHGAP 11 B. We think such findings provide little leeway for robust and specific genetic control of various high-end neocortical primary sensory and affective functions.
>
> (Panksepp et al. 2017, p. 199)

These findings are a massive blow against classical Jungian theory, as they imply that as far as there are patterns which could be called instinctual in humans in the sense of the aforementioned primary emotion systems, these exist independently from all higher cognitive processes, and the latter are totally dependent on experience and learning. It also has to be noted that Panksepp's use of the term "instinctual" for these mechanisms is highly controversial in the neurosciences. The majority of authors active in this field do not follow this definition (e.g., Mark Solms). So Jung's conception of basic patterns which then evolve into individual representations, images, narratives, etc., in the course of life – as is suggested in the following quote – has to be refuted.

> Nonetheless, [the instinct] is psychologically important because it leads to the formation of structures or patterns which may be regarded as determinants of the

human behaviour. . . . The immediate determining factor is not the . . . instinct but the structure resulting from the interaction of instinct and the psychic situation of the moment. The determining factor would thus be a modified instinct. . . . Instinct . . . would play the role of a stimulus merely, while instinct as a psychic phenomenon would be an assimilation of this stimulus to a pre-existing pattern. A name is needed for this process. I should term it psychicization.

(Jung, CW 8, para. 234)

This quote clearly demonstrates that Jung's general idea is that the instincts, as originally physiological processes, are connected with higher order psychological processes and thus become part of the psyche as stimulating factors.

In contrast, these higher order processes are actually activated by just a single gene (Panksepp et al. 2017, p. 199). We also know from neuroscientific research that in the first months of life in the infant brain, a large number of synapses is built so that at eight months of age, the human brain has the highest density of synaptic connections ever in life. Thereafter, only those synapses remain which are used and thus strengthened. The others vanish. The rule is "use it or lose it". It seems that the massive growth of synaptic connections in the first year of life is activated by only the single gene mentioned earlier. This implies that there is no genetically encoded specificity in the sense of content regarding cortical structures.

On the other hand, these findings demonstrate that consciousness and subjectivity, on a basic level, are primary and in so far as they are rooted in affects which are inherited. There actually is an innate base for consciousness and subjectivity. This has a funny consequence that, as Solms and Panksepp (2012) point out, the "Id" (das Es) is conscious. It should be noted that this basic consciousness and subjectivity has no connection to what, over the life course, evolves into a sense of self, in the sense of memorized experiences, etc.

Nevertheless, psychologists have used the findings of affective neuroscience to support Jung's ideas of archetypes (Alcaro et al. 2017). This is a good example of the misinterpretations which arise from the unclarified definitions of archetypes. One can only argue in the form of the paper just mentioned, if one automatically equates innate mechanisms with archetypes.

Attachment theory and research

The vast body of findings that have been produced by attachment research strongly supports the hypothesis of universality of the attachment needs and patterns. In every study in European and Western as well as non-European countries, children were observed to show attachment behaviour in stressful circumstances and to have a preferential bond with one or more caregivers; nevertheless, there is space for intercultural differences and culture-specific forms of attachment bonds and behaviours as well as childrearing structures (Mesman et al. 2018, p. 866). The findings of attachment research also support other hypotheses of universality. The normativity hypothesis states that the distribution of attachment patterns (e.g., secure versus insecure) is more or less equal cross-culturally, which could be clearly empirically supported (Cassidy & Shaver 2018). This demonstrates that secure attachment and also insecure patterns are not an invention of Western societies. Furthermore, insecure patterns are not only related to so-called civilized cultures, which means that insecure patterns can also be found in so-called primitive societies. These are often thought to be closer to nature – especially in Jungian and Post-Jungian thought (see previous section). Also, the sensitivity hypothesis could be supported, which argues that the differences in attachment security are related to the sensitivity of the caregivers in responding to the needs of the child. This again, of course, supports the general notion that the formation of the personality is by no means genetically determined but the result of experiences, especially in the interaction with caregivers (Rothbaum et al. 2000).

Attachment and evolution: Environment of evolutionary adaptedness (EEA)

For most of our evolutionary history, humans were hunters and gatherers who lived in small, cooperative groups. Most people within a tribe were biologically related to one another, and strangers were encountered rather infrequently, mainly during intertribal trading, social contact, or war. Though people occasionally migrated in and out of their natal groups, most remained in the same tribe their entire lives. Men and women formed long-term care bonds, but serial monogamy was probably most common. Children were born approximately four years apart and were raised with considerable help from extended family and perhaps even non-kin; few children were raised exclusively by their biological parents. Humans, in fact, were probably cooperative breeders who shared childrearing with their kin [see also Hrdy 2009; CR]. . . . Participation in the daily functioning of small, cooperative groups may in fact have been the predominant survival strategy of early humans. These likely features of the social EEA must be considered when conceptualizing attachment theory within an evolutionary framework.

(Simpson & Belsky 2018, p. 96)

A large body of evidence supports this model. Following this model, the main evolutionary function of early social experience is to prepare children for the social environments they are likely to encounter during the lifetime. With this background, it also can be assumed that the mating model of long-term pair bonds seems to be the most reasonable since it provides the highest probability for the offspring to survive under these harsh conditions; also, it is probably the most suitable environment for the development of complex social competencies. On the other hand, this implies that the quality of the environment early in life can exert long-lasting effects on psychosocial development, including social competency and the development of specific mating and parenting strategies in both males and females.

Human infants would not be able to survive without the care of a more experienced adult, who is able to regulate their basic physiological needs as well as their stress levels, because young infants cannot take care of these basic physiological and psychological needs by themselves. The early environment of evolutionary adaptiveness among humans required the basic ability to become emotionally attached in order to survive and enhance inclusive fitness. Since the environment of humans consists mainly of situations with a high need of cooperation and complex social interaction, these are the competencies which human children must be prepared for. Thus, the evolutionary adaptiveness of humans involves the acquisition of complex social and interactive competencies, which is only possible through experiences in a social network itself. It cannot be preformed by genes. The genetic makeup only prepares the infant to be highly sensitive for social interaction.

On the other hand, the following is depending on the quality of the early social interactions provided mainly by the caregivers:

> Infants differ rather drastically in the quality of their attachment relationships, and attachment theory hypothesizes that this attachment performance is largely, albeit not exclusively, environmentally determined . . . as a consequence of childrearing experiences with parents and other caregivers. . . . The parallel to language development is useful here. Every child is born with the capacity to learn a language, but the specific language environment determines the kind of language to be learned.
>
> (Bakermans-Kranenburg & van Ijzendoorn 2018, p. 155)

So the general rule is that young children's attachment security is not heritable (ibid.).

The findings of attachment research also point to the fact that the development of the Self of human beings is almost exclusively based on interpersonal processes. The new-born infant has just some basic abilities to draw the caregiver into a form of interaction (e.g., by imitating the face expression or giving other signals which are then interpreted by the caregiver as an initiative to communication). But on the one hand, a development starting from these fundamental initiatives will only take place as long as there is a caregiver who is aware of the signals and responds to them in a sensitive way. If this happens, the child can increasingly rely on the presence of the caregiver and use the adult person to regulate its needs and emotions. The way in which the adult caregiver responds (e.g., sensitive or not) will determine the internalized representations of these interactions (Daniel Stern: representations of interactions generalized). So the Self which is formed in such processes is constituted by interpersonal processes, by interactions. There is no way how the child could develop his/herself individually and independently. Even when children have formed an early form of the Self, they still apply what is called social referencing: when confronted with a new experience, the first thing they do is to look on the face of the caregiver for signs of how to interpret this experience. These ideas have been put together in the theory of the social brain (Pfaff 2013; Fink & Rosenzweig 2015), which basically points out that the brain of humans is largely a social construction.

This is, by the way, also an argument against the classic conceptions of evolutionary psychology in the sense of Dawkins or Wilson, who argued for a basic egoism in humans.

The dialogical Self – Jung and Buber: The general idea of this interpersonal process which shapes the Self can, in an early form, be found in the works of Martin Buber. Interestingly, when Martin Buber was invited by one of the members of the Psychological Club in Zürich in the 1920s, Jung attempted to keep the other members of the club from attending this lecture and did not take the opportunity to have a dialogue with Buber (Bair 2003). It could be interpreted that Jung somehow felt Buber's conception to be absolutely contrary to his own, as he proposed an individualistic view of development, whereas Buber strengthened an interpersonal view. The individualistic view on development Jung shared with one of his Swiss compatriots, Jean Piaget, who designed his theory of cognitive development in a very similar way, as if the child investigated its environment all on its own – a view which was strongly criticized later in the course of developmental psychology.

The social brain: Cooperation and reciprocal altruism

As we have seen earlier, the environment of evolutionary adaptedness of human beings is that of a group of humans who form close social/interpersonal relationships and who cooperate for hunting and gathering but also for childrearing. The high quality of cooperation in human beings was apparently a strong advantage under Stone Age conditions for more effective hunting and thus provided a selection preference. We can also assume that in these early human groups, the described individuals were preferred and had a selectional advantage. Concerned are persons who were reliable in cooperation, who applied fairness when it came to the sharing of hunting game, who could coordinate well in shared activities, etc. This is the reason why, as evolutionary anthropologists argue (Tomasello 2021; de Waal 2019), a genetic makeup, which prepared well for these complex forms of cooperation, sociality and complex communication, was selected in human evolution.

Evidence exists that in humans, there is an inborn tendency/preparedness for cooperativeness towards other human beings. This has been demonstrated by empirical research, mainly through the studies of Michael Tomasello (2021), President of the Department for Comparative and Developmental Psychology at the Max-Planck-Institute for Evolutionary Anthropology in Leipzig for 20 years. It can be demonstrated that already, infants in their first year of age show cooperation and altruism in the sense of supporting others without being asked for it and that this is not a result of socialization. The evolutionary basis for this behaviour is the need, under Stone Age conditions, for human communities to cooperate and support each other in order to survive as a group. This inborn tendency to cooperate contains several basic elements: human infants from the first days after birth have the ability to imitate face expressions of their caregivers and thus go into resonance with them. They can do so due to the existence of mirror neurons; therefore, it can be said that the human infant is preformed for interpersonal resonance (Bauer 2019). Human infants have the ability to create what is called the referential triangle, meaning they are able to cause another person (e.g., the caregiver) to focus on a third object together with the infant. They can do so by using eye contact, pointing at things and later, by talking. This shared focus, of course, enables cooperation and reciprocal support (Tomasello 2021). In contrast, primates like chimps do not have this ability (de Waal 2019). Another area which is, of course, fundamental to cooperation and reciprocal support is the ability for language. At the age of three years, there is another achievement in children, as they now are able to understand that they are members of a group (e.g., a family). To be a member of the group or family is one of the basic needs of humans. Children at this age start to focus on the rules that are shared in the group and tend to correct other children when they do not obey to the rules. Especially children, but also adults in human groups, have a very strong tendency to conformity, to be a respected and accepted member of a group and to understand and follow its rules. Already at the age of five years, children have a sense of fairness, solidarity and identification with others. At the age of seven or eight, in traditional cultures, children usually start to take over tasks for the group (e.g., watch over a herd of sheep) (Tomasello 2021).

This line of studies does not deny that there is also a certain amount of egoism within humans. But in this tradition of research, it has been pointed out that the strong egoism we have in modern, especially Western, societies, which has led to the formation of capitalism and free welfare, seems to be a product of the Neolithic age, in which agriculture, trade, civilization, settlements and ownership of land and other goods started. Anthropologists, who first came into contact with traditional peoples, usually report that they were welcomed very friendly and received support, even without having asked for it (Hrdy 2009). Even in civilized cultures all over the world, hospitality is one of the highest values.

Transactional causality: How culture impacts evolution

We have already seen earlier that the genetic code in the sense of the human genome alone does not determine processes of gene expression but that these processes are modulated by epigenetic factors. Tomasello (2021) adds a further perspective on these processes: not only is the expression of genes influenced by epigenetic factors and thus is activated through environmental factors but also, the timing of these epigenetic influences plays a crucial role since they can cause very different sequences of the expression of whole sets of genes. The sequence, in which such genes are activated, can make large differences in the phenotypic effects. Now Tomasello argues that, as has been demonstrated earlier, the genetic makeup of infants prepares them in different ways for complex social interactions, for being interested in other human beings, for being able to understand emotional signals in the face, to give signals themselves, etc., but this is only the beginning. It needs a highly competent social other on the other end to react to these initiatives. And it is not only the presence of a competent social other but also the fact that human infants are born into a culture, a complex sociocultural context. Tomasello argues that cultures and sociocultural institutions are designed to come into play at crucial points in the development of a human child to activate specific genetically pre-formed social competencies which would not develop (or not in such a complex way) if there were no culture. And because in an earlier stage of development, specific capacities have already developed (e.g., communication by language because there is a caregiver present to talk to the child), the human child is capable of developing further competencies in the course of ontogeny. The reason being that on a later stage, specific cultural conditions activate these preformed capacities. So for example, in the first three years of life, human children usually develop interpersonal, social and communicative competencies in a dyadic interaction with their primary caregivers. Based on this development as well as on processes of maturation of the organism, with three years of age, they become capable of form-ing social relationships with other children of their age in groups. They built the competency to coordinate with others in play, etc. (therefore, at this age, we usually send children to kindergarten). This is called transactional causality. Capacities, which evolve through maturation, provide the foundation for new forms of experiences and learning, and subsequently, these learning experiences are the direct cause for further development. Human cultures have evolved to optimally support this process.

So Tomasello, referring to the work of Vygotsky, argues that human culture and the human genome closely interact in ontogenesis to form the unique human capac-ities of sociocultural cooperation. Human cognitive and social ontogenesis depends on these transactions between the individual and its surrounding rich cultural ecol-ogy. This transactional model has also been called the theory of developmental systems or evolutionary developmental psychology. This transactional approach is in sharp contrast to viewpoints which could be called nativist – among them Jung's – which argue that certain abilities are solely inborn (which could also be called a too-simple nativism). The transactional approach presented here, in contrast, assumes that there are only genetically preformed behaviour tendencies which, in a certain way, "presuppose" the existence of certain cultural institutions (e.g., schools for teaching) which then activate a sequence of social and cognitive developments.

This is based on the unique human capacity to form a "We", a shared actor with shared intentions, knowledge and sociocultural values. These processes, vice versa, have influenced the evolution of mankind. Because early human groups, under Stone Age conditions, were more successful when they could cooperate in complex ways, the need to prolong the period of children's education arose. Henceforth, instruction and teaching were invented, leading to the formation of a human culture in which parents provide food and information far into adolescence, enabling children to acquire huge amounts of cultural information. All of the afore-mentioned genetically preformed abilities for cooperation, understanding and shar-ing intentionality, altruism, etc., are directed towards making the development of a shared intentionality on the base of cooperative activity possible. This includes the ability to take the perspective of others, to view the same thing from different per-spectives, to exchange information via signals, to think about the future in the sense of making plans for cooperative action, to help others so as to make sure that they are in good shape when their cooperation is needed, to develop a sense of fairness, to take over a role in a play in the sense of taking a position in a coordinated action (e.g., hunting) and to understand the inner world of others in the sense of empathy and mentalization. Consequently, groups consisting of such individuals form con-ventions over time, in the sense of systems of rules (e.g., for how the hunting game is shared). They form shared systems of symbols for exchange and hierarchies in the sense of systems of different positions/status in coordinated action (e.g., chief – follower) – to put it simply: culture. On the other hand, being a member of such a group/society/culture makes it necessary to understand and adopt the system of rules of this group in the course of development. Therefore, it was a selection advantage for children to be able to imitate elders, to take up instruction and teach-ing and to have a tendency to conform with the rules and values of one's group for building a sort of group identity.

By the way, this approach also explains why in human groups, only about 50% of the caregiving for children is performed by their own mothers. This is due to the fact that they are cared for by a whole group of adults – called cooperative breed-ing (Hrdy 2009) – providing a unique environment for the development of complex social cognition, as the children have to adapt to different other human beings and understand different states of mind, etc.

This viewpoint is also supported by empirical findings, which show that in con-trast to other mammals, also primates, the human infant's brain has just 20% of the weight of an adult brain. This exemplifies that the brain substance of an adult human being is formed by experiences and the information taken up during sociali-zation and culturalization. The comparably slow growth of the human brain dur-ing childhood and adolescence is an adaptation to the culturized way of living of human beings, implying that humans have to acquire a huge amount of competen-cies and knowledge to become a full-grown member of their kind.

Polyvagal theory

Another interesting finding is that this sharing of experiences and viewpoints, by taking the perspective of the other, as a result, equalizes the inner states of the individuals involved. This again supports the development of attachment relation-ships. In contrast to reptiles, for example, mammals evolve auditory systems that enable them to respond to airborne acoustic signals, an important requisite for increasingly complex modes of social interaction. The result was the emergence of a capability for a dynamic social engagement system with social communication features: head movements, production of vocalizations, hearing and understanding vocal communication. Human babies, already in the first weeks of their life, have a tendency to smile at the face of any other human being (which even primates do not do). This usually has the consequence of instigating an interaction, drawing the adult into a social relationship with the baby.

Humans share with other mammals an evolutionary development which resulted in a face-heart connection, in which the striated muscles of the face and head were regulated in the same brainstem areas that evoked the calming influence of the myelinated vagus. In effect, meeting others does not automatically activate defensive mechanisms but, in contrast, creates a need for being close to others of the same kind, having a calming effect. These evolutionary developments provided setting conditions under which social behaviours could have a significant impact on cognition and health. In the human nervous system, specific features of person-to-person interactions are innate triggers of adaptive biobehavioural systems, which in turn can support health and healing (Cozolino 2006).

Biocultural theory

In Jung's model, there is a basic misconception about the role of genes in development. To put it simply, Jung assumes that in the genetic code, the archetypal structure (in the sense of the matrix of the crystal) is already defined and leads directly to behaviour by organizing perception into certain images, a tendency to be prepared for certain behaviours, etc. So the general idea is that genetics provide similarity. Based on contemporary insight in genetics, it can be said that also the opposite may take place. This has to do with the fact that in humans, as well as in almost every species, for some genes, there exist a number of different variants. This is an example from mating behaviour:

> The tendency to cheat on the partner within romantic relationships, by having an affair, actually seems to be dependent on certain gene variants, meaning there is a certain hereditary factor. In a study conducted in Finland (Zietsch et al. 2015) it was found that there are considerable differences in the tendency to commit adultery. These differences showed connections to hereditary factors in the family of origin. The interesting point was that there was not a significant difference between the sexes, but within each of the sexes. This tendency is called polyamorous or socio-sexuality. So, the genome in this case is not responsible for creating similarity in human beings, but for creating considerably sharp differences.

The same was found for the tendency to be a good father, respectively, mother. In both sexes, there are two different hereditary phenotypes, which are responsible for a tendency to take over responsibility for the offspring or not (Wlodarski et al. 2015).

Another important finding is that the heredity of a genetic trait is not automatically given but is dependent on the quality of the environment. In environments that are poor in resources without much space for individual freedom, different genetic predispositions cannot produce such strong effects in the phenotype compared to open societies with a variety of behavioural options (Charmantier & Garant 2005; Guo & Marcus 2012). This means that cultural environment and genetic variations interact with each other. As an example, the development of different phenotypes of styles of seeking sexual contacts: in modernized, liberal societies, different genetic variants have more opportunity to express and produce individual differences in sexual orientation. This is called biocultural interplay of genetic variation and cultural environment.

So the attempt by the protagonists of sociobiology (e.g., Edward Wilson [1975] or Richard Dawkins) to subsume sociology and psychology under the natural sciences and, namely, biology has to be regarded as failed (Richter 2005). Interestingly, Dawkins (1976) in his later publications points out that human behaviour cannot be seen as genetically determined and introduced the term "meme", the cultural equivalent of the gene. This concept was further expanded by the British psychologist Susan Blackmore (1999); it is defined as the smallest unit of cultural information capable of being replicated and passed on to subsequent generations. For these processes, of course, language and the capacity to symbolize is crucial.

> Our evolution differs from other species because it has been dependent on two lines of transmission of species specific information, not one. Once the capacity for symbolic representation develops, first through images and then through words, there is introduced into the evolutionary process a new means for disseminating intergenerational information.
>
> (Kugler 2003, p. 273; see also the discussion about dual inheritance theory in the section on anthropology)

The example of mating behaviour/couple bonding

Müller-Schneider (2019) presents a detailed account of biocultural theory in his attempt to understand the interplay of the biological basis for human mating behaviour and the social forms that we can find in postmodern society in the sense of different models of romantic relationships. He starts from the interesting observation that even though postmodern societies have a maximum of personal freedom and unfolding of the individuality, the large majority (in a number of studies, even more than 90%) seek a monogamous, long-term couple relationship based on love, exclusivity and reciprocal fidelity.

Müller-Schneider (2019) compiles very convincing evidence by summarizing findings and insights from several disciplines (anthropology, human genetics, behavioural biology, etc.) that there seems to be a biological basis for human mating behaviour and couple bonding. In general, it can be said that humans have a predisposition to form long-lasting monogamous couple relationships. In evolutionary biology, the ultimate reasons for this form of couple bonding have been intensely discussed. It was found that long-lasting couple bonding is a necessity to form the basis for parental cooperation to secure the survival and the reproductivity of the offspring. The human infant is born in an extremely immature and, therefore, vulnerable and dependent state, which makes it necessary for the mother – and other caregivers – to care for the child for many years. This immature state is, on the other hand, necessary so that the infant can develop differentiated social capacities for interaction and cooperation, which are the crucial advantage of the human species. But under Stone Age conditions, the mother alone would not be able to provide this care for several years, so there is a necessity to include the father (and all the other group members) into a stable system of childcare.

So in contrast to prevalent prejudices in modern societies, it was found in ethnographic studies that in hunter gatherer societies, usually, the fathers and, in general, the men of the group are incorporated into a shared system of childcare (Chapais 2011). In some cases, even a larger amount of childcare is provided by the fathers/ men in the group, and in these cases, even hunting is conducted by the women, along with gathering fruit, etc. Another theory, resulting from these studies and findings, argues that with the development of arms, male competition for women would have resulted in devastating fights and loss of human lives, which would then have weakened human societies. Therefore, stable couple bonding was supported in the evolution of human societies (see also the 10 Commandments in the Old Testament). This is as much a cultural achievement, as it is based in biology.

This demonstrates that, on a very basic level, there seems to be a biological basis of human couple bonding. However, it goes alongside social developments that human groups and societies must deal with certain social problems and find similar solutions to these problems. So regarding the question what is archetypal, here, it can be said that the prevalence of monogamous marriages is a result of a combination of biological and social processes. On the other hand, there is solid evidence that love and jealousy are clearly biologically determined (Müller-Schneider 2019).

The human capacity to form culture is part of the genome, but in effect, it forms a secondary system of heredity. This system is organized as collective knowledge or memory, but in contrast to Jung's theory, it is not based in the biology/genome. It is memorized in symbolic form and transmitted from generation to generation as knowledge in the form of language. This capacity to symbolize and to transmit knowledge in the form of language has contributed to an enormous rise in adaptability. It is no doubt that there is something like a genetically imprinted, biologically deep structure of human beings – in short: human nature. But this is not to be confused with a reductionist understanding in the sense of that human behaviour is directly genetically imprinted. Human nature means there are species-specific innate tendencies (e.g., the human tendency to cooperate).

The evolutionary development of mankind in contemporary models and theories is seen as a co-evolution of genes and culture (Pinker 2010). In this sense, development is not a one-way street. This has to do with the extremely high plasticity of the brain which responds to experiences in the sense that certain experiences, especially in early socialization, act as feedback for the expression of certain genes. Some genes even need certain experiences, in the form of cues from the environment, to be activated. It also has to be noted that there are large differences between different parts of the genome, in so far as some are extremely plastic and respond to environmental cues, whereas others follow genetically highly structured synaptic arrangements (e.g., Panksepp's neuroaffective systems). But in general, it can be said that all structures that are connected with meaning or produce meaning or are experienced as meaningful are the product of experience and socialization and, therefore, come from outside, from experience, socialization and enculturalization, not from the genome.

This line of theorizing is very clear in pointing out that there are no such things as instincts in human behaviour. Those entities which are genetically based are on the level of motivations. So for example, there is the basic human need or motivation for finding a mate. How to do that, in which contexts, etc., is prescribed in social scripts.

At the core of all human motivations, there is the need to receive interpersonal acceptance, appreciation and care. In this sense, at the core of human nature is the tendency to social resonance and cooperation. Humans receive direction in regard to these motivations from their emotions. So in general, it can be said that even if there is a genetic predisposition for certain motivations, genes do never directly activate certain behaviours but only via the activation of emotions, which serve as signals for different aims or dangers. These emotions in turn activate certain behaviours.

The Self is relational: Relationship is primary, not the individual[4]

So it becomes more and more clear that the genetic makeup of humans is oriented towards interaction with other human beings and sociality. Even Charles Darwin, the founder of evolutionist theory, was aware of this:

> It has often been assumed that animals were in the first place rendered social, and that they feel as a consequence uncomfortable when separated from each other, and comfortable whilst together, but it is a more probable view that these sensations were first developed in order that those animals which would profit by living in society, should be induced to live together, . . . For with those animals which were benefited by living in close association, the individuals which took the greatest pleasure in society would best escape various dangers; whilst those that cared least for their comrades and lived solitary would perish in great numbers.
> (Darwin 1871, p. 80)

The most elaborate concept and theory resulting from these considerations is attachment theory and attachment research. The findings reported earlier, which were conceptualized into the transactional approach, have also influenced other theoretical approaches, as for example, what has been called the "Social embedded brain" (Northoff 2015) and cultural neuroscience. CN is an interdisciplinary field that investigates the relationship between culture (e.g., value and belief systems and practices shared by groups) and human brain functions and aims at elucidating the intrinsically biosocial nature of the functional organization of the human brain (Shihui et al. 2012).

From these insights, in psychoanalysis, the relational and intersubjective schools have developed, which are based on the infant research conducted by the Boston Process of Change Study Group, with concepts as Stern's "representations of inter-actions that have been generalized" (Stern 1985). The general idea here is that the psyche is structured and practically built from the early interactional experiences of the child in its relationships with caregivers. It also has to be noted that the term drive, so fundamental to orthodox psychoanalysis, meanwhile has been discarded in the contemporary schools of the Freudian tradition and has been reformulated as the concept of motivations (e.g., Lichtenberg et al. 2009):

> Post-Freudian's, for instance, have replaced Freud's pleasure principle as the primary biological drive with the idea of the need for relationship and related-ness as our most basic human longing. Wherever we turn across the psychody-namic spectrum, we see therapy more concerned with engagement, and more critical of all forms of disengagement, especially narcissism and other disorders of relatedness.
>
> (Tacey 1998, p. 228)

These ideas have already found their way into some schools of Jungian psychology:

> For relational analysts, the social aspect of our being is fundamental to psy-chological life – it is not an add-on or a separate domain of our existence. This leads to a critique of what Stolorow and Atwood call "the myth of the isolated mind". . . . It is not simply that the mind develops in the social context of rela-tionships with others; there is a more fundamental idea here that the mind itself is social and that the private subjective self, the intrapsychic inner world, is sub-sequent to and contingent upon the relational context in which it is embedded.
>
> (Colman 2018, p. 130)

It should be noted that these ideas are more or less the contrary of how Jung imag-ined the development of a person, putting the emphasis mainly on what comes out of the individual ("the myth of the isolated mind"). Archetypes here mean prefor-matted patterns and structures which develop independently from experiences in interactional relationships, what Jung calls "autochthonous development".

These insights, of course, have far-reaching implications for the practice of Jungian psychotherapy. If, as in the classical school, the therapist waits for an autochthonous development to unfold out of the person independently, based on biologically/genetically imprinted archetypes, this may not happen, as the find-ings and insights presented earlier would suggest. Should the emphasis not be much more on creating a certain quality of relationship, as the relational schools in psychoanalysis suggest? But if so, what is the relationship between the idea of archetypes and an archetypal development of the person in the course of psychotherapy on the one side and the contribution of the therapeutic relationship on the other? It seems to me that this relationship is not really clarified even in contemporary schools of Jungian psychology. These questions will be discussed further in the final chapter on the process of psychotherapy.

Conclusion

In this chapter, the state-of-the-art in the fields of human genetics, developmental psychology, neurosciences and their interplay were presented. In sum, these findings and contemporary conceptualizations clearly refute what has been described as Theory 1: A biological conceptualization of archetypes. There is no doubt that in humans, there are innate capacities and behavioural tendencies, but they are the opposite of what Jung imagined to be biologically rooted archetypes; all of these innate elements are not structures and contents but only capabilities which are all directed towards creating relationship, participating in relationships and groups, initiating interaction and participating in communication, cooperation, sociality, etc. In sum, they are directed towards social relationships. This is, as I have pointed out, the contrary of what Jung imagined, as he claimed a biological foundation of archetypes. The archetypes Jung had in mind cannot be conceptualized as biologically or genetically founded in the face of the earlier theories and findings.

In the debate with George Hogenson at the IAAP Congress of 2001, Anthony Stevens argued: "Evolutionary psychologists and psychiatrists on both sides of the Atlantic have announced the presence of neuropsychic propensities which are virtually indistinguishable from archetypes. They use such terms as 'evolved psychological mechanisms' and 'innate propensity states'" (Stevens et al. 2003, p. 370). In the same manner, contemporary Jungian authors often make the mistake of using some of the findings presented earlier as evidence for the biological theory of archetypes for conceptions of innatism, biological preformationism, etc., without taking into account that the archetypes of classic archetype theory – anima and animus, the wise old man, the trickster, the divine child, the journey of the hero, etc. – are totally different from the capabilities that were found to be biologically rooted. So I would conclude that Theory 1 is, in a certain sense, legitimate, which means that there actually are biologically preformed mental or psychological capacities in humans, but this has nothing to do with archetype theory. Archetype is not a biological concept and cannot be described or explained by referring to concepts from biology. So when authors in AP still argue that there is evidence for innate psychological propensities, it has to be said that this is correct – see previous section – but is by no means evidence for the archetypes of AP being biologically rooted. Theory 1 is not part of archetype theory and should not be confused with it. It presents a totally different concept: a theory of innate psychological qualities and capabilities having nothing to do with archetypes. I would also suggest not to use the term archetype anymore for the concepts and findings presented earlier, as this creates confusion instead of clarification.

Why, at all, is it so important to describe the archetype as a biological concept, even for contemporary theorists? It is as if the theory, when armed with dubious concepts and findings from natural sciences and highly questionable pseudo-biological argumentations, became a better theory. Does that not mean to make the same mistake as Jung: to conceptualize archetype theory as a part of the natural sciences, namely, biology, in an attempt to defend the theory against criticism, to make it a "real scientific theory"? We have seen that very early in the development of AP, a number of scholars clearly pointed out that this attempt was a defensive strategy by which Jung attempted to be regarded as a scientist, without caring for the state-of-the-art in biology, yes, without even being interested. The attempt to ground archetype theory in biology was a misconception from the beginning – owing partly also to Jung's academical background as a medical doctor and thus a natural scientist and his conviction that psychology was a natural science. From my point of view, it is time to abandon this theory and to clearly acknowledge that AP and also archetype theory are not part of the natural sciences. There is no need to continue such attempts to create a biological foundation for archetype theory, as it does not make it a scientific theory. In contrast, such attempts have become highly questionable and make archetype theory unscientific. Of course, this does not mean that archetypes have nothing to do with what could be called human nature. The biological and genetic makeup of humans plays a role in what kind of behaviour patterns, social rules and cultural contexts we develop. But it is not necessary – and I would argue it is even not possible – to investigate what is meant by the term archetype on the level of genes, gene-environment interaction, instincts and patterns of behaviour, etc. This is what in philosophical epistemology is called a category error. From my point of view, for decades, AP has been caught in useless academic debates of discussing different biological pathways in the desperate attempt to find a biological explanation for how archetypes come about. The overarching question, from the viewpoint of archetype theory, would instead be the following: What is appropriate and characteristic for human beings? This question has been investigated in depth in the discipline of anthropology; therefore, in the next chapter, the state-of-the-art in this field of research will be discussed.

Notes

1 "If something happens in life which equals an archetype, the archetype is activated with a certain compulsiveness, which, like an instinctual reaction, prevails against reason and human volition" (CW 9/1: para. 99).
2 Confirmed by interview with Prof. Dr. Tebartz van Elst (Freiburg/Germany), Neuropsychiatrist.
3 Confirmed by interview with Prof. Dr. Michael Müller-Schneider, Universität Landau/ Germany (see also references).
4 Confirmed by interview with Prof. Dr. Joachim Bauer, Neuroscientist, International Psychoanalytic University Berlin.

Chapter 6

Anthropology

Jung's theory around archetypes contains ideas from and references to the field of anthropology, specifically, very general and far-reaching assumptions regarding human universals that can be found in peoples from all over the world and from different epochs. He claims that there are similarities to be found cross-culturally in social rules and patterns, cultural habits and symbols/images, religious beliefs and ideas, mythological motifs and narratives, etc. In the course of such argumentations, Jung frequently refers to theorists and researchers in the field of anthropology and points to ethnological findings for such cross-cultural similarities, as well as to findings from prehistoric human societies and cultures. It seems that Jung had knowledge of a number of theories within the field of anthropology of his time, as far as they are cited in his published works. But the picture that is presented still in contemporary publications[1] that Jung systematically investigated mythologies and other products and ideas of indigenous societies is, from my point of view, part of the legend around Jung and his way of performing science. In the passages of the *Collected Works*, which make reference to anthropological theories and findings, I can see no systematic in the sense of an open-mindedly search for evidence speaking for or against his own theory; he even did not make systematic use of the findings reported by ethnological field researchers available already in his time. In contrast, it seems that he very selectively only presented the material which he thought was suitable to support his ideas. An example is the 1964 publication, *Man and His Symbols*, by Jung together with his followers – von Franz, Henderson, Jacobi and Jaffé (Jung et al. 1964) – which could be characterized as one of the already mentioned just-so explanations. The focus lies on Jung's theory, which is illustrated with examples from cultures and religions but only those which fit into the theoretical frame. There is no methodology applied, no systematics of data collection and no reference to other anthropological theories or studies. Even the citations are almost exclusively from Jungian authors or just sources for the myths and fairy tales discussed. This is phantasizing in the disguise of a scientific study.

As I have already pointed out, the few references that Jung makes in the *Collected Works* to ethnological researchers (Eliade, Mauss, Levy-Bruhl, Paul Radin, Baldwin Spencer, James Stevenson, Winthius) are often even only footnotes. Jung was apparently very fond of Levy-Bruhl (1912/1921) and quotes him more than

DOI: 10.4324/9781003348191-6

60 times in his works, referring mainly to the concept of participation mystique. But Levy-Bruhl is more an anthropologically orientated philosopher in the tradition of 19th century science than an empirically oriented anthropologist. The most important researchers and theorists of his time – Marcel Mauss and Bronislaw Malinowski – Jung only mentions once. This means he knew of their works but chose not to use them. This is quite surprising, especially in the case of Malinowski (1924), as he conducted research about the occurrence of the Oedipus complex in different cultures of the world. This should have been of interest to Jung. Claude Levi-Strauss (1949) does not get mentioned, even though he created an interesting alternative theory to Jung's archetype theory and began to publish these ideas in the 1940s.

My impression is that this approach to the use of findings and theories in anthropology has continued in AP, namely, in the works of Erich Neumann, and up to the present day, as the earlier quote (Boechat 2022) demonstrates, which is currently presented on the website of the IAAP in a section with recent summaries of the major concepts of AP.

There is no doubt that Jung was very much interested especially in indigenous cultures, and he undertook adventurous travels (e.g., to Mount Elgon in Africa and Taos Pueblo in the Southwest of the United States) in order to personally meet such peoples and learn more about their worldviews. But the way in which he collected data and interviewed individuals from these indigenous peoples can by no means be characterized as proper ethnographic research – even though systematic methods for such research where very well available already in his time. Again, it seems, he was not really interested in such a kind of systematic research, with proper collection of data, a careful testing of hypotheses, etc., but more in finding proof for his already pre-conceptualized ideas, and consequently, he interpreted what he found according to his own framework of thought.

The homology of phylogeny and ontogeny

In Jung, there is a basic idea which parallels phylogeny and ontogeny, which is of major importance for understanding the endeavour Jung undertook in his works. The basic idea is that the archetypes have formed over thousands of years in the history of mankind and can thus be reconstructed by investigating early cultures and prehistory. They can also be found in so-called primitive peoples, their rituals, beliefs and mythologies, and they are repeated in the individual development of humans today. The archetypes (as structures of the collective unconscious) form the basis of all these different forms of development, historic, cultural, mythological, religious and individual. This very fundamental idea in Jung's works was later unfolded in detail in Erich Neumann's (1949) *The Origins and History of Consciousness*.

This theory entails an idea which has been characterized as the homology of phylogeny and ontogeny. The development of the individual (ontogeny) recapitulates the history and evolution of the species (phylogeny). The idea was introduced into biology by the German biologist Erich Haeckel, and the concept, in fact, correctly applies to the prenatal embryonic development of human beings but only on a biological level (e.g., the human embryo passes through developmental phases in which, for a short time, it develops features like gills, etc.). Already in the 19th century, this originally biological concept was expanded to the field of psychological anthropology, which means that the psychological development of the individual recapitulates the evolutionary and cultural development of mankind as a whole. Included in this idea is the assumption of a scale of different levels of maturity of development from archaic/primitive to developed/civilized, which can accordingly be applied to individual development as well as to the development of cultures and societies.

In Jung's worldview, there was a clear distinction, if not to say a hierarchy, regarding the differentiation of culture and, connected with this, psychological development and functioning. He was convinced that traditional/indigenous peoples were on a more primitive level of culturalization as well as of individual psychological development and that this was evident in their mythologies, social and religious practices, but also in their mental functioning.

An example: in his 1920 publication, *Psychological Types*, which remained uncorrected up to the last edition of 1949, he writes:

> An incident in the life of a bushman may illustrate what I mean. A bushman had a little son whom he loved with the tender monkey love characteristic of primitives. Psychologically, this love is completely autoerotic that is to say the subject loves himself in the object.
>
> (CW 6, p. 403; see also Samuels 2017)

This viewpoint or model includes the assumption that so-called primitive people live on the same level of psychological development as earlier forms of Homo sapiens (e.g., Stone Age hunter gatherer groups on the one hand and as little children on the other) (e.g., CW 8, para. 95–98). Even more, this perspective includes the assumption that in psychopathology, a degeneration, regression or dissolution of the so-called civilized state of mind of Westerners takes place which results in a state of mind on a more primitive level, which in this model is equated with the state of mind and psychological functioning of phylogenetically earlier, more primitive peoples and/or that of children.

A good example of this way of thought in Jung's works can be found in his text "On the energetics of the soul" (CW 8) in the chapter on "The primitive concept of libido". Here, Jung argues, based on a compilation of quotes from anthropology, that in the psyche of the so-called primitives, there is a powerful energetic principle, for which Jung coins the term "Mana". This finally leads him to argue that the described phenomena in primitives is what Levy-Bruhl (1912) has called "participation mystique". Levy-Bruhl even calls the primitives "les sociétés inférieures" (the inferior societies). Jung argues that primitives cannot distance themselves from the effects of this energy nor can they reflect on it, the same as children. He even argues that they do not have a concept of it but only experience it as a psychic phenomenon. This is what Jung calls "primitive mentality" (see also the text under the term "archaism" in the "Definitions" in *Psychological Types*, CW 6, para. 754).

> In us (Westerners) it would be a psychological concept of energy, but in the primitives it is a psychic phenomenon, which is experienced as being connected with the object. There is no abstract idea in primitives, generally not even simple concrete concepts, but only imaginations.
>
> (CW 8, para. 127; transl. C.R.)

Jung clarifies in this text that he sees the so-called primitives on a lower level not only of cultural development but also of psychological development as well. In another text, Jung (CW 8, para. 668) argues that he sees the little child and the primitive on the same level of psychological development, without any evidence of ego consciousness, being strongly impressed by the expressions of their own psyche and falling prey to magical beliefs.

Referring to Levy-Bruhl's concept of participation mystique – here translated as "identity" – Jung writes:

> The identity is grounded in the notorious unconsciousness of the little child. This is also the connection to the primitives: they are to the same extent unconscious as the child. The unconsciousness causes the non-differentiation. There is no clearly separated ego yet existent, but only happenings, which are related to me or someone else.
>
> (CW 17, para. 83; transl. C.R.)

Jung then discusses what would happen if children were not to go to school:

> The children would stay to a high extent unconscious. . . . It would be a primitive state, which means that if such children would grow up, they would be, in spite of all natural intelligence, primitives, i.e. savages, like the members of an intelligent Negro or Red Indian tribe. They would not be just silly, but only instinctively intelligent, they would be unknowing and therefore unconscious of themselves and the world. They would start their life on a significantly lower level of culture and would be only slightly different from the primitive races.
>
> (CW 17, para. 104)

A parallel example from Neumann, who uncritically shared this view:

> As the ego of the child recapitulating this phase is weak, easily fatigable, emerges only in single moments from the twilight of the unconscious and falls back into it, in the same manner the man from the early history experiences of the world. Little, weak, sleeping most of the time, i.e. mostly unconscious, he floats in the instinctual like an animal.
>
> (Neumann 1963, p. 92)

Giegerich's critique

As early as 1975, the famous Jungian author Wolfgang Giegerich (1975) pointed out the problems inherent in this idea of homology very sharply. He fundamentally criticizes the aforementioned attempts by Jung and Neumann and clearly distinguishes between cultural development and phylogeny. He concludes that it is impossible to argue for any kind of psychological evolution in history and characterizes Neumann's work as fiction and speculative construction. These ideas are characterized as in itself a myth, an archetypal fantasy. The problem is that these myths are presented as science. He also accuses Jung of a reduction of the mythological, as if it were not enough to present it as something cultural, to give the impression of a scientific theory. The author maintains that, as psychologists, it is not our business to look for historical or biological facts but, instead, for the psychological truth.

There is a number of authors who argue in the same line and criticize Jung's models as the product of a longing for a conflict-free oneness, a lost paradise, and argue for an archetypal psychology which is free from mistaken ontological reductionisms (e.g., Papadopoulus 1992). It is interesting that, although Giegerich's critique was formulated as early as 1975, in recent publications still, Neumann's approach is defended, and the central argument in the critique is not really understood. Walch (2005), in a paper given at a conference in Vienna celebrating the 100th birthday of Neumann, accuses Giegerich of misunderstandings and a destructive tendency when he tries to confront Neumann's assumptions with insights and facts from studies in mythology. The central argument here, again, as in so many papers in AP, is that the archetypes are located in the collective unconscious and can, therefore, not be compared, described or explained with empirical facts or insights from so-called "positivistic" sciences.

The homology-hypothesis in the history of anthropology

The idea of homology presented earlier was quite common and widespread in 19th and early 20th century anthropology. In German romantic thought, this idea can be found early as the beginning of the 19th century (e.g., in Wilhelm von Humboldt and Johann Gottfried Herder), presented as "Volksgeist" (Wolfradt 2021). With the 1888 publication of his "Völkerpsychologie" (peoples' psychology), Wilhelm Wundt became the main protagonist of this universalist viewpoint and, as we know, was highly influential for the development of Jung's ideas. Wundt proposed the evolutionist idea of a level theory: 1. Primitive phase, 2. Totemic phase, 3. Age of heroes and gods and 4. Development towards humanity. Likewise important for Jung were the ideas of Adolf Bastian (1881), who presented the concept of "elementary thoughts", which are the foundation of a "psychic unity of mankind" – a concept which obviously laid the ground for Jung's archetype theory (for more details on Bastian, see next section). Lastly, Levy-Bruhl (1912) – of whom Jung was very fond of – assumed that "primitive peoples" were only capable of illogical ways of thought and, therefore, prone to magical beliefs, a viewpoint which Jung adopted without any reflexion. These ideas had an important role in the justification of the politics of colonialization well into the 20th century. Since this approach was based on a biological/evolutionist perspective, it attempted to connect psychological qualities of indigenous versus European societies with physiological characteristics, as for example, the form of the head, facial expressions, etc., attempts that were continued by the Nazis in their "Rassenlehre" (race theory). These approaches were based on two fundamental misconceptions: first, the biological development was equated with sociocultural developments, and second, there was a fundamental lack of systematic empirical methods and, consequently, of respective studies and findings (Wolfradt 2021).

In contrast to Jung, his fellow countryman, Jean Piaget, who also described a level of cognitive development in children characterized by animism and magical beliefs, did not go as far as paralleling this with the psychological state of mind of the "primitives" and can provide a lot of empirical evidence for this way of psychological functioning in children. This stands opposed to Jung, who just repeats widespread assumptions in the anthropology of his time.

It should be noted that this view of indigenous people had devastating effects in practical politics. The German psychiatrist Heinz (2019) demonstrated in a thorough investigation of this historical viewpoint that it was strongly supported by Eugen Bleuler, head of the psychiatric hospital at Zürich University and Jung's boss and academical supervisor in the years from 1903 until he left the university. Bleuler developed these thoughts in his famous work on dementia praecox/schizophrenia, which was also influential for the development of Jung's ideas. In this famous work, which had strong influences on the development of psychiatry in the 20th century and on the concept of schizophrenia, Bleuler speculates in a highly racist way about the primitive psychological functioning of Negroes. These ideas played a certain role in the war and the following attempts of extermination of the peoples Nama and Herero in the German colony in Southwest Africa, a war which was headed by Imperial Commissioner Ernst Heinrich Göring, the father of the Nazi leader Hermann Göring. Such ideas were used by the German racists as a justification for the treatment of indigenous African tribes and peoples, as they were considered to be living on the level of wild animals. It is obvious that Jung's thinking about the primitives and the primitive state of mind were influenced by these thoughts and perspectives and were never really reflected upon during his lifetime. This is sad because Jung would have had the opportunity to correct his thinking. The anthropologist Bronislaw Malinowski, who lived with the "primitive" people of Melanesia during the time of the First World War, published his reports about these people as early as the 1930s (available in Malinowski 1948/1974; it has to be noted that Jung knew Malinowski because he quotes him). He provided a lot of ethnographic evidence which speaks clearly against the assumption that these colonialized peoples were subject to an evolutionarily more primitive, irrational way of thinking, which was thought to be categorically different from the thinking of modernized people in the Western world. He provided evidence that these assumedly primitive people were absolutely capable of goal-directed thought, rationality and even empirical studies (e.g., in the search for healing substances in plants). He also demonstrated that the seemingly irrational rituals and practices of these peoples were in general goal-directed and made a lot of sense as soon as one tried to understand their function in the relevant context.

An example: as a Polish citizen, Malinowski was interned in Melanesia during the First World War since this region was a British protectorate. Being an anthropologist, Malinowski decided to make use of this time by choosing to live on the Trobriand Islands to study the indigenous people there, who had had practically no contact to modern civilization up to that time. He participated in the life of the Trobriands (a way of conducting ethnographic research which was later termed participative observation), which included lots of daily rituals. Practically, the whole of everyday life was permanently accompanied by religious rituals. At first glance, this structuring of everyday life seemed to support the aforementioned ideas that these indigenous people were not able to conduct daily life without permanently appeasing wrathful deities. But there were interesting exceptions from that rule: the Trobriands were fishermen and very competently sailed the open seas surrounding their islands in fragile wooden boats. Malinowski observed that while on the sea, no rituals were conducted. When asking for the reason, he received the answer that only crazy people would conduct rituals on the open sea, where you need all your senses and intelligence to master the dangers of the wild ocean. This clearly demonstrates that these so-called primitive people were well capable of differentiating situations and of distancing themselves from the influence of magical powers and thus to act highly rationally.

Also, in psychiatry, the aforementioned viewpoint was strongly criticized as early as 1930, as it could be demonstrated that this model provided no satisfying explanation for the development of schizophrenia (Storch 1930).

Racism in Jung

The anti-Semitic comments Jung made during the 1930s have been criticized for quite a while (Kirsch 2004; Spillmann & Strubel 2010). More recently, racist statements Jung made about Africans (he believed they had inferior cognitive abilities compared to white people) have been discussed (Group of

Jungians 2018). In the year 1934, Jung published his article "Die gegenwärtige Lage der Psychotherapie" ("The current state of psychotherapy", CW 10). In a crucial passage, he speaks about the differences between the Jewish and the Aryan unconscious and that the Aryan unconscious has a superior potential compared to the Jewish one. He then speaks in a very devaluing way about Freud and that he was not able to understand the potential of the Germanic race. This is the most problematic quote but, by far, not the only one. In the essay *Wotan* (Jung 1936, CW 10), as in other publications and statements from the time, Jung continues this line of argumentation. In the 1990s, the German Society for AP conducted a research project, collecting all the anti-Semitic statements and publications by Jung (Tann & Erlenmeyer 1993). It clearly demonstrates that Jung's anti-Semitic thinking can be found in many of his works and public statements and covers a period of at least 25 years. My point here is not to prove that Jung was an anti-Semite. What I am trying to point out here is the fact that these statements are closely linked with a certain point of view in Jung, a mindset, which is based on his biological understanding of archetypes and the aforementioned homology idea. This leads to figures of thought which can objectively be called racist (Haymond 1982).

Jung himself admits to having declared his support for "Rassenpsychologie" (race psychology) long before the Nazis came into power (Dalal 1991). There are actually earlier examples of his anti-Semitic and racist thinking like his essay *Über Unbewusstes* from 1918, as well as a lecture given to the Zürich psychoanalytic society on January 24, 1913, called *Die unbewusste Psychologie der Neger* (*The Unconscious Psychology of Negros*) (Shamdasani 1998, p. 15).

Recently, a group of Jungians in the *British Journal of Psychoanalysis* collected and criticized relevant statements about the inferiority of Africans in comparison to Europeans based on his archetype theory. They emphasize that Jung's circle had already warned about his problematic views on the subject, but Jung would not listen (Group of Jungians 2018; Dalal 1991).

In the essay *Nach der Katastrophe* (*After the Catastrophe*), Jung begins to deal with his own thoughts, but no real self-reflection is happening (Erlenmeyer 2001). Even after the war, Jung says:

> It is however difficult to mention the antichristianism of the Jews after the horrible things that have happened in Germany, but Jews are not so damned innocent after all – the role played by the intellectual Jews in the pre-war Germany would be an interesting object of investigation.
>
> (Bair 2003, p. 444)

This again is a highly typical anti-Semitic line of reasoning, claiming that the Jews are responsible for their own persecution.

The most personal form of confession can be found in the following wording: "Jawohl, ich bin ausgerutscht" ("Yes, I slipped"; transl. by the author) (Jaffé 1985). This problematic expression insinuates that the problem does not lie within his own character but in the unstable ground below him, therefore, his only mistake being to not have been careful enough not to slip. This does not match the extent to which he was caught up in anti-Semitic and racist ways of thinking, which can be seen throughout his work ever since 1913.

Aniela Jaffé (1985) has already shown that Jung did not really reflect on the problematic nature of his thoughts and especially the consequences of his statements at that time:

It has to be seen as a severe mistake that Jung emphasized the specialness of being Jewish in a time when it was life-threatening to be Jewish, and that at the same time he put psychological -racist differentiations on the scientific program of the International Association. Any statement pointing to Jewish otherness at that time was provoking more fanaticism.

(p. 72; transl. C.R.)

In the same line:

It is not enough to say, when we look at Jung's racism, sexism, anti-Semitism and so forth, "Well he was just a man of his time". The problem with that, especially in relation to the anti-Semitism, is that he wasn't. There was a wide acrimonious debate about what he was doing and saying in relation to Jews and Germans at the time. In 1936, when it was proposed to give him an honorary degree at Harvard, there were virtual riots. . . . So it was not as if Jung could not have done anything else. People at the time knew that he had various options open to him.

(Samuels 1998, pp. 24–25)

In my opinion, Jung was never really an anti-Semite at heart – considering the fact that a lot of his students came from Jewish backgrounds and always had a warm and heartfelt appreciation for one another (e.g., Erich Neumann, Sabina Spielrain, James Kirsch, Jolande Jacobi and Carl Alfred Meier to name a few) (for an overview, see Kirsch 2002, 2016).

But Jung as a person is not the point here. It may even be difficult or impossible to find out what he really thought and felt. What I am trying to point out here is that Jung's racist and anti-Semitic arguments are connected with his theory of archetypes, namely, its biological foundation. Jung takes a biological view on archetypes, which is built around the idea that humans have a phylogenetic evolutionary heritage which necessarily forms their behaviour and personality to a large extent. This means, because of one's belonging to a specific race and due to the fact that, according to Jung, genetics form the personality, the form of a person's psyche corresponds with the racial heritage. In the case of black Africans and Jews, Jung connected this with a value judgment. That brings Jung's theory close to fascist ways of reasoning, which also believe in a biological foundation of national characters and base their supposed superiority on this line of argumentation (Lesmeister 2001). So to argue that archetypes are based in one's biology and, therefore, if there are biological differences between ethnic groups, to argue that they are psychologically different "by nature" is a pattern of thought generally used by fascist and racist theories. As well as there are biological differences between the races, from his point of view, there are also inherited psychological differences between the races. This is, without any doubt, a racist argumentation, independent of what Jung as a person thought about Africans or Jews. It also has to be considered that this argumentation has been scientifically disproved quite a while ago. There are, for example, no biological differences in intelligence between the human races. The corresponding investigations were conducted by Franz Boas as early as 1910 by using questionnaires he tested whether the children of immigrants to the United States adapted to the habits and the way of thinking in their new home country and could provide evidence that after one generation, there were no differences detectable anymore between these second-generation immigrants and the native population (Wolfradt 2021). Based on these findings, Boas supported an antiracist anthropology (see next section for more details).

In recent times, it has even been questioned whether there are different human races because investigations in the genome have made clear that all so-called races share a large amount of similarities – which are the result of migrations and mixing of different ethnic groups in the history of human development – so we all are more or less "hybrids" and the descendants of migrants (see also chapter "Prehistory"). Certainly, there is no such thing as a "pure race" (e.g., Aryan). The strange thing is that Jung could have used his archetype theory – since archetypes are thought to be universal – for putting the emphasis on the equality of all humans. Instead, he chose the racist point of view.

Evidence speaking against the homology-hypothesis

The view described earlier, which could be characterized as "colonial thinking", was not only strongly questioned in anthropology but it can also be said that this viewpoint has been refuted in contemporary ethnology. The German term "Naturvölker", which translates as natural peoples, was even eliminated from contemporary publications in anthropology, as the assumption included in the term that traditional peoples live closer to or in identity with nature – as they are closer to the animal level regarding their mental development – is by no means supported through ethnographic findings. In general, it can be said that there is an independence between technological development of a traditional people and the complexity of their cosmologies. So for example, the indigenous peoples of the Amazon basin lived on a Stone Age level of technology but had extremely complex and multilayered cosmologies. It is a widespread romantic fantasy that these so-called natural people live in ecological harmony with their environment. And this belief is inherent in Jung's archetype theory since he argues that problems of modern man have to do with the alienation from nature, in general as well as regarding our own human nature:

> It [the archetype] throws a bridge between present-day consciousness, always in danger of losing its roots, and the natural, unconscious, instinctive wholeness of primeval times.
>
> (CW 9/1, para. 293)

Here are some findings from archaeology which speak against the inherent prejudice, the phantasy of a "natural, unconscious, instinctive wholeness":

> Archaeological findings in North America point to the fact that when the first hunter gatherers arriving from Asia via the Bering Strait land bridge, in a period of less than 1000 years they had eradicated all the big mammals living on the continent, except from bison, deer and caribou, because these were either too aggressive or retreated into forests or polar regions. Killing these large mammals (e.g., mammoth) was so easy because these animals had no schema for protecting themselves against human hunters.

> Whereas the extinctions took place probably before 30,000 years ago in Australia, they occurred around 17,000 to 12,000 years ago in the Americas. For those extinct American mammals whose bones are available in great abundance and have been dated especially accurately, one can pinpoint the extinctions as having occurred around 11,000 BC. Perhaps the most accurately dated extinctions are those of the Shasta ground sloth and Harrington's mountain goat in the Grand Canyon area; both of these populations disappeared within a century or two of 11,000 BC.
>
> (Diamond 1997, pp. 46–47; see also Mithen 2003 for a detailed account)

What is today known as the big prairies in North America originally was forest land, but the immigrating hunter gatherers from Asia burnt down these forests completely so as to be able to hunt their game more easily in the grasslands. This took place more than 10,000 years ago and is considered to be one of the largest destructions of biosphere in the history of mankind.

Similar extinction patterns can be found for Australia and New Guinea:

> All of those Australian/New Guinea giants (the so-called megafauna: a 400 pound ostrich-like flightless bird, big reptiles, including a 1 ton lizard, a giant-python etc.) . . . become extinct after humans reached Australia. . . . In contrast, most big mammals of Africa and Eurasia survived into modern times, because they had coevolved with proto-humans for hundreds of thousands or millions of years. They thereby enjoyed ample time to evolve a fear of humans, as our ancestors' initially poor hunting skills slowly improved. The dodo, moas, and perhaps the giants of Australia/New Guinea had the misfortune suddenly to be confronted, without any evolutionary preparation, by invading modern humans possessing fully developed hunting skills.
>
> (Diamond 1997, pp. 42–43)

The extinction of Eurasia's woolly mammoth and woolly rhinoceros may have similar reasons, as around 20,000 years ago, human hunter gatherers were able, even in the face of ice age climates, to move northward due to the development of the technology of needles and sewing, which allowed for the production of warm clothes protecting against the cold (Diamond 1997, p. 44). One could even argue that in modern humans, there is a much greater awareness for the sensitivity of their ecological environment and for the devastating impact humans can have on it.

"Survivals" and "human fossil" societies: The way of thinking outlined earlier, prominent in the evolutionary school of anthropology, led to the idea that there can be found human groups or societies which are remnants of the Stone Age because they have been relatively isolated. These societies were thought to be representatives of a racial purity and their social system being a kind of living fossil that could reveal information about prehistoric human groups and societies and, in general, about the development of mankind. An example for this approach is Radcliffe Brown's investigation of the peoples of the Andamanese Islands. Here, he divided their cosmology into a tripartite schema, consisting of sea/water, forest/land and skies/trees, which should explain their religion as well as their system of social hierarchies and functions (Wunn 2019). Another example of this way of thinking is Edward B. Tylor's theory about primitive religion (see next section for details on these outdated theories). Contemporary anthropologists strongly criticize this viewpoint and stress the point that these views are not shared any longer in anthropology.

> The evolutionary school in anthropology saw a uni-linear progression from more primitive societies to more civilized ones. Accompanying this progression was a similar proposed progression from magic to religion to science. Myths were seen as belonging to the primitive period, with sacred myths being replaced by secular folktales until finally dying out altogether in civilized societies. It is important to remember that anthropologists no longer believe in such an evolutionary progression or that peoples can be classified as primitive or civilized.

Theorists from the evolutionary school assumed that modern people living in small-scale societies lived and thought the same way that earlier European societies had. They compared myths found in many different cultures, looking for common elements from which they could reconstruct an assumed original form of myth from which all others had arrived. It was believed that doing this could help explain puzzling aspects of modern European society.

The work of James George Frazer is a good example of this approach. He collected as many examples of myths and magical practices from around the world as possible and published them as a 13 volume work entitled "The Golden Bough". Although modern anthropologists criticize the information in the Golden Bough is taken out of its cultural context, the book is still widely read [and was highly important for Jung's archetype theory, with many references in the CW; CR.]. . . . Since Frazer's time, further studies of myths have found that no single myth exists cross-culturally, but characteristic versions of the story may be found in specific areas.

(Stein & Stein 2008, p. 41)

Jung and the grand theories of the 19th and early 20th century

The general assumptions inherent in Jung's archetype theory, as for example, the aforementioned homology and the general idea of a scale of development from primitive to civilized, were not Jung's invention but can be found in a number of other theories in anthropology, which were formulated in the 19th and early 20th century. In the following, these will be characterized as the grand theories of anthropology (for an overview, see Bowie 2004). Many of these thinkers were strongly influenced by Darwin's ideas of the process of evolution in biology and attempted to apply these findings to the explanation of the development of societies, religion, rituals, etc., and in general, on the development of human history itself. These approaches can, therefore, be characterized as evolutionistic (the following account is based on Beer & Fischer 2017; Stein & Stein 2008; Bowie 2004; Harris 1975).

Herbert Spencer (1876), a 19th century British social and political thinker, had the general theory that all things move from simpler to more differentiated complex forms on the path of a universal evolution. Spencer attempted to apply this idea to the explanation of the development of religion and assumed that ancestor worship was at the root of every religion.

Edward Burnett Tylor, however, emphasized the role of the soul in his account of religious origins and coined the term animism, which describes the idea that all beings, animate and inanimate objects, have a soul. This idea became very influential in anthropology and is still used as a general descriptive term for primitive or indigenous religions. Also, Jung heavily referred to this idea. Tylor's work *Primitive Culture* (1871), which summarized these ideas, became very influential in 19th and early 20th century anthropology. He developed the notion of three stages of social evolution, going from animism over polytheism to monotheism. Interestingly, though, Tylor did not assume a biological base for these developments but coined the idea of diffusion, the transmission across time and space of cultural elements and traits. He also developed the idea of "survivals", which means that some of these primitive elements remain even in advanced or civilized societies and are connected to an earlier evolutionary stage. Tylor was convinced that in so-called primitive cultures, there was not a variety but uniformity, and he even expressed a certain extent of boredom when referring to the similarities: "the same story everywhere". Not only is this devaluing account problematic in Tylor but also, the value judgments that he gave to his scale of stages of cultural development poses a difficulty.

Very much the same way of argumentation can be found in L.H. Morgan's (1877) influential work *Ancient Society, or Researches in the Lines of Human Progress from Savagery Through Barbarism to Civilization* – a title which summarizes the general idea of a scale of development of human cultures. All of these theories, therefore, pose the idea of an initial primitive state of mind, society, religion, etc., from which civilization develops and which can be found still in so-called primitive peoples or societies, which means mainly contemporary hunter gatherer societies.

Another grand theory of that time can be found in James Frazer's seminal publication *The Golden Bough* (1890). In Frazer's account of the development of religion, the basic assumption is that magic precedes religion.

Leo Frobenius (1904, 1936), a German ethnologist and very popular author in his time, is exemplary for the reductionist views in these grand theories. Frobenius was a very active field researcher and gained international reputation with his copies of Stone Age cave paintings and rock art, which he collected in a number of adventurous expeditions to all parts of the world. Prior to that, he became widely known as a collector of mythologies from all over the world. He founded the discipline of "Kulturmorphologie" (morphology of cultures) connected with an institute, which still is active in Frankfurt/Germany. He followed the evolutionist viewpoint that, especially in the cave paintings as well as in the mythology of the peoples of the world, the development of culture itself could be identified; he saw the paintings as well as the myths as an expression of the archived nature of man itself. Interestingly, one of his publications on cave paintings has the title *Das Urbild* (*The Primal Image*) (Frobenius 1936), the same term that was used by Jung initially for his concept which he later called archetype. Frobenius also followed the aforementioned idea that there is a homology of Stone Age cultures with today's so-called primitive peoples, so the study of these contemporary hunter gatherer societies would provide information about the ways of living in the Stone Age. He even called the prehistoric rock art the picture book of the history of humanity. He stressed the point that also in modern humans, the archaic irrationalism is stronger than modern consciousness: "The I life is always stronger than that which is conditioned by consciousness" (Frobenius 1936, p. 139; transl. C.R.). Even though he became highly popular in his time, especially through his widely read publications, he remained an outsider in this scholarly field of anthropology. Jung heavily relied on Frobenius in his works, starting with his seminal 1912 publication, *Symbols of Transformation*, although Frobenius was a diffusionist (see next section in the section on mythology). It is quite clear that Jung was strongly influenced by Frobenius's ideas on the primal image, the archaic, etc., since it is obvious that he uncritically shared many of these viewpoints and also quotes him extensively. The same applies to the theories of Tylor and Frazer, who are quoted by Jung many times.

A similarity in all of these grand theories is the general assumption that laws taken from biology, especially the processes of biological evolution, need to be applied to all the other fields of anthropology, society, religion, mythology, etc. This is a view shared by Jung, who was convinced that psychology is a natural science and who took an evolutionist point of view, as I have pointed out earlier.

Contemporary criticism of the evolutionist school

All of the grand theories are heavily criticized by contemporary anthropologists:

> The "butterfly collecting" mythology, which juxtaposes information, often of a very dubious provenance, totally out of context, allows the author to prove almost any point he cares to make. This has not prevented the Golden Bough in its abridged edition from remaining almost constantly in print.
>
> (Bowie 2004, p. 15)

This point of critique could also be applied to Jung's works. Jung heavily relied on Frazer. Also, other contemporary anthropologists have taken this point of critique towards the 19th century classics, arguing that these theories were lacking any real evidence and that these theories were fallen to the "if-I-were-a-horse" fallacy, and their tales of origins of religion as "just so stories". The critique against these unilinear theoretical accounts was first formulated by field researchers, who could not find empirical evidence for these theories developed by scholars that often never left their university offices (Beer & Fischer 2017). Interestingly, Jung preferred to follow these ivory-tower thinkers instead of using empirical data of field researchers. From the perspective of field researchers, the similarities found in different peoples had strong connections to similar environmental conditions or to similarities in how they produced food (e.g., agricultural or horticultural societies), which were connected with specific social systems and hierarchies. In other words, specific social or cultural belief systems could be seen as adaptations to a certain environment or a certain way of life.[2] These insights formed a tradition in anthropology which could be characterized as finding systemic explanations for the similarities and differences between cultures (e.g., Marcel Mauss).

A good example of such a systemic approach to understand parallels and similarities between cultures is the theory of the **German anthropologist Klaus Müller** (1983). He starts from the insight that all human groups, because of their similar physiological and psychological conditions, are confronted with similar problems in life and, therefore, find similar solutions for these basic problems all over the world. In his theory, he attempts to describe in general form these invariable antecedent conditions as well as the invariants in individual and group behaviour, including cultural belief systems. In his investigations, he found that these orientating systems are stable and have the same topographical construction, which can be characterized by the elements of centre versus periphery and a dichotomy of a positively valued realm of cultural habits versus a negatively valued realm outside of one's own culture. These differentiations or separations are constructed by stabilizing mechanisms, of which he identifies seven: separation, rationalization, dogmatization, ritualization, negation and absolutization. These mechanisms make the social system immune against critique and questioning, so for example, religious ideas and rituals are considered in many societies as sacred and, therefore, not to be criticized (interestingly, this applies also to theories and procedures in psychoanalytic communities). Problems arise when transitions are needed from one realm to the other, for example, transitions in status (e.g., marriage, the transition from childhood to adulthood); therefore, these transitions are usually ritualized. Here, Müller fully agrees with Van Gennep's (1909) description of rites of passage (see chapter "Religion").

Another characteristic pattern in these grand theories for the explanation of the development of human culture and religion is the attitude to try to explain all the different forms by applying just one monolithic explanatory system. Often, these systems use binary oppositions. An example is Émile Durkheim's (1915/1976) work, *The Elementary Forms of the Religious Life*, for which he used an investigation of Australian aboriginal peoples (of which he believed that they represented the simplest form of society and could, therefore, serve as a model for the roots of human culture). In this system, the key distinction was between the sacred and the profane, interestingly, the same that was later used by Mircea Eliade (1959). Durkheim's theories were highly important for Jung in developing his own system of thought and again, in Jung, can be found such a binary opposition as the central explanatory concept here: the opposition between unconscious and consciousness. Another famous system in anthropology which uses a binary opposition is that of Claude Levi-Strauss's (1970, 1976) *Structural Anthropology*, which makes use of the distinction of the raw and the cooked.

Only later in the first half of the 20th century, the first anthropologists left behind these monolithic explanatory concepts, for example, Franz Boas (1922), who stressed the cultural differences in his ideas about historical particularism. He combined the emphasis on social functions with a focus on individual psychology. This leads to an understanding of characteristic cultural styles unique to each society. Consequently, Boas explicitly took an antiracist stance in anthropology. Interestingly, Jung chose not to use this theory, even though it was available to him, which could have changed the racist element within his concepts.

In general, it can be said that as soon as anthropologists started to use systematic methods of comparison in the second half of the 20th century, it quickly became clear that the earlier theories had to be refuted as they could not be backed by evidence. This also applies to later theories (e.g., Levi-Strauss's system), even though he makes use of a very detailed method of comparison:

> As with the earlier search for universals, the innate structures proposed by Levi-Strauss remain speculative and (like Frazer's Golden Bough) there is a danger of simply amassing data that repeat an argument without actually strengthening it. . . . Many critiques have in the end found that such an approach leaves too many important questions unanswered.
>
> (Bowie 2004, p. 20)

A basic result of these systematic comparative methods in anthropology is the insight that there is not one unifying concept which can explain the variety of cultural forms and ideas. Regarding Durkheim's binary concept of the sacred and the profane, Bowie (2004) states:

> Many anthropologists have pointed out that it is not always possible to distinguish in practice between the sacred and the profane, and this idea, so central to Durkheim's work has by and large been discarded, at least as a monolithic organizing principle.
>
> (p. 140)

In contemporary handbooks, anthologies of anthropology and the history of religion, Jung's ideas are mentioned, often together with Freud's assumptions about totem and taboo. Both are usually criticized for their far-reaching speculations and their limited use of empirical data.

> In part because Jung's archetypes are alleged to be universal and pre-cultural, he has received less attention in anthropological circles than Freud, whose theories are more amenable to cultural relativism. Anthropologists have also criticized Jungian analysis for rarely using data from non-Western sources.
>
> (Stein & Stein 2008, p. 45)

Bachofen's "Mutterrecht" and Jung's "great mother"

An especially drastic example of one of these historical grand theories, on which Jung heavily relied on, is Bachofen's (1861/2004) monumental work on *Das Mutterrecht* (published in English in 2004 as *The Law of Mothers*). Interestingly, he was a fellow townsman of Jung's. Bachofen was a renowned scholar and historian very much interested in mythology and symbolism. He assumed that in human history, there had been a period of matriarchy, which was thought to be also a period of political rule of women. This was thought to be followed by a period of destabilization initiated by invasions of patriarchal people introducing patriarchy in combination with a repression of all memory of those prior eras. Jung very much appreciated this theory and was looking for matriarchal symbolism in his own works and assumed matriarchy to be a stage in the development of consciousness. This was later taken up by Jung's follower Erich Neumann in *The Origins and History of Consciousness* and in his second monumental work, *The Great Mother* (Neumann 1963), in which he relied heavily on Bachofen's theory of early matriarchy. Neumann (1963) actually praises Bachofen as being the discoverer of the "deeper psychic layers of the development of mankind" (p. 92). Jung wrote the foreword to Neumann's first work and welcomed it since – as Jung argued – it grounded AP on a firm evolutionary base (CW 18, §521–522). Jung's ideas about the psychological feminine often are grounded in Bachofen's ideas. It has to be noted that these ideas, though they became popular again in the women's movement, have long been refuted, as there is absolutely no evidence of any kind for these ideas. Bachofen's ideas were mainly based on intuitions and phantasies (van Schaik & Michel 2020). We will come back to this topic in the discussion on prehistoric female figurines, which were also interpreted as evidence for matriarchy or at least for a universal cult of a great mother goddess (Gimbutas 1989) (see chapter "Prehistory").

Contexts are relevant

Another important point in which contemporary approaches to anthropology differ from the classic grand theories is the insight that religious ideas, beliefs and rituals are closely interconnected with social organization, political interests and power regulation, hierarchies, etc., on the one hand and, on the other hand, with environmental conditions and the needs and pressures that result from it.

> Cosmologies are not, of course, pulled out of the air to suit the convenience of the communities to which they are attached. They are conditioned by many and various historical, environmental, technological, psychological, and social factors. A flourishing community is likely to involve a bright, self-affirming cosmology, and the languishing communities likely to see the world in darker shades.
>
> (Mathews 1994, p. 13)

If investigated without any prejudices, it becomes apparent that societies and their belief systems as well as cosmologies are directly connected in complex ways with the environment in which it is located and with social attitudes. Therefore, it has to be acknowledged that cosmologies and other religious elements serve certain functions in societies. This is also another argument against the aforementioned notion of a scale of primitive to civilized:

> An irrational view of the world as peopled by spirits may be more adaptive than a scientific view that sees the world in mechanistic terms.
>
> (Bowie 2004, p. 122)

In general, contemporary anthropologists take the viewpoint of how adaptive a cultural belief system is to the needs of a people and their situatedness in a certain environment.

Culture before biology

Lastly, there is a contemporary tradition in anthropology which stresses the inter-relatedness of human biology and culture in the sense that not only the biological conditions of humans produce certain cultural elements (e.g., a religious belief system) but also that culture has a strong impact on the development of humans (Beer & Fischer 2017). One example is language and how the specifics of a certain language shape the way an individual as member of the respective culture views the elements in the environment. Even in cognitive ethnology, which originally attempted to find universal cognitive structures, again in the search for human universals, finally found that even cognitive structures or procedures are heavily influenced by cultural conditions and socialization (Norenzayan & Heine 2006). Also noteworthy is that human beings cannot develop or even survive without being integrated into a social group. Any social group always has culture. In this sense, culture is an a priori to human development. Each individual, as soon as he or she is socialized into a specific culture, is limited in how he or she can react to certain stimuli or conditions on the base of the patterns the culture provides. In this sense, culture is part of human evolution and, in many aspects, has a much stronger influence on human development than the biological outfit. This viewpoint is even supported by biologists and geneticists investigating human evolution: as was pointed out earlier in the chapter on biology, it was discovered that early Homo sapiens groups relied more and more on cooperative hunting since this provided higher nutrition reservoirs for the group. This made the capacity to cooperate and to be capable of complex social interaction a selection criterion for evolution. In fact, culture and societal structures became an environment to which the genome had to adapt.

These insights have been summarized in the so-called dual inheritance theory (Paul 2015):

> Unlike other forms of life, human life, which takes place in social groups, requires a massive quantity of additional instructions beyond what is contained in the DNA; this information is collectively the culture of the social group, and is composed to a highly significant degree of systems of symbols. Symbols, the constituent units of that which is transmitted via social learning, that is, culture, or bits of information just as are genes etc. that compose the instructions inscribed in the DNA. . . . Culture is built up from symbols arranged into symbol systems differ from society to society, as do the forms of social organization that are enabled by the symbol systems. . . . Genetic variation, though it very probably plays some role in the variation among human groups, is not significant enough to account for the observed variation in human sociocultural

systems. Homo sapiens is a single species, but one whose sociocultural forms differ widely across time and place. These differences between societies and their cultural systems are thus the result of differences in the cultural symbol systems themselves, not of genetic information. To take an obvious example, all human groups have language, the capacity for which is no doubt a genetic trait; but languages, which are systems of symbols, vary widely and are mutually unintelligible; this variation is in the symbols, not in the genes. Both genetic instructions encoded in DNA and cultural instructions encoded in symbols are required for the construction of a complete person. DNA does not give a human organism enough information for it to survive and flourish.

(pp. 6–7)

Indeed, and this is crucial, the symbols, from the point of view of the developing child, are out there in the world before they are in the brain. . . . So while it is true that symbols from the world can be re-transcribed in the course of learning and enculturation into neuronal codes and stored in the brain, they do not originate there, nor is that their only or even primary location.

(pp. 71–72)

This theory, therefore, stresses the importance of institutions in constituting human society, which means the existence of collective realities stands above the level of individuals.

It is therefore a fundamental principle of social and cultural anthropology that institutions such as matrilateral cross-cousin-marriage or male initiation rituals can be understood, analysed, and compared on their own terms and need not be thought of only as a collection of individuals with brains containing such and such instructions packed into them.

(p. 73)

This is, of course, a direct blow against Jung's biological argumentation and demonstrates that forms of collective memory in anthropological terms can be theorized without recourse to biological argumentations.

There is no doubt that culture has developed, as it serves the function of providing an evolutionary advantage. First, it enhanced the human capacity for social cooperation. There is, as we have seen earlier, a biological preformation in humans for cooperation, but of course, through culture and sociality, the capacity for complex forms of cooperation is multiplied. The second adaptive advantage is that culture enables humans to adapt to new niches, situations, climates and ecologies (e.g., the development of the technology of knitting enabled humans to produce warm clothes and thus to inhabit northern climates as well as to survive the ice ages). It is, therefore, assumed that the development of cooperative social conditions and institutions have provided the social environment in which prosocial norms were favoured by selection and became part of the innate genetic endowment of constituent members of cooperative societies (see also de Waal 2019).

> People are endowed with two sets of innate predispositions, or social instincts. The first is a set of ancient instincts that we share with our primate ancestors. The ancient social instincts were shaped by the familiar evolutionary processes of kin selection and reciprocity, enabling humans to have a complex family life and frequently form strong bonds of friendship with others. The second is a set of tribal instincts that allow us to interact cooperatively with a larger, symbolically marked set of people, or tribe. The tribal instincts result from the gene-culture co-evolution of tribal scale societies by the process described above.
>
> (Richerson & Boyd 2005, pp. 196–197)

These theorists assume that there is no genetically hardwired human nature because to serve a high adaptability of humankind, it is required that the cultural system be mutable and, therefore, that the symbols that gave instructions for how to live in different environments needed to be just as mutable.

I have already pointed out that the aforementioned grand theories are part of what could be called colonial thinking: the unquestioned conviction that Western, especially European culture, is always superior over indigenous cultures, a belief which, as we all know, has produced devastating results for the majority of peoples in this world. Jung, though he was interested in indigenous cultures, was strongly embedded with his thinking in this colonial tradition. This made it difficult for him to find anything else than what fit into his system of thought.

After the Second World War, a general turn away from this colonial thought and its universalist viewpoint took place in anthropology towards an interpretive approach, which attempted to understand a culture out of itself. This necessarily implies interpretation and hermeneutics to be the major methodological approach in anthropology. It also means a turning away from assumptions that anthropology was something like a natural science. In this tradition (e.g., Clifford Geertz 1973), cultures or cultural products are always contextualized on the background of their historical, environmental, social, etc., conditions.

Contemporary approaches in anthropology to the question of intercultural similarities

Belmonte (1990) notes:

> The theorist of the forms of universal as opposed to local knowledge is rarely processed of a disciplined ethnographic or historical imagination. Freud, Jung, and Levi-Strauss are alike vulnerable to charges of mentalism on the one hand and biologism on the other. All deny the absolute autonomy of the cultural level and all reduce its multitudinous and emergent properties to a theory of neural

residues. Such theories, it must be admitted, have yet to attain the epistemological rigor of medieval alchemy.

(p. 46)

In the 19th century, theories and debates on how similarities between cultures come about were important points of discussion. There were some theorists who saw all or most human cultures resulting from the diffusion of ideas, either by migration or by physical contact. Others took the perspective that cultures evolved independently from one another because all human beings have a similar psychological makeup and that they, therefore, come up with the same solutions to social or environmental problems.

An opposite point of view was taken by the so-called **functionalist school of anthropology** which sees society as a self-regulating system, in which religion plays a certain role, keeping up social organization, establishing hierarchies and systems of morale. Since human societies in history as well as all over the world have more or less the same social problems and are under the pressure of survival, they often develop the same solutions to these problems, which can explain similarities. In this sense, religion serves the same psychological function all over the world (i.e., alleviation of anxiety in the face of life's uncertainties). But additionally, this viewpoint is criticized by contemporary anthropologists as simple guesswork, which also includes the works of Freud and his hypothesis of patricide (Beer & Fischer 2017).

The anthropologists of the functionalist school were interested in what the functions of the different elements of a culture were (e.g., magic, religion, rituals, etc.). Malinowski (1948/1974), one of the major proponents of this approach, investigated magic in the Trobriands and found out that magic is only applied when the people do not have full control of a certain field (e.g., agriculture) by use of their tools and practices; therefore, magic serves the function of gaining control (or at least the belief that there is control). The functionalist school assumed that elements of culture referred to a set of basic needs of humans (e.g., nutrition, security). Often, the answers they found were that the elements of a culture served to strengthen the social system, solidarity, etc.

Clyde Kluckhohn (1965), one of the leading anthropologists in the second half of the 20th century and a proponent of the view that the most important concept for anthropology and the understanding of human behaviour is culture, gives the following summary of the functionalist viewpoint:

I have maintained that anthropology, psychiatry, clinical psychology, and learning theory all tend to accept the following postulates:

1. Human behaviour is functional.
2. Behaviour always involves conflict or ambivalence.
3. Behaviour can be understood only in relation to the field or context in which it occurs.

4. Behaviour tends toward a state of maximal integration or internal consistency (homeostasis).

(p. 260)

But Kluckhohn is also an outstanding critic of the functional viewpoint. He stresses the importance of culture itself as a system that, once established, has its own dynamic in the sense of that it opens up certain developments but also closes down others. We will later see that the same viewpoint can be applied to the development of religion in the sense that once a religion is established, it develops its own dynamic, often independent from outside conditions as well as from human needs (see chapter "Religion"). This account sheds a critical view on the assumption, shared by Jung, that the development of culture can be explained by referring to human needs or other basic structures based in the biology of humans.

The viewpoint that culture itself produces a strong dynamic was even strengthened in the **structuralist school of anthropology**, which in general assumed that the repository of cultural beliefs and practices in a society, in which a person is socialized, determines to a large extent how this person acts and thinks and views the world. This set of cultural beliefs and practices is transmitted from one generation to the other by ways of socialization and culturalization. Nevertheless, also in the structuralist school, it was assumed that the structures transmitted by culture are, in the last end, produced by basic features of the human mind. But they do not rely on human nature alone, as they also stress the point of the categorization systems of cultures. Although they may mirror the basic features of the human mind, they also have their own systems of categorization and meaning and may also differ considerably from one culture to another. The most important proponents of this approach were Levi-Strauss, who developed a complex system of describing cultural beliefs and social practices based on a system of binary oppositions, as well as Émile Durkheim and Marcel Mauss among others. Levi-Strauss (1949) focused intensively on patterns of kinship, namely, rules of marriage, and found that on the one hand, they include universals of human reproduction but, in their final shape, are a product of culture-specific rules (e.g., the incest taboo is universal), whereas the specific rules from which group a bride is to be chosen are culture specific. In general, the rules which determine what is my own group and what are outsiders cannot be reduced to biological factors alone since there are considerable differences from one culture to the other. In the development of his works, Levi-Strauss increasingly made use of linguistic comparisons for analysing the basic structures of cultures. This method of analysis was also applied to mythologies. A crucial insight is that cultural belief systems as well as mythologies differ in respect to basic values which receive a dominant role in the respective system.

Important to note is that the same argument – culture has its own dynamic and shapes the human mind in depth – was already put forth within psychology by Jerome Bruner as early as 1990 (Bruner 1990). Bruner criticizes contemporary psychology for having forgotten that the main subject of psychology, as well as the world in which humans live, is characterized by meaning. This implies different ways of scientific analysis and theorizing would be necessary, as they are usually applied in academic psychology. Structures of meaning are fundamental for human life, and they are not provided by the biological outfit but are transmitted in social practices of narrations. The cultural narratives that a society provides deeply shape the psyche of the individuals. This is interesting because Jung himself, even though he strongly argued for a basis of his psychology in the natural sciences, practically was occupied throughout his life with hermeneutics and the interpretation of narratives (e.g., from mythology, alchemy). This points to what already has been characterized as the scientistic self-misunderstanding of his psychology.

I also happen to think that psychoanalysis is a hybrid discipline and that it is a science in the service of its hermeneutics, by which I mean that it uses the methods of science to study the meanings that humans create. . . . First, psychoanalysis, since the time of Freud, has aimed to study mental or psychological phenomena in a scientific manner; second, also since the time of Freud, psychoanalysis has attempted to study these things in a non-reductionistic way, one that preserves the autonomy of the psychological realm and that uses a bridging language, for too long Freud's outdated metapsychology attempted to link the psychological to the neurological. . . . Another way of putting this is to say that minds have intentionality (in the philosophical sense), meaning, and purpose but that brains, even highly complex ones, do not and that a psychoanalytic clinician is mainly interested in the meanings that he or she and other minds in the room are cocreating, not in the neural events that underlie them.

(Auerbach 2014, pp. 277–281)

Human universals: Isolationism versus diffusionism

As much as he took an essentialist and evolutionist perspective in his archetype theory, Jung also took a universalist point of view when it came to anthropology. In line with the aforementioned grand theories with an evolutionist background, he was also in search of universal structures to be found in all human societies and epochs, namely, archetypes. Similar, or at least comparable, concepts in the evolutionist theories were Adolf Bastian's (1881) concept of "elementary thoughts", "Volksgeist" (Herder), "genius of the people" (Boas) and Paideuma (Frobenius) (for an overview, see Beer & Fischer 2017). Already in the 19th century, striking similarities in the narrative motifs of ethnic groups living far apart from each other had been apparent for a long time and, from 1880, set into motion a decade-long debate about how this convergence of ideas in fairy tales and myths could be explained.

Two main models of explanation were competing for supremacy at the end of the 19th century. The diffusion and transference theory, often called diffusionism, claimed that the reason for the similarities lay in the actual physical contact between peoples in the sense of migration (Eisenstädter 1912). Some authors in this faction went as far as to assume that all peoples on earth stemmed from the same original tribe, the so-called "primal horde", which was supposedly located in an area between Caucasus and Central Asia (Baumann 1936). The opposing thesis was the theory of elementary thoughts, "Völkergedanken" (Bastian 1881), which stated that the mythological convergence expresses the psychological homogeneity of all people (for a detailed discussion, see chapter "Mythology"). It was precisely these thoughts, which were extremely popular in the scientific world in 1900, that Jung incorporated into psychology with his theory of archetypes.

Even contemporary Jungians arguing for the concept of the archetype, or applying it to cultural phenomena or case material, often refer to the concept of universals from anthropology but very often – at least in my estimation – without reference to actual empirical or state-of-the-art findings in anthropology. Some authors, as for example, Obrist (1990) in the following quote, present various lists of universals from different periods in the development of scientific anthropology, as if the referral to these lists would provide proof for the existence of Jung's archetypes:

> Universals of social behaviour are observed in the following areas: in the mother-child relationship, in the search for a relationship, in the formation of a hierarchy, in territorial behaviour, in the ownership and exchange of objects, in intra-species as well as curiosity/explorative aggression.
>
> (Obrist 1990, p. 112)

There are a number of problems connected with this approach. If one does go into the relevant literature in anthropology, the surprising result is that the findings on human universals are very limited. Beyond that, the universals that were found according to ethnological researchers are completely different from what, in AP, is considered an archetype (e.g., the anima, the wise old man, the great mother or the journey of the hero). Lastly, what is often not considered is that in anthropology itself, there has been constant controversy around the concept of universals, with the result that in present day, accounts of universals as a concept have been discarded (Norenzayan & Heine 2006). This is another striking example for the problematic tendency in AP to pull out a singular finding or concept from a specific discipline and present it as proof for the theory of archetypes, without fully taking into account the academical debate and its development over time in the respective discipline.

One of the first attempts to provide a list of human universals was presented by George Peter Murdock (1945), who later became the editor of the *Ethnographic Atlas*, evolving into the famous Standard Cross-Cultural Sample (see next section). Other lists were compiled by Kluckhohn (1953). Here are some examples from the list provided by Murdock (1945):

> Bodily adornment; Community organization, cooking, courtship, education, funeral rites, games, hospitality, language, music, dance, mythology, sewer concepts, surgery, toolmaking, visiting.

The most extensive recent effort to catalogue human universals was that by Donald Brown (1991), who constructed a list of hundreds of characteristics, incorporating both categories (e.g., marriage, rituals, language) and content (e.g., fear of snakes, coyness displays, having colour terms for "black" and "white") that are common to people everywhere. Brown's (1991) "Human universals", which gives an overview of the debate and includes all the empirical studies and theories on human universals after more than a century of anthropological research, presents the following list[3] (pp. 130–141):

> a language/system of communication, which allows for abstractions and symbolization, and enables lies, has some basic universal features on the level of grammar, and is used to create narrative and metaphor; separate terms for kin categories, including mother and father; binary discriminations, e.g. for sex terminology, elementary logical notions, conjectural reasoning (causality); universal recognition of facial expressions and the ability to mentalize, that is to get in the minds of others; toolmaking (note: even the use of fire is not universal!) and building of shelters; Patterns of preparation for birth, for giving birth, and for postnatal care; living in groups which claim a certain territory. . . . Marriage, in the sense of a person having a publicly recognized right of sexual access to a woman deemed eligible for child bearing, is institutionalized. Families have patterns of socialization, that is children aren't just left to grow up on their own; they favour their close kin, but have incest taboos to prevent sex between genetically close kin; there are statuses and roles, prestige, a division of labour, customs of cooperative labour, concepts of property etc., that is a social structure; men form the dominant element; trade, attempts to predict and plan for the future, government, leaders, laws, conflicts (usually structured around ingroup-outgroup antagonisms) and forms of conflict regulation, ideas about responsibility and intentionality, etiquette and hospitality including customary greetings and customs of visiting kin and others, religious or supernatural beliefs, e.g. around disease and death, and the practice of magic; rituals, especially initiation rites/rites de passage and mourning of dead; aesthetic standards, e.g. how to adorn bodies or shape hair, standards around sexual attractiveness, decorative art, dance and music.

It is obvious that these lists present very broad and general categories (e.g., that **there is** language, dance and music, that **there are** social hierarchies), but there are no specifications. It is very clear that these empirically found universals have nothing to do with the archetypes of AP. More interesting than what is included in the list is what is not included. For example, it has to be noted that the only rituals that seem to be universal are around marriage, initiation and mourning of the dead. Many people think, for example, that there are universals to childrearing, which is actually not the case. Even though this is so basic to human beings, no universal structures around childrearing could be found (Ahnert 2010).

And even a proponent of the universalist point of view such as Brown argues:

For a considerable period the term universal was used without anyone thinking it needed to be defined. During that period the implicit definition was approximately as follows: a trait or complex present in all individuals (or all individuals of a particular sex and age range), or societies, or cultures, or all languages, provided that the trade or complex is not too obviously anatomical or physiological or too remote from the higher mental functions. . . . I write at, and am a product of, a time when the distinction [between biology and culture] remains fundamental to most anthropologists – even though it is vaguely and falsely conceived. Nothing in human culture comes into being or gets transmitted without consideration of the specifically human genetic makeup. Yet significant aspects of human anatomy and physiology can only be fully understood with some consideration of human culture, which always and everywhere is a crucial part of the environment that interacts with human genes to produce human organisms. Any prophetically conceived boundary between the thoroughly genetically determined and the not too obviously biological is more likely to be a boundary between what has and what has not been interesting to anthropologists.

(Brown 1991, page 42)

Brown, in this paper, has obviously no problem to argue that many of the universals in his list are transmitted by ways of cultural exchange and socialization.

A relatively small number of causal processes or conditions appear to account for most if not all universals. These processes or conditions are

1) the diffusion of ancient (and generally very useful) cultural traits,
2) cultural reflection of physical fact,
3) the operation and structure of the human mind, and (behind the latter)
4) the evolution of the human mind.

(Brown 1991, p. 148)

An important exception to the general rule that human universals are very general and basic, lacking specification, is the striking similarities in fairy tales and myths found all over the world, which were well investigated in anthropology (Aarne & Thompson 1964). These will be dealt with in a special chapter on "Mythology" (see next section).

An important question, which is often not addressed in Jungian publications that make use of the concept of human universals, is how the term universal is actually defined: Does universal mean the element has to appear everywhere in the world, in every culture and in every individual (which would be an absolute universal in the terminology of Brown)? And if not in every individual, to which percentage of distribution can we talk about an element being universal?

The question of definition is discussed in detail in Brown's papers (1991, 2000). In his paper *Human Universals, Human Nature & Human Culture* (Brown 2004), he summarizes the findings from the publications mentioned earlier:

> There are severe methodological limitations on what can be known about universals in general. No one can really know the conditions in all societies, so that any statement about universality is based on some sort of sampling. In most cases this sampling has not been rigorous. Furthermore, the precision with which a real or alleged universal has been described often leaves much to be desired, in part because the original reports or descriptions were provided by different observers and sometimes at widely spaced intervals in time. Thus the confidence one can have in particular claims of universality is quite variable. Given the costs involved in studying even a single society, this range of problems will persist. . . .
>
> But only rarely have psychologists conducted their research outside the modernized and mostly western world, so that the cross-cultural validity of the numerous mental processes and traits that they have identified is often in doubt. And some cross-cultural research has indeed shown that psychological phenomena that one might think are unaffected by cultural differences – the perception of certain optical illusions, for example – are in fact not universal (many other examples could be given).
>
> Examples of universals of psyche or mind that were determined by cross-cultural study but without evolutionary theorizing are dichotomization or binary discriminations, the language acquisition device (as described by the linguist Noam Chomsky), emotions, classification, elementary logical concepts, psychological defence mechanisms, ethnocentrism or in-group bias, and reciprocity as a mechanism for bonding individuals to one another.
>
> Among the universals identified more recently through testing evolutionary propositions are a facial-template-constructing mechanism that generates a preference for faces that are near the population mean, a social-cheater-detecting mechanism, a mental mechanism for thinking about "human kinds," and a preference in males for skin colours in females that are lighter than the mean (because in the past it correlated with fecundity). Incest avoidance – a phenomenon found in many animal species as well as humans – straddles the boundary, as it is an evolution-minded re-thinking of what for long was one of the most frequently discussed and prototypically cultural human universals: the incest taboo.

(pp. 48–50)[4]

There is no doubt that the human being is not a tabula rasa at birth. Nowadays, nobody denies that there is an inborn capacity in children to learn language and grammar (language acquisition device), as well as a certain preparedness to be frightened of specific things (e.g., spiders) (for an overview, see Roesler 2021). In the chapter on biology, the empirical findings on innate mental capacities were already presented in detail. Again, the state-of-the-art findings in anthropology make clear that the universals being found – and which are, additionally, subject to a fundamental controversy about whether it makes sense at all to look for such universals (Norenzayan & Heine 2006) – have nothing to do with the archetypes of Jungian psychology. It would also make no sense to use the term archetype for these universals since it is very clear that these are very basic and far from what in Jungian psychology is regarded as an archetype (e.g., the myth of the hero), so it would only continue the confusion that was found in the definition of archetypes.

These problems, together with the fundamental misconception inherent in Jung's approach to anthropology, were pointed out earlier by critics from outside of AP, such as Petzold et al. (2014):

> This assertion of the culturally overlapping meaning of archetypes must, there-fore, also be critically considered. C. G. Jung assumes a collective unconscious of the human species, but it is based rather on culturally determined interiorised collectivities, for which Moscovicis' socio-psychological conception of a "col-lective mental representation" – conscious, preconscious, unconscious mentali-sations – offers an alternative for the explanation of myth forming structural elements.
>
> (archetypes, p. 439f.)

Subsequently, the author gives numerous examples of the same elements or sym-bols in various cultures having completely different meanings based on geographic or climate conditions. For example, in the north, the sun contains a warmth-giving motherly power, while in desert areas, it contains a threatening character and is assigned to the area of evil. It is argued further:

> The assumption of, as it were, genetically predisposed mythologems and arche-types of heroes and goddesses even comes into the realm of mythotropic con-ceptualization. What is powerful in archetypes, myths, and symbols must be current in the collective mental representation and passed down in a process of socio-historical transmission, otherwise it is not present. The attempt by Kerenyi, together with C. G. Jung, to see the figures of Greek mythology as pre-images of the human soul must, in addition to the criticism that it takes too little account of the socio-historical and socio-economic conditions of the ancient world or that it does not seek to create a connection between explanations in terms of mental history, counter the Eurocentrism associated with recourse to antiquity.
>
> (p. 441)

Universalism versus cultural relativism/particularism

The search for universals in anthropology was part of a general approach termed universalism, which was opposed by the viewpoint of cultural relativism or par-ticularism. As soon as anthropologists, instead of searching for universals, started to systematically look for differences that are dependent on cultural backgrounds, it became clear that the impact of culture is enormous. In fact, it shapes the psyche's fundamentals, the personality and the Self (Markus & Kitayama 1991, 1998; Richerson & Boyd 2005; for an overview, see Norenzayan & Heine 2006). The influence of culture can even be found in the imagery and the general shape of dreams that reflect cultural viewpoints on the Self, individuality and development of the personality (Roesler et al. 2021). As a result, the efforts to discern and taxonomize the universal human have been highly controversial throughout the history of anthropology. Some have questioned whether interesting human universals really exist (e.g., Benedict 1934), and others argued that such efforts to identify the lowest common denominator of humankind are either misguided or of dubious value (e.g., Geertz 1973). More recently, a growing number of voices in cultural anthropology have adopted a post-structuralist perspective, emphasizing the fluidity and ambiguity of culture. There is a marked scepticism in this view towards generalizing from the individual level to the cultural level, let alone generalizing to the level of what is universally human (for an overview, see Norenzayan & Heine 2006). One important insight to be pointed out: the biological development of humans cannot be thought of without taking into account the pre-existence of culture. As we have already seen in the chapter on biology, the genetical makeup of humans is oriented towards culture and society and incorporates deeply the social relationships and societal structures in which it develops so that one could say the environment of evolutionary adaptedness of humans is culture and society and not specific natural environments, as they are for animals. What is characteristic of humans is not that they are driven by certain instinctual motivations, which is more characteristic of animals, but their enormous adaptability and flexibility, their capability to adapt to practically all environments by use of cultural and technological achievements. Humans can even permanently stay in outer space and will soon be able to survive on the moon and maybe on Mars. This enormous adaptability is reflected in the equally enormous plasticity of the human brain.

The empirical foundation for human universals

Although the search for human universals may seem, on the base of the earlier discussion, a bit outdated, it may still be interesting for Jungians to learn about the actual empirical findings concerning such universals. In contrast to the grand theories that were characteristic of the 19th and the beginning of the 20th century – in which Jung's thought was deeply embedded – beginning in the 1930s and 1940s, a wealth of proper empirical descriptions of indigenous societies was accumulated, allowing for a more precise answer to the question about human universals today: "To answer these questions, anthropologists go out into the field, study particular communities, and write reports describing these communities. Questions of universality and variability can be answered on the basis of descriptions of hundreds of human societies" (Stein & Stein 2008, p. 3).

Explanatory systems, in the sense of universalist versus culturally relativist approaches, can and have to be tested thoroughly with the available data. Today, not only considerable masses of ethnographic data are available, they are also accessible in systematized comparative samples, such as the ones presented later. These can be investigated systematically regarding certain questions or comparisons focusing on assumed similarities.

The anthropologist George Peter Murdock, mentioned earlier, very early in the development of systematic comparative studies developed a list of human universals (see previous section), which over time developed into the so-called *Ethnographic Atlas* (Murdock 1967a, 1967b). This later became a university-based databank of detailed descriptions of independent indigenous societies, the **Standard Cross-Cultural Sample (SCCS),** a sample of 186 cultures used by scholars engaged in cross-cultural studies (Murdock & White 1969). The second widely used databank are the **Human Relations Area Files (HRAF)** (Ember 2000).

Both databanks can be accessed online, the SCCS by its open access online journal *World Cultures*, HRAF via Yale Univers ity: https://hraf.yale.edu.

When using these databanks for studying specific similarities across cultures, it quickly becomes clear that the list of true universals is, firstly, very limited and, secondly, very basic. Additionally, the majority of these similarities can well be explained by geographical closeness, similar environmental conditions or reciprocal cultural influences between similar cultures (Beer & Fischer 2017).

The degree of formal similarity observed among independent sociocultural units is a direct measure of the degree of genetic affiliation or cultural relationship among the units being compared.

(Binford 1971, p. 9)

In the following, I will provide detailed examples with a discussion based on the available literature in anthropology, as well as analyses based on the aforementioned databanks.

Religion

Religion is universal. Among the many theories that have tried to explain this phenomenon, there are also biological, respectively, evolutionary, approaches which argue, more or less in the same manner as Jung does, with the similar makeup of the human brain. There are even theories that argue for a religious gene or a number of such genes – the so-called God Module – but this approach has been criticized strongly and can, on the base of contemporary research in genetics, be discarded (Stein & Stein 2008). What is universal is the fact that there is religion, but the contents of the specific religions are definitely not universal. Nevertheless, for a discussion of archetype theory, religion is such a crucial field with such far-reaching implications for an evaluation of AP as a whole, for the topic will be dealt with in a special chapter later.

Incest taboo

There is, presumably, no other concept of such importance for the historical development of the psychoanalytic schools as the incest taboo. And in fact, it seems to be a universal motif or idea. In a comparative study of 50 randomly selected cultures, the motif of incest can be found in 39 of these mythologies (Kluckhohn 1960). It has always been argued that the incest taboo has a biological basis in the sense that it inhibits genetic defects in offspring from biologically close relatives. But the matter seems to be more complex, as the detailed ethological and anthropological investigation by Bischof (2020), "The riddle of Oedipus", demonstrates. There is a variety of rules around incest and sexual relations of close relatives in different cultures. In some cultures, these relations are even supported, as they are thought to produce supernatural powers. This is evidence for the fact that these biological inhibitions can be transcended by societal rules. The author provides an explanation based on general systems theory that makes no use of any biological predeterminations. In that sense, he points out, the incest taboo is a cultural achievement.

Chapais (2011) has tried to explain the universality of the incest taboo as an evolutionary achievement, linking human development with patterns in primates. This approach was strongly criticized from many sides in anthropology (e.g., Barnard 2014) based on the insight that the incest taboo is a product of categorization, in terms of kinship, which is not to be found in primates. In general, the existence of an incest taboo is often discussed in anthropology in connection with kinship patterns. In the works of Levi-Strauss (1949/1969), kinship patterns are regarded as one of the major categorization principles which characterize human culture. So although we have seen earlier that a tendency to categorize seems to be an innate capacity of humans, the structures and contents of the categories applied are consensually seen as a cultural product and can show considerable intercultural variation.

The incest taboo has often been linked in anthropology with initiation rites (see also chapter "Religion"). Jung, for example, was strongly influenced by Freud's theory of the Oedipus complex and thus saw male initiation rites as serving the function to resolve Oedipal conflicts, as well as establishing masculine identity. He contends that in societies, where the mother-son bond is particularly strong, elaborate and painful ceremonies are needed to vigorously and decisively break a male child's identification with his mother (and hence, with other women). Furthermore, to install him in the psychological and social company of his father's group. This arguably explains why initiation rites seem more important for males than for females. This view is in line with functional viewpoints in anthropology – and surprisingly, in contrast to Jung's usual biological reasoning – which argue that initiation ceremonies and their cross-cultural similarities are viewed from the perspective of their social function (Young 1965).

Burials and funeral rites

Concerning burials and the accompanying rituals, a search in databanks as well as in literature shows great variability, as well as in the understanding of death and the hereafter connected with the ways of dealing with the dead. Societies were even found, which have now vanished, that disposed of their dead with the garbage.

> Funeral rituals differ from other rituals in one major respect: there is a dead body. All societies have ways of disposing of the corpse in one way or another. Burial is quite common, but there are a number of variables such as where the grave is located, what the body is buried in, what objects are buried with the body, and so on. Bodies can also be placed in trees to decay, and later the remains may be cleaned and buried. Bodies can be cremated, and the remains kept in a container, buried, or scattered at sea.
>
> (Stein & Stein 2008, p. 11)

The authors give a list of a variety of forms of burials and funeral rites. Different forms of burial exist: in specialized graveyards, in necropolis, but also close to or even beneath the floor of the house. The custom of secondary burials exists in certain regions. This means there is a first burial following the death of the person. Then after some time, when the corpse has decayed, the bones are gathered from the ground and buried a second time, sometimes in special houses. In some cases, these specialized houses are even divided in places for the skulls and places for the rest of the bones. In contrast to burials, there is cremation, and there is also a variety of forms to dispose of the ashes: some preserve them in boxes, others scatter them over the sea or into the wind, etc. Then there is mummification and exposure of the body, either to the elements of nature or to be consumed by animals. Even though this may seem archaic, this custom is still used in the very highly developed religion of the Zoroastrians in Iran. This also demonstrates that the archaism of a specific burial rite is not necessarily connected with the complexity level of the respective religion.

> Funerals vary among cultures in a number of ways: the form of expression of grief, the role of the ritual in terms of what will happen to the individual in the afterlife, the ritual ways in which the family and community separate themselves from the dead to avoid contamination or illness, how the living are reorganized in society to accommodate for the absence of the deceased, and the method of disposal of the corpse.
>
> (Stein & Stein 2008, p. 194)

For example: in the prairie tribes of the Native Americans, a very long time of mourning for the dead is common, whereas in the Pueblo peoples, the deceased are supposed to be quickly forgotten. It has even been argued that the existence of forms of burials do not necessarily imply that there is an idea of a hereafter or life beyond. It could also be an expression of the difficulties the living have with letting go of their dead relatives (Wunn 2019). This could also be the reason why, in some cultures, the remains of the dead relatives are buried below the floors of the houses, so as to keep them close to the world of the living (see also chapter "prehistory").

Mating behaviour, couple bonding and marriage rules

As was pointed out earlier (see chapter "Biology, genetics and inheritance"), there seems to be a biological basis for the human tendency to form stable, long-term, monogamous couple bonds (Walker et al. 2011). In a study conducted with the Standard Cross-Cultural Sample (see previous section), it was found that in the over 850 societies investigated, in which more than 80% theoretically allowed for polygamy (which means that men in marriages are allowed to be married to more than one wife), only a minority of 5% to 10% of the men acted on this (Fletcher 2013; Marlowe 2003, 2005). 70% of all the hunter gatherer societies in this sample were mainly monogamous, allowing only slightly for polygamy. The theory behind these findings is that in the development of Homo sapiens, early hunter gatherer societies tended to be more polygamous, whereas with growing cultural differentiation, cooperation and the development of technology, the societies become more and more monogamous. In this context, an interesting finding is that the highest percentage of polygamist societies – and in that sense, less-developed (i.e., more characterized by hunting gathering economies) – is found in Australia. This would speak for the hypothesis that immigration into the Australian continent via the South Asian/Indonesian land bridge, which ended about 40,000 years ago, created a more "primitive" hunter gatherer society in Australia compared to the development in Eurasia. Also, genome analyses of the ancestry of several hunter gatherer societies speak for the fact that monogamy was the dominant couple model since the emigration of Homo sapiens from Africa 60,000 years ago and was transferred from there all over the world (Müller-Schneider 2019, pp. 93–98) (see also chapter "Prehistory").

There is another social advantage which arises from monogamous couple bonds. In combination with the incest taboo (see previous section), marriage rules lead to the fact that different social groups (e.g., hunter gatherer groups) become connected through kinship relationships. This supports the development of larger societies and civilizations and is a hindrance to continuous warfare, which would have weakened early human societies. So there is no empirical support for the widespread prejudice of the "promiscuous primal horde", or the idea, also present in Jung, that humans originally had a promiscuous and polygamous orientation.

These findings demonstrate that there seems to be, at least on a very basic level, a biological basis for human couple bonding. Still, monogamous marriages are by far not universal; more than 20% of the world's indigenous societies practice other models. Also, as was demonstrated earlier, the reasons that these models have developed are not only biological but result from the development of societies and the social problems they have to deal with. So in sum, these findings do not support the idea of an archetype of marriage/monogamy, at least not in the sense of an autochthonous development all over the world. Another finding also speaks against this assumption: there are some societies in the world which have polyandrous models of couple bonding, which means that one woman is married to several men. The societies are almost exclusively to be found in the region of Tibet and the surrounding Himalayas. This provides strong support for the assumption that seemingly archetypal patterns have been distributed via migration and cultural exchange.

Male and female societal roles, power and dominance

Sanday (1981), in her book *Female Power and Male Dominance: On the Origins of Sexual Inequality*, systematically investigated gender roles by making use of the Standard Cross-Cultural Sample in order to look at the cultural context of sex-role configurations. Of the 186 societies which were included in the sample, 156 could be used for direct comparisons. One insight was that in regulating secular power and dividing it between the genders, sacred symbols played a crucial role. Also, many religions deal with the question of how the differences between the sexes came about and how men and women should relate to one another and to their environment. The author comes to the conclusion "that male dominance is not an inherent quality in human sex-role plans, as many feminist writers of the 1970s had assumed, but a response to particular environmental pressures, whether social or physical" (Bowie 2004, p. 130). Sanday found that in many cultures, female is associated with nature, whereas male is associated with culture and dominance. Nevertheless, the author points to the permeability between the categories of female and nature in some societies but not all, and secondarily, men are not unequivocally aligned with culture so that in a number of societies, there is a reciprocal flow regarding the power roles.

> The variations in sex-role plans found in different societies show that they are cultural constructions rather than genetic. . . . Historical and political factors, as well as the environment in which people live, will affect the ways in which they interact. Sex-role plans will in turn change the social and natural environment.
>
> (Bowie 2004, p. 131)

Hewlett and Hewlett (2008) provide an example for this culturally influenced diversity by comparing African hunter gatherer (Aka) versus agricultural (Ngandu) societies, which live geographically closely together. Looking at sex roles, love and couple bonding, they found the following:

> In the Aka hunter gatherer society, there is equality on all levels, couples are monogamous in majority, have an emotional style of bonding with flexible roles; men are involved in child-rearing and education in the same manner as women. The search for nutrition is equally divided between men and women; all everyday activities happen together and violence between partners is very rare.

In the Ngandu agricultural society, very rigid hierarchies, rules, etc., exist, with a strong ancestor cult. Marriages are often polygamist, and relationships rely on material support with very rigid sex roles. Childrearing and education happens exclusively through women and elder siblings, and also the provision of nutrition is in the responsibility of women. Meals are taken separately, while men receive more calories, and often also, sleeping happened separately. Marital violence is widespread.

Conclusion

It can be summarized that in the field of anthropology, Jung referred to theories which were highly problematic, from a contemporary point of view, even flawed, and which were outdated and strongly criticized even in Jung's lifetime. From these, Jung also favoured the most problematic, namely, Bachofen's and Frazer's. Beyond that, these theories, and as a consequence, also Jung's thoughts, contained racist elements, as they are part of what has been characterized as colonial thinking (i.e., a devaluation of indigenous societies as being on a lower level of cultural as well as psychological development).

In the summary of contemporary viewpoints and insights in the field of anthropology, it was clarified that these take a view on cultural characteristics being largely influenced by environmental and context conditions and also by developments on a societal level and not so much by the biological makeup of humans. Adaptability itself is seen as the truly human characteristic. In so far, cultures are always adaptations to certain environments and conditions, as well as to certain societal structures and ideas and beliefs about hierarchies, sex roles, etc. A seemingly archaic indigenous tribe (e.g., San bushmen) can be seen as better adapted to their environment than, for example, civilized Europeans.

In general, contemporary anthropological theories emphasize diversity and question the assumption of universality of basic characteristics of human societies. Even where universals were found and are still supported by contemporary viewpoints in anthropology, these empirically supported universals can by no means be equated with Jung's archetypes or used as "proof" for archetype theory. The universals in the sense of cultural patterns and symbols that Jung claims to be (e.g., in Jung et al. 1964) actually do not exist!

This tendency to emphasize the impact of dynamics on a societal and cultural level over biological influences, which can be found also in theories from the first half of the 20th century, has gained more and more influence in the development of anthropology. It points to a problem – as far as I can see – in Jung to take into account sociological and cultural perspectives. It is well-known that Jung was critical of the dynamics of groups and emphasized the role of the individual in psychological as well as cultural development. I would go as far as stating that Jung had considerable difficulties to include – maybe even to understand – sociological argumentations, as can be seen, for example, in his negative attitude towards Durkheim's theory, which is still regarded as valuable in contemporary sociology. To put it very simply: Jung always regarded biology as more important than culture and seems to have had no theoretical understanding of the dynamics of society and culture, whereas in anthropology in general, there has been a seminal shift from the emphasis on evolutionary factors to today's emphasis on contextual factors and dynamics inherent in societal structures and cultures themselves. I assume that this owes to Jung's academical training as a physician and thus as a natural scientist, which seemingly limited his knowledge and understanding of theorizing from the viewpoint of social and cultural sciences. In this sense, Jung's anthropology does not transcend the limits of evolutionary biology and thus gets entangled in the contradictions and errors outlined earlier, whereas anthropology, at least from the mid-20th century on, has become a science of culture.

I would, therefore, conclude that what was defined as Theory 2 inherent in Jung's theorizing around archetypes (an anthropological theory about human universals which come about through the biological makeup of humans, including the assumption of homology of phylogeny and ontogeny; see Chapter 3) has to be regarded as refuted, if not deeply flawed and misconceptualized from the beginning. Furthermore, I would propose not to use the term archetype anymore for any kinds of anthropologically defined human universals, if there are any, as this would further continue the confusion around the definition of the term archetype, as pointed out earlier. Instead of continuing the misleading use of the term archetype for the investigation of cultural similarities and characteristics – which I still see as one of the major topics of AP – I would propose to use the concept of cultural complexes for this kind of research. The concept of cultural complexes, as presented by Singer and Kimbles (2004a, 2004b), is very much in line with contemporary theories in the social sciences and in cultural studies; it is much more careful than archetype theory in making far-reaching assumptions; it has a clear definition and methodology; and finally, it succeeds in including an analytical viewpoint on unconscious factors into a useful interpretation scheme for societal and cultural phenomena (see also final chapter).

Notes

1 "From that time onward, Jung would set out on a constant search for evidence for his hypothesis. . . . Jung carried out an extensive study into the mythology of peoples from all over the world . . . This research revealed the emergence of similar primordial images (*Urbilden*) across a range of different cultures. . . . The only possible explanation for this was an autochthonous sprouting of these primordial images from a supra-personal unconscious. Jung could also observe the constant appearance of collective, archetypal images in his patients' phantasies and dreams, as well as in his own unconscious material. Based on these various evidences, Jung proposed a hypothesis on the existence of a *phylogenetic unconscious* common to all mankind" (Walter Boechat 2022: The collective unconscious. https://iaap.org/the-collective-unconscious-2/).

2 This critique was also put forward against Jung's notion of archetypes as biologically rooted: "We have seen that such a demonstration requires eliminating the possibility that common human experience could account for similar archetypes in widely scattered individuals and in diverse cultures, and this is exceedingly difficult" (Neher 1996, p. 86).

3 An overview from 1991 may seem outdated, but the relevant empirical research in the field of anthropology came to an end before that because research into human universals needs to investigate societies which had no – or at least not much – contact with civilization. It is very unlikely that in the meantime, strikingly new insights were found in the field.

4 There is a detailed discussion later of the incest taboo and other allegedly universal entities which are of interest to AP and archetype theory.

Chapter 7

Religion

It has already become clear in the chapter on anthropology that Jung's ideas about universalities and cross-cultural similarities also refer to the field of religion:

> Rebirth is an affirmation that must be counted among the primordial affirmations of mankind. These primordial affirmations are based on what I call archetypes. In view of the fact that all affirmations relating to the sphere of the suprasensual are, in the last analysis, invariably determined by archetypes, it is not surprising that a concurrence of affirmation concerning rebirth can be found among the most widely differing peoples.
>
> (CW 9/1, para. 207)

On the other hand, in comparison to the universals already discussed earlier, the field of religion has its own dynamics and peculiarities. Jung published extensively on religion. The previous quote stems from his text on the – assumed – archetype of rebirth, which is explicitly a religious concept. It will be pointed out later, with reference to comparative studies in religion, that the idea of rebirth is not universal, as Jung claims.

Jung's impact on religious studies has been and still is immense (Dourley 1990). Unfortunately, it cannot be said that the same is true vice versa, which means that since Jung's days, AP has only very little taken into account the developments in religious studies, at least not when it comes to archetype theory.

Eliade's monolithic approach and its legacy

When we investigate the field of religion, the question whether there are universalities in religion, in how religions develop and how they can be categorized, there is no way around the seminal works of Mircea Eliade, a scholar of comparative religion. In several encyclopaedic works, he investigated the religions of the world (Eliade 1954, 1959). He was already mentioned as one of the founders of so-called grand theories, even though he was active well into the second half of the 20th century. But his approach and how it is structured belongs to the systematic of older approaches, in so far as he applies monolithic schemas for the explanation

DOI: 10.4324/9781003348191-7

of the development of religions. One is the binary opposition of the sacred and the profane (Eliade 1959). On the other hand, he discovered a schema that seems to be almost universal, which consists of a triad: firstly, there is a great god who is unknowable and ineffable. In most of the simpler religions, this god remains unworshipped and has, therefore, been called the lazy god. Secondly, there are his sons, his messengers, who act as the intermediaries between man and the great god. Thirdly, there are humans.

Eliade has been enormously influential in the development of the anthropology of religion, so have been his works on the concept of cosmogony (Eliade 1954, 1959). Cosmogonies are sets of myths in the sense of sacred narratives explaining how the world and man came to be in the present form. Creation myths give out service to the most profound human questions, such as who we are, why we are here, what is the purpose of life and death and how are humans placed in the world and cosmos in time and space. According to Eliade, rituals are the reproduction of original creation myths but on a microcosmic scale. Thus, by participating in a ritual (e.g., a ritual of the end of the world and its recreation), the participant was born anew, began life over and over again, as if it were the moment of birth.

Eliade's monolithic schema of interpreting the historical development of religion has been criticized strongly by a number of contemporary authors (e.g., Oestigaard 2011):

> Moreover, anthropologists, sociologists, and historians of religion have either ignored Eliade or simply dismissed his works, claiming that his method is uncritical, arbitrary, and subjective and hence his works cannot be taken seriously. His sweeping generalizations and universal structures are not historically falsifiable, and his phenomenology is as normative as theology. Eliade's approach is, however, consistent in the way that his aim is to interpret trans-historical meaning and religious experiences making ontological claims about human nature and being as such, although this is difficult within the history of religion as a human science. Eliade has, nevertheless, precisely emphasized the irreducible character of religious experience, and he has stressed that it is impossible to grasp the essence of religious experiences by means of physiology, psychology, sociology, etc. Nevertheless, although one may be sympathetic to his position where one aims to understand religion on religious criteria only, to accept religion in its own terms is really to deny that it has any ideological function, since all religious phenomena are historical and all data are conditioned and consequently religious phenomena cannot be understood outside of its history.
>
> (p. 80)

Nevertheless, the concept of cosmogonies is useful in differentiating between different types of religions, namely, transcendental religions (e.g., Christianity or other monotheistic religions) and cosmogeny-centred religions, which can often be found in hunter gatherer or other early human societies. In cosmogeny-centred religions, sacrifice as a ritual practice has a major religious function and is one of the central features. In early human societies and civilizations, the idea was to return the life-giving energy back to its divine sources by way of sacrifice, whereas in transcendental religions, the creator god exists independent of his creation, or the energy bound in that creation.

This demonstrates that there are important differentiations to be made between different forms of religions. This is also the main problem in Eliade's approach and other monolithic theories which try to explain assumed similarities or even a common source of religion. The empirical data have shown more variation than Eliade and these other early theorists were willing to incorporate into their theories.

> Moreover, when Eliade claims that the only function of myths is to create a sacred cosmos from the primordial chaos, and that all rituals are repetitions of the cosmogenic myths, he gives these structural patterns a privileged ontological status and denies that religion can be understood in other premises in terms of social, cultural, or psychological factors.
>
> (Oestigaard 2011, p. 85)

Eliade knew the theories of Jung and, in some instances, even refers explicitly to his works. He was also eager in his works to provide support for Jung's conceptualizations. But even though he took this attitude, he clearly states that religion is always a matter of social, linguistic and economic factors. It is, therefore, formed by humans and by human societies in their respective contexts. Even though he tried to reduce the different religions from all over the world to some basic interpretive schemas, he clearly points out that there is an endless variety of forms of religion and religious practices and that no unitary formula or ultimate definition will do justice to these labyrinthic compositions. He emphasizes the multifaced and sometimes even chaotic conglomeration of practices, beliefs and ideas which can be subsumed under the phenomenon religion and that any hypothesis which tries to find simple, elementary forms of religion is just an unproven hypothesis (Eliade 1959).

Comparative religion: From the grand theories to contemporary approaches

As was demonstrated earlier, a general problem in 19th- and early 20th-century theories in anthropology, which attempted to explain the development and origins of religion, is the ethnocentric viewpoint the theorists take, as well as the problem that they applied the already mentioned scale of primitive/savage to civilized/developed. Bowie (2004) provides an account of such a distinction between "primal" and "world religions":

The supposed features of a world religion:

- it is based on written Scriptures.
- it has a notion of salvation, often from outside (a coming deliverer).

- it is universal or has universal potential.
- it can subsume or supplant a primal religion.
- it often forms a separate sphere of activity.

The supposed features of primal religions:

- they are oral – the culture is illiterate, the religion lacks written Scriptures and formal creeds.
- they are this-worldly in orientation.
- they are confined to a single language or ethnic group.
- they formed the basis from which world religions have developed.
- religion and social life are inseparable and intertwined, and there is no clear division between the sacred and profane or natural and supernatural.

These categorizations are not without utility, or they would not have survived so long. They do, however, as numerous scholars have pointed out, beg many questions, and are at best intellectual constructs rather than descriptions of reality. To take the world religions first, to what extent can Taoism or Confucianism be considered to have universal potential? They are both commonly referred to as world religions, but are largely confined to Southeast Asia.

(Bowie 2004, p. 26)

It can definitely be stated that the fact that humans have religion is universal. Even contemporary theorists speculate about the evolutionary and genetic background, respectively, function, of this universal fact. It has to be noted, though, that what is seen as universal is the mere fact of the existence of religion and religious beliefs, and this is by no means support for the far-reaching assumptions of archetype theory in the sense of the previous quote that the contents of religious beliefs and ideas are universal.

In this sense, brains have been disposed by evolution to belief and even evolutionary materialists concede that religion plays a role in human well-being. It is easy to see how these converging mechanisms rapidly came to be used to rationalize or solve existential problems that otherwise have no worldly solution, such as the inevitability of death or the threat of deception by others. Research in this area based on cognitive psychology, neuroscience, cultural anthropology, and archaeology is beginning to reach maturity, and a number of generalizations can now be seen to be shared between all modern religious systems. In a phylogenetic sense these shared beliefs are best explained as deriving from our evolutionary origins. These universals include:

- the cosmos and its living creatures have inherent worth
- religious and ecological preservation are integrally linked: individuals and communities have responsibility towards the environment.

- The world is infused with supernatural agency: humanity is spiritually linked to and affected by the cosmos.
- Individuals maintain social relationships with supernatural agents.
- Individuals generally entertain highly anthropomorphic expectations about the supernatural agents.
- The minds of supernatural agents are implicitly expected to function like our own, even thou this is at odds with our explicit beliefs about them.
- Individuals are usually willing to subscribe to the religious norms of their own social groups, at the expense of being viewed as wrong by other groups.
- Individuals are only aware of some of their beliefs; a large amount of implicit, unconscious tenets underlies them.
- Religious beliefs are often concerned with issues of purification and danger, invoking ritual behavior designed to deal with these.

The most obvious use of religion is to encode and preserve ecological information. The origin of deities and other supernatural agents may, therefore, be seen as personifications of ecological processes. . . . Religion therefore involves a costly commitment to a counterintuitive world of supernatural agents who are believed to master existential anxieties.

(Pettitt 2011, pp. 330–332)

It also has to be noted that contemporary scholars of religious studies clearly state the following: religions are transmitted from one generation to the other by means of communication and learning processes (Wunn 2019). There is also definitely no continuity in the shape of religion from prehistory until today (Wunn 2005). Even though religions seem to have their inherent dynamics of evolution, recent theories criticize earlier conceptions and ideas which were based on far-reaching speculations with practically no evidence, including conceptions of bear cults, fertility rituals, goddesses, widespread cannibalism, etc. Eliade, for example, based his far-reaching assumptions about the connections between Palaeolithic cave paintings, shamanism and contemporary forms of so-called primitive religion on just one painting in the French cave Trois Freres – that of the "shaman-like" so-called great sorcerer (Witzel 2012, p. 255). There are also problems concerning terminology and differentiation:

One can standardize the words taken from a primitive vernacular, like totem, and use it to describe phenomena among other peoples which resemble what it refers to in its original home; but this can be the cause of great confusion, because the resemblances may be superficial, and the phenomena in question so diversified that the term loses all meaning.

(Evans-Pritchard 1981, p. 12)

Again, as we have seen previously, those earlier theories, which were characterized as the grand theories of the 19th and early 20th century, have been dismissed by contemporary research. It is also criticized today that these earlier speculations referred to far-reaching comparisons with recent hunter gatherer societies.

Examples for misconceptions

Hunting magic as Palaeolithic religion: The scholar of mythology Joseph Campbell (1971), who in his seminal work on the myth of the hero strongly referred to Jung and took up major ideas from his works – and by doing so wished to support Jung's theories and ideas – was one of the scholars who presupposed a parallelism of the mythologies and religions of Palaeolithic human groups and societies with those of recent hunter gatherer peoples. The precondition of his conclusions, though, is his conviction, even his strong insistence on the idea of a biological and cognitive-spiritual identity of mankind over thousands of years. Based on these presuppositions, Campbell – as well as other authors – have insisted that Palaeolithic groups had a differentiated religion which was mainly based on hunting magic. Contemporary scholars clearly reject these ideas since there is absolutely no evidence for practices which could be interpreted as hunting magic (Hodder 2001; Wunn 2005).

> A claim that evidence was found for Middle Palaeolithic animal worship c 70,000 BCE (originating from the Tsodilo Hills in the African Kalahari desert) has been denied by the original investigators of the site.
>
> (Narr 2021)

The earlier misinterpretations can be explained in so far as they referred to archaeological reports, which were based on unsystematic and even poor excavation methods, which were widespread in the archaeology of the 19th and early 20th century, and which were only changed by what today is called new or experimental archaeology (see chapter "Prehistory") (Binford 1983). But even without these poor archaeological findings, Campbell's approach can be characterized as a circular conclusion in so far as he assumed – without any evidence – that Palaeolithic hunters practiced hunting magic, as it can be found in recent hunter gatherer societies, and that, therefore, these early human groups and societies shared the same mythology with contemporary ethnicities.

The "prehistoric bear cult": Another example of widespread misconceptions about prehistoric religion is the theory of a prehistoric bear cult, which was formed in the first half of the 20th century. It refers to findings of bear bones and skulls in caves which were thought to have been inhabited by prehistoric humans. These bones were found in a certain systematic order, which was then interpreted as the remains of a religious cult of the cave bear with specific rituals connected with it. This theory assumed a continuation of these assumed prehistoric bear cults to practices in the Arctic regions of Siberia and North America of comparable bear cults, which have been documented in detail in anthropology. The theory argued that these bear cults originated in prehistoric times and that these were spread over all of Eurasia and North America and continued up to the present day, as they could be found in the rituals and religious practices of peoples living in the Arctic region. These ideas and theories have been rejected by contemporary scholars based on two insights (Wunn 2005, pp. 74–79):

> The early theories had been founded on very poor excavation practices in caves mainly in Germany. It has to be noted that the caves in which the bones and skulls were found are subject to periodical flooding, which then lead to processes of sedimentation. Contemporary reconstructions could demonstrate that the positions of the skulls and other bones can be well explained by such processes of sedimentation, transportation of the bones and skulls through water, and other physical processes which take place without any influence from human beings – so the seemingly meaningful placements are just the result of natural fossilization processes.

The second reason for the rejection of these earlier theories are detailed comparisons by contemporary anthropologists regarding the different forms of hunting magic and bear cults found in contemporary Arctic societies (e.g., Ainu). These investigations could demonstrate that there are actually large differences between rituals and beliefs of different contemporary ethnicities so that it is not possible to draw a line of continuity from earlier practices to the contemporary ones. Contemporary rituals of hunting magic and bear cults in Arctic societies are embedded in their complex religious belief systems as well as their environmental and economic conditions. It can be summarized that there is no evidence for any kind of bear cults and other practices and rituals of hunting magic for the middle and upper Palaeolithic.

The same applies to ideas which attempt to draw a line from assumed hunting magic practices to more elaborate forms of animism – the religious veneration of animals or lords of animals as well as the identification of the hunter with an animal ghost or soul, called totemism. There is no doubt that such practices and beliefs do exist in contemporary hunter gatherer societies and go back well into history, but consider the following:

> It is not possible to determine to what extent animalism had already assumed the character of true totemism in the Palaeolithic Period; the early existence of clan totemism is improbable because it occurs primarily among peoples who are to some extent agrarian, and possibly a certain kind of sedentary life was prerequisite to its development.

(Narr 2021)

Cannibalism: Another popular theory in the first half of the 20th century was the idea of a common, if not universal, practice in prehistoric peoples to eat the bodies of their enemies and of their deceased relatives, an idea which is ironically referred to in contemporary anthropology as the man-eater myth. It could be demonstrated that these ideas were founded on accounts of adventurers, which could by far not be interpreted as serious archaeology or ethnography. Even if these practices were reported by ethnographers, they were usually not reported as eyewitness accounts but were referring to secondary sources. Accumulations of shattered bones and destroyed skulls found in archaeological excavations were quickly interpreted as the remains of prehistoric cannibalism. As in the case of the previously reported bear cults, the position of the bones and other remains could, in fact, well be explained by natural processes (e.g., they could be identified as the remains of hyenas living in caves in the times of the lower Palaeolithic) (Wunn 2019). Cuts in the bones and distracted skulls, which were in earlier accounts interpreted as the remains of the use of knifes and attempts to open the skull and eat the brain, could again be interpreted as sedimentation and fossilization processes (e.g., when bones are pressed in the sediment against sharp stones or moved in the ground) (Wunn 2005). In general, the same explanations could be found in contemporary accounts for earlier ideas about funeral rites and the positioning of human skulls in the middle Palaeolithic. This is notwithstanding that in some contemporary hunter gatherer societies, ethnologists reported such practices as eating the remains of deceased relatives in the context of funeral rites, but they are definitely not universal.

> This obsolete conception, still held by some scholars today – i.e., that cannibalism is an especially "primitive" phenomenon and therefore very ancient – must be abandoned. Ethnological studies show clearly that cannibalism appears almost exclusively in the practices of agrarian peoples, that is, in a later cultural stage, and evidently is essentially bound up with religious or magical conceptions in which cultivated plants play a large role. Even if a Palaeolithic cannibalism existed on a large scale, it could not be explained by means of concepts that originated in a cultural stage so differently structured.
>
> (Narr 2021)

In general, it can be summarized that contemporary archaeology and the conclusions that are drawn from the findings in contemporary theories of the anthropology of religion are much more cautious in interpreting the material. They attempt not to carry preconceptions and monolithic explanatory models into the documentation of the findings, etc. In sum, this leads to the insight that our knowledge about the religion in the Palaeolithic is very restricted and may remain so in future since it is almost impossible to reconstruct religious beliefs just from the very restricted archaeological findings we can have of that time.

The theory of religious evolution

Instead of assuming that religion develops out of evolutionary features of the human mind or even genetic foundations, the scholar of religion Robert N. Bellah (1964) developed a model of how religions develop out of their own structural dynamics in a form of evolutionary process; these ideas were based on the concepts of the evolution of social systems developed by the sociologist Talcott Parsons.

The general idea in this theory is that religions develop over five distinct stages from primitive beginnings lastly to the individualized belief systems of present times. The factors driving this evolution are processes of differentiation inherent in religion itself. Bellah assumes five stages: primitive religion, archaic religion, historic religion, premodern religion and modern religion. Primitive religion, for example, is characterized by the lack of religious organizations, which are separated from other societal organizations. There is no church nor any priests. Differentiation in society is organized based on age, sex and kinship relations. Women are not excluded from religious life but may have their own rituals. Religion takes an important role in society; it creates solidarity and introduces the members into their rights and duties. What is very important for a discussion of archetype theory is the insight, which Bellah could present convincingly, that these developments are not connected with features of the human brain, but they are closely connected with the economic system and social organization of the respective ethnicities and groups, which again relate to the environment they were living in.

This is different from the earlier grand theories of the 19th and early 20th century which assumed a teleological process, which could be observed in every part of nature as well as in society, which leads necessarily from primitive structures to lastly perfect forms. An example of this is Lamarck's idea of a universal drive to perfection, an idea which strongly influenced Jung's psychology. Inherent in these older theories is the general assumption that European civilization and religion are the crown of the creation, a viewpoint that has already been characterized as colonial thinking. Contemporary approaches do not include such value judgments in the sense that so-called primitive religions can have extremely complex cosmologies compared to much simpler modern religions, as for example, Christianity.

> In evaluating all such attempts it must be remembered that even seemingly primitive tribes, so one used to say, such as the headhunting Dayaks of Borneo, have myths and ritual tales that . . . amount to some 15,000 pages, once collected.
>
> (Witzel 2012, p. 369)

If we call prehistoric religious practices primitive, this does not necessarily mean that they consist of simple forms; they may even have very complex cosmologies. The term primitive refers to the social institutions that are inherent in the religious forms, as for example, the institutions of priests, religious organizations, etc. Additionally, it has to be noted that societies with primitive forms of religion may have elaborated technologies in practical life, whereas peoples living on a technologically simple level may have quite complex religious beliefs and practices (Wunn 2005).

In the view of Ina Wunn (2019), anthropologist of religion, religions have developed in adaptation to the respective peoples' natural environment as well as their social and political organization. They have not developed out of assumed – and up to date, not verifiable – functions of the human brain or other physiological conditions but on the way of cultural tradition (i.e., processes of communication). Usually, members of a society learn religious beliefs from their mothers on a vertical line of transmission from one generation to the other. Only if there is horizontal communication between different social groups with different religious points of view there will be change in religious ideas because otherwise, the processes of transmission are very stable over long time. Based on these processes, religions have developed into a great variety, which may have some features in common. But contemporary scholars stress the fundamental differences between contemporary religions as well as between religions from prehistoric times and contemporary hunter gatherer societies or other small-scale societies (Wunn 2005). This also means that the religions of today's hunter gatherer societies or those of simple agricultural civilizations cannot longer be seen as the original religions. Instead, they are also at the end of a long series of developments in the form of religion. Contemporary theorists would also clearly deny ideas such as that religions develop somehow automatically on a unilinear scale, following undeniable natural laws – an idea that characterized the aforementioned grand theories. Such ideas and approaches today are regarded as refuted (Wunn 2005). Since religions always serve certain needs of the peoples that developed them, they are also subject to change, as also the environments and contexts as well as the social organization and technological level of these peoples change over time.

The evolution of first religions

Based on these fundamental considerations, Ina Wunn (2019), one of the leading scholars in the field of history of religions, presents a history of the development of the first religions in Palaeolithic times, which is summarized in the following account. She stresses the point that, in contrast to the earlier, aforementioned grand theories, she applied a systematic method of comparison which is based on a detailed analysis of the environmental contexts in which the respective peoples and societies lived, and this is additionally paralleled with the respective archaeological findings. By archaeology, the author refers to what is called new archaeology or experimental archaeology which makes use of systematic scientific methods to analyse the data and findings (see chapter "Prehistory" for details). This also includes a thorough analysis of the living conditions, technology and practices of contemporary hunter gatherer societies, not in the sense that she parallels their beliefs with prehistoric belief systems or religions but in the sense of understanding the living conditions and the means for securing survival in societies which are reliant on hunting. These studies enabled archaeologists to understand what the typical remains of a hunter gatherer group look like in their usual context to become able to analyse and interpret archaeological findings from prehistoric hunter gatherer groups. Unfortunately, even in many contemporary accounts of the development of religions, earlier insufficient methodologies in archaeology are still referred to, which has led to the situation that in the anthropology of religion many of the aforementioned outdated ideas and approaches have remained.

About 90,000 years ago, the first humans began to bury their dead but without having any ideas that could be called religious. Wunn assumes that the burials had a territorial aspect, as they demonstrated the claim of the hunter group over certain hunting territories. That is also the reason why the dead would be buried in the village or even in the ground beneath the floor of the houses, a practice which lasted until Neolithic times. On the other hand, the burials were a means to cope with the sorrow and bereavement about the loss of a relative. Out of this practice developed first beliefs of a life beyond death. So at the base of the development of religions are, on the one hand, territorial claims, on the other, ways of coping with existential fear. In the upper Palaeolithic, these developments led to the painting of caves, which can also be understood as a way of demonstrating a claim on this habitat. The pictures that were used make use of universal threat and appeasement (apotropaic) signals, mainly, the presentation of an erect phallus or a vulva, often combined with the presentation of the female breast as a sign of appeasement. Both elements are combined in the female figurines with large breasts presenting a vulva (e.g., Venus of Willendorf). Anthropologists of religion were able to understand these universal, biologically based gestures and signs based on ethological research. These apotropaic signals include the presentation of the genitals, the female breast, the hand held out in defence, the menacing stare of the eyes, etc. These signs or gestures contain the same meaning independent of language and can be understood in all human societies (in this sense, they are, according to Wunn, truly universal). This can explain the use of these apotropaic signs in art and sculpture from prehistoric times way into antiquity, in the form of ancestor figures, temple guardians, border posts, demons and talismans. The presentation of the buttocks, in contrast, signals the willingness for coupling and can, therefore, be understood as a submission gesture.

These considerations of fundamental human gestures which are thought to be universal is partly supported by Witzel (2012, pp. 271–272). He provides the following list of "pan-human gestures", which he believes are derived from our primate ancestors and are, therefore, independent of language: pacifying smile; threatening bearing of teeth; threatening staring of the eyes; the demonstration of the erect penis as a threat and power gesture with its modern variation of raising the middle finger; the exposure of the female posterior as an invitation to sex and as a demonstration of submission; the presentation of the vulva, knees raised and spread out as a gesture of female dominance; the demonstration of female breasts as a pacifying gesture; and the presentation of a raised palm is used as a sign of denial and as a protecting device. All these signs can be found in abstract form already in Palaeolithic art. But he also adds some gestures which are in fact not universal but have different meanings in different cultures: the shaking of one's head, which in some cultures means yes, in others, no; and the Tibetan projection of the tongue as a greeting. The same applies to some symbols which (for example, in Jungian psychology) have been interpreted as being universal:

For example, in contemporary West Africa the ubiquitous Indian, Buddhist, Jain, Amerindian, and so on swastika sign has no relation to the course of the sun, as it does in many other cultures, but rather, indicates monkey's feet.

(Witzel 2012, p. 274)

The described form of proto religion developed in Europe during the ice age, migrated from there to the East and reached the Near and Middle East, the so-called Fertile Crescent, by around 10,000 years ago. When in the Fertile Crescent agriculture was invented, these religious ideas developed into first conceptions of a realm of the dead and a female figure which was responsible for birth and death, for growing and decaying and for the renewal of life itself. The territorial claims developed into practices of ancestor cult, which was practiced by conserving the bones of the dead, keeping their skulls, sometimes visible in erect position or later through methods of mummification. This became even more important for the development of agriculture, which created a need for legitimation of the claims on agricultural land (Bellwood 2004). But from this time onward, regional differences develop and lead to significantly different religious ideas and traditions. So regarding religion in the upper Palaeolithic, it can be summarized that the only plausible interpretations of the findings speak for the existence of the first ideas of a life beyond death and the existence of an idea of a primal mother responsible for the creation of life – but nota bene, only in Europe and the Fertile Crescent. These primal mother figures were not thought of being universal goddesses but were worshipped as individual ancestors of a specific family or group. In later times, when the first cities and states were formed in Mesopotamia, the need arose to unify these divergent groups and tribes and their specific ancestor figures, and this happened by creating unified mythologies which incorporated the specific mythologies of the divergent groups. The same happened to the figurines of worship, which were melted into one great goddess of life/creation on the one hand. On the other hand, this was the birth of polytheism, as all the divergent gods and goddesses were melted into the polytheistic pantheon.

Since agriculture, as can be demonstrated convincingly, was invented originally in the Fertile Crescent, it can be assumed that with the proliferation of agricultural techniques from the Near and Middle East to Europe, Asia and other parts of the world, this polytheistic religion migrated with the technological developments and thus spread over considerably parts of the Old World, it namely influenced religion in Greece and the Mediterranean as well as in Iran. On the other hand, the described development also happened parallel (e.g., in Egypt) under the same conditions – that is, the pressure to create larger political units and establish political hierarchies. The different development of Israel/Judah shows that there were a variety of possibilities to deal with the same problem. In the case of Israel, the authorities, instead of creating a polytheistic pantheon, chose a way to unite their divergent protective gods and goddesses of the different tribes and towns into one god figure. This went parallel to the extinction of older cult places and temples, which were intentionally destroyed and levelled, so as to give authority to the Temple in Jerusalem.

Wunn (2019) summarizes:

This model of religious evolution proves that religions cannot be scaled as more or less developed, and therefore cannot be connected with a scale based on value judgments. Instead, each religion of a people has to be regarded as an ideological adaptation to the respective environment. . . . This not only speaks

clearly against the assumption of a – up to date not verifiable – brain function which generates religion, moreover it can explain why the human brain
does not bring about the same kind of religion in all times – because religion
does not automatically develop out of physiological conditions, but because
religions are cultural accomplishments and are inherited on the same way
as all culture: via communication processes. . . . Religion does not develop
because the brain automatically produces certain connections, but instead
because from earliest childhood on we learn religion. Together with ethical
norms, the foundations of our social behaviour, we also take over religion, and
this happens mainly on the base of vertical communication from the mother
to the child.

(pp. 332–334; transl. C.R.)

Even though this account of the development of religions is one of the most elaborate and well empirically grounded, it is not undisputed. There is an extensive critical discussion of Wunn's hypotheses in Witzel (2012, pp. 255–261), even though
he agrees with many of her fundamental assumptions.

No universal/primal religion to be found

Based on these fundamental considerations in contemporary approaches to the history and development of religions, some basic elements in the anthropology of
religion can now be reconceptualized.

Totemism

The 19th- and early 20th-century theories that were discussed earlier and were
characterized as grand theories – among them the theories of Frazer and Durkheim –
relied heavily on the concept of totemism (along with shamanism) to describe
and explain assumed universal features of religions and, especially, the origins of
religions. Totemism was regarded as the earliest form and the root of religion.
This view was based on an evolutionary perspective that carried the assumption
of a progression from primitive – that is, animistic – to modern, civilized religions
that were monotheistic. They attempted to provide evidence for this assumption by
looking for data about the most primitive societies.

Despite having occupied many leading anthropologists for the best part of
the century, totemism as a concept is now seldom discussed, and by many is
dismissed altogether. The association of totemic systems with early or primitive societies has been unfortunate, leading to the use of Australian aboriginal
beliefs as a representative of prehistoric types of cosmology. While Australian aboriginal cultures may have maintained greater continuity over time than
Western cultures, there is no evidence that they are in any sense ancestral to

non-Australian peoples, or that their belief systems were once universal. These views imply that simpler societies are ahistorical and static, which is very different from claiming that they are both adaptable and conservative. . . . The idea of totemic sacrifice as a primary and universal religious act does not find cross-cultural support.

(Bowie 2004, pp. 137–139)

So for contemporary scholars in anthropology and the history of religion, totemism is not a universal form of religion but a specific religious practice in societies characterized by a clan structure and is, therefore, seen as just one way among many to form a religious system and to relate to the surrounding environment.

Animism

The same that was said earlier about totemism applies also to animism and the theories accompanying this phenomenon. In the aforementioned grand theories, there was the common notion that animism – meaning that also inanimate objects are thought to have a soul – is a specific feature for so-called primitive societies as well as for primitive modes of thinking, as can be found in children as well as in the mentally insane, which was apparently the same idea Jung had in his theory. These ideas are continued in theories attempting to explain the development of religions referring to evolutionary forces. These ideas parallelize the ways of thinking in early Homo sapiens in the Palaeolithic and that of children respectively thinking in states of regression and psychopathology. Insoll (2011) summarizes the debate and also points out the problems with such cognitive processualist approaches to religion because of the "universalizing perspective employed, that is a defining hey-presto moment of religious complexity subsequent to a number of evolutionary stages" (p. 1009), which is not supported by contemporary scholars. He also points out evidence which speaks against such assumptions. Cross-cultural studies have found that some hunter gatherer groups do not depict animals in visual art. In some cases of rock art and cave paintings, some animals appear wounded by spears, which would be incompatible with the respect that would be due to a totem.

The utility of the terms animism and totemism is questionable, and various anthropological observers have commented upon their problematical status and that of related terms such as ancestor worship and shamanism. Geertz, for example, has described all these terms when applied to religious traditions as denying their individuality and as insipid categories by means of which ethnographers of religion devitalize their data. Similarly Wendy James has noted that such concepts as totem, taboo, animism, ancestor worship, tribal gods, and so on carry too much of a burden from older evolutionary thinking about religion.

(Insoll 2011, p. 1004)

Ancestor cults

The same as was said about animism and totemism applies also to the idea of ancestor cults when referring to findings from the Palaeolithic:

> Interpreting the presence of ancestor cults based on archaeological materials has validity in some contexts, but if ancestors and ancestor cults are deemed interpretively relevant for archaeology then ethnographic analysis usually tells us that they should not be thought of as operating in isolation, but, as already stressed earlier, as part of a multiple package of phenomena, practices, and beliefs whose configuration and importance can change over time. For instance, the study of the Baktaman clearly indicates that the interlinking between sacrifice and ancestor veneration in stating that the focal operation in every Baktaman ritual is sacrifice. Similarly, among the Tallensi, complex configurations of ancestors exist, as described, but believes in these and their associated ritual practices operate alongside other frames of reference such as earth cults and totemic observance. It is when we privilege singular ancestral interpretations with supposed universal applicability that interpretive complexity and subtlety is lost.
>
> (Insoll 2011, p. 1055)

Ritual

Eliade (1954) based his explanatory system of religion on the analysis of mythology, and for him, ritual is a re-enactment of primal myths, so they can be seen as performances of cosmogonic events brought into the present. As with other forms in the field of religion, rituals are also seen by contemporary anthropology from the perspective of their function, for the individual as well as for groups or societies. This means that they are seen to be closely connected with organizational forms of groups and societies, power relations and the forming and guidance of behaviour to provide social harmony and balance and, on the personal level, to modulate emotions. Thus, all rituals, including religious rituals, seem to be grounded in the everyday human world and serve certain functions in everyday life conduct.

Contemporary anthropologists also point to the problem that it is often not easy to identify a ritual as separated from other everyday practices, and it seems that it depends very much on the definition of the anthropologist. This means that a certain activity which is called ritual is not automatically and universally recognizable, but it is more a category for analysis and interpretation by Western observers; the difference between ritual and non-ritual is relative rather than absolute (Bowie 2004). So there is also not a single or simple explanation of ritual, but it has to be recognized that rituals are multifaceted.

> Ritual is not, however, a universal, cross-cultural phenomenon, but a particular way of looking at and organizing the world that tells us as much about the

anthropologist, and his or her frame of reference, as the people and behaviour being studied. This does not mean that as a category ritual has no explanatory or interpretive value, but we would do well to beware universal, essentialist interpretations of actions defined by the anthropologist as a ritual.

(Bowie 2004, p. 151)

It also has to be noted that religious rituals are driven by the same cognitive system that guides everyday practice, which could explain the difficulty to differentiate between the two when looked at from an outside perspective.

Another fundamental distinction is often made between religious and nonreligious rituals. . . . However, the distinction between the sacred and the profane, or the supernatural and the social, is often difficult to make and in many contexts even not present at all. For instance, since the fundamental work of Durkheim, it is acknowledged that religious rituals have important social functions, with regard to, for example, social cohesion, uniting people by their belief, the establishment and maintenance of power structures, making social differences appear as supernatural.

(Verhoeven 2011, p. 118)

It has been argued that to the modern Western rational mind, rituals are often regarded as distinctly sacred, non-functional and irrational. This kind of perspective is not found in all societies. In fact, it is by now well known that strict separations, as for example, between the sacred and the profane, nature and culture, etc., are utterly meaningless to many traditional small-scale communities all over the world.

Given the many different definitions, attributes, typologies, and approaches used by researchers, as well as the fact that in many societies ritual and religion are inextricably bound up with every aspect of life, it has been argued that ritual is not only a multidimensional, but also a holistic phenomenon. Thus, in many contexts rituals are basic mechanisms for the proper operation of the sociocultural universe, relating social and supernatural domains. Ethnocentric assumptions regarding the sacred and profane, or other taken for granted distinctions should therefore be treated with suspicion, especially when dealing with small-scale prehistoric societies. The many dimensions of ritual make it not only a very interesting but also a rather difficult subject, especially for archaeologists.

(Verhoeven 2011, p. 127)

Rites of passage

An important position in the debate about ritual takes Arnold van Gennep's (1909) work on rites of passage, in which he investigates transition rituals, which mark a change of status and which are performed in ritual actions. These rites of passage can be observed in different societies and deal with passages around birth, initiation, marriage and other changes of social status. He developed a framework which is applicable to practically all ritually performed passages, assuming these have a threefold structure: the first stage is that of separation from the current state or status, followed by a middle "liminal" stage, in which the person is betwixt and between, before in the final stage of reintegration, the transformed person is reintegrated into the group with a new status (summary in Bowie 2004, p. 163).

> Our interest lies not in the particular rites but in their essential significance and their relative positions within ceremonial wholes – that is, their order. . . . The underlying arrangement is always the same. Beneath a multiplicity of forms, either consciously expressed or merely implied, a typical pattern always recurs – the pattern of the rites of passage.
>
> (Van Gennep, quoted in Bowie 2004, p. 167)

So here seems to be a universal pattern which is not fundamentally questioned even by contemporary anthropology. It has to be noted, though, that the supposed threefold structure is an explanatory concept, an analytical tool, and should not be reified. Also, any assumptions about a biological foundation of these patterns have been dismissed in anthropology (and also by Van Gennep himself). Instead, the emphasis lies on the social functions of these ritual forms. Van Gennep himself, as early as 1909, criticized the aforementioned theories and their colonial thinking as well as their evolutionist viewpoint. First, he criticized the characterization of indigenous societies as primitive, which he saw as far-reaching speculation since in his own investigations, he found that they were neither uniform nor homogeneous and, in regards to their social mechanisms, as complex as so-called civilized societies. Second, he criticized the method (e.g., found in Frazer's *The Golden Bough*) to draw elements out of the context and interpret them by looking at surface similarities, instead of investigating their inner mechanisms in depth. This is interesting, because Jung knew Van Gennep's seminal work and also used it in his argumentation but seems to have not acknowledged this critique. In this sense he misused Van Gennep as a support for his universalist, evolutionist ideas.

Van Gennep's ideas were further developed by the anthropologist Victor Turner (1974, 1991) in his studies on initiation rites. These theories were later criticized since they drew heavily on male initiation rites and were not applicable to female initiation. Bruce Lincoln suggested an alternative threefold structure for women's experiences and rituals including the stages of enclosure, metamorphoses, and emergence. He emphasizes the transformative effects of such rituals. Bowie (2004, p. 184) summarizes:

> Rituals attempt to enact and deal with the most central and basic dilemmas of human existence – continuity and stability, growth and fertility, mortality and immortality or transcendence. It is the potential of rituals to transform people and situations that lends them their power. . . . Symbols and sacred objects are

manipulated within ritual to enhance performance and to communicate ideological messages concerning the nature of the individual, society, and cosmos. . . . They can be used to control, to subvert, to stabilize, to enhance, and to terrorize individuals and groups. The study of ritual can indeed provide a key to an understanding and interpretation of culture.

Instead of assuming that rituals, even if they seem to have a universal structure, are based in the psychobiology of humans in the sense of a collective memory with a genetic base, this account implies that rituals have a universal structure because they aim at the psychobiological makeup of humans to activate or channel, yes, even to manipulate, human emotions to serve certain functions. This is paralleled by the insight, mentioned earlier, that human behaviour is not genetically coded, but humans have a set of preformed emotional systems which, when activated, lead to specific preformed action patterns. So human behaviour can be activated, transformed, but also manipulated by activating certain emotions. It seems that rituals are designed to do just that.

Shamanism

Shamanism is one of these terms which is often used very broadly, referring to many different phenomena, some of which bear little relationship to one another or to any original derivation. Most writers, however, agreed that shamanism is a technique rather than a religion, and that the shaman is a religious specialist existing within many different religious and cultural contexts.

(Bowie 2004, p. 190)

Halifax (1991), in her summarizing work on shamanism, gives a list of defining features: there is an initiatory crisis, often connected with illness or a disability; a vision quest; ordeals that the apprentice has to undergo, which can include experiences of dismemberment or even symbolic death followed by regeneration; the idea of a sacred tree or axis mundi; spirit flight; the ability to travel transcendental worlds by entering ecstatic trance; and the function of a healer and intermediary between the tribe/people and a reality beyond.

In anthropology, there have been several theorists who assumed that shamanism is something as the original or primal religion, which already existed in the Palaeolithic. An outstanding protagonist of this way of thinking is Mircea Eliade with his encyclopaedic work on *Shamanism: Archaic Techniques of Ecstasy* (1964). He assumed that shamanism is a specific phenomenon which can be found all over the world in ancient as well as contemporary religions. Also, contemporary religions include shamanic elements, but Eliade postulates that there is something as an original and pure shamanism.

In popular works on archaeology, cave paintings from the Palaeolithic have been interpreted as products of shamanic rituals or practices, and there has been the interpretation of these paintings and carvings as ornaments of sacred chambers in which shamanic rituals were conducted. There is also a debate which sees shamanism as the Celtic religion ("Druids") which is interpreted as the predecessor of contemporary European religions.

> Such claims are very difficult to verify and owe more to 19th-century theoretical evolutionist debates then to contemporary anthropological discourse. Eliade's work has, however, been extraordinarily influential and is widely quoted by writers on shamanism, most of whom accept his definitions and classification of shamanism without question.
>
> (Bowie 2004, p. 193)

Shamanism has been investigated thoroughly by Russian anthropologists, also because it is mostly found in the Arctic region, namely, Siberia (Hultkrantz 1993). These investigators usually have been more cautious in interpreting shamanism and regarded it not as a single, unified religion but a cross-cultural practice of religious rituals and healing procedures. In this scholarly tradition, a more restricted definition of shamanism is used, which is seen as a specific cultural practice and worldview characteristic of the circumpolar or Arctic complex. Parallels can be found throughout the Americas and in Southeast Asia, although there are wide divergences between the practices in these regions and those from the Arctic.

In the Russian scholarly tradition, definitions were specified which apply exclusively to this circumpolar complex of shamanism: the shaman is a master or mistress of spirits, which he/she can get under his or her control by a complex of methods and techniques which are transmitted from master to apprentice. Shamans have a special social position in their community and can give a theory about their practice (Bowie 2004).

Practices characterized as shamanism may be widely distributed but are showing different constellations of traits which do not occur in Siberian shamanism (Hultkrantz 1992). In general, contemporary anthropologists tend to restrict the definition to the circumpolar complex with a certain degree of cultural continuity (e.g., Bowie 2004).

> The desire to reserve the use of the term shamanism to the circumpolar regions, with the recognition of related concurrences in Asia and the Americas, is, however, confined to scholars writing for the academic market. So handy a term, which can mean almost whatever you want it to mean, has achieved a broad currency in popular literature and in the popular imagination.
>
> (Bowie 2004, p. 196)

Witchcraft

As with other examples described earlier, in contemporary anthropological accounts of religious ideas about witchcraft and the respective social and cultural practices, which are indeed found in a variety of cultures, these can well be explained by the social context and the social relationships in which they are embedded in. It is assumed that witchcraft reflects interpersonal behaviour between people in stressful situations and that stressful behaviour is frequent in particular social relationships. Bowie (2004) gives an example for these relationships from the Nupi and Gware of the Guinea Coast culture area:

> According to our hypothesis that witchcraft accusations are signs of difficult social relationships, we might want to examine differences in interpersonal relationships in the two groups. Among the Nupe the general picture is one of antagonism between men and women, reflected in the fact that witches are always women and men have the ability to control the activity of female witches. Further study reveals a major difference in marriage relationships in the two groups. Among the Gwari, marriage is generally free of tension, but this is not the case with the Nupe. This is likely due to the differences in the economic systems. Among the Nupe, married women can become itinerant traders and have the potential of economic success. Their husbands are often indepted to their wifes, and wifes take over certain economic tasks that usually fall within the sphere of activity of man. These include paying for feasts and gathering together the bride wealth for sons. Men are angry and resentful over the situation but really cannot do anything about it. In addition, among the Nupe, itinerant traders can be married women who leave young children in the care of extended family, and even refuse to have children, to be free to ply their trade. Although men condemn this activity as immoral, once again they are helpless to do anything about it. It is this anger and hostility that are projected into the world of witchcraft, in which witches – interestingly, visualized as itinerant traders – are women who can be controlled by the men. Thus, men have power over women in the realm of witchcraft but not in the real world.
>
> (pp. 229–230)

Compared to European and North American ideas about witchcraft and the practices of witches (Evans-Pritchard 1981), it becomes clear that there are many differences compared to ideas in small-scale societies. Again, it can be demonstrated that these differences can be well explained through the social context in which the phenomenon appears. Interestingly, contemporary studies about the persecution of witches in Europe in late medieval times, which made use of court documents of trials against witches, found out that most accusations against these women came from their female neighbours, which could be interpreted as speaking for the aforementioned hypothesis that witchcraft is associated with stressful interpersonal relationships, in this case, presumably jealousy and female rivalry (Lütz 2018). Evans-Pritchard (1981) concludes that beliefs around witchcraft serve a number of functions in societies; it provides explanations for the unexplainable, especially for misfortune and how to deal with it; and it serves to define morality.

Conclusion

Bowie remarks: "What such comparisons do teach us is that religious behavior may have universal elements, but that it is also highly dependent upon its social and physical environment" (Bowie 2004, p. 214).

Again, as was found for anthropology in general, it can be summarized that beyond the mere fact of the existence of religion, no truly universal elements in the field of religion could be found; the same applies to the idea of a primal religion, which actually does not exist. It could be demonstrated that earlier ideas regarding assumed universals (e.g., about shamanism or hunting magic), as well as theories constructing a linear scale of development from primal or original to contemporary religions, were based on poor documentation and data analysis or were prejudiced misconceptions from the beginning. Similarities as well as differences found in cross-cultural comparisons can well be explained by the social, economic and political contexts as well as natural environments in which these phenomena occur and, to a great extent, also through cultural exchange (see also chapter "Prehistory"). Contemporary accounts of the anthropology of religion have departed from assumptions that specific religious beliefs and practices come about through the biological makeup of humans. This does not imply, on the other hand, that there is not such a thing as a universal and fundamental human need for spirituality and transcendence. It is also not denying the idea inherent in Jung's theorizing around archetypes that the study of religions can teach us what – broadly speaking – is "good for us humans". So for example, a number of religions have explicit diet rules (e.g., the rule in Judaism as well as Islam not to eat pork meat, which makes a lot of sense since in the climate of the near East and Arabia, this kind of meat can quickly develop dangerous bacteria). Religious rules and practices can also serve human needs on a psychological level (e.g., rites of initiation can help loosen the strong bonds between children and their mothers and can thus help to take the step into adulthood, and it can be demonstrated that cultures with a lack of such initiation rites have more problems with adolescence) (Zoja 1989). In that sense, the study of religions and religious practices and beliefs, as has been practiced in AP for decades, can provide psychological insights which can be of help in the practice of psychotherapy. But it is not necessary for this approach to insist on problematic assumptions that such helpful rules come about through the biological makeup of humans or are universal at all.

Chapter 8

Prehistory

In the analysis of Jung's statements and definitions around the concept of archetypes, a basic element was identified: the idea that archetypes have developed in the prehistory of humans as a "precipitation of experiences" of early men. They are a heritage that has come upon us modern humans from early times, in some sense, as our archaic nature, linking us to our ancestors in prehistory. So together with the aforementioned idea of homology of phylogeny and ontogeny, Jung's theories about archetypes contains a whole set of ideas and assumptions about the life and development of humans in prehistoric times. Therefore, the state-of-the-art in studies of prehistory, or palaeoanthropology, will be summarized in the following – with a special emphasis on aspects of religion.[1] This will provide further evidence for what was presented in the chapter "Religion".

Problems in the archaeology of prehistory

There are some general problems that archaeologists of prehistory are confronted with when having to interpret findings from prehistory:

> When assessing potential evidence of ritual and religion in the upper Palaeolithic – the period from roughly 40,000 to 10,000 years ago – it is often difficult to decide whether one is seeing something of deep significance or instead something mundane: was all cave art necessarily profoundly meaningful and mystical? Do footprints in deep caves do represent ritual visits, or simply the bravado of youngsters? Was the breakage of an object a ritual, or an accident? Were bone fragments stuck into cave walls and floors as part of a ritual or for practical reasons? Is the positioning of a bear skull part of a mystical rite, or the result of a child playing with it? It is all too easy to project our own preconceptions and wishful thinking on to the mute archaeological evidence, and one could cite countless examples of unwarranted and purely speculative hypotheses involving ritual in this period. The evidence requires a more objective and sober assessment.
>
> (Bahn 2011, p. 344)

DOI: 10.4324/9781003348191-8

When assessing the state-of-the-art in prehistoric studies and the historical development of theories and concepts in this field, one becomes aware of the endless sequence of highly speculative, in some cases, even bizarre, theories and ideas that have developed over the last 150 years in the discipline.

An interesting example for such misconceptions and misinterpretations was reported in the German scientific journal *Bild der Wissenschaft* of July 2014:

> Palaeontologists investigated a cave in South Africa which contained paintings on the walls, including colour handprints; this cave was especially interesting since it contained footsteps of a number of people. These must have been conserved from the time in which the paintings were created, from the upper palaeolithic. The researchers engaged three professional hunters and trackers of the San Bushmen, who had the ability to interpret footprints, and asked them to provide their expertise on the possible occurrences in that cave. The results were quite sobering: in contrast to earlier interpretations by scholars, who assumed that the paintings and the footsteps where the remains of a prehistoric ritual, presumably a dance, the Bushmen experts found out the footprints to belong to of a group of children with one female adult. They also analysed the sequence of footprints and assumed that this was a group of children in play supervised by an adult, and as part of the play they had created coloured handprints on the walls. So instead of being the remains of a prehistoric ritual or shamanistic dance, their interpretation was that of something like a prehistoric kindergarten, in which the supervising adult tried to engage and occupy the children with different forms of play, maybe while waiting for the other adults to return from hunting or gathering.

When it comes to prehistory, we also have to take into account that what has been found may not necessarily be representative for the everyday life and culture of that time (Wunn 2005, 2019). So for example, in the case of cave paintings, these were preserved only in caves of which the entrance was blocked in very early times; thus, the climate in the cave was constant and the paintings were preserved. Some scholars even assume that in the Palaeolithic, the inhabited landscapes were covered all over with paintings and rock art, as can be still found today in the Sahara Desert as well as in Australia. In Europe and other northern regions, nothing of the sort was preserved due to the humid climate (Trachsel 2008).

To explain findings from the Palaeolithic, very often, parallels have been drawn to contemporary hunter gatherer societies based on the assumption that both lived on the same cultural level and can thus be compared. This approach has been strongly criticized from many sides:

> Care should thus be taken, with Wunn and against Eliade, not to mechanically compare modern hunter gatherers with their ancestors many thousands of years ago. The few hunter gatherers remaining today are, like us, modern humans with

a long history, and the current state of mind cannot automatically be projected back to 50,000 years ago or to more recent times. If some of the ancient patterns have been maintained by their myths better than in other mythologies, this must be the object of additional, detailed study.

(Witzel 2012, p. 261)

Care has to be taken if models are imported and, without any verification, are applied to prehistoric cultures of Europe. This approach is based on some assumptions which are often not made explicit, and which can be characterized as follows:

- the spectrum of human behaviours follows certain basic rules and laws, and therefore under comparable conditions similar cultural characteristics develop [it is not difficult to identify the basic pattern of Jung's thinking in this description, C.R.]
- the spectrum of [contemporary; C.R.] ethnographic examples cover all possible conditions, which are to be found in the prehistory of Europe. So, one only has to find the appropriate model.

It has to be noted, that the conditions and the characteristics of human behaviour alone leave enough space for different cultural solutions. Individual accomplishments, charismatic personalities, natural events, cultural feedback (e.g., taboos) or merely chance may lead to individual history, on the base of which similar conditions lead to very different developments. Cultural structures have historically developed and are therefore mostly more individual than one would assume from the perspective of theoretical models. Also, it is more than likely that those societies which were ethnographically described, may cover only a part of all the possible cultural models. . . . Lastly, it has to be pointed out that in prehistory some imported models from ethnology are still in use, which there have already been refuted, a fact that may not have been acknowledged in the field of prehistory.

(Trachsel 2008, p. 223; transl. C.R.)

Mithen (2003) makes clear:

There are no isolated stone age tribes in the world today. . . . We must, as always, be cautious of such accounts. Archaeologists must not be tempted by the present; they must keep returning to the analysis of artifacts and the pursuit of excavation. There are no shortcuts to the prehistoric past.

(p. 358)

These warnings may lead us to the sobering insight that there are considerable limits to what we can learn about prehistory. In fact, many things (e.g., what the religious beliefs of these people were) we will probably never know because it is impossible to be reconstructed from the few remains that we have of these illiterate societies. As was pointed out earlier, the remains we can find and investigate are only those able to survive the impact of climate, sedimentation, etc., over tens of thousands of years, and these are probably not representative of the everyday life, the culture and the belief systems of the people.

To provide a basis of knowledge of the development of humans over what is called the Stone Age, on which later more detailed discussions of certain aspects can build, the most widely accepted theory in palaeoanthropology of the development of Homo sapiens will now be presented.

The migration of Homo sapiens out of Africa and over the world

In prehistory, palaeoanthropology and archaeology, it is standard knowledge today that anatomically modern humans, Homo sapiens, first appeared in Africa some 300–130,000 years ago and started to migrate out of Africa and all over the world around 60,000 years ago – the so-called Out-of-Africa theory. This period coincides with the beginning of the ice ages, which made the northern parts of Europe and Asia uninhabitable, forcing the Homo sapiens to live on hunting mainly large animals (e.g., mammoth, wild horses, reindeer, etc.). This in turn made cooperation between the hunters necessary, and this supported the development of cooperative abilities (see also chapter "Biology"). Migration of the Homo sapiens along the shores of the continents followed, and only in periods of receding glaciers was it possible to inhabit northern zones and to move across the Bering Strait land bridge into the Americas. On the other hand, because there was so much water frozen in the glaciers, the sea level was much lower, which created land bridges connecting Southeast Asia with Indonesia, Australia and Papua New Guinea on the one hand and Siberia and Alaska over the Bering Strait land bridge (Witzel 2012; Wunn 2005).

The anthropologist Michael Witzel (2012) provides a detailed overview of this theory of the Homo sapiens' migration and the empirical evidence which backs this concept. The theory can be regarded as very well established in anthropology, as there are empirical findings on several levels, leading to parallel results and supporting the reconstruction of the migration routes of Homo sapiens out of Africa into the different parts of the world (see also Buss 2015). There is evidence on the following levels:

- archaeological findings
- genetic analyses
- to a certain extent, comparisons of physiognomy/physical anthropology
- comparative linguistics
- these findings go parallel with investigations in comparative mythology, which demonstrate that similarities and differences in mythological motifs as well as in whole systems of mythologies can be well explained by these routes of

migration; these findings will be presented in detail in the chapter "Mythology" (see next section)

Archaeological findings

Already in the 19th century and – intensified – in the 20th century, there have been many archaeological findings of remains of early humans, mostly bones, skulls or in some cases, only teeth, which can be traced back to the different forms and pre-forms of members of the species homo according to their anatomical features. These findings can also be dated (e.g., by making use of the so-called C-14 method) (for details, see Witzel 2012). There have been many findings which allow for a reliable and coherent reconstruction of the first occurrence of anatomically modern humans, Homo sapiens, in Africa and the migration over thousands of years of these early groups into the Near and Middle East, Asia and Europe. The spread of humans to large parts of Eurasia took place during the warm period between the second to last ice age (52,000 to 45,000 years ago) and the last one (25,000 to 15,000 years ago). The findings of human remains (bones) goes parallel with findings of stone tools as well as places of periodical settlements (fireplaces, remains of hunting, etc.). Especially the stone tools can be placed on a timescale of technological development and can thus be dated. Yet another level of archaeological findings is early rock art found in France/Spain, the Sahara, central India and Timor as well as in South Africa, New Guinea and Australia. This appearance of the first form of human art around 40,000 years ago is often connected with the development of the human capacity to symbolize and to be creative, which is called the "symbolic revolution".

There is, of course, a major problem here, as such archaeological findings must be interpreted; they do not speak by themselves. This is especially important in so far as we are interested in the present context with findings pointing to archetypes, so we are dealing here with symbolic, even spiritual, data. Many religions and rituals, for example, in Australia, use perishable materials or may even not use any materials at all which could persist. It would be even difficult for contemporary rituals to be observed (e.g., by Pygmy, San or Australian aborigines) to interpret them only by the material remains.

In general, in modern archaeology, the experts are much more cautious, compared to the earlier mentioned grand theories, in interpreting the findings. There is a good overview in Harrod (2006) which demonstrates the careful methodology applied by contemporary archaeologists. The general idea is to very carefully collect and document the findings before applying any theory or interpretation to the findings, so as to prevent the excavation from overseeing or destroying material that would speak against a certain theory. The same care is applied in the interpretation of the findings; again, the general idea is to allow the support of different theories without excluding an explanation rashly or prematurely (Witzel 2012, pp. 257–258)

It also should be noted that we can only form theories today on the base of the remains that were found. We cannot rely on the fact that what was found is representative for what has been in prehistoric times. The rule is the absence of evidence is not evidence of absence. When we go back as far as Palaeolithic times, it is also the question whether what could remain over such long periods of time tells us enough about what is really important. These limitations of archaeology have to be kept in mind when we use archaeological evidence to support or refute any contemporary theories. Nevertheless, in the present context, the most important point for our discussion of archetype theory is the fact that the migration routes of Homo sapiens over the world can be reconstructed with sufficient reliability.

Regarding the aforementioned route (Witzel 2012, pp. 245–246), of course, the most copious remains of Homo sapiens are found inside Africa, whereas only very few early artifacts and bones have been retrieved along the aforementioned exodus path along the southern shore of Asia. This is due to the fact that the sea level in that time was some 50 m lower because of the large amount of water frozen in the ice age glaciers. Since these early humans were so-called beach combers, which means they collected large amounts of their proteins in the form of seashells and other maritime foods, they stuck very close to the seashore. So it can be assumed that their remains are today covered by seawater, if they are not totally destroyed. But there have been found respective remains on one major inland route, the so-called Narmada Valley corridor, which transgresses central India from the west coast to a small strip of land that leads to the Ganges Plains near Patna. In this corridor, many ancient remains and rock art have been found, the latter supporting the aforementioned theory. Also, the arrival in Australia is well-documented by early finds and can be dated to 43,000 BCE. Papua New Guinea, which was then part of the Australian continent, was settled by 32 kya and the Solomon Islands by 28 kya. Regarding Australia, there is reliable archaeological evidence for a much later immigration from Southeast Asia by around 3000 to 1000 BCE, which is also documented by the introduction of the dingo dog. It can also be traced back by the so-called x-ray style of painting in cave paintings, which is well preserved and still executed in Northern Australia. This also speaks for very early prehistoric capacities of humans to cross the oceans by boat (see also next section for maritime contacts).

The central and northern sections of Eurasia were inhabited, as is now believed, by around 52 to 45 kya, after the end of an earlier ice age allowed settlement in these northern territories. Europe was reached via the near East, which was repeated later after the Neolithic Revolution, when agriculture was introduced into Europe from the Fertile Crescent – that is, the Levant, southern Anatolia and Mesopotamia (see next section). Northern China, Mongolia, Siberia, Korea and Japan were reached by settlements around 42 to 39 kya, as can be documented by the discovery of a Homo sapiens skeleton at Zoukoudian near Beijing. Central Asia, in contrast, was inhabited comparatively late as well from the East as from the West, probably due to harsher climates there.

Immigration into the Americas via the Bering Strait/Aleutian land bridge is now believed to have started around 20,000 BCE in three different waves. As has been pointed out earlier, these first immigrants into the Americas very quickly transgressed the whole continent and reached the southern parts of South America by around 12,500 BP, as is documented by findings at Monte Verde in Chile (Diamond 1997).

It is important to note that the last of these waves must have happened just before the breakup of the land bridge from Siberia between 11 and 7 kya. This immigration consisted of the group of Na Dene–speaking peoples (Athabascan, Navajo, Apache), which certainly brought with them Siberian types of religious ideas and practices as well as mythologies. These groups remained in the northern parts of Canada and in Alaska for thousands of years until they finally moved into the Southwest of the United States into their today known territories, probably due to climate changes, and expelled the ancient Anasazi culture from there. Still today, there are strong tensions between the descendants of this ancient culture, the Pueblo and Hopi people, and the Navajo.

> In sum, the available archaeological evidence largely agrees with that provided by genetics, linguistics, and comparative mythology. It closely follows the two geographically and ultimately climate based migration patterns of middle and upper Palaeolithic humans: first, around 65,000 BCE, an early exodus out of Africa up to Australia . . .; then, another move northward, during the interglacial period round 40,000 BCE, and into the Americas after 20,000 BCE.
>
> (Witzel 2012, p. 251)

Genetic analyses/archeogenetics

In general, there are two ways of how analyses of the genome could be used to reconstruct the genealogy of Homo sapiens. The first way is to compare the genome of contemporary living humans: all of today's living human beings share a high amount of gene sequences in their DNA, albeit minor differences. There are special sections of the genome which are known to change (mutate) faster than others. For some of the sections, the speed of change over time can also be computed (especially for the mitochondrial DNA, mtDNA). Thus, from the number of differences in these sections, the distance of different individuals or peoples from the next common ancestor can be reconstructed (via principal component analysis; for details, see Witzel 2012, pp. 207–231).

> Over the past two decades, it has become well-known that anatomically modern humans (Homo sapiens sapiens) can be traced back to a single woman in Africa who lived well over 100,000 years ago. We all share derivatives of her mitochondrial genetic features (mtDNA) . . . The date of our ultimate common female ancestor can be estimated at some 130,000 years ago. Two derivative versions of her mtDNA endured in two major types (haplogroups L1A and L1B) in Africa, while all other humans descend from the East African subgroup, L3. These people departed Africa around 65,000 BCE, crossed the then much narrower street of Aden, moved eastward along the Indian Ocean shore (the

southern route), and reached Southeast Asia and Australia within a few thousand years. Based on studies of bottlenecks in the gene pool, it is believed that initially only some 10,000 or even as few as 2000 migrants were involved. Over the next 40,000 years, these hunter gatherer and beachcombing groups continued to spread from their outposts along the shores of southern Eurasia all across the rest of the world.

(Witzel 2012, p. 210)

These analyses, for example, allow to differentiate between the general European population and some remnant populations which have been isolated during the last ice age, namely, the Basque and the Sardinians. Consequently, genetic traits can be shown that stand out against much of Europe and so do their languages and also their mythologies (or what remains of them).

The second way to make use of genome analyses in Paleohistory was recently made possible through advances in genome sequencing. For a number of years now, it has become possible to extract the DNA from prehistoric bone findings, even human remains more than 100,000 years old. From these remains, the genome could be extracted and sequenced. As was pointed out earlier, there are enough archaeological findings of human remains on the route described earlier, which makes it possible to reconstruct, by referring to the aforementioned changes in the human genome, the genetic development of Homo sapiens starting from his exodus from Africa and even before.

This approach to genome analyses is called archeogenetics. Johannes Krause, director of the research group for archeogenetics at the renowned Max-Planck-Institute for Evolutionary Anthropology in Leipzig, Germany, which was at the forefront in the scientific research in this new field, has given a comprehensive overview of the history of this research and a summary of the findings (Krause 2019). In sum, the findings of archeogenetics strongly support the aforementioned model of the spread of Homo sapiens over the world starting in East Africa. Based on comparable theoretical models about the speed of mutations in certain parts of the human genome, it was possible to reconstruct the migration routes from archaeological findings of human remains from the different parts of the world. The starting point of this Exodus around 65,000 to 60,000 years ago is supported. Since the northern part of the Eurasian continent was covered largely with ice or was in general uninhabitable until the end of the second to last ice age, immigration into Europe did not start before 40,000 years ago. It could be reconstructed that the route the immigrants took followed the Danube River from the shores of the Black Sea into Central Europe. The arrival of these modern humans in Europe goes parallel with the emergence of Palaeolithic art in the sense of cave paintings, rock art and small figurines (see next section). From these findings of artistic objects, and also from the genome analyses, it could be reconstructed that firstly, there was quite a large population in Europe at that time, and secondly, these human groups seemingly had plenty of food from hunting so that they could find time for artistic creations. The postglacial planes and forests of Central Europe were then filled with hunting game, and since these Homo sapiens hunters had high competencies in cooperation, they were able to provide lots of nutrition for their groups and tribes. These findings apply to the period between the two last glacial periods (i.e., roughly between 40,000 years and 25,000 years BCE). When the last ice age started, the European hunter gatherers had to move southward again and brought their genes back into Anatolia. This again clarifies that there was not just one direction of migration of Homo sapiens, but there were, mainly due to the climate changes, several movements forward and backward over the last tens of thousands of years. This can be reconstructed through the archeogenetic genome analyses. It is important to note because it can explain similarities in artistic objects, cave paintings and religious beliefs, such as burials, **by physical contact and cultural exchange.** After the end of the last ice age, the genetic analyses even speak for the fact that this mobility and cultural exchange was intensified. After the invention of agriculture in the Fertile Crescent and southern parts of Anatolia, this mobility brought, together with the genes of these peoples, the technology of agriculture and ceramics to central and northern Europe via the Balkan and the Danube corridor.

It was even possible to reconstruct the last common ancestor of Europeans and Americans: in the Baikal region north of Mongolia, the so-called boy of Mal'ta was found, who lived 24,000 years ago. His genome is the missing link between Europeans and the native Amerindians because both groups share the same amount of his genome. It could be reconstructed that the common ancestors of Europeans and Amerindians, the northern Eurasians, inhabited the large region in Central Asia 24,000 years ago, which includes the steppes north of the Black and the Kaspi Sea of Kazakhstan and Mongolia and moved from there to the West into Western Russia and Europe as well as to the east, to Northeastern Siberia and via the Bering Strait land bridge into the Americas. The genome of contemporary Europeans consists to a large part (c. 40%) of the genes from these northern Eurasians as well as from immigrants from the Fertile Crescent (c. 60%), which immigrated into Europe after the invention of agriculture.

Human remains from Stone Age times are often to be found together with stone tools, in some cases, even together with artistic objects or signs for burials. This allows for drawing parallels between genetic developments, migration routes and cultural developments. In general, it can be summarized that for Neolithic times (11,000 BCE until historic times), there is clear evidence for intensive exchange between human groups over large distances; for example, there are findings of ceramics and early gold products which were produced in the Fertile Crescent and were seemingly exported to the north of Europe, to the British Isles and even to Scandinavia. The same applies to East-West trade routes. But even for Palaeolithic times, there is clear evidence for trade over long distances, so for example, ornaments made from seashells from the Atlantic were found in central Germany (Trachsel 2008). There is evidence for even earlier contacts in the form of trade of early shell bead necklaces, which were found in Israel as well as in Algeria, which speak for trade contacts over large distances, at least in the north of Africa as early as 130,000 to 100,000 years ago (Diamond 1997, p. 39).

A very important consequence of the findings of archeogenetics is the insight that there are no pure human races on earth, and they may even never have existed. All human beings today share a large amount of genes, the differences are very small and even differences in physiognomy (e.g., skin colour) can be partly explained by differences in gene expression (i.e., epigenetic variations). Lastly, we are all the offspring of immigrants. This research also makes clear that to assume something as "Jewish genes" existed (which Jung still believed) is nonsense. From the viewpoint of human genetics, it has even become impossible to speak of human races. Also, the role of genes for typical human characteristics, especially mental capacities, should not be overestimated; for example, variations in intelligence are not due to genetic factors, variants of the respective genes are similarly distributed all over the world and individual differences can be well explained by differences in environmental conditions (in this case, education).

It is possible to further support the findings from genetic analyses with reference to anthropometric data in the sense of shape of the head, facial features, skin colour, etc. (Cavalli-Sforza 2001).

Comparative linguistics

In comparative linguistics, it is possible to place a certain spoken language on a scale of closeness versus distance to other languages and thus create a family or genealogical tree of the relationships and, in part, also origins of languages, a so-called cladistic pattern. Witzel (2012) provides a detailed overview of the findings of comparative linguistics, which allows for a reconstruction of the development of the languages of the world and, parallel to that, of the routes of migration of Homo sapiens. It could also be reconstructed through archeogenetic analyses that the Homo sapiens groups that left Africa around 65,000 years ago already were capable of speaking a complex language (Krause 2019) (e.g., genes for the innervation of tongue, lips and other muscles responsible for controlled modulation of the voice, as well as for the aforementioned language acquisition device). It is impossible to speak of different levels of development of contemporary languages in the sense of more primitive versus more elaborate languages since it can be demonstrated that all languages have developed over a comparable period of time from one shared predecessor, which is most probably the language of the early humans that left Africa at 65 kya. For our context, the crucial point is that these findings, which are well established in comparative linguistics, strongly supported the aforementioned account of the routes of early humans in their spread over the world. We will later see, in the section on mythology, that these language families are closely related to the families of mythologies which were reconstructed by Witzel (2012, p. 231). This, of course, has to do with the fact that myths need to be told in a certain language.

It can be summarized that the overall model of the spread of Homo sapiens from Africa around the world, the routes of migration as well as the dates of inhabitation, is very well empirically founded. Data and findings from different fields of research go parallel and support this model, as outlined in detail by Witzel (2012). This model is well established in anthropology and is supported by the leading scientists in the field (Krause 2019; Diamond 1997; Buss 2015; Cavalli-Sforza 2001; Trachsel 2008).

Prehistoric maritime contacts

There is some surprising evidence for prehistoric maritime contacts between the continents that is transoceanic contact (Witzel 2012; Mair 2006; Trachsel 2008; see also Sorenson & Johannessen 2006) – which provides even more support for the assumption of physical contacts and cultural exchange in prehistoric times.

The use of boats to travel from one coast to another across the open sea must have been practiced by humans as early as 35,000 years ago because without this, the inhabitation of Australia would not have been possible; it can even be reconstructed that from the Indonesian Isles, which are closest to the Australian continent, it was never possible to see the Australian coastline. This implies that the immigrants to Australia departed into the unknown (Diamond 1997, p. 41) – which, from my point of view, tells us a lot about the spirit of these early humans.

The inhabitation of the islands in the Pacific (Polynesia, Hawaii, Easter Islands) took place in the first, partly even in the second, millennium BCE (Witzel 2012; Diamond 1997). Early maritime – and thus, cultural – contacts are also evidenced by the introduction of certain animals and plants (for details, see Sorenson & Johannessen 2006; Witzel 2012; Diamond 1997):

1. the dingo dog was introduced into Australia by maritime contacts from India around 3,000 years ago
2. pre-Columbian spread of Polynesian chicken and of the sweet potato to South America
3. from 13th-century Hawaii, there is a traditional account of a Japanese shipwreck
4. traditional accounts by Native Americans of sightings of Japanese ships on the West Coast of North America before 1700 AD
5. Findings of antique Chinese anchor stones in California and other findings that speak for very early prehistoric Chinese transoceanic expeditions, for which there are also written reports in China (Cheng Ho)

There have been findings of European Solutrean culture types in Topper in South Carolina, Cactus Hill in Virginia and Meadow Croft in Pennsylvania, and these sites are dated to 14,250 to 15,200 BP. This raises the question of whether there were very early European immigrants – traveling over or along the then still existing ice shields covering the North Atlantic – that contributed to Northern Amerindian culture and myths (Witzel 2012).

This is a thesis strongly supported by the anthropologist and adventurer Thor Heyerdahl (1978). Already in the 1930s and 1940s, Heyerdahl argued that there had been prehistoric maritime contacts across the oceans, namely, from South

America to the islands in the Southern Pacific, as well as from Europe/North Africa to the Americas. He became famous in the attempt to support these theories by reconstructing prehistoric boats and using them in tests to cross the oceans. He succeeded: the Kon Tiki expedition with a wooden float from Peru to the Easter Islands and Polynesia and the reed boat Ra by which he travelled from Egypt along the North African coast and across the Atlantic Ocean to South America. These expeditions provided the evidence that technically, it was possible in prehistoric times to cross the oceans. Apart from these quite adventurous footings, Heyerdahl provides a large amount of highly convincing evidence for prehistoric maritime contacts and cultural influences across the oceans and between continents, namely, between ancient Mediterranean cultures and Meso and South American cultures and between Peru/Chile and Polynesia. Among this evidence are some of the already mentioned crops that apparently have been introduced into prehistoric cultures from faraway lands, namely, the sweet potato, the coconut, the squash, cotton, chili pepper and others (for details, see Heyerdahl 1978, pp. 228–237). Of the more speculative kind may be Heyerdahl's thesis that the earliest high civilizations in Mesoamerica, the Olmec, were actually immigrants from the Mediterranean. It actually is still an unsolved riddle in prehistory why the Olmec civilization appears all of a sudden on the Mexican/Caribbean coast around 1200 BC (Meggers 1975). There is clear evidence that all the later Amerindian high cultures (Maya, Aztec, Inca) are descendants from this early culture. There are surprisingly many parallels/similarities between characteristics of the Olmec culture and ancient Mediterranean cultures, namely, Egyptian, Hittite and Phoenician (especially the latter were well known for their high technical capacities in shipbuilding and navigation). The list of highly specific parallels between these two cultures contains more than 40 elements: a social hierarchy, in which the kings claim to be descendants of the sun; brother-sister incest marriage in the royal family; a striking similarity in the system of hieroglyphs of early Mexico and the Hittite culture; a habit of producing colossal statues showing the face of a bearded man, who fights a colossal snake which stands on its tail, surrounded by hieroglyphic inscriptions (and it has to be noted that Amerindians do not have beards, so the question is from where they knew this motif); a specific technology of weaving and specific weaving patterns; a singular way to tie and knot ropes; etc. (Heyerdahl 1978, pp. 87–90).

Even if one may view this theory as speculative, there is no doubt that Heyerdahl provides very convincing evidence that there has been oversea migration and trade in prehistoric times, and as soon as there is trade, there is also an exchange of cultural ideas and beliefs.

Isolationism versus diffusionism revisited

The central point about these findings for our discussion on archetype theory is the very convincing evidence, which speaks for diffusion in a broader sense and thus for physical contact and cultural exchange on a broad level for very early periods in prehistoric times. As pointed out earlier, there is evidence speaking for trade connections over large distances for periods as early as 100,000 years ago. Even if these connections may be speculative, the experts agree that at least for the upper Palaeolithic, well-established trading connections and cultural exchanges over large distances on all continents have to be taken for granted. Above all, since we are all descendants of the first human groups which left Africa about 60,000 years ago, these groups apparently had a complex language and, presumably, as a consequence, also social rules and practices as well as mythological stories. It cannot be ruled out that basic similarities between distant cultures are remnants of this common ancestry.

It certainly has to be noted that there is a much greater influence of local developments, societal, climatic and other environmental conditions as classic archetype theory usually allows to consider. Nevertheless, the evidence for the aforementioned theory of the spread of Homo sapiens over the world is so well grounded in empirical evidence that it is difficult to deny it.

For the discussion of archetype theory, this has far-reaching consequences, as it clearly speaks against the theory of isolationism and, therefore, also against Jung's assumption that similarities in culture, religion, mythologies, etc., are the result of autochthonous developments based on innate archetypes. The ideas of innate archetypes as well as of isolationist development ("autochthonous development" in Jung's terms) are based on the assumption, even the logical requirement, that any physical contacts and cultural exchange can be excluded. But as soon as there is such convincing evidence, as presented earlier for migration, physical contact and cultural exchange, this assumption can no longer be maintained. The similarities in religious ideas and practices, social patterns, mythologies, etc., then can well be explained by physical contact and cultural exchange.

It is generally assumed in research in prehistory that as soon as humans and goods migrate, so do ideas and ideologies (Trachsel 2008, p. 249). Often, the line of development or the roots of migration can be reconstructed, as in the account presented earlier. The case is more difficult if similar developments appear in different regions at the same time.

> One such case is the invention of the wheel. The idea behind it is, although ingenious, but also just functional, which is the reason why different peoples at different times could have the same idea.
>
> (Trachsel 2008, p. 249; transl. C.R.)

In this context, the famous cultural virus theory (Cullen 2000) should be named, which argues that similar to biological viruses, certain ideas or cultural elements can spread in a viral form from one person to another or from one human culture to another. This is interesting because this theory includes the three main principles of biological evolution: reproduction, which means that cultural elements are transmitted via repeated practice (e.g., in the case of rituals); variation, which means that cultural elements are not reproduced always in the same form, as they are adapted to local conditions; and selection, which means that those cultural elements are transmitted and survive which serve existential needs or improve the adaptation of humans to their environments.

This theory is also supported by the studies of Cavalli-Sforza (2001), who found that the development of mankind is based on the transmission of information through communication and learning, which applies to all the aspects of human life, including religion. She demonstrated that based on these fundamental considerations, the similarities can be explained by migration and communication processes of cultural exchange over time, which can be paralleled with genetic, linguistic and cultural findings (Cavalli-Sforza et al. 1994, 1995).

Trachsel (2008) points out that with the arrival of Homo sapiens in Europe around 40,000 years ago, cultural development goes much faster than biological development, which means that the habits and capacities humans acquire from that time are a consequence of cultural exchange and education and not of biological imprinting. This can also be seen in the considerable regional differentiation, which even speeds up with the beginning of the Neolithic and agriculture (see next section).

Religion in the palaeolithic

Based on the previous insights, we will now turn to some elements in the field of religion in the Palaeolithic, which were discussed intensively in palaeoanthropology and which are of interest for the discussion of archetype theory.

As a rule, in prehistoric research, the following archaeological findings are usually seen to be connected with cosmological ideas and beliefs (i.e., religion in the broadest sense) (Trachsel 2008, p. 226):

1. graves
2. manipulations on human remains
3. depositions
4. a special treatment of symbolic or prestige goods
5. artifacts/buildings without any obvious profane use
6. representations/buildings with astronomic references
7. figurines/representations of all kinds

Sources for understanding prehistoric beliefs around death are scarce and can only be reconstructed with a considerable amount of speculation. It seems that in prehistoric times, concepts of death included two steps. First, a non-material part had to be extracted from the physical body, which was dealt with in the first part of a funeral rite. The second part focused on the body, which was either transformed through cremation, pulverization, etc., or was brought out of sight by burial, etc. So death is a change of status in the sense of Van Gennep's (1909) rites of passage, and thus, ritual must deal with this status change. In this, grave goods have a certain function, which may include farewell, deposing of goods that have become impure through death, a signifier of status, means for the journey, an entrance fee or equipment for the other world or a signifier of status in the other world. A general insight of research in prehistory is that the forms of burials, grave goods and the characteristic of remnants show significant regional variation as well as over time, without any systematic to be detected – so they could also be seen as a kind of fashion (Wunn 2019; Trachsel 2008).

Burials

It seems that burial rites incorporating grave goods were invented by early Homo sapiens 100,000 years ago and were spread to other groups of hominids when Homo sapiens spread from Africa to the Near and Middle East. Before these "Out-of-Africa" Homo sapiens groups reached other parts of the world, no places referring to burials could be found in these regions. (Liebermann 1993, p. 163).

It can be stated that burials seem to be one of the universal practices, even though there is a great variety of how the dead body was placed, whether there was the use of grave goods or not, the postures and orientations of skeletal remains and tombs, etc. Narr (2021) provides an overview of the endless variety of burial customs but warns:

> From these facts it is not possible to infer the existence of a definite belief in souls; it is also not possible to determine the advent of such concepts from archaeological evidence. . . . it is not possible to connect particular burial customs with particular notions of the beyond, or to any other religious conceptions.
>
> (Narr 2021)

Nevertheless, this made scholars infer that when burials existed, it meant there were also ideas about a place beyond, a life after death, a soul, etc., but Taylor (2011) warns:

> these often conflate four things: i) the emergence by whatever means of religion; ii) the increasing emotional impact of death with increased intelligence (as pining becomes concrete bereavement and is then formalized by mourning); iii) specific treatment patterns for corpses, some of which may be, more or less accidentally, more archaeologically visible; iv) some belief in souls.
>
> (Taylor 2011, p. 97)

The already mentioned grand theories of the 19th and early 20th century acknowledged the fact that there was an extraordinary global diversity in indigenous religious beliefs in relation to death practices, although Van Gennep applied his tripartite model of rites of passage also to burials and the treatment of death. Taylor (2011) states that for anthropologists, internment is a puzzling phenomenon and gives a short overview over the multiple forms of burials found by archaeology: 128,000 years ago, anatomically modern humans in the near East were buried with pigs jaws and burnt flint tools; 60,000 years ago in Iraq, a Neanderthal was perhaps buried with a garland known as the grave of flowers; and 25,000 years ago, there were elaborate burials of adults and children with hundreds of drilled seashell beads and deer-antler tools. There are triple burials of women who were apparently not capable of becoming pregnant buried with two men on both sides, one of them touching her pelvis. As a consequence, anthropologists have inferred that burials in Palaeolithic times may not have been practiced with all members of a community but only with special persons, perhaps those of higher rank in the hierarchy. There is also a wide variety of practices of dealing with the dead, ranging from burial in the ground, cremation, dismemberment, etc.

> But it may be that it is often a mistake to attempt to "read" the patterns for any particular archaeological culture as reflective of a unitary religious practice.
>
> (Taylor 2011, p. 95)

In contemporary standard comprehensive overviews of prehistory, no author will miss to point to the immense diversity and global variation of forms of burials and funeral rites, which is usually interpreted as speaking for the fact of different regional developments in culture and religious practices (e.g., Trachsel 2008; Narr 2021).

Palaeolithic cave paintings and rock art

In the European upper Palaeolithic (between 40,000 and 12,000 years ago), rock art and cave paintings appear between 36,000 and 10,000 years before our time and go parallel with the appearance of Homo sapiens in Western Europe. Stone Age art in the sense of cave paintings can be found in southern France and Spain, the Sahara and Upper Egypt, but there are also equally old paintings found in the Urals (Belaya River), central India (Bhimpetka area), New Guinea, Australia and eastern and especially southern Africa, for example, in caves in Namibia dating about 27,000 years ago. Australian aboriginal rock art is primarily totemic and thus inherently different from at least European cave paintings. There have been a number of attempts to interpret this art, ranging from hunting magic, totemic signs, mythological markers, art for art's sake, shamanism, etc.

Witzel (2012) uses these findings for his argumentation on the different levels of development of mythological systems since this Palaeolithic art appears rather suddenly around 40,000 BCE, which has also been called the creative explosion, and he sees it as evidence for his theory off the development of northern or Laurasian mythology as a later and more developed form of mythological systems (see next chapter, "Mythology", for details). He criticizes older accounts (e.g., by Joseph Campbell), who argued that this explosion is first attested and would be originating from late Palaeolithic Europe.

Together with this art, the first image and sign systems appear. It can be demonstrated that already in the upper Palaeolithic in the settlements of the ice age hunters and in the caves used for settling and painting, the first mnemotechnies systems of images and symbols can be detected. It has been claimed in Jungian circles (e.g., Jung et al. 1964) that in these first sign systems, universal (i.e., "archetypal") symbols appear, for example, the spiral. In a special issue of the German scientific journal *Bild der Wissenschaft* (2013), the global findings of such symbols were presented in a map, providing evidence that there is not even one truly universal sign or symbol to be found in prehistoric caves, respectively, rock art. The sign found most often (70%) was the line. Even the most orthodox Jungian would not argue that the line is an archetype. Spirals were only found in 7% of all the places and, by far, not on all continents.

The assumed connections between cave paintings, shamanism and altered states of consciousness

It was already mentioned that there have been a number of interpretations of the meaning of Palaeolithic cave paintings, starting with the assumption that these reflect hunting magic practices and rituals.

> But this interpretation is highly speculative, and it remains uncertain what these drawings mean. It is just as difficult to decide whether or not other pictures, sculptures, abstract symbols, amulets, and similar objects were used to make magic in this and later periods.
>
> (Narr 2021)

It was already demonstrated that ideas of Palaeolithic hunting magic practices and rituals were based on poor excavation methods and misinterpretations of archaeological findings and are today rejected by scholars in palaeoanthropology. Another problematic interpretation was proposed by André Leroi-Gourhan (1964), who argued that the paintings and especially the symbols should be understood as sexual symbols, a viewpoint based on Freud's psychoanalysis – a viewpoint that has been dismissed by contemporary archaeology. The next step in the line of interpretations was to draw a connection between the cave paintings and assumed early forms of shamanism. The general idea, as presented by Lewis-Williams and Clottes (1998), was that shamanism was the characteristic and universal religion of Palaeolithic times. These prehistoric shamans used techniques of ecstasy (e.g., music and dancing but also hallucinogenic substances). These states of ecstasy, as was argued, were interindividual similar (altered states of consciousness, ASC) all over the world and thus created the experience of universal images, which were then painted on the walls of the caves, which were thought – in this model – to have been sanctuaries or ritual places for such ecstatic experiences, which is also known as the neuropsychological model.

> Crucially, it was argued that this process was hardwired into the human brain and that the types of images, or entoptic phenomena, seen in the ASC could be classified in clear stages ranging from initial vortexes and geometrics to final forms that were determined by cultural context. Thus the paintings were argued to represent not just the emergence of shamanic beliefs, but also a vital moment

of human cognitive evolution embodying the brain's ability to enter trance and invest it with cultural significance.

(Proce 2011, p. 991)

There are two major problems with this model, the reason why it is rejected by contemporary palaeoanthropologists: firstly, the assumption of a worldwide distribution of shamanism, which sees shamanism as a primal or universal religion; and secondly, the belief that there are typical, universal images hardwired into the human brain, which can be released by certain ecstatic techniques or hallucinogens.

> Lewis Williams points out that when people enter altered states there are some experiences that appear to be universal, because they result from the biology of the brain. One is the sensation of flying. Another is that of being drawn into a vortex, which is often perceived as the entrance to a tunnel that leads to another world such as an underworld. He theorizes that upper Palaeolithic peoples saw the caves in terms of such experiences. They were the entrails of the underworld. The walls of the caves were seen as a membrane between the everyday world and the world of the spirits.
>
> (Stein & Stein 2008, p. 112)

In some cases, so-called theriomorphic figures can be found in the cave paintings, which depict figures with a human body but an animal head (e.g., a bird's head or the head of a deer). In the line of argumentation mentioned earlier, these are seen as pictures of shamans conducting rituals in the caves (Lewis-Williams & Clottes 1998).

This parallelization of cave paintings with recent shamanistic traditions and practices has been strongly criticized recently (e.g., Wunn 2019) because this is based on the widespread mistake in anthropology to parallel a recent religion (e.g., that of the bushmen in southern Africa) with the religion of Palaeolithic groups, although these are separated by several thousand kilometres of distance and lived in very different natural environments: tropic savanna versus subarctic steppe. Finally, they are separated by at least 30,000 years of history of religious development.

In an overview of research on shamanism, Proce (2011) investigates the phenomenon, its distribution and the connection of contemporary forms of shamanism in indigenous peoples with Palaeolithic/prehistorical religious forms. Historical papers about shamanism, which took an ethnocentric or even racist perspective, tended to perceive shamanism as a primitivism characteristic of lower races, a viewpoint which is definitely not shared by contemporary scholars. Also, Mircea Eliade's widely used publication, *Shamanism: Archaic Techniques of Ecstasy*, first published in French in 1951, which is actually still quoted very often – also, Jung referred to it – has a number of shortcomings which are not shared any longer by contemporary scholars. Especially problematic is the focus on ecstasy, whereas in recent publications, shamanism is seen as a collection of practices deeply embedded in the social and cultural structure of the respective ethnicities. It was argued by earlier scholars, and this is in the same line as the typical Jungian argumentation, that by shamanistic practices and rituals, and especially the use of hallucinogenic substances, these would activate neuropsychological structures of the brain which then produced similar states of consciousness in prehistoric man as well as in contemporary subjects. This neglects the fact that different hallucinogenic substances produce very different states of consciousness, but more importantly, in the actual practices of shamans as they were documented in ethnographic research, it is more the ritual itself than any substances which produce ecstatic states.

The problematic focus on ecstasy, ultimately deriving, we must remember, from a work written in the 1950s, is also the primary reason why the modern, popular definitions of shamanism are so broad, extending far beyond what many anthropologists would accept.

(Proce 2011, p. 991)

Where there is some evidence for connections between prehistoric forms of religion and shamanism in general, other findings speak clearly against the – also Jungian – hypothesis that this reflects basic universal structures of the human mind/psyche. The main point is that shamanism in its precise definition (as it is used in contemporary anthropology) can be found in a defined world region, which is called the circumpolar region, broadly including the northern regions of Europe, Asia and North America:

The archaeological support for the idea of the circumpolar shamanic complex is very clear. . . . There are also more clearly quantified details. One example comes from the work of Karl Schlesier who in studying Tsistista (Cheyenne) religion has demonstrated an astonishing 108 direct parallels with features of Siberian shamanism.

(Proce 2011, p. 991)

The author points out more examples (e.g., the idea of a world pillar, which is found throughout the Arctic as well as in Northern Amerindian). This speaks for the fact that shamanism has migrated with the latest wave of immigrants from Asia over the Bering Strait land bridge into the Americas (Na Dene) and that the influences have been bidirectional. This would again support the migration hypothesis of religious ideas and practices, pointing against Jung's assumption of a biologically based universality of certain ideas.

The earlier interpretations are even more strongly criticized by the palaeontologist Paul Bahn:

Unfortunately, this entire approach proved bogus, being founded on a distortion, misuse, or misunderstanding of the term shaman and the phenomenon of shamanism; on outdated, distorted, or utterly erroneous neuropsychological data; and on highly selective and distorted data from southern Africa as rock art motifs and ethnographic testimony. The supposed three stages of trance, one of the cornerstones of this approach, and copied endlessly from author to author without the slightest effort to check their validity, only occur when one has ingested a very small range of hallucinogens, most notably LSD, and certainly has no applicability whatsoever to ice age art. The resulting obsession with trance interpretations led to some amazing claims – for example, that the supposedly mutilated hand stencils in France's Gargas cave were the result of people cutting their fingers off so that the pain might help induce altered states of consciousness. Besides, the above-mentioned careful planning of much cave art and the tremendous artistry involved in its production cry out against it being simply an accumulated record of images seen in trance. Moreover, trance – which is never clearly defined, there are over 70 kinds – is in no way a reliable indicator of true shamanism, most often in Siberia, the shaman simply pretends to enter an altered state of consciousness. One of the favourite pieces of evidence used by the proponents of the shamanic hypothesis was the therianthropes, half man/half animal figures, which they naturally saw as depicting shamans. Unfortunately, such figures are extraordinarily rare in cave art (about six are known) so they cannot possibly be seen as a representative of ice age art, let alone a key to its understanding. In any case, why should one see them as shamans rather than mythical beings, or gods, or sorcerers, or men dressed as animals, or simply creatures of the imagination?

(Bahn 2011, pp. 350–351)

This line of criticism in contemporary anthropology could be continued endlessly. Lewis-Williams was criticized heavily, for example, because of grounding his theory in a selection of only 40 out of thousands of cave paintings. Again, as already seen in the chapter on anthropology, such theories attempt to explain the endless variety of a phenomenon from Palaeolithic times with just one monolithic explanatory model, making it necessary to deny obvious contradictions and falsifications. For example, a maximum of 40% of the depicted animals have been hunting game and were edible by the Palaeolithic hunters – so it makes little sense to interpret them in the context of hunting magic. It is much more likely that these prehistoric humans, when creating art, pictured what was impressive in their natural environment, which was their world of living. So the interpretation favoured by most of the contemporary anthropologists is that the animals depicted were chosen as they symbolized strength and power, maybe life itself (Renfrew & Bahn 2004).

Another interesting finding of contemporary systematic and unprejudiced investigations: typical artistic styles characteristic of a specific time period or region can be detected in the paintings. Typical for the Gravettien, 27,000–23,000 BP, are reddish silhouettes of animals and the so-called hand negatives; both motives do not appear later.

In the Solutréen, 23,000–17,000 BP, the typical motifs are three-dimensional animals in action; reddish colour was no longer used, whereas black being a favourite. Typical for the Magdalénien, 17,000–10,000 BP, were three-dimensional black animals at rest, often with crossed legs. Such fashions speak again clearly for the hypothesis of cultural exchange. In a defined period of time, all of the paintings show the same style from Spain to Ukraine. Apparently, these early hunter gatherer groups migrated over long distances. It is known from the Inuit of Greenland and North Canada even from historic times that they travelled for thousands of kilometres just to meet other groups or relatives and have festivals (Züchner 2009).

Wunn (2005) also argues against the interpretation of cave art as being representative of hunting magic. A large percentage of the animals pictured in the paintings do not belong to the usual hunting game (e.g., lions and other large carnivores). The majority of the cave paintings do not show direct correlations with the pictured species of animals and the preferred hunting game of the respective human populations. She also points out that in the Palaeolithic cave paintings, only 4% of the paintings show humans or humanlike figures. Even these are often very schematic, and it's not clear why, as many cave paintings show high artificial capacities of the painters in picturing animals, even using perspective, etc. The abstract signs and symbols found in many caves originally were interpreted as simplified presentations of weapons, tools or cabins, but again, since the painters were able to picture animals of their environment very naturalistically, this hypothesis was given up again. What she criticizes strongly is that many early interpretations are based on the very poor quality of documentation of the findings of the cave paintings, which were often documented in the late 19th and in the first half of the 20th century. So for example, the drawings of Henri Breuil, on which many interpretations were based, are viewed from today's perspective as being strongly influenced by artistic fashions of his age and, even more problematic, also include first interpretations of the paintings. She argues that based on this poor documentation in many cases, many of the interpretations are flawed. In sum, she argues, from a contemporary point of view of anthropology and with modern careful methods of interpretation of such findings, it may not be possible to reconstruct the world of ideas of these Palaeolithic painters that are behind the cave paintings (e.g., only one of 1,000 strokes in such paintings can be interpreted with certainty). Also, the parallelization between these cave paintings and the level of cognitive development of its artists with the art and cognitive development of children is not scientifically tenable. As pointed out earlier, the Palaeolithic artists as early as 36,000 years ago (e.g., Grotte Chauvet) were able to use perspective in the presentation of different kinds of animals. She points out that the later female figurines, which were highly abstracted, are a later development, which would mean that the simpler artifacts are products of a later period. So it is not possible to draw a line from so-called primitive ways of thinking and a certain form of art connected with it to the development of thinking and artistic behaviour in contemporary children and adults (e.g., in indigenous populations). So the argumentation in many earlier theories that Palaeolithic art is the result of a generally lower or even more immature level of consciousness (which can also be found in Jung and Neumann) today is clearly refuted.

Wunn also strongly denies the interpretation that some of the abstract signs and symbols (e.g., arrows, etc.) are the product of inborn archetypal patterns in contrast. She interprets them as being the expression of acquired schemata, which were widespread in the respective world of ideas of Palaeolithic humans.

She also explicitly refers to the interpretation of pictures which mix elements of animals and humans, as for example, the famous painting from Trois Freres, as the representations of early shamans. She denies this interpretation, referring to the studies of Victor Turner (1991), who found that in contemporary indigenous peoples, such mixed forms are used (e.g., in initiation rites) to stimulate the initiands to think about the differences between humans and animals so that these paintings may best be interpreted as ways of grappling with these differences and what it is that makes one a human being.

Her general interpretation of Palaeolithic cave art is that it represents the strength, aggressiveness and power which these prehistoric humans experienced in the animals of their environment and by which they were fascinated. They are also used as symbols or signals of defence, and that could be the reason why they are used in caves, of which many were found to have been used as settlements, so the paintings would have served as a means of protection of these safe places.

Bahn (2011) summarizes the debates around the meaning of cave art with the following harsh commentary:

> All of the blanket explanations put forward so far for cave art are deeply flawed, usually bending the facts to fit the theory, grossly exaggerating the frequency of certain pet themes, or employing erroneous data on neuropsychology and ethnography. Clottes has even claimed that all decorated caves are the result of magical religious practices; but it is hard to see what can justify such a statement. Those who make such claims tend to ignore the open air rock art of the upper Palaeolithic, perhaps because it looks more secular; but we know from studies of rock art in places such as Australia that open air rock art can be just as mystical, powerful, or dangerous as anything in deep caves. Future discoveries and studies will doubtless bring new questions as well as new theories, but it is vital that the evidence be assessed soberly and objectively, without preconceptions or fantasy.
>
> (p. 351)

So for the discussion of archetype theory, it can be summarized that the contemporary state-of-the-art research in prehistoric cave paintings does not support the ideas of archetypes behind these paintings. Following Whitley, it can also be summarized that nothing speaks for the existence of a uniform primal religion:

> Rock art is often conceptualized primarily as a hunter gatherer phenomenon, hence the occasional use of the generic term cave art, implying just this association. Although hunter gatherers commonly made this art, it was also produced by agriculturalists, occasionally even in state-level societies. Given the diversity in religions that this implies, a similar wide range of variation is known for the

described origins of this art, what it symbolizes, which social and gender groups made it, and how it was used ritually -with distinctions sometimes existing even between why the art was made and how it was subsequently employed. Further complicating this circumstance, the origin, meaning, and use of rock art does not perfectly correlate with specific kinds of religious systems (such as shamanism versus totemic cults versus formal priestly religions).

(Withley 2011, p. 308)

Prehistoric female figurines and the myth of a great mother

Another important topic from palaeoanthropology, which has often been used to argue for archetype theory, namely, the existence of a universal religion of a great mother goddess, are the findings of female figurines from a large period of time covering the upper Palaeolithic as well as the Neolithic.

Small female figures, the so-called Venus statuettes, appear for the first time in the Upper Palaeolithic Period. In some cases, they are very schematically formed, and it is often difficult or impossible to recognize female attributes. In other cases, however, they are naturalistic representations of corpulent women whose secondary sexual characteristics (their breasts and buttocks) were given special prominence, though their faces, feet, and arms were almost completely neglected. Such strong emphasis on the anatomical zones that are related to the bearing of children and nourishing them easily conveys to one the idea of female fertility. Nevertheless, it is not necessarily true of all these small figures.

(Narr 2021)

An example for such universalist interpretations of the findings is the theory proposed by Helen Benigni (2013). In her book *Emergence of the Goddess*, she argues that the consistency in design of these featureless, large-breasted, often pregnant figures throughout a wide region and over a long period of time suggests they represent an archetype of a female Supreme Creator. Prehistoric humans, she argues, connected women as creators innately tied to the cycles of nature. Through this, it was believed that women's birth and menstrual cycles aligned with lunar cycles and tides.

In AP, Neumann (1949) in his history of consciousness attempts to locate its beginnings in the Stone Age cultures of the great mother goddess, the animal mistress. He draws a line to the later agricultural societies of the Neolithic era that also worshipped still fertile femininity in the mystery of the germination and growth of plants from the seeds, which these societies depended on for their existence.

Zabriskie (1990), in her paper on "The feminine", provides a good example for the classic conception in AP concerning the role of the feminine in the shape of the great mother goddess and its role in prehistory, connecting it with far-reaching assumptions about the roles of men and women, and male and female, in the history of societies:

> A Great Mother from whom the race came was imagined. . . . As human groups consolidated into tribes; tribes into cities; and cities into states, kingdoms, and empires, hierarchical structures, perceived as masculine, evolved apart from nature, which was increasingly perceived as feminine. . . . Physical size and strength and phallic, single-minded aggression were admired and idealized. . . . As male rulers and conquerors of ascendant civilizations sought to have their agendas and appetites reinforced by male gods, goddesses in many cultures lost primary status to increasingly patriarchal and domineering father gods. As the Western world evolved, the female deities of its cultural cradles and nurseries were diminished or suppressed.
>
> (pp. 268–269)

The theory that a great mother goddess was worshiped in the upper Palaeolithic and in the Neolithic, for which the female figurines were thought to be evidence, was put forward by the archaeologist Marija Gimbutas (1989). She interpreted the figurines that were found as being evidence for a universal prehistoric religion that was later destroyed by presumably Indo-Germanic tribes invading the Eastern Mediterranean and near East. This theory was strongly connected with ideas of a matriarchy, characterized by a peaceful society concentrating on fertility rites, and that the memory of this golden age was later destroyed by male historians.

The archaeologist and excavator of the famous Anatolian Neolithic site Catalhöyük, Mellart, supported such ideas with his interpretations of the figurines that were found in this Neolithic settlement. But the archaeologist Ian Hodder (2014), who continued Mellart's excavations in Catalhöyük, could not confirm these interpretations. The only enthroned goddess that was found was an isolated find and thought to be a protecting figure for a granary. Figurines that could be interpreted as a mistress of the animals were only found thousands of years later in the Bronze Age. All the other representations in the Neolithic settlement were centred around hunting and wild nature and not around agriculture or fertility (Hodder 1987). So the newest interpretations even question the role of a female goddess or great mother as being of high importance for the Neolithic agricultural societies (Goodison & Morris 1989; Hodder 2014; Fehlmann 2001). In the same line, Narr (2021) points out:

> No known direct continuum connects these earlier Palaeolithic figures to similar ones of the early Neolithic and later periods. . . . Not all female figures can, however, be understood merely as fertility symbols; rather, in many cases they are assumed to be house gods or representations of ancestors, and, especially when appearing in graves, as substitutes for the bodies of maids, wives, and concubines. An appearance of a large number of smaller figures suggests a votive or magical usage.
>
> (Narr 2021)

One interpretation came from McCoid and McDermott, who suggested that because of the way these figures are depicted, such as the large breasts and lack of feet and faces, these statues were made by women looking at their own bodies. They suggest that women during the period would not have had access to mirrors to maintain accurate proportions. This theory also provides an explanation as to why many of the Venus figures do not have faces or heads, as the creators would need mirrors to do so. However, Michael S. Bisson critiqued this theory by suggesting that alternatives, such as puddles, could have been used as mirrors (Fagan & Beck 1996).

In general, contemporary scholars are much more careful in interpreting these findings, and some are even highly critical, characterizing earlier far-reaching assumptions of a primal religion of the great mother goddess as being just fantasies without any evidence.

> Some scholars believe that early human religion centered on fertility, a lunar circle as opposed to a solar one, and the worship of a goddess. This is largely speculated and based on findings of small carvings of female figures with exaggerated characteristics thought to be connected to fertility. Although matriarchy, or rule by women, never existed in the past.
>
> (Stein & Stein 2008, pp. 210–211)

We have to be careful, as Julian Thomas (2011) points out, referring to the ideas:

> of a Great Goddess that had been developing within romantic thought during the previous century. As Hutton points out, the association of the earth with the female sublime is a thoroughly modern conception, dressed up as a rediscovered primal truth. The various elements of the Goddess theory (a central female deity presiding over a golden age of matriarchy that was eventually destroyed by patriarchal warrior bands from the North) were eventually pulled together by the classicist Jane Ellen Harrison at the start of the 20th century [who was actually quoted by Jung, CW 11, para. 197, and praised as "very instructive"; CR]. In Britain, the vision of the great goddess was championed by Jacquetta Hawks . . . As with her reliance on Jungian psychology this reveals a willingness to see Neolithic religious practices as having been underpinned by symbols and themes that remained unchanged for millennia, and which relate to fundamental human dispositions. This kind of essentialism was characteristic of its time. . . . Like Hawks and Crawford, Gimbutas tended to conflate material from over a wide geographical area, in the service of a rather grand vision. The cost of this was a degree of insensitivity to the contexts from which figurines were recovered, and the practices in which they may have been engaged. Despite these failings, Gimbutas continued to have a massive following in the eco-feminist movement, for, however flawed her methodology, the image of a peaceful matriarchal past is a deeply attractive one.
>
> (pp. 347–375)

Jung and Neumann, of course, were very much drawn to this fantasy theory, as they already favoured Bachofen (1861/2004) and his ideas about matriarchy. In the same line as Thomas, a number of contemporary scholars criticize those interpretations as being in total neglect of the context of the findings.

> There also are widespread sculptures of the erroneously so-called mother goddess. . . . Some of them are typically corpulent, and others, rather slender. As they commonly lack feet, they must have been inserted into the ground or in some other kind of pedestal or niche and would then be classified as cult objects. The interpretation as mother goddesses is, however, very much open to question.
>
> (Witzel 2012, p. 260)

Wunn (2005) takes a comparably critical stance and points to far-reaching speculations around these female figurines in earlier theories. From her point of view, these Palaeolithic figurines were depictions of individual females and not a generalized type, certainly not a goddess. She criticizes that in earlier speculations, the context of the findings was not considered. For example, in Eastern Europe, these figurines were found in the context of the houses and close to the hearth, which, from her point of view, point to the fact that they were used as protective (apotropaic) devices and guardian spirits. Interpretations as a depiction of goddesses are not justified. She also strongly criticizes early interpretations as being quickly inserted as interpretation of these figurines being goddesses, without considering alternatives. Even for the Neolithic cultures in Anatolia and the Fertile Crescent, she denies the existence of a ruler or lady of the animals (which, for example, Neumann stresses in his account of mythology), as she questions the existence of such a clearly developed form of religion and the existence of defined gods and goddesses in such an unstratified society. At best, it can be assumed that these figurines in the Anatolia Neolithic were seen as depictions of a primal mother in the sense of a far ancestor, which was worshipped.

In the same way, Lauren Talalay (1993) is critical of such interpretations: "While most of the interpretations are provocative, many are simplistic, ignoring the profound social and, perhaps, political complexities that likely motivated the manufacture of figurines in early, nonliterate societies" (p. 37). They may be idols and may have had the function of religious sacrifices but could also have been just toys for children.

In Hacilar, in Anatolia, a figurine was found which shows the meeting of a female and a male, which was quickly interpreted as being a representation of the hieros gamos (holy marriage). Wunn (2005) takes this as a good example for carelessness in the interpretation of such archaeological findings. In a more detailed investigation, it was found that both figures wore clothes, which would exclude the interpretation of holy marriage.

It can be summarized that the interpretations of the female figurines that were found, and that stem from various periods of time ranging from the middle Palaeolithic to the Neolithic, range from being evidence of the universal cult of the great mother goddess on one end to just being toys for children on the other end. These interpretations were often closely connected with far-reaching speculations about matriarchy, which all contemporary historians argue has never existed in reality (von Schaik & Michel 2020). Even if there were cults of a female goddess, this does not necessarily mean that there was also a political rule of women. It also has to be noted that these figurines were found in a territory from the Pyrenees to the Ural, covering a period of more than 20,000 years; that they were found in very different contexts (e.g., graves, houses, garbage holes, etc.); and that these female figurines present only 3% of all the representations of humans and animals from the Palaeolithic and Neolithic that were found. Also, the interpretation as speaking for the existence of fertility cults is problematic since in hunter gatherer societies, a high fertility is not welcome because it may lead to problems in providing enough food for the group. For Neolithic societies which use mainly agriculture to provide their nutrition, there is certainly a connection to fertility cults, but the fertility refers to the crops and not to humans. There are figurines which are interpreted as being connected with pregnancy, childbirth, etc.; these were probably worn as amulets and served the function of protecting the mother-to-be. It also has to be noted that in the large Neolithic temple site Göbekli Tepe, which is considered the first religious temple of mankind, not even one female figurine was found.

The Neolithic

Conditions for the life of humans changed considerably at the end of the ice ages. Larger areas of Europe and Asia were inhabitable. For the late hunter gatherer societies, this seems to have been a platitude of game to hunt. In the region of the Fertile Crescent, which is today the southeastern part of Turkey/Anatolia, Syria and the eastern coast of the Mediterranean (Levant) as well as what is known as Mesopotamia, which is mainly today's Iraq and parts of Iran, the conditions were so comfortable that hunter gatherers societies started building the first temples, which were excavated in the last two decades, namely, Catal Hüyük and Göbekli Tepe (Schmidt 2016).

In this region, agriculture was invented (Lewin 2009); it can be demonstrated empirically that the original wild forms of the culturalized crops known today together with the wild forms of today's domestic animals have their origin in this region, which speaks for the fact that agriculture was invented here and not independently but simultaneously at different places in Europe, Western Asia, etc. (Schmidt 2016). Even the hill is known on which the originally wild form of wheat, as it is known today, was found: "In 1997 the wild wheat still growing on the Karacadag (in Anatolia close to Göbekli Tepe) was identified as being the closest known genetic relative of modern domestic wheat" (Mithen 2003, p. 67). From this region of the Fertile Crescent, agriculture together with the whole culture of the Neolithic and its religious ideas wandered into Europe, Asia and into the north of Africa (Lichter 2005; Witzel 2012). Other scholars (Trachsel 2008) point to the fact that rice was domesticated from several forms of wild rice at different places in

Asia almost at the same time – that is, independently in China, India, etc. The same applies to the cultivation of corn in the Americas. So what was said earlier applies mainly to Europe and Western Asia as well as North Africa.

The main finding for the discussion of archetype theory is the insight that, once agriculture had developed, it quickly spread from there together with other technologies and religious ideas and social practices (e.g., hierarchies), which has been called the "Neolithic package" (Trachsel 2008). This Neolithic package – first identified by Gordon Childe (1958) – included, apart from the technologies of agriculture and herding of domesticated animals, ceramics; architecture of settlements; and specified religious beliefs, namely, the cult of a great mother goddess (Mithen 2003). This cult centres around cycles of life, death and renewal, the seasons, etc., because agricultural societies are dependent on these cycles and deal a lot with the right time for the sowing of seeds ("burial of the dead body") which "die" in the ground, but miraculously, their life is renewed in spring (see, for example, the Demeter cult and the mysteries of Eleusis). It should be noted that, contrary to Jung's and Neumann's statements, the idea of a great mother goddess is not universal but restricted to those territories which received the Neolithic package originating in the Fertile Crescent, so it can only be found in agricultural societies in Europe, Western Asia and North Africa, which were influenced by the near East cultures (Witzel 2012). The same applies to the idea of rebirth – according to Jung, a universal archetype – which is closely connected with the mythological structures around the idea of the great mother goddess (i.e., ideas of a cycle of death and renewal). These can only be found in Neolithic cultures influenced by the Fertile Crescent and later spread with the missionary activity of Buddhist monks along the Silk Road to other parts of Asia and as far as Korea and Japan.

There is more evidence for the close connection between agriculture and the mother goddess: the Neolithic temple at Göbekli Tepe in the foothills of the Southern Anatolian highlands. This first Temple of mankind, built in a period starting 12,000 to 9,000 years ago, before the invention of agriculture, contained images of a number of animals – among them foxes, bulls, snakes, spiders, birds, lions and wild boars – but no mother goddess, not even one female. There are only male figures. Some of them bear irrigated phalluses, which reminds us of the apotropaic figurines and symbols of the upper Palaeolithic. Therefore, palaeontologists (Schmidt 2016; Wunn 2005) interpret these images of animals on the temple walls, again, as guardian figures protecting the place from evil powers, etc. Since the constructers of the temple were still hunter gatherers, the imagery provides evidence that the cult of a mother goddess is initiated with the invention of agriculture. This would also clearly speak against the assumption of an archetypal nature of the great mother, as it can be demonstrated how closely connected this belief is with the conditions of an agricultural society, and it, therefore, is not to be found in hunter gatherer societies (Mithen 2003).

The reason for the quick spread of agriculture and its associated practices could be that agricultural societies grew faster and needed new territories but also that the quality of living improved so much through agriculture that hunter gatherer groups that came in contact with these technologies quickly changed to this new form of existence. Also, climate changes played some role (for details, see Narr 2021; Diamond 1997). Whatever the reason, we have to note that as soon as a society has taken over agriculture and its technologies, it can be found that the societies have intensive social and political contacts with neighbouring societies and also with regions far away via trade.

These trade connections and activities were intensified after the invention of metallurgy, as tools from metal were so immensely effective, and on the other hand, the technology to produce metal was quite elaborate (Trachsel 2008). There is even some evidence pointing to the fact that in a territory including the whole of Europe, Western Russia, Anatolia and the near East, there was a standard measure for cast ingots made of bronze. These standard casts were found all over that territory, and it is assumed that since metal does not decay, they were used as a standardized currency, which also allowed for an accumulation of property as a result from successful agriculture (Trachsel 2008, p. 66). The intensification of long-distance trade connections also applies to the trade of salt (e.g., Hallstatt culture) and amber; there are also signs for a veritable ceramics industry with an intensive export economy. In burial mounds of the local elite of that time, so-called "Fürstengräber" (princes' tombs) (e.g., in Ukraine but even as far away as in Sweden) imported ceramics from Greece as well as gold jewellery from the Mediterranean can be found.

This is interesting for a discussion of archetype theory. In so far as if there are trade connections, it can be assumed that this was accompanied by an exchange of ideas and practices. On the background of these insights, it has to be assumed that cultural exchange between the near East, the Mediterranean, the rest of Europe, the north of Africa as well as way into Asia was established as early as 8,000 years ago, which makes it almost impossible to argue for an isolationist position, as Jung does.

As a result of the Neolithic Revolution about 6,500 years ago, the first civilizations developed, and in contrast to the pre-Neolithic nomadic societies, these now developed hierarchies of gods, whereas it is assumed that non-sedentary societies do not have polytheism since these pantheons mirror the hierarchical structure of societies (Narr 2021).

Summary on religion in the Stone Age

Wunn (2005, 2019), in her detailed overviews of archaeological findings and the different interpretations around prehistoric religion, pledges for a very careful approach to these matters. She concludes that, to the present point, it may not be possible to reconstruct the religious world of these prehistoric human populations, if they even had religion at all – of the latter, we cannot be sure. There are many alternative interpretations for the findings presented earlier. She is, therefore, in general, very critical of earlier accounts such as those of Tylor (1871) or Eliade (1954, 1959, 1964). This applies to the following constructs, theories and interpretations:

The assumption of widespread **cannibalistic practices** in the Palaeolithic were found to be misinterpretations and could not be verified with the findings, but were the product of preconceptions. The same applies to the assumptions of **hunting magic** practices, which did not withstand critical follow-up examinations. There is absolutely no archaeological evidence which could justify these interpretations. The assumed sacrifices in the aftermath of hunting are mere speculation and can even not be found in contemporary hunter gatherers as for example the San bushman of the Kalahari or the pygmies in the Congo. **Palaeolithic cave paintings** are understood as a form of action art, by which the prehistoric humans attempted to understand their environment. Therefore, they tried to paint those beings, mainly animals, in their surrounding environment which impressed them most. It is probably the same with the **female figurines**: Wunn argues that in the beginning these depictions were representations of individual women and only later became more abstracted, and were used for protective purposes. She is very critical of the interpretation which sees these female figurines as expressions of a Palaeolithic great goddess or mother goddess, as she argues that such developed forms of religion in the sense of a Pantheon or individual gods and goddesses did not exist in that time. This would only start with the Mesolithic, where sculptures can be found of the vulva presenting or heraldic female (e.g., Catal Hüyük). They can be seen as a continuation of depictions from the upper Palaeolithic which served the function of protection (apotropaic). These presentations clearly can be interpreted as expressions of a cult of a primal mother or female goddess. But again, and in contrast to typical Jungian interpretations, it can be demonstrated that this cult of a female goddess initiated in Anatolia and spread from there, together with the technology of agriculture, to Europe, into Asia and partly into North Africa. It has to be noted, also in contrast to Neumann's assumptions, that the cult of the mother goddess is neither universal nor pan-human but restricted to those regions in Europe and Asia (and partly North America) that were influenced by the religious ideas and technology initiated in Anatolia and the Fertile Crescent. So, already in Anatolia, not only a mistress of the animals can be found, but also a lord of the animals. So, it is not fully clear, whether the female goddess had a position of primacy. It can even be generally said that the Neolithic religion developed in the Fertile Crescent and from there spread into those regions and territories which also took over the new technology of agriculture – and in those territories which remained to be hunter gatherer societies no signs for this developed Neolithic religion can be found. It also has to be pointed out that, even where the Neolithic religion was taken over, it was partly strongly adapted to regional practices and ideas, as can be seen for the different consecutive cultures in Europe which can be identified by their ceramics (Linienbandkeramik, Glockenbecherkultur etc.), some of which can clearly be differentiated from the Anatolia Neolithic. From a certain point on, the European cultures also developed their own original forms of cults/religious practices, as can be seen in the megalithic culture which originated in the West of Europe (Brittany etc.).

With the Neolithic culture of Stichbandkeramik in Central and Western Europe, the first **megalithic structures and stone circles** can be found. It has to be noted that megalithic structures can be found only in Europe and the near East. These stone circles are oriented along the cardinal points and other important astronomical data in the course of a year, the most important of which is the winter solstice. But these astronomical points are not the main focus or use of the stone circles, as has been argued in a number of dubious publications, some of which even assumed that the stone circles and other megalithic structures were something as early astronomical centres (Burl 1999). In contrast to this assumption, contemporary archaeologists assume that the stone circles were mainly burial grounds, and the astronomical orientation points were used as a calendar serving the aim of memorizing the dead.

> It surely would be a mistake, however, to look for a uniform interpretation of all megalithic monuments or even to speak of a distinct megalithic religion. The megalithic monuments are rather to be understood as a complex of grandiose manifestations of ideas that could well have been diverse, but among which the cult of the dead, nevertheless, played an important role.
>
> (Narr 2021)

Apart from this important religious function, they were also used as a calendar for important agricultural data, such as when to sow the seeds. Another important function certainly was to mark territorial claims (which became especially important in Neolithic times with the first agricultural societies); therefore, the structures are often to be found on hilltops, where they could be seen from afar. This is also the reason why the structures had to be gigantic, so to present the strength and power of the building group. There is also an interesting economical interpretation of why at a certain point in the Neolithic, these megalithic cultures suddenly emerge: after a few thousand years of agriculture, the soil had become impoverished, which led to a situation of food deprivation, making it even more important to mark the claims on certain territories.

In some of these megalithic graves, rock carvings of menacing eyes were found, which by contemporary anthropologists of religion are connected with the aforementioned mother goddess of the Fertile Crescent, which in Central and Western Europe took over the role of a goddess of the underworld. The menacing eyes have the function to protect the buried from evil influences. The same applies to representations of necklaces or pairs of female breasts. This goddess of the dolmen, a goddess of the underworld, also had the function of a goddess of fertility, which reflects the close connection of death and life which was already present in the figurines from the Fertile Crescent. A remainder of this early goddess is the goddess Demeter of Greek antiquity, which also connects these two qualities and is thus a goddess of agriculture. Beyond these obvious functions, we are not in a position today to be able to reconstruct the religious beliefs and mythological stories which were certainly connected with these megalithic structures.

Again, there are considerable regional differences, as for example, the early mother goddess in Eastern European Neolithic cultures does not develop into a goddess of the underworld but becomes a protector of the home and the hearth. There is also a different development on the islands of Malta due to their geographical isolation. These islands were populated around 6000 BCE by settlers from Sicily/Sardinia, who brought, together with the technology of agriculture, the religious beliefs and practices which can also be found in Anatolia. Initially, the Maltesians continued the religious practices which they brought along, mainly funerals and connected rituals, together with the belief of a goddess of the underworld. Starting from these practices, the people on these islands developed a very complex religion around a death and temple cult, building large stone temples with megalithic structures, which served as a place for collective burials and a highly developed ancestor cult. Speculations about astronomical functions of these temples could not be confirmed.

It is clear that very early, there were **burials**, but again, it is not necessary to assume that they were connected with religious beliefs. Prehistoric humans certainly have realized very quickly that the remains of dead humans were quickly attacked by scavengers and other animals. So it may have been the case that they were just mourning their loved ones and relatives and tried to protect them from being torn apart by animals; thus, the burials may have just had the function to protect the dead body. It could also be the case that burials were a consequence of practices to support the mourning process. But it is also quite reasonable to assume that from a certain point on the burials served a religious function and were connected with beliefs about a life after death or a world beyond. This again may have served the function to make the reality of death acceptable. This religious dimension of the burials becomes quite clear in the upper Palaeolithic, where there can be found more complicated ways of burying the dead, of keeping up the memory of the ancestors, partly even findings of tools, weapons, etc., in the graves which point to the idea of a world beyond, to which the deceased go. These practices increase in the Mesolithic (ca. 12,000 BCE). Now burial grounds can be found, and in some graves, dogs are buried with their owners. In the Mesolithic settlements that were found in Anatolia (e.g., Catal Hüyük), the dead were buried beneath the ground of the houses, which again shows the need for staying close to the deceased. Here, first signs of rituals can be found, which increase in the transition to the Neolithic. In Anatolia and in other places now, remains can be found which point to a practice of preserving the skulls of the dead (probably as the location of the mental power), which were cleaned from the flesh, separated from the rest of the remains and, in some cases, were resurrected and worshipped as representations of the ancestors. But it also has to be noted that even in the Neolithic, there are findings of practices which point to a mere disposal of the remains of the dead into garbage pits. It is, therefore, questionable whether all of the human populations in the Neolithic had ritual burials and the connected ideas of a life after death. Also, there are many regional differences. Wunn summarizes:

> This development of religion did in no way develop from the primitive to the elaborate, from the simple to the complex. Instead, our cultural ancestors took a certain way in terms of religion and beliefs of a beyond with their care around the fate of the dead, which for the following thousands of years dominated religious beliefs. . . . From this care for the dead and the associated ideas about transcendent beings the whole variety of prehistoric religions developed, on which the religions in historic times have built.
>
> (p. 465; transl. C.R.)

The overview presented by Wunn clearly shows that in some cases, there is a clear historical continuity in the sense of cultural transmission of certain patterns (e.g., the belief in a primal mother, which developed into a mother goddess and goddess of the underworld), whereas in other cases, there is a sequence of clearly unrelated practices, which develop seemingly out of nothing and vanish again (e.g., funeral practices). In Europe alone, there is a great variety of forms of burials: deposition in the garbage, individual burials versus collective burials, burials in the ground, below the houses and in specialized burial grounds and graveyards. There are graves with the bodies lying stretched out, alone, a man with two women on both sides, with dogs, horses, weapons, ceramics, ships or without anything, in an embryo position, sitting, in the squat, in caves, in temples, etc. – in short: an endless variety. There is definitely no evidence speaking for the manifestation of any kind of archetypes which manifest autonomously and in isolation again and again.

Very much in the same line, Narr (2021) summarizes these insights in the following conclusion, which again sheds a light on the equation of prehistoric humans and their practices with contemporary "primitives":

> Religion is always closely related to other realms of life, such as economic activities. These relations are partly direct and partly mediated by social forms. The latter are, on the one hand, at least partially dependent on economic conditions; on the other hand, social structures influence the formation of religious phenomena and often serve as models for their elaboration. . . . It is inconceivable, for example, that the religious conception of simple hunters and gatherers included an elaborately organized hierarchy of gods with detailed division of labour between the individual figures. Similarly, it is a mistake to attribute to hunters and gatherers conceptions that are bound up with agriculture and the fertility of fields. . . . In fully agrarian cultures, on the other hand, ideas about the fertility of fields and cultivated plants play an important part; they are connected with other notions about fertility and influence other spheres of life.

A study of very simple hunters and gatherers of recent times shows that several religious conceptions generally considered to be especially "primitive" (e.g., fetishism) hardly play an important part, but rather that, among other things, the supposedly "advanced" conception of a personal creator and pre-server of the world does play an important part.

(Narr 2021)

Conclusions

As far as archetype theory is concerned, from these descriptions and insights, the following conclusions can be inferred:

1. Jung parallels historically early forms of religion, rituals, social practices, etc., with forms found in so-called primitive cultures of recent times. This conclusion is refuted in contemporary prehistoric sciences since recent primitive cultures apparently have much more complex religious belief systems and practices. As a result of these changes in the viewpoint of archaeology and prehistory, the term primitive is not used recently for present-day hunter gatherer societies.
2. As the previous descriptions and insights point out clearly, the ideas and imagery of early religious forms is closely connected with the environmental, social and economic conditions of these early human groups. So for example, the idea of death and rebirth only comes up in agricultural societies of the Neolithic, which is, of course, connected with their experience of "burying" the seed which is paralleled with its death and its rebirth at the beginning of vegetation.
3. **There is no such thing as a primal religion.** Early forms of religion and reli-gious practices (e.g., in the sense of burials) can be found as early as 70,000 years BCE, maybe even earlier – although findings of burials do not necessarily imply religion, as was pointed out earlier. As we know from archeogenetic research, since that time, Homo sapiens has migrated, starting from Africa, practically all over the world. So the most plausible explanation for similarities in early forms of religion is the theory of diffusion. On the other hand, Jung's idea of "autoch-thonous development" of such ideas in different places of the world stemming from archetypal structures being rooted in biology/genetics is not only not plau-sible, it is also not necessary since the first explanation is sufficient and can well explain similarities where they can be found. This refers to the principle of economical explanations in the sciences (also known as "Ockham's razor"): if there are alternative or competing explanations, the most economical one should be favoured (i.e., the one which has the fewest prerequisites or makes the fewest assumptions). Since the evidence for the Out-of-Africa hypothesis (i.e., migration and diffusion) is so overwhelming and contemporary insights in all of the aforementioned fields of knowledge (biology, anthropology, etc.) clearly speak against Jung's assumptions, the choice to be made here is quite clear. Even more than that, the migration of certain ideas and beliefs in the field of religion, namely, the cult of a great mother goddess and of rebirth – both of

which are clearly not universal or pan-human, which means not archetypal in Jung's sense – can be reconstructed in detail from their origins in the Fertile Crescent to all of the other parts of the world where they could be found. These migrations of ideas can be reconstructed in much more detail for mythologies, which will be the topic of the following chapter.

Note

1   The summary and conclusions of studies in prehistory presented here were confirmed by interview with Prof. Dr. Brigitte Röder, Professor of Pre- and Early History, University of Basel/Switzerland.

Chapter 9

Mythology

The controversy of isolationism versus diffusionism starting in the 19th century initially centred not so much on religious ideas and social practices but on the striking similarities found in mythologies from all over the world (for striking examples, see Witzel 2012, pp. 2–9, who also provides a definition of myth as a narrative). The majority of the fairy tales found throughout the world can be arranged into just about 100 categories, and for each type, examples can be found from completely different parts of the world (Aarne & Thompson 1961; Üther 2011).

In the 19th century, there was a prominent school in anthropology which assumed a close link between myth and ritual. This was also called functionalist school and saw myths as a justification for beliefs, customs or social institutions, which are, therefore, closely related to social needs and are used to stabilize patterns of local society.

In ethnology, striking similarities in the narrative motifs of ethnic groups living far apart from each other had been apparent for a long time and, from 1880, set into motion a decade-long debate about how this convergence of ideas in fairy tales and myths could be explained (Eisenstädter 1912), which was already referred to as the isolationism versus diffusionism debate. A large-scale collection of individual motifs of which myths are built was investigated by Stith Thompson already in the 1930s (Aarne & Thompson 1961), although he was later criticized for a heavy bias towards Europe, the near East, Asia and the Americas, neglecting sub-Saharan Africa, New Guinea and Australia (Witzel 2012).

The outstanding proponent of isolationism was the theory of elementary thoughts, "Völkergedanken" (Bastian 1881) which stated that the mythological convergence expresses the psychological homogeneity of all people.

> From all sides, from all continents, we encounter in similar conditions a homogenous human thought, an iron necessity of how the plant forms cell ducts or milk vessels depending on the phases of growth, drives out leaves, sets knots, flowers unfold. The fir of the north is different under climatic or local variations, the palm of the tropics is different, but nevertheless the same growth law is present in both.
>
> (ibid. p. 14; transl. C.R.)

DOI: 10.4324/9781003348191-9

This quote also demonstrates the deeply evolutionist viewpoint inherent in isolationism. This general idea that the similarities in mythologies go back to universal innate characteristics of the human psyche, and therefore, similar motifs and ideas develop independently and autochthonously, were repeated again and again in the 19th century (Witzel 2012). It was precisely these thoughts, which were extremely popular in the scientific world in 1900, that Jung incorporated into psychology with his theory of archetypes.

The aforementioned Stith Thompson and his school supported the diffusion theory in so far as they argued that motifs and tale types with the same motifs arranged in the same order spread from a common centre. So for example, myths from North American Amerindians have strong similarities with those of Siberia and northern Europe, and this can be explained through physical contact over the Bering Strait land bridge that existed until around 11,000 years ago. In the same manner, the Russian anthropologist Yuri Berezkin (2005) has collected motifs from all over the world and presented them in a large number of maps, which allows for the investigation of the spread of single motifs (e.g., from North and Central Asia to the Americas) (Witzel 2012). The classical form of diffusion theory goes back to the German anthropologist and Africa specialist L. Frobenius (1904; quoted by Jung at least 50 times in his works, while he apparently ignored that this was the counter position to his own), who argued that the worldwide similarities have spread via diffusion from the great ancient civilizations, meaning mainly those of European and near East antiquity. The theory became even more popular through his famous student H. Baumann (1936), who assumed a "world myth" that existed around 3000 BCE, which he located in some archaic high cultures between the Nile and the Indus; this world myth then spread from the centre to Iceland, China and Peru. It is important to note that from this time on, diffusion theory specifically meant a worldwide distribution of myths in the form of a gradual dispersal from a known or assumed centre. The problem is that this theory was not very difficult to be refuted since it was not possible to identify such a centre of all mythologies. In the course of this debate, the more general idea of diffusion, which means a cultural transferral via physical contact or migration, without arguing for a cultural centre of these ideas, was rejected together with the classical form of diffusion theory.

Related to Jung's ideas is Joseph Campbell's (1971) approach, who argued in a similar fashion with biological/cognitive similarities which lead to similar motifs in mythologies. Problematic in this approach is the distinction Campbell makes between reasoned classical ancient near Eastern and European mythologies opposed to primitive mythologies of peoples in sub-Saharan Africa – again, the general idea that in contemporary indigenous people, there is a primitive mode of thinking and living preserved comparable to that of Stone Age times. Witzel (2012) criticizes this assumption:

> It assumes that certain ethnic groups of modern Homo sapiens lived or still are living at different levels of consciousness! But all anatomically modern humans can look back to some 130,000 years of psychic and religious development. . . .

> In sum, it is not different levels of consciousness but the physical and social environment as well as the position and importance of local spiritual leaders that condition local systems of mythologies.
>
> (pp. 14–15)

Another important approach to the similarities in mythologies is that of Claude Levi-Strauss (1976), who argued with his central concept of binary structures, which are used by all peoples in the world to structure their experience of the world. Levi-Strauss was very sceptical of explanations referring to historical developments but instead stressed the tendency to organize human experience in binary sets of opposites which appear in many societies. This organization into binary opposites is used for the purpose of understanding the world and explaining its origin and its condition. This allows for the typical structuralist method of analysis which is applicable to all myths and texts. The structures are inherent in humans and their languages, comparable to the features of language as they are seen in the works of the structuralist Noam Chomsky (1978), so that myths think themselves without human awareness. Levi-Strauss was convinced that the binary tendency reflected our bicameral mind, a viewpoint that is strongly criticized by Witzel (2012), who stresses the point that the structures are the choice of the societies involved, and these affect local social structures. Levi-Strauss was also criticized because his theories dealt mainly with Amerindian mythologies, which restricted the possible pool for comparisons.

> In sum, both currently fashionable explanations cannot explain the extraordinary amount of global similarities and congruencies of myth, whether such explanations supposed diffusion (Frobenius, Baumann, S. Thompson), psychic archetypes (Jung, Campbell), or bare-bone, binary structures of mental arrangements (Lévi-Strauss). Such continuities are found in large areas of the world, but they are neither thinly distributed nor found on all continents.
>
> (Witzel 2012, p. 15)

Predecessors of Jung's thinking on mythology can be found especially in the work of Edward B. Tylor (1871) on primitive religion. Tylor was fascinated by the correspondences between mythologies from all over the world. He first developed the idea that these similarities can be explained by the identical structure of human consciousness and the human mind in general, which under similar conditions produces the similarities. On the other hand, Tylor did not exclude the possibility of diffusion as an explanation for the similarities. Tylor systematically investigated similarities in myths from all over the world and assumed that they are based on a commonly shared stock of motifs, which have developed over time in the course of the development of human society. One of these motifs are the so-called nature myths, which, following Tylor, are the result of an infantile, immature mind which attempts to find explanations for natural phenomena, such as thunder. The childish, immature mind tends to personify and anthropomorphize these phenomena, thus producing the idea of a thunder god. In general, the result of these human tendencies is animism.

This theory and the general approach behind it have been strongly criticized by contemporary scholars of religious studies. The problem is that the theory, which then leads to a classification of objects (here, myths), is first, and the empirical findings are squeezed into that schema. A second problem is that inherent in the classification scheme are value judgments, which are not reflected. These earlier theorists did not reflect the fact that every classification depends on a theory. In Tylor's case, he did not reflect that his classification is based on the idea of a progressive cultural development, which leads to a certain way of classification. This classification, in return, can then not provide evidence for the existence of such a development. This is a mistake which has been repeated by many of Tylor's followers in the 19th and early 20th century (Wunn 2019). It has to be noted, though, that Tylor did not make one mistake which Jung has fallen to. He clearly separates the evolution of religion and religious ideas, including myths, from the biological evolution of man.

So the crucial question is that of the evolving unit (i.e., What is it that evolves?) (see also chapter on religion). Here is an example for this viewpoint from contemporary anthropologists of religion:

> Oral myths often exist in multiple versions, sometimes corresponding to different interests of different narrators (for example, different groups laying claim to the same land). Myths may also change to account for new circumstances or events. Gregory Bateson gave an example from Bali of the development of a new myth that blended several previous stories. The new myth linked certain gods as siblings in order to provide a regional basis for different sociopolitical groups coming together.
>
> (Stein & Stein 2008, p. 38)

The authors also provide an example taken from Polynesia, where a new element that was brought with the colonizers from Europe – metal – was included into a pre-existing myth, providing evidence for the fact that even in traditional societies, mythologies can change according to changes in the environment (Stein & Stein 2008, p. 38).

So Jung, as has been pointed out earlier, did not only fall to the epistemological mistake of Tylor but even to further mistakes. Jung himself did not systematically investigate mythologies, as was already demonstrated with the example of Jung's classic *Symbols of Transformation* (CW 5) in which he draws parallels between the psychopathological development of a female patient, based on her notebooks, and mythological motifs, in this case mainly the myth of the hero's journey. The unsystematic way of his researching in this work has been strongly criticized by a number of scholars. Homans (1979, p. 66) clearly demonstrates that in this text, Jung has produced a report of his own fantasies rather than a systematic interpretation of myths and symbols.

Jung himself did not provide a systematic analysis and overview of mythology as a whole and of the similarities and congruencies in the mythologies and mythological motifs from different parts of the world. This was left to his follower Erich Neumann (1949), who first put together an overview of mythologies of the world and interpreted them in line with Jung's psychology. Jung seemingly very much approved of this work, as can be seen in his foreword to the first publication, where he clearly states that Neumann created the work he himself did not succeed to undertake in his lifetime. The general idea in this work, in line with Jung's general thinking about archetypes, is that biologically rooted archetypes are behind the myths and mythological motifs, which, therefore, can be found all over the world, and, importantly, that these mythological stories and images reflect the phylogenetic as well as the ontogenetic development of the human mind and consciousness. The general development goes from a primal unconscious, which is equated with the great mother or the female sublime, out of which consciousness slowly emerges, which is mainly pictured by the journey of the hero. The whole interpretation is intriguing, and this work has gained major importance in AP and has also received respect from scholars outside of AP. Nevertheless, there is also massive criticism, which is summarized by Bischof (1996).

Bischof accuses Neumann of being only a little more systematic than Jung in his analysis, but what is even more problematic, he provides evidence that Neumann intentionally left out material which did not fit into his scheme of interpretation. More fundamentally, he criticizes that Neumann – and also Jung – are epistemologically naïve (pp. 193–196). In Neumann's interpretation, there is the unreflected claim that myth owns transcendental objectivity. The next major problem is that Neumann – with Jung – assumes that the cosmogonies described in mythology which explain the origin of the world and its development reflect the historical development of human consciousness from prehistoric times and, parallel, the individual development of consciousness in human development from childhood to adulthood. This, of course, follows the well-known pattern of equating phylogeny with ontogeny. Bischof argues that this is not only epistemologically naïve but it has also been, for a long time, empirically refuted in ethnological research. He points out that Neumann's basic interpretation schemas are heavily influenced by Bachofen's (1861/2004) romantic philosophy which assumes a prehistoric matriarchy which has been destroyed by patriarchal societies. Bischof plainly condemns this as nonsense – like the mainstream of contemporary anthropology (see chapter "Prehistory"). He accuses Neumann of producing fantasies more than solid research. If Neumann had referred to solid research and the state-of-the-art in anthropology and comparative mythology, he would have realized that there is absolutely no evidence which could justify such interpretations. Bischof himself then undertakes a comprehensive interpretation of the world's mythologies as reflecting individual psychological development, which actually has some parallels to Jung's and Neumann's thoughts but is much more systematically grounded in anthropological research.

Nevertheless: Universal motifs

It was already pointed out earlier, in the section about the grand theories of the 19th and early 20th century, that theories from that time attempted to find the origin of all myths, an approach which contemporary anthropology has discarded. Nevertheless, it has to be noted that there are striking similarities in the story plots of myths coming from very different parts of the world. For example, in myths of origin, a common element is the birth metaphor. In the case of a female creating power, this is often pictured as a spontaneous and independent birth, whereas in male creators, the birth is more symbolic (e.g., the god vomits or sacrifices parts of his own body). Contemporary accounts of such similarities usually refer to the process of diffusion, and it can actually be demonstrated that certain culture areas shared narrative elements. An example is the idea of the primordial egg as an element in creation stories in Asia. In contrast to this motif, common throughout North America is the motif of the emergence, in which the earth slowly develops through layers of dark, chaos, etc. (Witzel 2012; Stein & Stein 2008).

Another widespread motif are myths about a primordial flood; this is often explained in contemporary anthropology as a result of the real experience of floods.

At the end of the last ice age, approximately 12,000 years ago, the water that was enclosed in the massive glaciers melted very quickly. As a consequence, sea levels changed considerably in comparably short time. It has to be noted that during the so-called last glacial maximum (LGM), the sea level is believed to have been 100 to 150 m lower than today. Geologists found out from sediments in Alaska that 11,000 years ago in a period of only 400 years, the sea level rose for 18 m – which also sheds a new light on the consequences of today's climate change. So anthropologists assume today that the human groups living in that time were affected massively through these changes, especially because they were so-called beachcombers. Usually, humans in that time lived close to the seashore since it was easy there to gather high-protein nutrition (e.g., crabs, seashells, etc.) (Diamond 1997; Witzel 2012; Buss 2015). It is very likely that in some regions with flat shores, the coastline changed massively over just one generation. It is also known today that some regions, which were cut off from the oceans during the ice age, from a certain point on were suddenly flooded by the rising ocean level. This is well established for the Black Sea, where suddenly, the Mediterranean flooded the Dardanelles and the lower area behind, which is today the Black Sea. The same applies to the Persian Gulf. So as a consequence, myths about flooding could actually have a historical experience in the background.

A seemingly universal pattern, which is also described in Jung, is the motif of the trickster god, which can be found in stories from all over the world, and this figure also has common attributes (e.g., it is often part human, part animal). It also has a dark as well as a positive side, so it is described as adventurous, searching for sexual pleasures, lazy and easily bored, dishonest and impulsive, but at the same time, it is responsible for bringing important elements into the world, such as fire or other tools that are important for human beings. The method of this figure to obtain its goals is deceitful. Nevertheless, the outcome can be of benefit to the world. In that sense, tricksters are also transformers (Stein & Stein 2008).

The theory of common origin (Witzel 2012)

Harvard anthropologist Michael Witzel (2012) has presented a detailed and thorough investigation not only of the world's mythologies and their similarities but also of their origins based on the aforementioned insights about the spread of Homo sapiens from Africa all over the world. In contrast to Jung, who only claims to have systematically investigated similarities in mythology, Witzel provides a highly detailed account of similar patterns in the world's mythologies. This approach is different in so far as it does not repeat either diffusionism nor isolationism theories but assumes that the similarities have common origins (and is, therefore, in contrast to the aforementioned diffusion theory called theory of common origin), which can be traced back, step by step, in the sense of establishing a cladistic or family tree of a host of mythological tales. It is also different in so far as it does not look at isolated motifs but focuses on narratological structure and a common shared narrative scheme. The mythologies from the different parts of the world do not only share similar contents in the form of motifs but they are also arranged in the same or at least in a very similar fashion. So the main focus here is that of a common storyline of whole systems of myths and their comparability. This allows for the comparison of whole systems or collections of myths belonging to individual populations.

> Worldwide similarities between individual myths are habitually explained by diffusion or by common human psychic traits (see Jungian archetypes). However, the current proposal supersedes these approaches as it involves a whole system of myths, notably one characterized by a narrative structure (storyline) from the creation of the world to its end. This mythology has been spread not by diffusion but above all by the constant advance of humans: after their exodus out of Africa into northern Eurasia and beyond after the past two ice ages, respectively.
>
> (circa 52,000 to 45,000 BCE and 10,000 BCE,
> Witzel 2012, p. 35)

This approach is first and foremost descriptive and comparative. It assembles the similarities not only in motifs but also attempts to establishing a storyline and the fundamental structure of the mythologies involved. This approach is, on the other hand, historical, as humans and their myths have evolved over many tens of thousands of years. This is a very clear pledge for a viewpoint which denies an autochthonous and isolated appearance of similar motifs in different places again and again, based on a biological foundation, but sees similarities in mythologies as a consequence of cultural developments, physical contact, cultural exchange and migration not only of peoples but also of ideas.

This argumentation follows the aforementioned theory of the migration of anatomically modern humans, Homo sapiens, out of Africa and all over the world. As has been demonstrated earlier, this spread of Homo sapiens over the world followed specific routes, which can be marked geographically and also in terms of time. For the theory presented here, it is crucial to understand that on the way of this spread of modern humans over the world, these early human groups reached Australia, Melanesia and Tasmania already 40,000 years ago. Also, the earliest immigrants into the Americas reached the southern parts of South America by about 20,000 years ago. These immigrations were possible because of the land bridges that were formed during the ice age, which allowed traveling (mostly) overland into Australia, Papua New Guinea, Tasmania and other islands belonging to Melanesia, as well as over the Bering Strait land bridge from Asia into North America. After the end of the last glacial maximum, these land bridges were lost; therefore, these territories were cut off from Eurasia and the developments in the mythologies that occurred here. The same applies to sub-Saharan Africa, which was also in general cut off from the northeast of Africa, the origin of Homo sapiens and the developments that took place in the territories north of the Sahara Desert. Witzel points out that these territories, sub-Saharan Africa, Australia, Tasmania, Melanesia, Papua New Guinea, as well as the largest part of South America, have significantly different mythologies from the peoples in territories that belong to Eurasia, including the islands of Japan, Polynesia, Micronesia, Hawaii and the Easter Islands, which were inhabited later. The same applies more or less to North and Central America since the immigration of populations (e.g., Inuit, Na Dene) across the ice into North America and way into the South was possible even after the loss of the Bering Strait land bridge.

> In sum, archaeology, linguistics, population genetics, and studies of paleoclimate all present scenarios overlapping with a very similar to that assumed by comparative historical mythology.
>
> (p. 277)

Witzel differentiates three major systems of mythologies:

1. There is the oldest, in some way original, form of mythologies in the state it was when Homo sapiens left Africa around 60,000 years ago and started to migrate along the southern coastline of Eurasia towards the east, to South Asia and also into Europe. This original form, of course, needs to be reconstructed, which he admits is also debatable, as since then, it has undergone major changes in the different parts of the world. This system of mythologies is called by Witzel

Pan-Gaean (the term that is used in geology to describe the prehistoric single continent which then split into parts).

2. On the way Homo sapiens took out of Africa into the world, this original Pan-Gaean system of mythology migrated over the land bridges into Melanesia, Papua New Guinea, Australia and Tasmania on the one hand; over the Bering Strait land bridge into the Americas; and also from the centre of origin of Homo sapiens in East Africa into sub-Saharan Africa. Regarding America, it could be demonstrated that when the first groups of Homo sapiens arrived in North America, it took only 1000 years until they arrived at the southern tip of South America, in Tierra del Fuego. Witzel assumes that in these parts of the world, which were cut off from the Eurasian continent/mainland, the oldest forms of mythologies have survived or have at least developed differently from those systems in Eurasia. This is very clear for Melanesia, Australia, Papua New Guinea and Tasmania since the connection to South Asia was cut off at least 20,000 years ago. In a certain sense, it also applies to sub-Saharan Africa and South America, even though some influence from northern developments can be found in these mythologies. So we would expect to find the oldest forms of mythology, especially in Australia and Papua New Guinea. This system of mythology is called by Witzel **Gondwana**. It could also be called southern mythologies since they appear – more or less – only south of the equator. An interesting finding is that these older Gondwana mythologies have also survived in remote territories which actually belong to the next mentioned northern or Laurasian system of mythologies which are more developed, at least in terms of storylines. These remote territories/peoples can be found among the tribal peoples of the South Indian Nilgiris, in Malaya, in the Philippines, in Highland Taiwan, in Sakhalin/Hokkaido, in the Pamir Mountains, Caucasus and Pyrenees (Basque). This provides further evidence for the theory presented here since the respective peoples/tribes lived in very remote areas which were probably cut off from the usual migration routes and further developments in their surrounding territories, and they can also be differentiated from the surrounding cultures by linguistic and genetic features.

3. The most developed system of mythologies has developed on the Eurasian continent, presumably in greater Southwest Asia, and spread from there into Europe as well as into the South and Far East of Asia. Since the Bering Strait land bridge disappeared only around 11,000 years ago, it is also assumed that some elements of this Eurasian system of mythology migrated into the north of America (especially through the last wave of immigrants from Asia, the Na Dene family of tribes/languages, Athabascans, Navajo and Apache) and can, therefore, be found in North American Amerindian mythologies, partly also in Central America. It is also found throughout the islands in the Pacific, as it is well-established that the Polynesians moved out of their homeland, which was influenced by these northern mythologies, already by 1200/1000 BCE and spread from there over the whole Pacific, up to New Zealand, Easter Island and

Hawaii. This system of mythologies could be called northern, as it can mainly be found in parts of the world north of the equator, especially in Europe, Asia and North America. It is called by Witzel **Lauresian** mythology.

What is very important: the differences described here between the respective systems of mythologies are paralleled in detail by the findings described earlier about the routes of migration of early Homo sapiens and the development of its inhabitation of the different parts of the world. The differences in mythologies are totally parallel to differences in linguistics and genetics and are also backed by archaeological findings. In so far, this approach to the explanation of similarities and differences in mythologies is very well empirically established.

Another important consequence derived from these analyses is that already around 60,000 BCE, when Homo sapiens began to spread over the world, these migrating groups seem to have had first elements of mythologies, cosmogonies and, eventually, also religious ideas. This is further supported by the insight from genetic analyses that these humans, at least anatomically, had the capacity for a complex language (see previous section).

Laurasian or northern mythologies

These mythologies include those of the populations speaking Altaic, Japanese, Uralic, Afro-Asiatic, Indo-European, Tibeto-Burmese and Austric (South Asian, Southeast Asian and Polynesian). They are also the basis for the old written mythologies of Egypt, the Levant, Mesopotamia, India and China. It also strongly influenced the Inuit and American Indian mythologies, including Athabascan, Navajo/Apache, Pueblo, Algonkian, Aztec, Maya, Inca, etc.

These mythologies have a very clear narrational structure which differs clearly from the older aforementioned southern or Gondwana mythologies. This narrational scheme encompasses the ultimate origins of the world, subsequent generations of the gods, an age of semidivine heroes, the emergence of humans and, later on in time, even the origins of noble lineages. Very importantly, it also includes a violent end to the present world, sometimes with the hope for a new world emerging out of the ashes. The universe is often seen in comparison to the life of humans, as a living body, which is born (sometimes from primordial incest), grows, develops, comes of age and has to undergo final decay and death.

This structure distinguishes the northern mythologies clearly from those of the southern part of the world (Gondwana), especially in the narrative structure which in the latter has no pattern of a development of the universe, sometimes not even of the creation, and definitely, there is no end to the universe. In these mythologies, the world is regarded as eternal. Any account of an end of the world is missing.

In this sense, Witzel argues the northern mythologies are the most developed since they form something that could be called a novel, whereas in southern mythologies, such a clear line of development, is missing. They are more a collection of motifs and isolated stories.

In this context, Witzel also deals with Jung's ideas and clearly criticizes them:

> If Jung's analysis were correct, the archetypes would constitute, taken together, a brief history of the human mind, not unlike the many seemingly prehuman (amphibious etc.) stages that an embryo seems to go through in its development. . . . However, some archetypes are neither evenly nor generally distributed all over the world, such as the assumed worship of the generative power of a universal mother. Nor does an archetype lead to a full-fledged myth and even less so to a well structured mythology, and certainly not to one with a storyline, such as the Laurasian one.
>
> (Witzel 2012, p. 24)

It also has to be noted that since the described northern system of mythologies is at least 20,000 years old, it cannot be said that prehistoric, Palaeolithic societies have primitive religious systems since the systems described here include very complex worldviews which incorporate both nature and society.

An initial collection and comparison of similarities in mythological motifs allows for the following list:

1. the origin of the universe and our world
2. the several generations of deities
3. the creation of light
4. the killing of the dragon or of a similar monster
5. the emergence of humans, along with their faults
6. the involvement of the gods in human affairs
7. a great flood and the re-emergence of humans
8. an age of semidivine heroes, often overlapping with
9. the origins of local tribes and the later noble lineages and, as such, of local human history
10. a violent end to our present world

(Witzel 2012, p. 53)

Now in the northern system of mythologies, these elements are put into a coherent storyline:

1. creation from nothing, chaos, etc., father heaven/mother earth created
2. father heaven engenders: two generations (e.g., Titans/Olympians)
3. four (five) generations/ages: heaven pushed up, sun released
4. current gods defeat/kill predecessors: killing the dragon, use of sacred drink
5. humans: somatic descendants of sun god, they (or a god) show hubris and are punished by a flood
6. trickster deities bring culture, humans spread, emergence of nobles
7. local history begins
8. final destruction of the world
9. new heaven and earth emerge

(Witzel 2012, p. 183)

The underlying historical framework entails that mythology is characterized by an inherent narrational scheme that recalls, in succession, all events from the creation to the end of the world. In other words, the scheme has a recognizable pattern, it follows a red thread, it has a distinct storyline. . . . In sum, this mythology, reconstructed along these lines, represents our oldest complex story. It is a novel of the creation, growth, and destruction of the world, of divine and human evolution and decay, from birth to death, from creation to destruction.

(p. 54)

The occurrence of this structure in all of the aforementioned parts of the northern mythology system is illustrated by Witzel with a number of detailed examples, including the occurrence of the motive of the marriage of sun and moon in mythologies from Finland, India/Iran, Korea, Japan and Guatemala (kekchi) and the myth of the hidden sun, which can be found in Europe, West and East Asia and the Americas.

In contrast to this limited spread of motifs belonging to the northern system, the motif of a great flood is a truly universal pattern found all over the world (see next section).

More evidence for this distribution of mythological systems is the occurrence of the word for dog, Indo-European kuon (Witzel 2012, pp. 265–266). It is found in many languages of the world but, interestingly, only in those which belong to the here-mentioned northern or Laurasian mythology systems. This has to do with the fact that dogs were domesticated only around 15,000 BCE. Therefore, they did not reach societies as in Australia, which was by then cut off from the Eurasian mainland. Even though the dingo dog seems to have been introduced into Australia by maritime contacts from India around 3,000 years ago, it did not become domesticated with Australian aborigines. The same applies to sub-Saharan Africa. In the northern mythologies, in contrast, the dog appears as a mythical figure and symbol (e.g., as the guardian of the underworld or the gates of hell). This, apparently, has practical reasons because dogs were used as guardians and for hunting and were able to detect wounded gain or that which just had been killed by the weapons, therefore, the connection to death.

The same applies to the motif of horses, which are common in Eurasian mythologies (belonging to the northern system) in the form of sun horses/horses drawing the chariot of the sun (e.g., prominent in Greek and early Indian myth). Horses were domesticated around the fourth millennium BCE in Europe and the near East and used for vehicles even later. The seminomadic Central Asian tribes and the near Eastern peoples added the horse to their mythology, and some American Indians of the prairies did so much later, in the latter half of the second millennium, as soon as they were confronted with domesticated horses that were left by the Spanish invaders.

In contrast to that, there is a relative absence of chickens and pigs in Eurasian mythology, which speaks for the fact that these systems arose in West Asia, whereas chickens and pigs are both animals clearly domesticated first in Southeast Asia, where they can be found as motifs in mythologies.

Southern or Gondwana mythologies

These mythologies can be found in sub-Saharan Africa, the Andamans, New Guinea and Australia/Tasmania as well as greater Melanesia. It can be demonstrated that the Andamans were settled early, and archaeology and genetic evidence have recently shown that the Andamanese belong to some of the early immigrants from Africa. They can also be found in so-called remnant populations, which seem to have persisted in remote areas, such as the San bushman, the Pygmies, the Semang of Malaysia or some population in the highlands of southern India (Toda) and Taiwan. The Gondwana mythologies seem to have existed already at 40,000 BCE and thus have migrated with Homo sapiens into Australia, Papua New Guinea and southern Africa, whereas the aforementioned Laurasian mythologies seem to have developed not before 20,000 BCE, which could not have reached the territories mentioned here.

The most striking difference of Gondwana mythologies in comparison to the aforementioned northern mythologies is the absence of a coherent storyline. These mythologies do not tell of the creation of the world but only of that of the surroundings and of humans. Most notably, they do not know an end of the world. The interest of Gondwana mythologies clearly lies with the origins of humans. The first man and woman are sometimes created by the high god; however, in many other cases, they simply emerged from trees: a split tree, a tree stump or a bamboo. Even where this is not clearly stated (e.g., in Australia), it is symbolized in ritual where the tree plays a great role in initiation and burial. These mythologies also know an ultimate high god, which is an otiose god, far removed and not interested in human affairs, apart from creating descendants, such as a trickster or a totem deity. Typically, there is no creation. The earth already exists. The otiose high god moves to heaven, from where he sends down his son or other beings to create humans. These show hubris and are, therefore, punished by a flood. Trickster deities bring culture to them. There is no final destruction of the world.

Gondwana traditions share the motif of a primordial misdeed or hubris of the early humans, usually a broken food taboo, which leads to the emergence of death. This mistake in many instances is punished by a great flood. All of these elements, of course, occur also in Laurasian or northern mythologies, but there, they are put into a continuous and coherent storyline, which draws a line from the creation of the earth to its end, in the sense of causal connections.

Northern or Laurasian myth seeks to explain the origins of things, gods and humans as a means to understand them fully. In contrast to this, the ultimate questions on first origins are not asked in the Gondwana myths. They are, at best, interested in the origins of one's land or of humans and their condition.

In the north, there is enormous emphasis given on the power of the word (e.g., as it is used in magic and ritual). One can establish verbal and material equivalences and correlations between all entities and use them in magic and sorcery (e.g., in the Gospel: "In the beginning, there was the word"). In contrast, in Gondwana mythologies, there is no distinction among word, thought, discourse and action. The word is enduring, a solid reality. In sorcery and magic, there is no emphasis on words but on objects (e.g., ones used as fetishes). In Laurasian myth, there is the insistence on the word of origins, on the secret or sacred tales of origins, whereas in Gondwana, there is emphasis on remembering the first ancestors in ritual (e.g., the Australian dreamtime).

Pan-Gaean myths – the truly universal motifs

From a Jungian point of view, and also for the discussion of archetype theory, it is most interesting what the truly original and, therefore, universal myths of human-kind are, which Witzel summarizes under the term Pan-Gaean.

> It is here that truly human universals emerge, as imagined and postulated by Jung and his followers.
>
> (Witzel 2012, p. 357)

The idea is that these myths have already existed, at least in rudimentary form, at the point in time 65,000 years ago when the first Homo sapiens groups left Africa and spread over the world. As has been pointed out earlier, they have survived in the Gondwana systems of mythology, although it can certainly not be said that these mythologies, now very ancient, are in the same state as they were when the first humans left Africa. Also, these older southern mythologies, of course, have undergone certain developments over time and adapted to the environments and conditions of the peoples and societies in which they were transmitted. Neverthe-less, Witzel argues that it is possible to reconstruct some of these oldest mythemes.

One of them is the **myth of a flood**, which is apparently truly universal and is part in Gondwana myths as well as in Laurasia mythology. The truly universal motifs in this myth include:

> In sum, both the Laurasian and the Gondwana flood myths share the topic of retribution by a divine or human being. It often is caused by some sort of mis-take made by one or more early humans and is executed by excessive rain. Some people escape by float or boat, usually to one or more high mountains. In some cases, a new race of humans develops from the saved primordial people.
>
> (Witzel 2012, pp. 348–355)

Another truly pan-human motive is the ubiquitous **trickster** figure that brings human culture (e.g., Prometheus as the thief of fire, etc.) as well as the motif of the origin of humans from trees or clay. The interesting point is that some of these old motives can be found in later Laurasian mythologies, where they can clearly be identified, as they simply do not fit into the common storyline. They appear as elements somehow strange and alien to the rest of the story, which identifies them as very old remnants of earlier mythological systems. They stand out as archaisms that can easily be isolated. These culture heroes or tricksters receive a different role in the later Laurasian mythologies, as they are not the sons of heaven as in the older myths but belong to a later generation – that of the grandchildren of heaven. This is due to the need to find the reasonable place for them in the Laurasian mythological storyline.

Witzel provides a list of other pan-human, universal mythological motifs. There is a (male) **high god**, but he is often a deus otiosus, moved far away from humans and retreated into heaven. **Creation**: interestingly, there is no idea of the creation of the earth or the universe. The only question that is of interest is how the earth can be shaped properly so as to make human life possible. Later Laurasian myth, in contrast, is strongly interested in understanding the origin of everything, the universe, etc. A very old remnant, which could be called pan-human, is the motif of the **primordial giant made of stone** and the accompanying worship of large stones, rocks and stone pillars. Another very old motive for the origin or emergence of humans is the idea of a reservoir of souls, in the sense of a **well of souls**. For example, in Australia, the souls of unborn children are believed to come from certain totem welds, and the motif still exists in current Germanic belief about babies coming from the big pond, from where they are brought by a stork. This motif is not found in the official Laurasian mythologies but appears in folktales and legends.

In all the mythological systems described here, humans are described as being by nature full of **hubris** and that their arrogance usually leads to the origin of death due to some mistake or misdeed, often committed by a woman. This seems to be a very old idea. At least the idea of the **emergence of death** is seemingly another important Pan-Gaean or pan-human motif. The linking of life-giving women with death is widespread, as can be seen in the traditional role of midwives being responsible for birth as well as for the care of the dead. In sum, this old motif could be characterized as the search for the origin of death and who to blame for it.

In the history of comparative mythology, there have been several proposals for lists of universal myths, for example, by Van Binsbergen (2007), who identifies 20 universal motifs from various time periods, as well as the Russian anthropologist Berezkin (2005), who has pointed out ancient links among African, Australian and South American myths. Witzel criticizes these approaches in so far as they only focus on isolated motifs instead, as he does, on overarching and continuous storylines. He argues that individual motifs could have travelled easily and, therefore, be diffused, whereas the coherent mythological systems in the sense of a narratological point of view appear more robust against influences. Be it as it may, Witzel can convincingly demonstrate that on the one hand, there are truly universal mythological motifs or storylines, but he can also clearly demonstrate that they have been spread by migration, physical contact and cultural exchange and are not products of a supposed universal structure of the human brain or the biological makeup of humans.

While this might speak for the Jung/Thompson proposals, these facts receive a new interpretation in light of the Laurasian theory. . . . More importantly, what is significant about the few newly emerging, truly universal motifs is not just their worldwide spread; rather, it is the fact that these universals also occur but are isolated in Laurasian myth. They often go against its grain and are superfluous variants of topics treated comprehensively and systematically in Laurasian myth. As mentioned earlier, frequently these variants are not part of the official local storyline but occur as isolated myths, generally in the form of folktales or *märchen*. . . . They allow us a first glimpse of the mind of early humans and of the human condition as experienced by our most distant ancestors, after they moved out of Africa around 65,000 BCE and before that, perhaps as far back as 160,000 to 130,000 BCE, the time of the African Eve.

(Witzel 2012, pp. 371–372)

Conclusion

Again, as in the fields of anthropology and religion, it can be summarized that the universal patterns or motifs that Jung had in mind do actually not exist, at least not in the shape he imagined them. There are motifs that Jung claimed to be universal, which, in fact, are not, namely, that of a powerful mother goddess, the slaying of a dragon or the idea of rebirth. Where there are universal motifs (e.g., the trickster or the motif of a flood), their universality can well be explained by migration and cultural exchange. The overall model presented here, on the background of the Out-of-Africa theory and the spread of Homo sapiens over the world, can explain in detail the similarities as well as the regional and cultural differences in mythology on the background of the routes of migration. Again, it has to be clearly stated that Jung's isolationism position has been refuted. The powerful findings presented earlier are accomplished when a human sciences approach is applied to cultural phenomena, such as mythologies, narrative patterns or cosmogonies. It also has to be noted that in the comparative research on mythologies of the last decades, in contrast to Jung and AP, the myth of the hero's journey plays virtually no role. This is not to say that such a story pattern does not exist, but there is a strong contrast between the importance it has gained in AP in comparison to the research focus of comparative mythology. From the perspective of comparative mythology, it seems that this mythological motif does not have such a central role in the mythological storylines and cosmogonies of the peoples of the world. It is possible that Jung, again, has fallen into the trap of ethnocentricity – that is, a European point of view – which is on the background of the development of individualism in the Western world, beginning already in Greek antiquity and heightened since the Renaissance. This story pattern has gained enormous importance as a metaphor for explaining psychological individuality, and it may only have a minor role in all of the other societies and cultures, namely, indigenous societies, in the world. This has far-reaching consequences for the whole model of classic archetype theory since the whole concept of psychological development is based on the idea that consciousness develops out of the unconscious, and this is pictured in the mythologies and images of the so-called great mother and the path of the hero – which are definitely not universal motifs or story patterns. So the universal applicability of the whole model is thus in question. Again, the problem is that Jung had his preformed fantasy of archetype theory and made use only of those myths and motifs which fitted into his concept – instead of systematically and open-mindedly investigate the mythological motifs which actually exist in the world. Again, it can be demonstrated that Jung's pre-conceptualized innatism made him blind for the actual diversity to be found in the mythologies of the world.

Another far-reaching consequence is the following: the practice of Jungian psychotherapy is based on the aforementioned model and the idea of autochthonous development of these – supposed-to-be healing – motifs out of the individual psyche. Now if the research presented here clearly speaks for the fact that the existence of mythological motifs is a consequence of cultural transferral not only on a historical level but also on the individual level (usually, from mother to child; see chapter on religion), then Jungian psychotherapists cannot count on the pre-existence of these motifs in every one of their clients. If a specific client has never been told about the stories or has incorporated them in other ways (e.g., subliminally), then the whole approach may seem misleading to wait for the emergence of such motifs and ideas in the course of therapy.

Nevertheless, there are not only universal motifs but also universal cosmogonic storylines, as Witzel has pointed out. Even if there are striking differences between what he calls Laurasian versus Gondwana mythologies, there is still a surprising continuity in these super-narratives. Although they most probably have been diffused via migration and cultural exchange, the most interesting question still remains: How could these storylines and their contents survive for literally tens of thousands of years? I will attempt to provide an answer in the following final chapter.

Chapter 10

Conclusion

The core theory – a theory of psychological transformation

The starting point of this discussion of archetype theory was the insight that still today, there is no standard definition for archetypes. There is still confusion, with definitions presented which are completely incompatible and lead to unresolved questions concerning the core concept of AP, but it seems as if large parts of the community are not even interested (Mills 2018). Therefore, it is not clear what anybody is referring to when making use of the term archetype, even in contemporary publications. It was also pointed out that the confusion begins with Jung. The heart of the problem is that Jung put forward a theory – and tried to defend it against any form of, even justified, criticism – which basically goes like this: archetypes are embedded in the biological makeup of humans, like instincts/patterns of behaviour in animals. They have formed in the prehistory of mankind, and because they are biologically rooted, they appear "autochthonously", without any influence through culture and socialization, in every human being, at least potentially. These biologically rooted archetypes are, therefore, responsible for similarities and convergences in the fields of religion, cultural patterns and social practices. They are finally responsible for the psychological development of the individual. In this theory, Jung attempted to bind together all the four theories that were described in Chapter 3 and all the fields of expertise which were investigated, namely, biology, anthropology, religion, prehistory and mythology, into one unified explanatory concept for the development of mankind, its cultures and religions as well as for the individual psyche, which – as was demonstrated – is impossible. This theory of Jung's must be characterized as being a grandiose fantasy. It seems to me that this unifying approach is so fascinating that it is still highly attractive to many people, inside as well as outside of the Jungian community, so that there is a strong tendency to cling to this belief system.

It seems that Jung was fixated to this theory, in the face of critique or even contradictions that were pointed out already in his lifetime. As I have pointed out, the state-of-the-art in anthropology, religious studies, archaeology and palaeoanthropology clearly demonstrates that the assumed similarities or primary forms (e.g., of religion) do not exist. Where there are parallels (e.g., in what anthropology has characterized as universals as well as in the field of comparative mythology), these can well be explained by migration, physical contact, cultural exchange, the

DOI: 10.4324/9781003348191-10

interplay between regional environmental conditions and the dynamics inherent in culture and society itself. Jung was blind to such viewpoints because he was convinced that archetype theory was a biological theory and, as such, part of the natural sciences, which in his eyes was the only possibility to make this theory a truly scientific theory and defend it against critique. Ironically, this very approach has made archetype theory questionable, even unscientific, and has put it under massive critique.

What is irritating is the fact that the criticisms that I have summarized have been put forward, at least partly, already in Jung's lifetime and later in the scholarly debate in AP again and again, with seemingly very little effect. In the survey conducted as part of this study, viewpoints have been presented which still continue what could be called naïve innatism. At least as irritating is the realization that the insights which have developed in the relevant disciplines, namely, anthropology, religious studies, comparative mythology, etc., have virtually played no role in the debate in AP. It has to be noted that Jung's far-reaching nomothetic statements about the universality of the so-called great mother and the hero myth connected with it, being images for the development of consciousness out of the unconscious, are not just some ideas in archetype theory. They are in fact at the centre of the architecture of the whole theory. This is an aspect which again has been rarely discussed in AP that the debate is not only about the existence or nonexistence of certain archetypes but that Jung's ideas form a coherent explanatory system which links all the aspects discussed here: assumptions about the distribution and universality of certain aspects of cultural life, of religious ideas, of social patterns as well as of individual psychological processes and behaviours being rooted in the biology of humans and thus creating specific psychological processes (e.g., in the context of psychotherapy). All of these aspects play a role in the construction of the whole of the theory; they build a coherent architecture. In the face of the evidence speaking clearly against a universal distribution of these ideas and images, namely, that of the so-called great mother and the hero, practically, the architecture of the whole of Jung's archetype theory has collapsed. Again, it seems, nobody has noticed. Although archetype theory not only in the shape which Jung presented but also in present-day form (see, for example, the teaching at the institutes, introductory texts presented on the website of the IAAP, etc.) makes far-reaching, even nomothetic, statements about matters in the field of anthropology, religion, comparative mythology, etc., it has lost contact to the development and state of scholarly knowledge in these fields or has even totally neglected it. This neglect is not only ignorance but appears as a sort of arrogance, as if AP would not need these other disciplines and their insights, as if it were above such research often characterized as "positivistic", as if it were in the possession of the truth. As a consequence, the foundation of the whole theoretical construct of archetype theory has evaporated, and the architecture of the theory has collapsed. So even if there were some evidence for certain aspects or proof that some psychological features are actually genetically encoded, it would not save the whole of the theoretical construct from being refuted.

In fact, the situation is even worse: the racist and devaluing viewpoints, which were characteristic for colonial thought, are not only deeply embedded in Jung's theorizing around archetypes but these viewpoints have also been continued in AP up to the present day with only marginal critique (Group of Jungians 2018). My impression is that the majority in the Jungian community is even not aware that large parts of the theory convey these highly problematic viewpoints further.

There is even a certain renaissance of publications which more or less uncritically continue a biological line of argumentation (see the debate in the 2023, Vol 1, issue of the *Journal of Analytical Psychology*, Goodwyn 2023; Roesler 2023). I do not question that also in human beings, there are processes which can be described by gene-environment co-action (Goodwyn 2020a, 2020b). But how can these processes, which well explain development of bacteria, explain the coming about of complex symbolic and even narrative structures in the human mind, such as the great mother and the myth of the hero's journey? Contemporary conceptualizations even in human biology clearly refute what has been described as the biological conceptualization of archetypes (Theory 1). There is no doubt that in humans, there are innate capacities and behavioural tendencies, but they are the opposite of what Jung imagined to be biologically rooted archetypes. All of these innate elements are not structures and contents but only capabilities which are all directed towards creating relationship, participating in relationships and groups, initiating interaction and participating in communication, cooperation, sociality, etc. In sum, they are directed towards social relationships. This is, as I have pointed out, the contrary of what Jung imagined when he claimed a biological foundation of archetypes. The archetypes Jung had in mind cannot be conceptualized as biologically or genetically founded in the face of contemporary knowledge. It also has to be noted that Jung again and again stressed the point that biology/the genes **determine** human behaviour and imagination. This is very different from the pathways that authors such as Goodwyn describe (Merchant 2020). This is, again, a result of the fact that there is no consensus about the definition of archetypes, so evidence for biological/genetical pathways for mental capacities in humans are used to argue that such findings provide proof for Jung's archetypes being biologically rooted. The problem is that it is not clearly defined what is archetype.

Contemporary Jungian authors still make the mistake to use such as the aforementioned findings as "evidence" for the biological theory of archetypes, for conceptions of innatism, biological preformationism, etc., without taking into account that the archetypes of classical archetype theory – anima and animus, the wise old man, the trickster, the divine child, the journey of the hero, etc. – are something totally different from the capabilities that were found to be biologically rooted. I have already argued that it is legitimate to hold on to a theory which argues that there are biologically preformed mental or psychological capacities in humans, but this is by no means evidence for the archetypes of AP being biologically rooted. Therefore, again, I would suggest not to use the term archetype anymore for biologically preformed mental propensities in humans, as this creates confusion instead of clarification.

Why, at all, is it so important to describe the archetype as a biological concept, even for contemporary theorists? It is as if the theory, when armed with dubious concepts and findings from natural sciences and highly questionable pseudo-biological argumentations, became a better theory. This would mean to continue Jung's mistake to conceptualize archetype theory as a part of the natural sciences, namely, biology, in an attempt to defend the theory against criticism, to make it a "real scientific theory". We can acknowledge that today as being a defensive strategy by which Jung attempted to be regarded as a scientist and immunize his theory against criticism. There is no need to continue such attempts to create a biological foundation for archetype theory, as it does not make it a scientific theory. In contrast, such attempts have become highly questionable and make archetype theory unscientific. From my point of view, AP, for decades, has been caught in useless academic debates of discussing different biological pathways in the desperate attempt to find a biological explanation for how archetypes come about. But it is not necessary – and I would argue it is even not possible – to investigate what is meant by the term archetype on the level of genes, gene-environment interaction, instincts and patterns of behaviour, etc. We will certainly not find archetypes in the genes or on the level of biological processes.

The question is this: What is the appropriate level of investigation, of observation and of theory building adequate for the formulation of a theory of archetypes?

What is the adequate level of investigation?

The biological as well as genetic makeup of humans certainly plays a role in what kind of behaviour patterns, social rules and cultural contexts we develop. But even if we start from what biology and, namely, ethology say about what could be called human nature, what we find is that human beings are biologically prepared not for certain natural environments but for a life in social groups and relationships. The human capacity for building complex social relationships and large groups, even civilizations, for interaction, communication and cooperation, for trusting each other, building shared goals and following these goals together, is what makes our species so successful and what is the outstanding characteristic of humans. Therefore, there is no specific environment for us on this world. We can actually survive practically everywhere on this earth, in the Arctic, in high mountains, in deserts and in jungles. There are even ethnicities who live continuously on the water, and today, we can even survive on the moon and in outer space. The environment we are genetically designed for, so to say, is the human group and culture we are born into, and our biologically preformed capabilities aim at making us a competent member of this group and culture. There is no symbolical content inscribed in our brains, as the neuronal growth is unspecific (see chapter "Biology, genetics and inheritance"), but we are prepared to fully take in the contents, rules, structures and stories of the culture we are born into.

On the other hand, there certainly are similarities in structures and patterns that have developed in a considerable number or even in all the cultures and societies in the world (e.g., in mythologies and in the field of religion. Although it could be demonstrated that these similarities have come about through cultural developments and cultural exchange, nevertheless, the crucial question is this: How could these patterns, ideas and structures survive over such a long time? As Goodwyn (in print) puts it: "Some stories/images are 'stickier' than others". In this case, I absolutely agree. We must consider that Witzel (2012) assumes some of these mythological motifs and storylines may have existed already when Homo sapiens left Africa (i.e., approximately 65,000 years ago) and are still part of stories told today.

I do not question that such patterns can tell us something about what is characteristic for human beings, for human societies, and they certainly have to do with the way we psychologically function. I have already pointed out that rules and patterns which have developed in religions seem to provide, in their specific way, information which helps to lead a good or at least a better life. This applies to the field of practical everyday life as well as to the field of psychology in general. Just take the 10 Commandments. Even though they may appear a bit simple and rigid from a contemporary point of view, nevertheless, they had an enormous effect in structuring social life, making it more peaceful and protecting human relationships, which, as we have seen, are so crucial for human well-being. This line of explanation of psychologically meaningful patterns could be continued with many more examples not only from the field of religion but also from other fields (see, for example, the discussion of marriage rules in the chapter on anthropology). This viewpoint will be taken up again in the next section which discusses the process theory.

I would like to put this idea into the following reformulation of archetype theory: archetypes are about what is appropriate for human beings in the sense that it helps to lead a good life and that it is helpful in supporting growth, even potentially healing.

But I would very strongly argue that it makes no sense to search for these patterns on the level of biology, in genes, instincts and the like. It is not only that it makes no sense, but it is also not necessary. It is sufficient to investigate human habits and institutionalized rules and procedures on the level of social practices, habits and customs, religious ideas and beliefs, ritual processes, mythological stories, etc., to be able to identify such truly universal patterns. It only needs an open-minded and unprejudiced approach, by which I mean an attitude which does not want to prove right everything that Jung said, whatever it may cost.

So as a conclusion on this level, I would argue that **archetype theory is definitely not the kind of theory Jung conceptualized, but it is part of cultural psychology.** Archetypes are, therefore, best described as a condensed form of psychological wisdom which has developed in human social practice, and they can be investigated on the level of cultural products, social processes and religious beliefs and ideas. Nevertheless, we still have to take a close look into such patterns and whether the compressed wisdom is applicable to the whole of the human condition or maybe just to specific social, cultural and environmental contexts (i.e., it implies to apply a cultural sciences approach, as it deals with cultural products). For example: it may still be a good idea to keep milk and raw meat apart from each other, especially in hot climates (Judaism), but with modern refrigerators and electric cooking facilities, this problem can be solved. It may still be a good idea to be careful with drinking alcohol, especially in hot climates (Islam), but contemporary societies may find more appropriate regulations. On the other hand, the practice to observe a fasting period at the end of the winter (Catholic) may still be a good idea, as it does a lot of good on the physical as well as on a psychological level. It enables the psyche to go through a period of "light depression" which, in fact, can serve as a protector against psychological disturbances. The latter is an insight which we can find in a whole number of religions in the form of veneration of deities that stand for melancholia and gloom and have periods associated with their adoration in which people walk "in ashes" (e.g., Saturnalia). Again, it is not necessary for understanding these psychological insights to search for the genetic or other biological determinants of these processes, although they may certainly exist but are probably multifactorial. The WHAT of archetype theory may be more important than the HOW it comes about.

In a reformulated approach to archetype theory, we could argue that religions, mythological stories, social practices, rituals, etc., encode what is good for us humans. This reflects biological basics, our "human nature" if you like, but is not determined by them, and as we have seen, humans are not only formed by their biology but as well by the culture they are living in. Then archetype could be described as a pattern which creates resonance in humans because it obviously has to do with being human. This would mean, for example, that we feel a resonance when we listen to a certain story or when we encounter certain cultural habits or participate in a religious ritual. It strikes a chord in us which we share with other humans.

But practices, beliefs, myths and images, although they may be archaic or are found in indigenous peoples, are not necessarily good or wholesome in the earlier sense. A striking example is provided by Paul (2015): when European researchers, relatively late, investigated the indigenous peoples in the remote highlands of Papua New Guinea, they found a tribe which held the belief that sexuality was dirty, weakened the mind and was thus below the dignity of the people. Consequently, this tribe did not practice sexuality at all, which created the problem that they had no offspring. So as not to die out, they developed a strategy to attack their neighbours, kill or enslave the adults, steal the children and make them their own. Since they practiced these strategies for hundreds, if not thousands, of years, they reached a high expertise in warfare and, feared by their neighbours, dominated the highlands. This is, by the way, striking evidence for the fact that indigenous peoples do not follow nature and that, in contrast to assumptions made in sociobiology, the drive to spread one's own genes is not the strongest motivation in humans. In this case, what is transmitted over generations is not the biological but the cultural heritage.

The process idea

As a consequence, from the discussions previously, it can be summarized that Jung's assumptions in the fields of biology, anthropology, mythology and religion are largely to be refuted or need to be questioned thoroughly. In contrast, his idea of a universal process of psychological transformation which can provide a map for the psychotherapeutic process needs to be highly valued, even today in the contemporary field of psychotherapy theories and psychotherapy research.

As a conclusion, I would like to focus in the following on what I would like to call the core theory inherent in archetype theory. It seems to me to be justified to call this the core of archetype theory based on the insight that AP is a psychology and a theoretical discipline with a practical application (i.e., psychotherapy, respectively, Jungian analysis). From my point of view, it is an ethical requirement for an applied discipline as psychotherapy, which works with clients who hope to find relief when making use of psychotherapy, to provide a theoretical model for its psychotherapeutic practice and, additionally, that this model is well grounded in contemporary insights in the relevant disciplines. Through the differentiation of the lines of thought inherent in Jung's theorizing about the concept of archetypes, it became clear that for Jung, in his theory of archetypes, the idea of the individuation process provided this background theoretical model for the practice of psychotherapy.

The idea of a psychological process assumed to be universal first appeared to Jung during his years in psychiatry when he studied the dynamics of psychosis:

> He noticed, however, that these dynamics need not cause destruction, but that they could, on the contrary, exercise a positive influence. By confronting these dynamics, Jung observed that psychological growth comes from the unconscious. Jung's twofold experience of psychotic patients and of psychic maturation let him to surmise, in what he wrote between the years 1919 and 1923, that unconscious factors are at the source of both psychic illness and psychic healing. . . . The presence of archetypes justifies the therapeutic question as to whether it is possible to relate to unconscious organizing schemas such that they can have a positive influence on life. The search for the answer to that question is at the foundation of Jungian analysis.
>
> (Humbert 1988, p. 103)

Although the previous quote still contains assumptions which have been demonstrated to be problematic on the background of contemporary knowledge, it still points out the central idea in Jung's archetype theory of archetypes being organizers, organizing schemas, yes, even transformers. The idea that archetypes serve as organizing structures has already been discussed by Van Eewynk (1991, 1997) in connection with the term attractors. To summarize this idea in contemporary language: there is an assumed dynamic inherent in the human psyche which manifests in a process, which, when activated, leads to psychological integration, growth and, eventually, healing – a goal which is usually in AP termed wholeness. The idea further contains the assumption that the stages of this process are universal and can be described in the form of typical images, respectively, psychological experiences circling around figures personifying psychological qualities. It is important to note this idea also contains the assumption that this process appears as if there were an autonomous – in the sense of independent from the conscious ego – factor behind the dynamic, which means there is an independent factor in the psyche/ unconscious responsible (i.e., the transformation is brought about), at least partly, by this factor (in AP, usually called the transcendent function). This idea, as much as it is characteristic for AP, also differentiates this psychology from other psychological and psychotherapeutic approaches. On the other hand, it had an enormous influence on the development of other schools of psychotherapy, namely, in the field of humanistic psychology and transpersonal approaches (Roesler & Reefschläger 2022).

Different models of process

Nevertheless, it has to be pointed out that even in this core part of Jung's theory, there are different viewpoints to be differentiated. It makes a big difference if, on the one hand, one speaks of this process as a centring process, for which the archetype of the Self is responsible and which can manifest in images in the shape of mandalas in the broadest sense, or if, on the other hand, the idea of this process contains a model of a sequence of stages which are clearly defined, as was pointed out earlier (the shadow, anima and animus, the wise old man, the great mother, etc.). The latter is a theory of a much higher complexity and makes more far-reaching claims in the sense of nomothetic statements, whereas the first theory would probably find agreement among a number of contemporary schools of psychotherapy (e.g., Rogers's approach, Gestalt therapy, practically all of the schools belonging to the experiential/humanistic approaches). In Abraham Maslow's model of self-actualization, more or less the same idea is elaborated (Roesler & Reefschläger 2022).

A very important part of this model is the idea of a self-organizing nature of the psyche. It implies a force or impulse that comes from the unconscious which takes a helpful stance in the development of the personality and which is behind the process that aims for the wholeness of the personality. So in this model, the Self and the unconscious actively contribute and collaborate for psychic recovery.

> The collaboration of the unconscious is intelligent and purposive, and even when it acts in opposition to consciousness its expression is still compensatory in an intelligent way, as if it were trying to restore a lost balance.
>
> (CW 9/I, para. 282)

A summary of the whole idea, respectively, theoretical model, called "individuation" is provided by Murray Stein (Murray Stein: Individuation; https://iaap.org/ individuation-2/) – again, containing problematic assumptions but nevertheless useful. This is a highly comprehensive account of what could be called the classic theory of development and the goals of psychotherapy in AP. It is also a more careful definition of the individuation process, as it emphasizes the centring nature of the process and does not delve into the whole sequence of assumed stages (e.g., anima/animus or the so-called Mana personalities). In so far, it is a good example of the first variant of the aforementioned process models in AP, whereas the second would include a detailed description of the stages involved in the process (to be found in the papers in CW 7). Very generally speaking, the first model is much easier to accept even for someone being sceptical about the validity of the assumed archetypal stages, whereas the second model includes several problematic assumptions (e.g., about the nature and qualities of the counter sexual inner image). The second model contains as the central element the idea that consciousness develops out of an unconscious matrix which is pictured in myths and images of the hero emancipating from figures connected with the great mother. This model, in its assumed-to-be-universal form, has been falsified on different levels: first, the development of the brain cannot be described as starting from an unconscious matrix. In contrast, consciousness is first (see chapter "Biology, genetics and inheritance"). Second, in the chapters on anthropology and mythology, it was demonstrated that Jung and Neumann chose their material very selectively and took a Eurocentric view. The idea of a great mother as the source of life is by no means universal. So it can be said in general that the whole of the second model with its sequence of stages is flawed and needs to be discarded.

It is interesting that recent accounts of the process which is assumed to unfold in Jungian psychotherapy often ignore the model of the stages containing the classic archetypes. For example, Kast (1999), in her ambitious attempt to reformulate the process in Jungian psychotherapy, successfully integrated the insights of infant observation and the concept of "representations of interactions that are generalized" (Boston Change Process Study Group, Stern 1985) but describes the psychotherapeutic process, although she calls it archetypal, without any reference to the classic archetypes (i.e., anima/animus, shadow, the wise old man, etc). The same applies to the publications by Mario Jacoby (1993, 1998), who also attempted to integrate the Jungian approach with the findings of the infant researchers and Kohutian self-psychology. In his publication of 1998 about the relationship in Jungian psychotherapy, the term archetype is almost totally abandoned. The conceptualization of the "Self" follows Stern (1985), not Jung. The only reference to the term archetype is to the "creative and ordering factor, which is called archetype" (Jacoby 1998, p. 89; transl. C.R.), which enables us to form a generalized representation of all the experiences in relationships. In his 1993 publication about the transference and its role in the Jungian model, again, the only reference to the term archetype is by mentioning the archetype of the wounded healer as a role model for the therapist in the therapeutic relationship (see next section for more details).

There are two major problems connected with these ideas of a universal transformational process: the first being the question of validity of these concepts, respectively, connected with it the question how Jung came to conceptualize this process in the form he presented it. The second question concerns the role the therapeutic relationship takes in this process, a question which will be discussed in detail later, referring to developments in the broader field of psychodynamic therapies and contemporary conceptualizations of the role of relationships in development and in psychotherapy.

Is Jung's model of the individuation process universal?

Jung claims that he developed his model of the process in psychotherapy from clinical material provided by his patients in what could be called a quasi-empirical process of theory building, as for example, in the following quote:

> The chaotic assortment of images that at first confronted me reduced itself in the course of the work to certain well-defined themes and formal elements, which repeated themselves in identical or analogous form with the most varied individuals. I mention, as the most salient characteristics, chaotic multiplicity and order; duality; the opposition of light and dark, upper and lower, right and left; the union of opposites in a third; the quaternity (square, cross); rotation (circle, sphere); and finally, the centring process and a radial arrangement that usually followed some quaternary system. . . . The centring process is, in my experience, the never-to-be-surpassed climax of the whole development, and is characterized as such by the fact that it brings with it the greatest possible therapeutic effect.
>
> (CW 8, para. 401)

This is what I have termed the model of a centring process, in contrast to the model which includes all the stages represented by the classic archetypes. The most detailed account provided by Jung of this second model can be found in "The relations between the ego and the unconscious" (CW 7). I have already commented that it is a shame that Jung did not document the material he used for the first model, not to speak of he never published it. As to the second model, including the archetypal stages, it seems to me that he developed these ideas during his so-called confrontation with the unconscious as part of the crisis after the break with Freud. There is no doubt that these ideas were in statu nascendi when he published his 1912 paper *Wandlungen und Symbole der Libido* (*Symbols of Transformation*, CW 5). But as I have pointed out, and many critiques have demonstrated, this text is by far not a systematic study but more a documentation of Jung's own associative processes. So the question arises: Did Jung develop this elaborate model of the individuation/psychotherapeutic process just from his personal experiences and, from then on, applied it to his cases in the conviction that what he had experienced was universal? The interesting point, when scanning Jung's *Collected Works*, is that those papers in which he demonstrated the validity of his model with case examples, he always presents only a selection of material and not the total of the material available. So for example, in "Individual dream symbolism in relation to alchemy" (CW 12), Jung discusses a series of approximately 40 dreams by which he demonstrates the appearance of the classic archetypal stages of the individuation process. It is well-known that the dreams were presented by Wolfgang Pauli in his analysis with one of Jung's followers, and Jung received the dreams to use them for his study. But the whole dream series contains approximately 1,300 dreams, as stated in Pauli's comments to Jung (Meier 2001). So the question is this: Why did Jung select the 40 dreams he used, and what is the material in the other dreams?

We know how, for Jung, his concept had unconditional validity, and he did not let anyone question it. What I am trying to point out is the following problem: having once declared a theoretical system of explanation as valid for oneself, it will impact or even form the way how we look at reality. So there is the danger of constructing a reality which is based more on one's own concepts than on the client's reality, when looking at a client with such a bias. In the history of AP starting with Jung himself, there has been a lot of effort to find validation and confirmation for Jung's statements. What is missing from my point of view is a more sceptical attitude and, with it, an active search for confirmation or refutation of the concepts. This could, for example, consist of research projects documenting in detail analytical processes with all the material included (i.e., dreams, phantasies, pictures, symbols, etc.) and then to investigate this material open-mindedly, testing whether the processes match with how Jung describes the individuation process, instead of publishing only exemplary cases. The latter, of course, is a problem not only in AP, as Westen (2001) points out:

> Narrative case reports . . . are invariably compromise formations. We hope they include a heavy dose of relatively accurate perception and memory. But as compromise formations, they are likely to reflect a variety of wishes and fears. Convincingly, to appear intelligent and clinically talented to one's colleagues, to establish one's identity as a member of the analytic community (or a subset of it), to express identification with admired others and with those whose admiration one desires, to express competitive or hostile impulses toward those with whom one disagrees or dislikes, and so forth. Among the most important limitations are lack of replicability, lack of reliability of inference, lack of control over variables that would allow causal inference, and unknown generalizability.
> (Westen 2001, p. 883)

Because of this attitude, Jung's case examples as well as many others published in the history of AP may have served the aim, first and foremost, to affirm the already existing model, instead of investigating it open-mindedly. In those cases in which a critical attitude was applied, it could be demonstrated that even classical cases of Jung's could be well explained without any reference to archetypes (e.g., Merchant 2019).

So as a consequence from these considerations, it would be interesting to find out how Jung actually proceeded when he practiced psychotherapy, how he dealt with the material as well as with the therapeutic relationship in practice as well as in theory.

Apparently, Jung could be very sensitive, present, compassionate and supportive in his therapies and, by doing so, helped his clients very much. We know that from a number of students, who were in analysis with him and later became training analysts and scholars of AP. But it seems to me as if there were a certain bias, as if mainly those ideal therapies are being passed on and remembered in AP. For a number of years, I have collected first-hand reports by former clients of Jung's, as far as they are available in the literature (e.g., Wheelwright 1984;

Shamdasani 1992; Medtner 1935; Douglas 1977; Bair 2003, pp. 376–400; Reid 2001; and Jaffé 1989). When I read those reports, I was stunned by the great number of sessions in which Jung did not even occupy himself with the material of the client but rather held lectures. In long monologues, he explained his theory and how it had to be applied to the client (e.g., Reid 2001). I would go as far as saying from a contemporary point of view, this is not psychotherapy at all but rather, education. Again, it can be seen here, from Jung's point of view, his theory had absolute validity. In many cases, he forced his view about their psyche on the patients even though some of them even fought against it. Rather extreme examples are Christiana Morgan and Henry Murray, who both left very detailed reports about their experiences with Jung (Douglas 1997b; Murray, without publication year). Henry Murray was a famous American psychologist and later head of the psychological department at Harvard University, so it can be said that he was someone who knew a lot about psychotherapy. Morgan went to see Jung because of her affair with Henry Murray, who was in analytical therapy with Jung at the same time. Murray himself complained that the concepts Jung was using were extremely autobiographic and that everything Jung talked about was rather about his relationship with Toni Wolff. He openly assumed that Jung's main interest was not the patient nor his development, and he, therefore, was not really paying any attention to the reality of his patients.

> He does not know how much he talks. He also writes that he lets the patient go on and on, then the patient arrives at what path he ought to take just by a sort of spontaneous process after going through alternative possibilities. He gives you a picture of taking a very listening part, not passive but not intervening. But he is intervening, every single minute. He tells you every minute what he thinks or very close what he thinks, even though he may not say it explicitly in so many words.
>
> (Murray, C.G. Jung Biographical Archive, Countway Library of Medicine)

Jung advised him explicitly to use his two partners (wife and affair) in the same way Jung did, giving the role of homemaker and mother to the one and the role of femme inspiratrice to the other, and to explicitly talk about this with both of them. In accordance with "Die Ehe als psychologische Beziehung" ("Marriage as a psychological relationship", CW 17), Jung tried to force his theory of the containing and the contained on his patient Christiana Morgan, Murray's lover, rather than taking any interest in her problem. He told her to take on the role of the femme inspiratrice for her lover because it was important for his development. He said to her, "You are a pioneer. Your function is to create a man. Some women create children, but it is more important to create a man. If you create Murray, you will have done something very important for the world" (Douglas 1997b, S. 151). She surrendered to this recommendation and gave up on her wish to marry her partner.

Jung and Toni Wolff even developed a theory based on the attribution of a role to the woman as inspiration for a man: "There are women who are not made for giving birth to physical children, but to help a man to find rebirth in a spiritual sense, which is a highly important function" (Jung in a letter to Carol Jeffrey, June 18, 1958; Jung 2012). Joseph Wheelwright reports that this viewpoint was very much supported in the early Jungian community: "We were told that women were not really capable of thinking for themselves. Women were supposed to make the thoughts of a man real and concrete" (Wheelwright 1984, p. 160).

What these reports tell us is that Jung, absolutely convinced of the validity of his concepts, was willing to force them onto his patients, instead of dealing with the material unprejudiced. This may not have been a problem for many followers who admired Jung and wanted to take over his views, so it becomes apparent only in those cases in which the clients opposed Jung's views (e.g., Henry Morgan). As far as it concerns archetype theory, what I am trying to demonstrate is that we should be careful regarding the clinical material Jung provides as footing for his theory.

Jung's view of transference

One of the strongest contradictions that can be found in Jung's works concerns his attitude to the concept of transference. In the beginning, during his cooperation with Freud, Jung emphasizes the importance of the transference for any psychotherapy. Later, the concept becomes less and less important. This development happens while he engages more and more in relationships with earlier clients, especially females. Then he argues the natural gratitude of the patient could turn into a personal friendship: "A personal human reaction to you is normal and reasonable, therefore let it be, it deserves to live; it is not transference anymore" but "harmless intercourse" (Healy 2017, p. 105). Analysts from his circle (e.g., Maria Moltzer) criticized this statement already at that time (Bair 2003). In contrast to this view, many of Jung's female patients continued to have extremely strong transferences towards him, and in some cases, he made use of this to his own advantage by letting them work for him and not resolve their strong transference (Kirsch 2004). Toni Wolff used to be one of Jung's clients in the beginning, as well as Marie-Louise von Franz, who came to him when she was 19 years of age. Jung knowingly used her transference to him and asked her to search material in libraries for a new project of his – the study of alchemy, which Toni Wolff did not want to help him with (Healy 2017). Von Franz herself talked about her extreme transference on Jung and how it affected her life:

> It made me isolated. I had no friends of my own generation. I was always alone, so therefore I could do his scholarship. I shed all to other people. I suffered a lot for that, because I never knew what was wrong with me, why I could not get on with my people (i.e., those of her own age). I lived in another world than they did. So it gave me a lot of time to study and work for Jung.
>
> (Bair 2003, S. 370)

In 1946, Jung revised the role of transference in psychotherapy completely and calls it marginal. As a result, dealing with transference was not a part of the training at the Zürich Jung-Institute. June Singer, one of the first generation of students, complains:

> We were never taught anything specifically about ethics in our seminars at the institute as far as I can recall. Most of what we learned about transference-countertransference was based on Jung's commentary on the Rosarium Philosophorum. Of course, we understood that this was all symbolic – you were not supposed to get into the bathtub with your analysand – but after the symbolism came and went, what actually was permissible? Somehow, with receiving the analyst's diploma, you were supposed to know.
>
> (Healy 2017, p. 106)

I am referring to these statements here because they demonstrate a problematic in Jung, on the level of personal life conduct (see the detailed account of his relationship to Toni Wolff in Healy 2017) as well as on the level of theory, when it comes to interpersonal relationships. From my point of view, there is no real concept of relationships in Jung's works, at least not in the sense of what kind of deeper meaning a relationship between two people has. To Jung, a relationship is only a projection screen for the individuation process, and when it has fulfilled its function, it is over.

In Jung's perspective, development of the personality happens almost exclusively from inside the individual autonomously. Relationships do not play a role beyond their being a projection screen. For example: "At the heart of marriage is the question whether one can live his true nature, and if one can give the other – being it husband or wife – the freedom for their individuation" (Jung in Jaffé 2021, p. 57; transl. C.R.). This means a relationship, such as marriage, at best, is not an obstacle to individuation.

This attitude is in drastic contrast to the state-of-the-art in human and social sciences – and in practically all the other psychoanalytic schools – that relationships are at the very beginning of individual development and are absolutely essential for the development of the personality. The research and contemporary insights into this model of a "relational self" were presented in the chapter "Biology". There is a lack of clarity in the theory of analytic psychology as to where development comes from, which role relationships play in the matter and what that means for the therapeutic relationship.

Meanwhile, there has been some theoretical development regarding the conceptualization of the transference and its role in psychotherapy, mainly in the British – so-called developmental – school of AP. But there is no match to the theoretical developments in the Freudian tradition (e.g., object relations theory, self-psychology, infant observation, etc.). From my point of view, it is still an open question how these viewpoints on the therapeutic relationship (Jungian and post-Freudian) can be integrated. So for example, what do the findings of attachment research mean for an archetypal perspective on the therapeutic process? In Germany, as far as I can see, in the training institutes, a modern approach to the transference is presented, which is based on object relations theory, self-psychology and relational perspectives, and in a separated section, there is teaching on archetypal transference, but it is not clear what the two have to do with each other. There is seemingly not even an awareness that the two models are, in a certain sense, contradictory.

The role of archetypes in the developmental school

Hester McFarland Solomon's (1997) comprehensive overview of the so-called developmental school in AP pinpoints the central problem in Jung's writings about psychotherapy, the therapeutic process and the therapeutic relationship.

> AP as elaborated by Jung and his immediate followers did not focus on the depth psychological aspects of the early infant and childhood development. Neither was there much attention paid to the usefulness of understanding the varieties of relationship that can occur in the consulting room between patient and analyst. . . . The lack of a clinical and theoretical tradition of investigation in these two important areas . . . with the resulting lack of interest in understanding their interrelationship via the analysis of the infantile transference, left AP impoverished in an important way. This would need to be rectified if AP was to go on developing as a creditable professional and clinical endeavor.
>
> (Solomon 1997, p. 119)

In her paper, Solomon traces the development in the London group of Jungian analysts who found what they missed in the so-called London object relations school, namely, in authors like Melanie Klein, Donald Winnicott and Alfred Bion (Zinkin 1991). Michael Fordham later enhanced this in his process model of disintegration-reintegration (for a detailed overview, see Roesler 2021). The general idea in Fordham includes the concept of a Self as first described by Jung, which can be seen as an original integrate or the unique identity of the child, which is present from birth. Through encounters with the environment, which in a certain sense question or confront this original integrate, processes of disintegration are initiated, which can only be reintegrated via the interaction with caregivers. In this model, in contrast to Jung, the role of interaction with caregivers and their capacity to help and support the infant in reintegration becomes crucial. This role can also be taken over by the analyst in psychotherapy. In both kinds of relationships, it is the interaction which provides the continuity of the Self, even though the integrity of the Self and its capacity for self-regulation and healing is given from the beginning.

It has to be pointed out that this new model that developed in the developmental school is fundamentally different from Jung's model, which puts emphasis on the aspect of self-regulation in the sense that the process comes out of the individual. The focus is more on interactions with inner figures (e.g., anima). In Jung's model, the other is nothing more than a projection screen on which the archetypal deintegrates are projected and, if the process is wholesome, can be acknowledged as parts of the Self, which then can be taken back and incorporated consciously into the personality.

More recent "Post-Jungian" approaches even go beyond that:

> What has impressed me is the way in which the two apparently opposed developmental and archetypal schools have reacted similarly in an iconoclastic, revisionary way to the expressed tenets of classical AP. The two wings are attacking the centre. . . . For example, both schools find the classical concept of the self to be overweighted by emphasis on potential and review of conflict conditioned by possibilities of resolution. Both schools have earthed the idea of individuation. . . . Crucially, both schools do not strive for wholeness as a psychological goal. Instead, a differentiation of psychic contents is stressed, equally well illustrated whether we speak of "polytheism" or of the "deintegrates of the self".
>
> (Samuels 1990, p. 294)

There is also another important point to be made: the model of the developmental school is more or less identical with the first of the aforementioned versions of the core or process theory, the idea that from the beginning, there is a preformatted identity or centre of the personality and that the process is of a centring nature. As far as I can see, there is no place in the developmental school for what I have called the classical archetypes, or the second version mentioned earlier that is a process which can be mapped as a sequence of stages, and these are clearly defined by their content.

Jean Knox (2009), in her paper which attempts to integrate Jungian, attachment theory and developmental perspectives into a theoretical model of the analytical relationship correctly stresses the point that it was Jung, who first in the history of psychoanalysis spoke of the mutual relationship between analyst and patient in which both descend into mutual unconscious entanglements and projections, out of which a conscious understanding and, eventually, individuation will emerge.

> Nevertheless, there remain sharp divisions between different groups in both psychoanalysis and AP about the relative importance of the relational and interpretive aspects of analytic work. These divisions partly reflect the differing perceptions of the nature of the unconscious.
>
> (Knox 2009, p. 6)

Although contemporary approaches in the psychodynamic psychotherapies, as for example, attachment theory, strongly support the idea that was already present in Jung's thought, as mentioned earlier, of a self-organizing principle in the psyche, these contemporary approaches differ from the classical viewpoint in Jungian psychotherapy when it comes to the role and shape of the therapeutic relationship.

It supports the view that the analytical relationship needs to be more flexible than either the classical psychoanalytic interpretive or the classical Jungian archetypal models would allow; in place of the uncovering of specific mental content (e.g. repressed Oedipal material or archetypes), an attachment orientated analyst accompanies the patient on the developmental journey, one that will sometimes require interpretation of such material but will also allow for new experiences to emerge in the analytical relationship.

(Knox 2009, pp. 8–9)

Knox points out that beginning with the object relations school in psychoanalysis, all of the contemporary relational approaches in psychoanalysis agree on the three fundamental developmental tasks that have to be accomplished in a successful therapy:

1. affect regulation
2. the capacity for mentalization
3. a sense of self-agency

These capacities, especially affect regulation and the capacity for mentalization, directly result from the relational interaction with the therapist/analyst, especially "the emotional regulation offered by the relationship creates the conditions necessary for the neuronal development in the orbitofrontal cortex and other areas on which affect regulation depends" (Knox 2009, p. 10). These tasks are very different from what Jung thought to be the aims of therapy. Here, the relational model speaks of mental capacities, whereas Jung speaks of clearly defined stages of a process – which has a parallel in what we found (in the chapter on biology) to be different in Jung's view of biologically inherited qualities (i.e., archetypes) as being specified by their content (e.g., anima, the wise old man, etc.) versus contemporary insights in innate qualities being mainly capacities for interaction, relating and communication. It is interesting that this differentiation repeats the insights from the discussion of contemporary developmental models in biology which also show that there are inborn mental capacities, but the emphasis is on capacity and not on content, whereas Jung's idea was that content patterns were preformatted.

Thus:

A developmental Jungian analysis may result in analyst and patient co-constructing a different kind of narrative from that which emerges in a more classical Jungian analysis, but in both approaches the patient's unconscious is seen as playing an active and creative role in the emergence of a meaningful analytic story.

(ibid., p. 14)

It also has to be noted that based on the research presented in the chapter on biology, which found that inborn capacities consist of interaction and relationship abilities, in contemporary psychodynamic approaches, the Self in development is always conceptualized as "Self-being-with-other" (Stern 1985) – which is fundamentally different from Jungian conceptualizations. Contemporary approaches see the relationship at the beginning, whereas the Jungian school assumes that the Self is preformatted and primary. This is an unresolved question: Where does development come from, from the relationship or from the preformatted Self being an autonomous process? This question includes also the therapeutic relationship: Where does therapeutic change come from, from the experience of the relationship with the therapist (which is then internalized as "good object"), or is the therapist and the therapeutic relationship just working as a catalyst for an autonomous process coming from within? I hope it becomes clear that these questions are absolutely crucial for the future of AP. If we will not be able to point out what is the specific about the Jungian approach in terms of how development comes about and how therapeutic change is effected, there is no reason why we should not just merge with the other psychodynamic schools – as publications like that by Kast, Jacoby and Knox imply.

Speaking of how change is effected in psychotherapy, there is another process model, or better to say, a process metaphor, inherent in Jungian theorizing, which is rarely mentioned but, from my point of view, probably the most important metaphor for psychotherapeutic change as contributed by Jung's thought, the **idea of death and renewal** being a basic image of how psychological change comes about, namely, by letting go of the aims of the conscious ego – Jung sometimes uses the term sacrifice – which makes change and renewal possible. Personally, I believe that this is the most important contribution Jung made to psychology, as it refers to the deep mystery of how change in human life is accomplished, and it also links Jungian psychology with the religious and especially the mystical traditions. It also distinguishes Jungian psychotherapy from all the other psychotherapeutic schools and puts it in a spiritual context (for more details, see Roesler & Reefschläger 2022).

The theory of archetypes as a hermeneutics

I believe that the process idea inherent in Jung's archetype theory can still be used for the psychotherapeutic process, but this requires that we give up on the biologistic and nomothetic, in many aspects, even positivistic statements that Jung made about archetypes. In contrast, the theory of an archetypal process which takes place in psychological transformations and which can be described by its stages has to be regarded as an interpretation schema, a template for what could be called a clinically applied hermeneutics. Such a viewpoint has already been discussed in the humanities:

> Consequently, it considers Jung's writings and analytic discipline of which they are the foundation as part of the cultural sciences, that is, as part of a comprehensive interpretive project in which Jung's interpretation of the self and its "textual" productions (dream, myth, vision, art) are inseparable from his hermeneutics of culture. Indeed, the archetype is the culture of the self.
>
> (Barnaby & D'Acierno 1990, p. XVI)

These authors argue about Jung:

> did develop an interpretative methodology in his analytical practice, a herme-
> neutics. . . . Consequently, a properly Jungian hermeneutics involves the deploy-
> ment of a flexible (pluralistic), comparative, and interdisciplinary exegesis that
> seeks out interpretive possibilities – not conclusions – and whose canonic pro-
> cedures amplify the symbol-text by adding to it a wealth of personal and collec-
> tive, historical and cultural analogies, correspondences, and parallels. In other
> words, the Jungian interpretation unfolds as a production – a positing of mean-
> ings in relation to and not the uncovering of "the meaning".
>
> (p. XVII)

Jung himself gives a very similar definition of this approach:

> The essential character of hermeneutics . . . consists in making successive addi-
> tions of other analogies to the analogy given in the symbol . . . . This procedure
> widens and enriches the initial symbol, and the final outcome is an infinitely com-
> plex and varied picture, in which certain lines of psychological development
> stand out as possibilities that are at once individual and collective. There is no
> science on earth by which these lines could be proved right.
>
> (CW 7, para. 287)

It has to be noted, though, and was pointed out earlier in detail that Jung himself
often violated this principle by making far-reaching, even nomothetic, statements
with the claim of stating facts in the way of a natural science. He even practiced –
and so did many of his followers – what could be called "vulgar Jungianism (the
mechanical and reductivist allegorical rewriting of a text according to the master
code of the archetypes)" (Barnaby & D'Acierno 1990, p. XXI). In contrast to this,
we have to discard the idea that the meaning is fixed to the symbol, an idea which
can only be characterized as a primitive form of naïve essentialist epistemology.
Instead, meaning is only produced in an interactive relationship between at least
two human minds. This is the reason why psychotherapy and psychotherapeutic
change need two persons. And this relationship is much more than just a projection
screen; it is a place where something new emerges. I believe that here, still, all the
wonderful imagery of alchemy can be applied, as has been brilliantly pointed out
by Nathan Schwartz-Salant (1998) in his *The Mystery of Human Relationship*. But
we always have to keep in mind that these images are just metaphors, not tools to
uncover "the meaning" but elements used to enrich the therapeutic relationship and
the process going on in the client. The images that we use, and the mythological
stories that have accumulated in human history, may be used as attempts to picture
or describe these psychic processes so difficult to describe in theoretical terms.

In this sense, we can find a new answer to the question: What kind of science is
archetype theory (and with it, AP)? I have already pointed out that Jung's attempt
to formulate archetype theory as if it were a natural science was misconceptualized

from the beginning, a "scientistic self-misunderstanding". Since at the heart of analytic practice in AP, that is when we deal with what we consider to be archetypes, we are concerned with images and other artistic creations, myths, fairy tales and other narrative texts, symbols and imaginations, we could characterize AP as being a poetic science – concerned with finding, and sometimes even creating, meaning. This viewpoint has been excellently described by James Hillman (1971, 1975, 1983), who never made the mistake to confuse the psychology of the archetype with the natural sciences but made clear from the beginnings of his archetypal psychology that he was speaking of a world of imagination.

The difference to classical archetype theory is that we no longer argue that behind these stories, images and cultural products are some innate patterns; the viewpoint that in these mythological stories, images, etc., there is some psychological insight condensed into metaphors is just an idea, an interpretation scheme, which we make use of in psychotherapy, but we should never forget about its hypothetical and interpretive character. In this sense, archetype theory could be reformulated as being a theory of cultural symbolization processes of psychological transformations.

What remains of archetype theory?

Based on the insights presented in this study, there is no alternative to discarding the majority of assumptions inherent in archetype theory. It makes no sense to search for a biological or even genetic foundation for what we call archetypes. It is also not an anthropological theory which can explain assumed universals, nor can it provide any explanations about "archaisms" which link modern humans with archaic humans from prehistory.

I believe that archetype theory can only survive if we radically reduce the theory, its claims and its scope of application. We should stop to make any assumptions about the "instinctual" foundation of the psyche or any other dubious biological conceptualizations. Therefore, theories which are discussed in the field of psychotherapy recently, as for example Panksepp's model of basic emotional and action systems, or the idea of basic needs, although they have a high explanatory value, are not the same as archetype theory and should not be confused with it (if one wants to do so, the question comes up why we should maintain the term archetype for these processes, since it is so much confused with other meanings; these ideas are also certainly not specifically Jungian). We should also stop to make statements and claims about facts and relations in the fields of anthropology, prehistory, history of religion etc. – as I have pointed out, these are clearly refuted. Archetype theory should be reduced to an explanatory model for the process of psychotherapy. I strongly believe – and here I would still call myself a Jungian – there is a deep truth in the idea that there is a universal and autonomous process in the psyche unfolding over the course of psychotherapy; I also believe that this process can be mapped. I am quite sceptical whether this map, when we have investigated well-documented processes open-mindedly, will look like what Jung described. Some elements may be supported; for example, it makes a lot of sense to me that the repressed aspects of one's personality appear as a shadow figure, and if a person succeeds in integrating these aspects the shadow will provide a wealth of qualities and energy to the person. I am not so convinced that the same applies to concepts anima and animus, the wise old man, etc., even though there may be something to these concepts. Also, it is not necessary to assume innate archetypes for understanding the processes around what we call the shadow; complex theory (Roesler & van Uffelen 2018) is absolutely sufficient for describing and explaining these processes (see next section).

But the general idea Jung proposed, that there is a helping force in the unconscious which supports the therapeutic process by presenting symbols, images and narrative patterns, e.g., in dreams, I see as one of the most important contributions to the field of psychotherapy in the 20th century. Jung's idea of the self-organizing principle of the psyche, what also could be called the "transcendent function", is the forerunner of a whole number of concepts at the heart of different contemporary schools of psychotherapy, among them the humanistic schools, the systemic approach etc. I would also stress the point that we can work with this approach without making dubious statements about its biological foundation, or by drawing questionable parallels to the fields of anthropology, religion, prehistory and the like. This does not mean that we cannot use knowledge from these fields, for example societal rules that have developed in indigenous societies or wholesame practices that have developed in the field of religion, as a form of wisdom which can inform the psychotherapeutic process – in the sense of that they tell us something about what it means to be human and what the psyche needs for healing and wholeness. We just have to keep in mind that if we use such elements they are just interpretations, i.e., forms of creating meaning, and not facts out there in the world. This attitude would imply to say goodbye to the reification of archetype theory. But when we practice psychotherapy, we are dealing with humans and human relationships, and this human world is characterized first and foremost by being a world of meaning.

What about the idea of a collective unconscious and its contents?

Mills (2019), in a profound analysis of the epistemological and theoretical problems inherent in Jung's concept of a collective unconscious, has demonstrated that this concept cannot be maintained in the form presented by Jung (see also Hunt 2012). I have already proposed (Roesler 2021) that instead of continuing Jung's questionable assumptions about a collective unconscious and its preformed contents, we could modernize these ideas by making use of the concept of cultural complexes as presented by Singer and Kimbles (2004a). It has to be noted that the idea of a cultural unconscious was introduced by Joseph Henderson (1991). This would allow for maintaining the idea that there is a collectively shared sphere which is unconscious and which can have massive impact on social groups and processes, yes, even on nations and societies – by way of its "numinous" qualities, if you like.

> We call these group complexes "cultural complexes" and they, too, can be defined as an emotionally charged aggregate of ideas and images that cluster around an archetypal core. . . . Group complexes are ubiquitous and one feels swamped by their affects and claim.
>
> (Singer & Kimbles 2004a, pp. 176–178)[1]

The crucial difference to the original concept of a collective unconscious is the point that cultural complexes are not conceptualized as being primal (i.e., before any experience). As it was pointed out, this assumption is more than questionable, if not refuted. Instead, they are built upon experience but not so much on an individual as more on a collective (i.e., societal and historical level). In that sense, the theory of cultural complexes is very much in line with contemporary approaches in the social sciences and does not continue the total neglect of social science viewpoints to be found in Jung's theorizing around the collective unconscious. The theory of cultural complexes can easily be integrated with concepts as the meme (see previous section), the cultural/collective memory and other concepts which are well established in the social and historical sciences (for details, see Roesler 2021). It can also be well aligned with conceptualizations in the broader field of contemporary psychoanalysis, such as "the field", the shared unconscious, etc. (for details, see Roesler 2013).

> Cultural complexes structure emotional experience and operate in the personal and collective psyche in much the same way as individual complexes, although their content might be quite different. Like individual complexes, cultural complexes tend to be repetitive, autonomous, resist consciousness, and collect experience that confirms their historical point of view. And, [. . .], cultural complexes tend to be bipolar, so that when they are activated the group ego or the individual ego of a group member becomes identified with one part of the unconscious cultural complex, while the other part is projected out onto the suitable hook of another group or one of its members.[2] [. . .] Finally, like personal complexes, cultural complexes can provide those caught in their potent web of stories and emotions with a simplistic certainty about the group's place in the world in the face of otherwise conflicting and ambiguous uncertainties. . . . It is a description of groups and classes of people as filtered through the psyches of generations of ancestors. It contains an abundance of information and misinformation about the structures of societies – a truly inner sociology – and it's essential building blocks are cultural complexes.
>
> (Singer & Kimbles 2004a, pp. 185–186)

Ironically, Jung's conceptualization of his archetype theory and how it has developed in the community of AP (i.e., the form it has taken of a belief system) could be called a cultural complex specific for the Jungian community.

Outlook: The directions of future research

> As a final note, my guess is that Jung would not have wanted a legacy of a group of followers who look upon his theory with reverence rather than with a critical eye. Jung was well aware of the intellectual atrophy that developed in psychoanalysis because of this problem. The question is, will Jungians be able to avoid this potentially fatal error?
>
> (Neher 1996, p. 89)

These conclusions imply specific directions for future research in AP. If we reconceptualize archetypes as being cultural products, we have to investigate them by making use of the methodologies developed in the cultural and social sciences (i.e., mainly qualitative and interpretive research methods) (see, for example, Roesler 2006, 2010a, 2010b, 2021). Such studies should always start from the insights and approaches which have developed in the respective disciplines, namely, anthropology, religious studies, comparative mythology, etc. Future research should also clearly depart from the idea to find eternal archetypes and instead incorporate the general viewpoints elaborated in the cultural and social sciences (i.e., that such structures and patterns always serve certain needs and interests on a collective as well as on an individual level and are thus subject to historical change).

There is especially a great need to conduct research on psychotherapeutic processes, in analytical as well as in other psychotherapies. As I have pointed out in an earlier report to the IAAP about future research strategies in AP (accessible on the website of the IAAP) the crucial point is to establish a comprehensive and standardized system of documentation to be applied to psychotherapeutic processes, so as to create a databank which would allow for detailed investigations of unconscious processes going on in psychotherapy. Only if we succeed in creating such detailed documentations we will be able to search for interindividually occurring patterns, structures, symbols, processes, etc., which then could support the aforementioned idea of a universal process taking place in psychotherapy – we may then call archetypal. In the following, I would like to provide an example of such a research process and its findings:

> For a number of years now I have been conducting research on dream series from analytical psychotherapies, investigating the connections between the structure and imagery of the dreams as they change over the course of therapy, the psychopathology of the dreamer and the results of therapy. For this reason, I have developed the method Structural Dream Analysis (SDA) (for details see Roesler 2020a, 2020b, 2019a, 2019b, 2018). We found that there is a clear connection between the initial psychological problem (i.e., the complex) of the client and the typical structure of the dreams in the initial phase of therapy, typically picturing the dream ego being threatened. In successful therapies there is a typical succession of dream patterns, with a middle phase in which the core problem/complex is worked on, and if this central pathological

complex can be integrated, the structure of the dreams rises to a mature level of ego functioning, emotion regulation and autonomy. We have found this typical development of dream structures in successful therapies in several independent samples, lastly in a sample of 150 case documentations from the Stuttgart Jung Institute. Now the interesting finding, from the viewpoint of archetype theory, is that when the integration of the central complex is successful and the therapy turns into its final phase, towards more mature dream structures picturing higher ego functioning and integration, at this turning point we have found for 40% of the cases a typical motif appearing in the dreams: a child appears for which the dreamer is supposed to care, or the child conveys wisdom, helpful information, or offers help. Of course, every Jungian is reminded of Jung's idea about the archetype of the divine child, which stands for the future or a new beginning, maybe even for the emerging Self. What makes me confident as a researcher is the fact that I did not expect to find this motif, nor did we even search for it. This is an example for what I would call an open-minded approach to investigating archetype theory.

Another interesting research question in the field of archetypes is how Jungian therapists actually work with what they consider to be archetypes, so as to get a more empirically grounded understanding of the actual practice of analytic psychotherapy in the Jungian context – a claim that is not new in AP:

> A second line of inquiry in clinical research concerns research into the clinical process. This would be mainly, though not exclusively, of interest to clinicians, and would focus, for example, on how practitioners employ the theoretical concepts with which they are equipped, or on how responses to particular kinds of material with which they are confronted by patients are managed differently by different practitioners on the basis of theoretical orientation and personal variables.
>
> (Samuels 1998, p. 26)

As I have argued in many places, what is needed to create such research approaches is, on the one hand, a more open-minded attitude in Jungians, which is not fixated on providing proof for Jung's theories whatever it may cost but instead is interested to find out how things really are, in this case, what really happens in the course of psychotherapy. On the other hand, as soon as this attitude is given, we need a common effort to collect data, to systematically document our psychotherapies and to build a solid databank for such investigations into the process of psychotherapy – whatever it is that we will find out in the end.

Notes

1 The term "archetypal core" can be understood here, in contrast to classical conceptualizations, as speaking for a matter of high relevance for humans in general, as for example, identity, self-worth, autonomy, etc.
2 This quality of cultural complexes would allow for maintaining the important idea in Jung's archetype theory of a complementarity of the archetype, as having a bipolar quality, which is responsible not only for projection processes but also has a healing potential. As a consequence, this would also allow for maintaining the idea of a compensatory nature of the unconscious, which aims at balancing one-sidedness and completing the personality. Again, it is not necessary for maintaining these viewpoints to cling to the idea of innate archetypes.

References

Aarne, A., & Thompson, S. (1961). *The types of the folktale: A classification and bibliography. Translated and enlarged by Stith Thompson* (2nd Rev.). Helsinki: Suomalainen Tiedeakatemia.

Adavasio, J. M., Soffer, O., & Page, J. (2007). *The invisible sex. Uncovering the true roles of women in prehistory*. Walnut Creek: Left Coast Press.

Ahnert, L. (2010). *Wieviel Mutter braucht ein Kind?* Heidelberg: Spektrum.

Alcaro, A., Carta, S., & Panksepp, J. (2017). The affective core of the self: A neuro-archetypal perspective on the foundations of human (and animal) subjectivity. *Frontiers in Psychology, 8*(1424), 1–13.

Atmanspacher, H., & Fuchs, C. (Eds.). (2014). *The Pauli-Jung dialogue and its impact today*. Exeter: Imprint Academic.

Atmanspacher, H., Römer, H., & Walach, H. (2002). Weak quantum theory: Complementarity and entanglement in physics and beyond. *Foundations of Physics, 32*(3), 379–406.

Auerbach, J. S. (2014). Review of psychodynamic psychotherapy research: Evidence-based practice and practice-based evidence. *Psychoanalytic Psychology, 31*(2), 276–287.

Bachofen, J. J. (1861/2004). *Das Mutterrecht. Engl. Version: Mother right: A study of the religious and juridical aspects of gynecocracy in the ancient world*. New York: Edwin Mellen Press.

Bahn, P. (2011). Religion and ritual in the upper paleolithic. In T. Insoll (Ed.), *Oxford handbook of the archeology of ritual and religion* (pp. 344–357). Oxford: Oxford University Press.

Bair, D. (2003). *Jung. A biography*. New York and Boston: Little, Brown & Co.

Bakermans-Kranenburg, M. J., & van Ijzendoorn, M. H. (2018). Attachment, parenting, and genetics. In J. Cassidy & P. R. Shaver (Eds.), *Handbook of attachment* (3rd ed., pp. 155–179). New York and London: Guilford.

Barnaby, K., & D'Acierno, P. (1990). *C. G. Jung and the humanities: Toward a hermeneutics of culture*. Princeton: Princeton University Press.

Barnard, A. (2014). Complex kinship patterns as evolutionary constructions, and the origins of sociocultural universals. *Current Anthropology, 55*(6), 766–767.

Bastian, A. (1881). *Der Völkergedanke im Aufbau einer Wissenschaft vom Menschen*. Berlin: Dietrich Reimer.

Bauer, J. (2002). *Das Gedächtnis des Körpers. Wie Beziehungen und Lebenstile unsere Gene steuern*. Frankfurt/M: Eichborn.

Bauer, J. (2019). *Wie wir werden wer wir sind. Die Enstehung des menschlichen Selbst durch Resonanz*. München: Blessing.

Baumann, H. (1936). *Schöpfung und Urzeit des Menschen im Mythus der afrikanischen Völker*. Berlin: Dietrich Reimer.

Beer, B., & Fischer, H. (2017). *Ethnologie: Einführung und Überblick*. Berlin: Reimer.

Bellah, R. N. (1964). Religious evolution. *American Sociological Review, 29*(3), 358–374.

Bellwood, P. (2004). First farmers: The origins of agricultural societies. *Journal of Field Archaeology, 31*(1), 109–110.

Belmonte, T. (1990). The trickster and the sacred clown. In K. Barnaby & P. D'Acierno (Eds.), *C. G. Jung and the humanities* (pp. 45–66). Princeton: Princeton University Press.

Belsky, J., & Pluess, M. (2009). The nature (and nurture?) of plasticity in early human development. *Perspectives on Psychological Science, 4*, 345–351.

Benedict, R. (1934). *Patterns of culture*. New York: Houghton Mifflin.

Benigni, H. (2013). *The mythology of Venus: Ancient calendars and archaeoastronomy*. Lanham, MD: University Press of America.

Berezkin, Y. (2005). The assessment of the probable age of Eurasian-American mythological links. *Archaeology, Ethnology and Anthropology of Eurasia, 21*(1), 146–151.

Bild der Wissenschaft. (2013). *Spezial: Archäologie, Geschichte, Kultur – Der kreative Mensch (special issue: Archaeology, history, culture – man creative)*. Berlin: Spektrum. www.spektrum.de

Binford, L. R. (1971). Mortuary practices: Their study and their potential. In J. A. Brown (Ed.), Approaches to the social dimensions of mortuary practices. *Memoirs of the Society for American Archaeology, 25*, 6–29.

Binford, L. R. (1983). *Working at archaeology*. New York: Academic Press.

Bischof, N. (1985/2020). *Das Rätsel Ödipus*. Giessen: Psychsozial.

Bischof, N. (1996). *Das Kraftfeld der Mythen*. München: Piper.

Blackmore, S. (1999). *The Meme Machine*. Oxford: Oxford University Press.

Bloch, M. (1998). *How we think they think: Anthropological approaches to cognition, memory and literacy*. Boulder: Westview Press.

Boas, F. (1922). *Kultur und Rasse (culture and race)*. Berlin and Leipzig: De Gruyter.

Boechat, W. (2022). *The collective unconscious*. https://iaap.org/the-collective-unconscious-2/

Bowie, F. (2004). *The anthropology of religion: An introduction*. Oxford: Blackwell Publishing.

Brown, D. E. (1991). *Human universals*. New York: McGraw-Hill Professional.

Brown, D. E. (2000). Human universals and their implications. In N. Roughley (Ed.), *Being humans: Anthropological universality and particularity in transdisciplinary perspectives* (pp. 156–174). Berlin: Walter de Gruyter.

Brown, D. E. (2002). Human nature and history. *History and Theory, 38*(4),138–157.

Brown, D. E. (2004). Human universals, human nature & human culture. *Daedalus, 133*(4), 47–54.

Bruner, J. (1990). *Acts of meaning*. Cambridge: Harvard University Press.

Burda, G. (2019). *Pandora und die Metaphysica medialis*. Münster and New York: Waxmann.

Burl, A. (1999). *Great stone circles. Fables, fictions, facts*. New Haven and London: Yale University Press.

Buss, D. M. (2015). *Evolutionary psychology. The new science of the mind*. London and New York: Routledge.

Cambray, J. (2002). Synchronicity and emergence. *American Imago, 59*(4), 409–434.

Cambray, J. (2009). *Synchronicity: Nature and Psyche in an Interconnected Universe*. College Station: Texas A&M University Press.

Campbell, J. (1971). *The hero with a thousand faces*. Princeton: Princeton University Press.

Carrette, J. (1994). The language of archetypes: A conspiracy in psychological theory. *Harvest, 40*, 168–192.

Cassidy, J., & Shaver, P. R. (2018). *Handbook of attachment. Theory, research and clinical applications* (3rd ed.). New York and London: Guilford.

Cavalli-Sforza, L. L. (2001). *Genes, peoples, and languages. The biological foundations of civilization*. New York: Farrar, Straus & Giroux.

Cavalli-Sforza, L. L., & Cavalli-Sforza, F. (1995). *The great human diasporas: The history of diversity and evolution*. Boston, MA: Perseus Books.

Cavalli-Sforza, L. L., Menozzi, P., & Pizaaz, A. (1994). *The history and geography of human genes*. Princeton, NJ: Princeton University Press.

Chapais, B. (2011). The evolutionary history of pair-bonding and parental collaboration. In C. Salmon & T. K. Shackelford (Eds.), *The Oxford handbook of evolutionary family psychology* (pp. 33–50). New York, NY: Oxford University Press.

Chapais, B. (2017). Primate origins of human behavior. In *Encyclopedia of behavioral neuroscience* (2nd ed., pp. 176–184).

Charmantier, A., & Garant, D. (2005). Environmental quality and evolutionary potential: Lessons from wild populations. *Proceedings of the Royal Society B: Biological Sciences, 272*(1571), 1415–1425.

Childe, V. G. (1958). *The prehistory of European society*. London: Penguin.

Chomsky, N. (1978). *Topics in the theory of generative grammar*. Den Haag: Mouton.

Colman, W. (2016). *Act and Image: The emergence of symbolic imagination*. New Orleans: Spring Journal Inc.

Colman, W. (2018). Bringing it all back home. How I became a relational analyst. In R. S. Brown (Ed.), *Reencountering Jung. AP and contemporary psychoanalysis* (pp. 129–145). London and New York: Routledge.

Conley, T. D. (2011). Perceived proposer personality characteristics and gender differences in acceptance of casual sex offers. *Journal of Personality and Social Psychology, 100*(2), 100–309.

Connolly, A. (2018). Sea changes. The iconic and aesthetic turns in depth psychology. In R. S. Brown (Ed.), *Reencountering Jung. AP and contemporary psychoanalysis* (pp. 68–82). London and New York: Routledge.

Cozolino, L. J. (2006). *The neuroscience of human relationships: Attachment and the developing social brain*. New York: Norton.

Cullen, B. S. (2000). *Contagious ideas – on evolution, culture, archaeology and cultural virus theory*. Oxford: Oxbow Books.

Dalal, F. (1991). The racism of Jung. *Race & Class, 24*(3), 1–22.

Damasio, A. (2010). *Self comes to mind: Constructing the conscious brain*. New York: Pantheon.

Darwin, C. (1859). *On the origin of species*. London: John Murray.

Darwin, C. (1871). *The descent of man, and selection in relation to sex*. London: John Murray.

Davis, K. L., & Panksepp, J. (2011). The brain's emotional foundations of human personality and the affective neuroscience personality scales. *Neuroscience and Biobehavioral Reviews, 35*(9), 1946–1958.

Dawkins, R. (1976). *The selfish gene*. Oxford: Oxford University Press.

de Sousa, R. (2015). *Love. A very short introduction*. Oxford: Oxford University Press.

De Waal, F. (2019). *Mama's last hug: Animal emotions and what they tell us about ourselves*. New York and London: Norton.

Dehing, J. (1994). Containment – an archetype? *Journal of AP, 39*(4), 419–461.

Diamond, J. (1997). *Guns, germs, and steel: The fates of human societies*. London: Jonathan Cape.

Diercks, C., & Skale, E. (2021). Vom Wert einer historisch-kritischen Freud Edition. *Psyche, 75*(12), 1131–1160.

Dorst, B. (2015). *Therapeutisches Arbeiten mit Symbolen*. 2. Aufl. Stuttgart: Kohlhammer.

Douglas, C. (1997a). The historical context of AP. In P. Young-Eisendrath & T. Dawson (Eds.), *The Cambridge companion to Jung* (pp. 17–34). Cambridge: Cambridge University Press.

Douglas, C. (1997b). *Translate this darkness. The life of Christiana Morgan, the veiled woman in Jung's Circle*. Princeton: Princeton University Press.

Dourley, J. P. (1990). Jung's impact on religious studies. In K. Barnaby & P. D'Acierno (Eds.), *C. G. Jung and the humanities. Toward a hermeneutics of culture* (pp. 36–44). Princeton: Princeton University Press.

Durkheim, E. (1915/1976). *The elementary forms of the religious life*. London: George Allen and Unwin.

Edinger, E. (1985). *Anatomy of the psyche. Alchemical symbolism in psychotherapy*. LaSalle, IL: Open Court.

Eibl-Eibesfeldt, I. (1987). *Grundriß der vergleichenden Verhaltensforschung*. München: Piper.

Eisenstädter, J. (1912). *Elementargedanke und Übertragungstheorie in der Völkerkunde*. Stuttgart: Strecker & Schröder.

Ekman, P. (1994). Strong evidence for universals in facial expressions: A reply to Russell's mistaken critique. *Psychological Bulletin, 115*(2), 268–287.

Ekman, P., Friesen, W., O'Sullivan, M., & Chan, A. (1987). Universals and cultural differences in the judgment of facial expressions of emotions. *Journal of Personality and Social Psychology, 53*(4), 712–717.

Eliade, M. (1954). *The myth of the eternal return*. New York: Pantheon books.

Eliade, M. (1959). *The sacred and profane: The nature of religion*. New York: Harcourt Brace.

Eliade, M. (1964/1988). *Shamanism: Archaic techniques of ecstasy*. London: Arcana, Penguin.

Ember, M. (2000). *Human relations area files for the 21st century*. New Haven, CT: Human Relations Area Files Inc.

Erlenmeyer, A. (2001). Nach der Katastrophe: Auschwitz in Jungs Texten. *Analytische Psychologie, 32*, 107–121.

Evans-Pritchard, E. E. (1981). *A history of anthropological thought*. London and Boston: Faber and Faber.

Fagan, B. M., & Beck, C. (1996). *"Venus figurines", the Oxford companion to archaeology*. Oxford: Oxford University Press.

Fehlmann, M. (2001). *Die Rede vom Matriarchat. Zur Gebrauchsgeschichte eines Arguments*. Zürich: Chronos.

Fink, H., & Rosenzweig, R. (2015). *Das soziale Gehirn*. Münster: Mentis.

Fletcher, G. J. O. (2013). *The science of intimate relationships*. Chichester: Wiley-Blackwell.

Fordham, M. (1955). Editorial note. *Journal of AP, 1*, 3–5.

Fordham, M. (1976). *The self and autism*. London: Karnac.

Foulkes, L., & Blakemore, S.-J. (2018). Studying individual differences in human adolescent brain development. *Nature Neuroscience, 21*, 118–125.

Frazer, J. (1890). *The golden bough: A study in comparative religion, two volumes*. London: Macmillan.

Frobenius, L. (1904). *Das Zeitalter des Sonnengottes*. Berlin: Georg Reimer.

Frobenius, L. (1936). *Das Urbild. Cicerone zur vorgeschichtlichen Reichsbildergalerie*. Frankfurt am Main: Forschungsinstitut für Kulturmorphologie.

Geertz, C. (1973). The growth of culture and the evolution of mind. In C. Geertz (Ed.), *The interpretation of cultures* (pp. 55–87). New York: Basic Books.

Giegerich, W. (1975). *Ontogeny = Phylogeny. A fundamental critique of Erich Neumann's AP*. New Orleans, LA: Spring Journal Books.

Gieser, S. (2005). *The innermost kernel. Depth psychology and quantum physics – Wolfgang Pauli's dialogue with C. G. Jung*. New York: Springer.

Gimbutas, M. (1989). *The language of the Goddess: Unearthing the hidden symbols of western civilization*. London: Thames & Hudson.

Goodison, L., & Morris, C. (1989). *Ancient goddesses. The myths and the evidence*. London: Routledge.

Goodwyn, E. (2010). Approaching archetypes: Reconsidering innateness. *Journal of AP, 55*(4), 502–521.

Goodwyn, E. (2012). *The neurobiology of gods: How brain physiology shapes the recurrent imagery of myth and dreams*. New York: Routledge.

Goodwyn, E. (2019). Comments on the 2018 IAAP conference on archetype theory: Defending a non-reductive biological approach. *Journal of AP, 64*(5), 720–737.

Goodwyn, E. (2020a). Archetypes and the impoverished genome argument: Updates from evolutionary genetics. *Journal of AP, 65*(5), 911–931.

Goodwyn, E. (2020b). Archetypal origins. Biology vs. culture is a false dichotomy. *International Journal of Jungian Studies, 13*(2), 111–129.

Goodwyn, E. (2023). Phenotypic plasticity and archetype: A response to common objections to the biological theory of archetype and instinct. *Journal of Analytical Psychology, 68*(1), 109–132.

Gordon, R. (1985). Losing and finding: The location of archetypal experience. *Journal of AP, 30*(2), 117–133.

Gras, V. W. (1981). Myth and the reconciliation of opposites: Jung and Levi-Strauss. *Journal of the History of Ideas, 42*(3), 471–488.

Group of Jungians. (2018). Open letter from a group of Jungians on the question of Jung's writings on and theories about 'Africans'. *British Journal of Psychotherapy, 34*(4), 673–678.

Guo, G., & Marcus, K. (2012). The social influences on the realization of genetic potential for intellectual development. *Social Forces, 80*(3), 881–910.

Habermas, J. (1968). *Erkenntnis und Interesse*. Frankfurt am Main: Suhrkamp.

Halifax, J. (1991). *Shamanic voices: A survey of visionary narratives*. London: Penguin.

Harris, M. (1975). *Culture, people, nature: An introduction to general anthropology*. New York: Crowell.

Harrod, J. (2006). Periods of globalization over the southern route in human evolution. A metareview of archaeology and evidence for symbolic behavior. *Mother Tongue, 11*, 23–84.

Haule, J. R. (2004). Archetypal memory and the genetic/Darwinian paradigm. In L. Cowan (Ed.), *Barcelona 2004 – proceedings of the international congress for AP* (pp. 150–160), Einsiedeln: Daimon.

Haule, J. R. (2011). *Jung in the 21st century: Evolution and archetype* (Vol. I). New York: Routledge.

Haymond, R. (1982). On C. G. Jung: Psychosocial basis of morality during the Nazi era. *Journal of Psychology and Judaism, 6*(2), 124–137.

Healy, N. S. (2017). *Toni Wolff & C.G. Jung. A collaboration.* Los Angeles: Tiberius.

Heinz, A. (2019). Psychiatrie – die Kunst mit dem Irrationalen und Impliziten umzugehen. In B. Haslinger & B. Janta (Eds.), *Der unbewusste Mensch. Zwischen Psychoanalyse und neurobiologischer Evidenz* (pp. 55–72). Gießen: Psychosozial-Verlag.

Henderson, J. (1991). C. G. Jung's psychology: Additions and extensions. *Journal of AP, 36*(4), 429–442.

Hewlett, B. S., & Hewlett, B. L. (2008). *A bio cultural approach to sex, love and intimacy in central African foragers and farmers.* Chicago: Chicago University Press.

Heyerdahl, T. (1978). *Early man and the ocean.* London: George Allen & Unwin.

Hill, K., Walker, R. S., Božičević, M., & Eder, J. (2011). Co-residence patterns in hunter-gatherer societies show unique human social structure. *Science, 331*(6022), 1286–1289.

Hillman, J. (1971). *The myth of analysis.* Evanston: Northwestern University Press.

Hillman, J. (1975). *Revisioning psychology.* New York: Harper & Row.

Hillman, J. (1983). *Archetypal psychology: A brief account.* Dallas: Spring.

Hodder, I. (1987). Contextual archaeology: An interpretation of Catal Hüyük and a discussion of the origin of agriculture. *Bulletin of the Institute of Archaeology, University of London, 24*, 43–56.

Hodder, I. (2001). *Archaeological theory today.* Cambridge: Cambridge University Press.

Hodder, I. (2014). *Religion at work in a Neolithic society: Vital matters.* New York: Cambridge University Press.

Hogenson, G. B. (2001). The Baldwin effect: A neglected influence on C. G. Jung's evolutionary thinking. *Journal of AP, 46*(4), 591–611.

Hogenson, G. B. (2003). From silicon archetypes to robot dreams: Evolutionary theory and Jung's theory of archetypes. *Harvest, 58*, 7–21.

Hogenson, G. B. (2004). Archetypes: Emergence and the psyche's deep structure. In J. Cambray & L. Carter (Eds.), *AP: Contemporary perspectives in Jungian analysis.* Hove, NY: Brunner-Routledge.

Hogenson, G. B. (2009). Archetypes as action patterns. *Journal of AP, 54*(3), 325–337.

Hogenson, G. B. (2019). The controversy around the concept of archetypes. *Journal of AP, 64*(5), 682–700.

Homans, P. (1979). *Jung in context.* Chicago: University of Chicago Press.

Hopcke, R. (1989). *A guided tour of the Collected Works of C. G. Jung.* Boston and Shaftesbury: Shambhala.

Horton, R. (1994). *Patterns of fault in Africa and the West.* Cambridge: Cambridge University Press.

Hrdy, S. B. (2009). *Mothers and others: The evolutionary origins of mutual understanding.* Cambridge: Harvard University Press.

Hultkrantz, A. (1992). *Shamanic healing and ritual drama: Health and medicine in native North American religious traditions.* New York: Crossroad.

Humbert, E. (1988). *C. G. Jung: The fundamentals of theory and practice.* Wilmette, IL: Chiron.

Humbert, E. (1992). Archetypes reprinted. In R. K. Papadopoulos (Ed.), *Carl Gustav Jung – critical assessments* (Vol. 2). London: Routledge.

Hunt, H. T. (2012). A collective unconscious reconsidered: Jung's archetypal imagination in the light of contemporary psychology and social science. *Journal of AP*, *57*(1), 76–98.

Huston, H. L., Rosen, D. H., & Smith, S. M. (1999). Evolutionary memory. In D. H. Rosen & D. C. Luebbert (Eds.), *Evolution of the psyche*. Westport: Praeger.

Huxley, J. (1948). *Evolution: The modern synthesis*. London: Allan & Unwin.

Hyde, J. S. (2005). The gender similarities hypothesis. *American Psychologist*, *60*(6), 581–592.

Insoll, T. (2011). *Oxford handbook of the archaeology of ritual and religion*. Oxford: Oxford University Press.

Izard, V., Sann, C., Spelke, E. S., & Streri, A. (2009). Newborn infants perceive abstract numbers. *PNAS*, *6*(25), 10382–10385.

Jacobi, J. (1986). *Die Psychologie von C. G. Jung: eine Einführung in das Gesamtwerk*. Frankfurt: Fischer.

Jacoby, M. (1993). *Übertragung und Beziehung in der Jungschen Praxis (transference and relationship in Jungian practice)*. Düsseldorf: Walter Verlag.

Jacoby, M. (1998). *Grundformen seelischer Austauschprozesse. Jungsche Therapie und neuere Kleinkindforschung (basic forms of psychic interaction processes. Jungian therapy and contemporary infant research)*. Zürich and Düsseldorf: Walter Verlag.

Jaffé, A. (1971). *The myth of meaning*. London: Putnam.

Jaffé, A. (1985). C. G. Jung und der Nationalsozialismus. *Analytische Psychologie*, *16*, 66–77.

Jaffé, A. (1989). *From the life and works of C. G. Jung*. Einsiedeln: Daimon.

Jaffé, A. (Ed.). (2021). *Streiflichter zu Leben und Denken C.G. Jung*. Einsiedeln: Daimon.

Jones, R. A. (2003). On innateness: A response to Hogenson. *Journal of AP*, *48*(5), 705–718.

Jones, R. A. (Ed.). (2014). *Jung and the question of science*. London: Routledge.

Jung, C. G. (1916). *Wandlungen und Symbole der Libido* (B. Hindle, Trans.). New York: Moffat, Yard & Company. (Original work published 1912)

Jung, C. G. (1919). Instinct and the unconscious. *British Journal of Psychology*, *10*(1), 15–23.

Jung, C. G. (1936). Wotan. In *Aufsätze zur Zeitgeschichte*. Zürich: Rascher Verlag.

Jung, C. G. (1973). *Letters* (Vol. I., G. Adler & A. Jaffé, Ed.). Princeton: Princeton University Press.

Jung, C. G. (1984–2008). *The Collected Works of C.G. Jung*. London: Routledge.

Jung, C. G. (1989). *Memories, dreams, reflections*. New York: Vintage.

Jung, C. G. (2012). *Briefe I-III*. Ostfildern: Patmos Verlag.

Jung, C. G., Franz, M.-L., Henderson, J., Jacobi, J., & Jaffé, A. (1964). *Man and his symbols*. London: Aldus Books.

Jung, C. G., & Meyer-Grass, M. (2008). *Children's dreams: Notes from the seminar given in 1936 to 1940*. Princeton: Princeton University Press.

Kast, V. (1999). *Die Dynamik der Symbole: Grundlagen der Jungschen Psychotherapie*. Düsseldorf: Walter.

Kirsch, T. (2002). Jungian diaspora. *The Psychoanalytic Review*, *89*(5), 715–720.

Kirsch, T. (2004). Cultural complexes in Jung and Freud. In T. Singer & S. L. Kimbles (Eds.), *The cultural complex* (pp. 185–196). New York: Routledge.

Kirsch, T. (2016). Jung's relationship with Jews and Judaism. In E. Kiehl, M. Saban, & A. Samuels (Eds.), *Analysis and activism: Political contributions of Jungian psychology*. London: Routledge.

Kluckhohn, C. (1953). *Universal categories of culture. In anthropology today: An encyclopedic inventory*. Chicago: University of Chicago Press.

Kluckhohn, C. (1960). Recurrent themes in myth and mythmaking. In H. A. Murray (Ed.), *Myth and mythmaking* (pp. 46–60). New York: Braziller.

Kluckhohn, C. (1965). *Culture and behavior*. New York: Free Press.

Knox, J. (2001). Memories, fantasies, archetypes: An exploration of some connections between cognitive science and AP. *Journal of AP, 46*(4), 613–635.

Knox, J. (2003). *Archetype, attachment, analysis: Jungian psychology and the emergent mind*. New York: Brunner-Routledge.

Knox, J. (2004). From archetypes to reflective function. *Journal of AP, 49*(1), 1–19.

Knox, J. (2009a). The Analytic Relationship: Integrating Jungian, attachment theory and developmental perspectives. *British Journal of Psychotherapy, 25*(1), 5–23.

Knox, J. (2009b). Mirror neurons and embodied simulation in the development of archetypes and self-agency. *Journal of AP, 54*(3), 307–323.

Krafft-Ebing, R. V. (1886). *Psychopathia Sexualis*. München: Kindler.

Krause, J. (2019). *Die Reise unserer Gene: Eine Geschichte über uns und unsere Vorfahren (The journey of our genes. A story about us and our ancestors)*. Berlin: Propyläen.

Krieger, N. (2019). A dynamic systems approach to the feeling toned complex. *Journal of AP, 64*(5), 738–760.

Kugler, P. (1990). The unconscious in a postmodern depth psychology. In K. Barnaby & P. D'Acierno (Eds.), *C. G. Jung and the humanities. Toward a hermeneutics of culture* (pp. 307–318). Princeton: Princeton University Press.

Kugler, P. (1992). The primacy of archetypal structures: The paradigm shift from substance to relations. In R. K. Papadopoulos (Ed.), *Carl Gustav Jung – critical assessments* (Vol. 4). London: Routledge.

Kugler, P. (2003). Psyche, language and biology: The argument for a co-evolutionary approach. In R. Withers (Ed.), *Controversies in AP* (pp. 265–277). Hove and New York: Brunner Routledge.

Lambert, K. (1992). Archetypes, object-relations and internal objects. In R. K. Papadopoulos (Ed.), *Carl-Gustav Jung – critical assessments* (Vol. 2). London: Routledge.

Le Doux, J. (2012). Rethinking the emotional brain. *Neuron, 73*(4), 653–676.

Leroi-Gourhan, A. (1964). *Les religions de la préhistoire: paléolithique*. Paris: Presses Universitaires de France.

Lesmeister, R. (2001). Neuer Mensch"und faschistische Ideologie – einige Entwicklungslinien und Konvergenzen in C. G. Jungs psychologischer Theorie. *Analytische Psychologie, 32*, 148–157.

Levi-Strauss, C. (1949). *Structures élémentaires de la parenté*. Paris: Mouton. (*The elementary structures of kinship*. London: Eyre & Spottiswoode, 1969).

Levi-Strauss, C. (1970). *The raw and the cooked. Introduction to a science of mythology* (Vol. 1). London: Jonathan Cape.

Levi-Strauss, C. (1976). *Structural anthropology*. New York: Basic Books.

Levy-Bruhl, L. (1912/1921). *Les fonctions mentales dans les sociétés inférieures*. Paris: Presses universitaire de France.

Lewin, R. (2009). The origin of agriculture and the first villagers. In *Human evolution: An illustrated introduction* (5th ed.). Malden, MA: John Wiley & Sons.

Lewis-Williams, D. J., & Clottes, J. (1998). The mind in the cave – the case in the mind: Altered consciousness in the upper Paleolithic. *Anthropology of Consciousness, 9*(1), 13–21.

Lichtenberg, J. D., Lachmann, F. M., & Fosshage, J. L. (2009). *Self and motivational systems: Towards a theory of psychoanalytic technique*. London: Routledge.

Lichter, C. (Ed.). (2005). *How did farming reach Europe? Anatolian European relations from the second half of the seventh through the first half of the 6th millenium BC. Proceedings of the international workshop Istanbul 2004*. Istanbul: Ege Yayinlari.

Lickliter, R. (2017). Developmental evolution: Rethinking stability and variation in biological systems. In N. Budwig, E. Turiel, & P. Zelazo (Eds.), *New perspectives on human development* (pp. 88–105). New York: Cambridge University Press.

Liebermann, P. (1993). *Uniquely human. The evolution of speech, thought, and selfless behavior*. Cambridge: Harvard University Press.

Loomans, P. (Ed.). (2020). *Licht und Schatten der Meister. Karlfried Graf Dürckheim und C. G. Jung (Light and shadow of the masters)*. Giessen: Psychosozial Verlag.

Lorenz, K. (1941). Vergleichende Bewegungsstudien an Anatiden. *Journal of Ornithology, 89*, 194–294.

Lorenz, K. (1965). *Evolution and the modification of behavior*. Chicago: University of Chicago Press.

Lorenzer, A. (1973). *Sprachzerstörung und Rekonstruktion. Vorarbeiten zu einer Metatheorie der Psychoanalyse*. Frankfurt am Main: Suhrkamp.

Lütz, M. (2018). *Der Skandal der Skandale*. Freiburg: Herder.

Machalek, R., & Martin, M. W. (2004). Sociology and the second Darwinian revolution: A metatheoretical analysis. *Sociological Theory, 22*(3), 455–476.

Mair, V. (2006). *Contact and exchange in the ancient world*. Honolulu: University of Hawaii Press.

Malinowski, B. (1924). *Mutterrechtliche Familie und Ödipus-Komplex: eine psychoanalytische Studie*. Leipzig: Internationaler Psychoanalytischer Verlag.

Malinowski, B. (1948/1974). *Magic, science and religion and other essays*. London: Souvenir Press.

Marcus, G. (2004). *The birth of the mind: How a tiny number of genes creates the complexities of human thought*. New York: Baisc Books.

Markus, H. R., & Kitayama, S. (1991). Culture and the self: Implications for cognition, emotion and motivation. *Psychological Review, 98*(2), 224–253.

Markus, H. R., & Kitayama, S. (1998). The cultural psychology of personality. *Journal of Cross-Cultural Psychology, 29*, 63–87.

Marlowe, F. W. (2003). The mating system of foragers in the standard cross-cultural sample. *Cross-Cultural Research, 37*(3), 282–306.

Marlowe, F. W. (2005). Hunter-gatherers and human evolution. *Evolutionary Anthropology: Issues, News, and Reviews, 14*(2), 54–67.

Mathews, F. (1994). *The ecological self*. London: Routledge.

McCully, R. (1971). *Rorschach test and symbolism*. Baltimore: Williams & Wilkins.

McDougall, W. (1908/1963). *An introduction to social psychology*. London and Edinburgh: Morrison and Gibb.

McDowell, M. J. (2001). Principle of organization: A dynamic-systems view of the archetype-as-such. *Journal of AP, 46*(4), 637–654.

McGuire, W., & Sauerländer, W. (2012). *Sigmund Freud, C. G. Jung, Briefwechsel. 5. Auflage*. Frankfurt am Main: S. Fischer Verlag.

Meaney, M. J. (2010). Epigenetics and the biological definition of gene x environment interactions. *Child Development, 81*(1), 41–79.

Medtner, E. (1935). Bildnis der Persönlichkeit im Rahmen des gegenseitigen sich Kennenlernens. In Psychologischer Club Zürich (Ed.), *Die kulturelle Bedeutung der komplexen Psychologie* (pp. 516–616). Berlin: Julius Springer.

Meggers, B. J. (1975). The transpacific origin of Mesoamerican civilization: A preliminary review of the evidence and its theoretical implications. *American Anthropologist, 77*(1), 1–27.

Mehl, M. R., Vazire, S., Ranirez-Esparza, N., Slatcher, R. B., & Pennebacker, J. W. (2007). Are women really more talkative than men? *Science, 82,* 317–321.

Meier, C. A. (2001). *Atom and archetype. The Pauli/Jung letters 1932–1958.* Princeton and Oxford: Princeton University Press.

Merchant, J. (2006). The developmental/emergent model of archetype, its implications and its application to shamanism. *Journal of AP, 51*(1), 125–144.

Merchant, J. (2009). A reappraisal of classical archetype theory and its implications for theory and practice. *Journal of AP, 54*(3), 339–358.

Merchant, J. (2012). *Shamans and analysts. New Insights on the wounded healer.* London: Routledge.

Merchant, J. (2016). The image schema and innate archetypes: Theoretical and clinical implications, *Journal of AP, 61*(1), 63–78.

Merchant, J. (2019). The controversy around the concept of archetypes and the place for an emergent/developmental model. *Journal of AP, 64*(5), 701–719.

Merchant, J. (2020). Archetypes and the impoverished environment argument: A response to Goodwyn. *Journal of AP, 66*(1), 132–152.

Mesman, J., van Ijzendoorn, M. H., & Sagi-Schwartz, A. (2018). Cross-cultural patterns of attachment. Universal and contextual dimensions. In J. Cassidy & P. R. Shaver (Eds.), *Handbook of attachment. Theory, research and clinical applications* (3rd ed., pp. 852–877). New York and London: Guilford.

Metzger, W. (1954). *Psychologie. Die Entwicklung ihrer Grundannahmen seit der Einführung des Experiments.* Darmstadt: Steinkopff.

Meyer, A. (2015). *Adams Apfel und Evas Erbe. Wie die Gene unser Leben bestimmen und warum Frauen anders sind als Männer.* München: Bertelsmann.

Miller, D. L. (1990). An other Jung and an other . . . In K. Barnaby & P. D'Acierno (Eds.), *C. G. Jung and the humanities. Toward a hermeneutics of culture* (pp. 325–339). Princeton: Princeton University Press.

Mills, J. (2018). The essence of archetypes. *International Journal of Jungian Studies, 10*(3), 1–22.

Mills, J. (2019). The myth of a collective unconscious. *Journal of the History of Behavioral Sciences, 55,* 40–53.

Mithen, S. (2003). *After the Ice. A global history 20 000–5 000 BC.* London: Weidenfeld & Nicolson.

Morgan, L. H. (1877). *Ancient society: Or, researches in the line of human progress from savagery through barbarism to civilization.* Chicago: C. H. Kerr.

Müller, K. F. (1983). *Menschenbilder früher Gesellschaften. Ethnologische Studien zum Verhältnis von Mensch und Natur.* Frankfurt am Main: Campus.

Müller-Schneider, T. (2019). *Liebe, Glück und menschliche Natur (love, happiness, and human nature).* Gießen: Psychosozial-Verlag.

Murdock, G. P. (1945). The common denominator of cultures. In R. Linton (Ed.), *The science of man in the world crisis* (pp. 123–142). New York: Columbia University Press.

Murdock, G. P. (1967a). Ethnographic atlas: A summary. *Ethnology, 6,* 109–236.

Murdock, G. P. (1967b). *Ethnographic atlas: A summary.* Pittsburgh: The University of Pittsburgh Press.

Murdock, G. P., & White, D. R. (1969). Standard cross-cultural sample. *Ethnology, 8*(4), 329–369.

Murray, H. (without publication year). Interview by Gene Nameche. C.G. Jung Biographical Archive. *Countway library of medicine, Harvard University.* Cambridge, MA. https://cms.www.countway.harvard.edu/wp/?p=3208

Naroll, R. (1965). Galton's problem: The logic of cross cultural analysis. *Social Research, 32,* 428–451.

Naroll, R., & Sipes, R. (1973). Standard ethnographic sample. *Current Anthropology, 14*(1), 111–140.

Narr, K. J. (2021, December 16). *Prehistoric religion.* Encyclopedia Brittannica Online. www.britannica.com/topic/prehistoric-religion

Neher, A. (1996). Jung's theory of archetypes: A critique. *Journal of Humanistic Psychology, 36*(2), 61–91.

Neumann, E. (1949). *Ursprungsgeschichte des Bewußtseins.* Zürich: Rascher. (*The origins and history of consciousness,* Princeton: Princeton University Press, 1966).

Neumann, E. (1963). *The great mother: An analysis of the archetype.* London: Pantheon.

Neville, B. (1992). The charm of Hermes: Hillman, Lyotard, and the postmodern condition, *Journal of AP, 37,* 337–353.

Nietzsche, F. (1967ff.). *Werke. Kritische Gesamtausgabe (KGW). Hg. von Giorgio Colli und Mazzino Montinari.* Berlin und New York: De Gruyter.

Noble, K. G., Housten, S. M., Brito, N. H., Bartsch, H., Kan, E., Kuperman, J. M., et al. (2015). Family income, parental education and brain structure in children and adolescents. *Nature Neuroscience, 18*(5), 211–218.

Norenzayan, A., & Heine, S. J. (2006). *Psychological universals: What are they and how can we know?* [Unpublished paper]. University of British Columbia.

Northoff, G. (2015). Sozial eingebettetes Gehirn (social embedded brain) und relationales Selbst. In H. Böker, P. Hartwich & G. Northoff (Eds.), *Neuropsychodynamische Psychiatrie* (pp. 59–66). Berlin, Heidelberg.

Obrist, W. (1990). *Archetypen: Natur- und Kulturwissenschaften bestätigen C. G. Jung.* Olten: Walter Verlag.

Oestigaard, T. (2011). Cosmogony. In T. Insoll (Ed.), *Oxford handbook of the archeology of ritual ad religion* (pp. 76–88). Oxford: Oxford University Press.

Panksepp, J. (1998). *Affective neuroscience: The foundations of human and animal emotions.* Oxford: Oxford University Press.

Panksepp, J. (2011). The basic emotional circuits of mammalian brains: Do animals have affective lives? *Neuroscience and Biobehavioral Reviews, 35*(9), 1791–1804.

Panksepp, J., Lane, R. D., Solms, M., & Smith, R. (2017). Reconciling cognitive and affective neuroscience perspectives on the brain basis of emotional experience. *Neuroscience and Biobehavioral Reviews, 76,* 187–215.

Papadopoulos, R. (Ed.). (1992b). *Carl Gustav Jung. Critical assessments. Vol. 2: The structure and dynamics of the psyche.* London and New York: Routledge.

Papadopoulos, R. (Ed.). (1992a). *Carl Gustav Jung. Critical assessments. Vol. 1: Jung and his method in context.* London and New York: Routledge.

Paul, R. A. (2015). *Mixed messages. Cultural and genetic inheritance in the constitution of human society.* Chicago: Chicago University Press.

Penke, L., & Asendorpf, J. B. (2008). Beyond global sociosexual orientations: A more differentiated look at sociosexuality and its effects in courtship and romantic relationships. *Journal of Personality and Social Psychology, 95*(5), 1113–1135.

Pettitt, P. (2011). Religion and ritual in the lower and middle Paleolithic. In T. Insoll (Ed.), *Oxford handbook of the archeology of ritual ad religion* (pp. 329–343). Oxford: Oxford University Press.

Petzold, H. G., Orth, I., & Sieper, J. (2014). *Mythen, Macht und Psychotherapie*. Bielefeld: Aisthesis.

Pfaff, D. W. (2013). *Neuroscience in the 21st century*. Heidelberg: Springer.

Pietikainen, P. (1998). Archetypes as symbolic forms. *Journal of Analytical Psycholgoy, 43*(3), 325–343.

Pigliucci, M. (Ed.). (2010). *Evolution, the extended synthesis*. Cambridge, MA: MIT Press.

Pinker, S. (2002). *The Blank Slate: The modern denial of human nature*. New York: Viking.

Pinker, S. (2010). The cognitive niche: Coevolution of intelligence, sociality, and language. *Proceedings of the National Academy of Science of the United States of America, 107*(2), 8993–8999.

Plomin, R., DeFries, J. C., Knopik, V. S., & Neiderhiser, J. M. (2013). *Behavioral genetics*. New York: Worth.

Polan, H. J., & Hofer, M. A. (2018). Psychobiological origins of infant attachment and its role in development. In J. Cassidy & P. R. Shaver (Eds.), *Handbook of attachment. Theory, research and clinical applications* (3rd ed., pp. 117–132). New York and London: Guilford.

Proce, N. (2011). Shamanism. In I. Timothy (Ed.), *Oxford handbook of the archaeology of ritual and religion* (pp. 983–1003). Oxford: Oxford University Press.

Reid, J. C. (Ed.). (2001). *Jung, my mother and I. The analytic diaries of Catherine Rush Cabot*. Einsiedeln: Daimon.

Renfrew, C., & Bahn, P. (2004). *Archaeology: Theories, methods and practice* (4th ed.). London: Thames and Hudson.

Richerson, P. J., & Boyd, R. (2005). *Not by genes alone. How culture transformed human evolution*. Chicago: Chicago University Press.

Richerson, P. J., & Christiansen, M. H. (2013). *Cultural evolution. Society, technology, language, and religion*. Cambridge: MIT Press.

Richter, D. (2005). Das Scheitern der Biologisierung der Soziologie. *KZfSS Kölner Zeitschrift für Soziologie und Sozialpsychologie, 57*(3), 523–542.

Rippon, G. (2019). *The gendered brain: The new neuroscience that shatters the myth of the female brain*. New York: Random House.

Roesler, C. (2006). A narratological methodology for identifying archetypal story patterns in autobiographical narratives. *The Journal of AP, 51*(4), 574–596.

Roesler, C. (2008). The self in cyberspace. Identity formation in postmodern societies and Jung's self as an objective psyche. *Journal of AP, 53*, 421–436.

Roesler, C. (2010a). *Analytische Psychologie heute: Der aktuelle Stand der Forschung zur Psychologie C. G. Jungs*. Basel: Karger Verlag.

Roesler, C. (2010b). Archetypal patterns in postmodern identity construction – a cultural approach. In R. Jones & M. Stein (Eds.), *Identities in transition*. London: Routledge.

Roesler, C. (2012a). Are archetypes transmitted more by culture than biology? Questions arising from conceptualizations of the archetype. *Journal of Analytical Psychoogy, 57*(2), 223–246.

Roesler, C. (2012b). Archetypen – Ein zentrales Konzept der Analytischen Psychologie. *Analytische Psychologie, 170, 43*(4), 487–509.

Roesler, C. (2012c). A revision of Jung's theory of archetypes in the light of contemporary research: Neurosciences, genetics and cultural theory – a reformulation. In P. Bennett (Ed.), *Facing multiplicity: Psyche, nature, culture. Proceedings of the XVIIIth congress of the international association for AP, Montreal 2010*. Einsiedeln: Daimon.

Roesler, C. (2013). Das gemeinsame Unbewußte – Unbewußte Austausch- und Synchro-nisierungsprozesse in der Psychotherapie und in nahen Beziehungen. *Analytische Psychologie, 44*(4), 464–483.

Roesler, C. (2014a). A research frame for investigating the appearance of synchronistic events in psychotherapy. In H. Atmanspacher & C. Fuchs (Ed.), *The Pauli-Jung dialogue and its impact today*. Exeter: Imprint Academic.

Roesler, C. (2016). *Das Archetypenkonzept C. G. Jungs. Theorie, Forschung, Anwendung*. Stuttgart: Kohlhammer.

Roesler, C. (2017a). Complex (Jung). In V. Zeigler-Hill & T. K. Shackelford (Eds.), *Encyclopedia of personality and individual differences*. New York: Springer.

Roesler, C. (2017b). Synchronicity. In V. Zeigler-Hill & T. K. Shackelford (Eds.), *Encyclopedia of personality and individual differences*. New York: Springer.

Roesler, C. (2018a). Synchronistic experiences in psychotherapy: An ongoing study. In C. Roesler (Ed.), *Research in AP*. London. Routledge.

Roesler, C. (Ed.). (2018b). *Research in analytical psychology: Empirical research*. London: Routledge.

Roesler, C. (2018c). Dream content corresponds with dreamer's psychological problems and personality structure and with improvement in psychotherapy. A typology of dream patterns in dream series of patients in analytical psychotherapy. *Dreaming, 28*(4), 303–321.

Roesler, C. (2019a). Theoretical foundations of AP – recent developments and controversies. Papers of the Basel IAAP conference. *Journal of AP, 64*(5), 658–681.

Roesler, C. (2019b). Jungian theory of dreaming and contemporary dream research – findings from the research project 'structural dream analysis'. *Journal of AP, 65*(1), 44–62.

Roesler, C. (2019c). Narratives of transformation: The structural dream analysis method. In R. A. Jones & L. Gardner (Eds.), *Narratives of individuation* (pp. 205–219). London: Routledge.

Roesler, C. (2020a). Jungian theory of dreaming and contemporary dream research – findings from the research project "Structural Dream Analysis". In E. Kiehl (Ed.), *Encountering the other. Proceedings of the twenty-first congress of the international association for AP, Vienna 2019* (pp. 51–68). Einsiedeln: Daimon.

Roesler, C. (2020b). The structural approach to the empirical investigation of the meaning of dreams – Findings from the research project „Structural Dream Analysis". *International Journal of Dream Research, 13*(1), 46–55.

Roesler, C. (2021). *The archetype concept of C. G. Jung – theory, research, and applications*. London: Routledge.

Roesler, C. (2023). Response to Erik Goodwyn's paper 'Phenotypic plasticity and archetype: A response to common objections to the biological theory of archetype and instinct'. *Journal of Analytical Psychology*. https://doi.org/10.1111/1468-5922.12881

Roesler, C., Konakawa, H., & Tanaka, Y. (2021). Differences in dream content and structure between Japanese and Western dreams. *International Journal of Dream Research, 14*(2), 195–201.

Roesler, C., & Reefschläger, G. I. (2022). Jungian psychotherapy, spirituality, and synchronicity: Theory, applications, and evidence base. *Psychotherapy, 59*(3), 339–350. https://doi.org/10.1037/pst0000402

Roesler, C., & Sotirova-Kohli, M. (2014). Das psychische Erbe der Menschheit – Forschungsstand und laufende empirische Studien zum Archetypenkonzept C. G. Jungs. *Forum der Psychoanalyse, 30*(2), 133–155.

Roesler, C., & van Uffelen, B. (2018). Complexes and the unconscious: From the association experiment to recent fMRI studies. In C. Roesler (Ed.), *Research in AP*. London. Routledge.

Rosen, D. H. (1992). Inborn basis for the healing doctor-patient relationship. *The Pharos*, 55(4), 17–21.

Rosen, D. H., Mascaro, N., Arnau, R., Escamilla, M., Tai-Seale, M., Ficht, A., et al. (2010). Depression in medical students: Gene-environment interactions. *Annals of Behavioural science and Medical Education*, 16(2), 8–14.

Rosen, D. H., Smith, S. M., Huston, H. L., & Gonzalez, G. (1991). Empirical study of associations between symbols and their meanings: Evidence of collective unconscious (archetypal) memory. *Journal of AP*, 36(2), 211–228.

Roth, G. (2019). Neurobiologische Grundlagen unbewußter Prozesse und Bedeutung für die Psychotherapie. In B. Haslinger & B. Janta (Eds.), *Der unbewußte Mensch. Zwischen Psychoanalyse und neurobiologischer Evidenz* (pp. 23–54). Giessen: Psychosozial Verlag.

Rothbaum, F., Weisz, J., Pott, M., Miyake, K., & Morelli, G. (2000). Attachment and culture: Security in the United States and Japan. *American Psychologist*, 55(10), 1093–1104.

Saban, M. (2019). Jung's personal myth and the two personalities. In R. A. Jones & L. Gardner (Eds.), *Narratives of individuation*. London: Routledge.

Samuels, A. (1983). The theory of archetypes in Jungian and post-Jungian AP. *International Review of Psychoanalysis, 10*.

Samuels, A. (1985). *Jung and the Post-Jungians*. London: Routledge and Kegan Paul.

Samuels, A. (1990). Beyond the feminine principle. In K. Barnaby & P. D'Acierno (Eds.), *C. G. Jung and the humanities. Toward a hermeneutics of culture* (pp. 294–306). Princeton: Princeton University Press.

Samuels, A. (1994). "A Jung club is not enough": The professionalisation of AP 1913–1957 and its implications for today. *Harvest, 40*, 155–167.

Samuels, A. (1998). Will the Post-Jungians survive? In A. Casement (Ed.), *Post-Jungians today* (pp. 15–32). Lomdon: Routledge.

Samuels, A. (2017). The future of Jungian analysis: Strengths, weaknesses, opportunities, threats (SWOT). *Journal of AP*, 62(5), 636–649.

Samuels, A., Shorter, B., & Plaut, F. (1986). *A critical dictionary of Jungian analysis*. London: Routledge and Kegan Paul.

Sanday, P. R. (1981). *Female power and male dominance*. Cambridge and New York: Cambridge University Press.

Saunders, P., & Skar, P. (2001). Archetypes, complexes and self-organisation. *Journal of AP*, 46(2), 305–323.

Sanderson, S. K. (2014). *Human nature and the evolution of society*. Boulder, CO: Westview Press.

Saunders, P., & Skar, P. (2001). Archetypes, complexes and self-organization. *Journal of AP*, 46(2), 305–323.

Schmidt, K. (2016). *Sie bauten die ersten Tempel*. München: Beck.

Schwartz-Salant, N. (1998). *The mystery of human relationship*. New York: Routledge.

Scull, A. (2021). American psychiatry in the new millennium: A critical appraisal. *Psychological Medicine*, 51(16), 1–9.

Seghier, M. L., & Price, C. J. (2018). Interpreting and utilizing intersubjective variability in brain function. *Trends of Cognitive Science*, 22(6), 71–82.

Shamdasani, S. (1992). Two unknown early cases of Jung. *Harvest, 38,* 38–43.

Shamdasani, S. (1998). *Cult fictions. C. G. Jung and the founding of AP.* London: Routledge.

Shamdasani, S. (2003). *Jung and the making of modern psychology: The dream of a science.* Cambridge: Cambridge University Press.

Sharp, D. (1991). *Jung Lexicon.* www.psychceu.com/Jung/sharplexicon.html

Shelburne, W. A. (1988). *Mythos and Logos in the thought of Carl Jung. The theory of the collective unconscious in scientific perspective.* Albany: State University of New York Press.

Shihui, H., Northoff, G., Vogeley, K., & Wexler, B. E. (2012). A cultural neuroscience approach to the biosocial nature of the human brain. *Annual Review of Psychology, 64*(1).

Shukurov, A., Sarson, G. R., & Gangal, K. (2014). The Near-Eastern roots of the neolithic in South Asia. *PLoS One. 9*(5), e95714.

Sidoli, M. (1989). *The unfolding self: Separation and individuation.* Boston: Sigo. Press.

Siegel, D. J. (1999). *The developing mind: Toward a neurobiology of interpersonal experience.* New York: Guilford Press.

Simpson, J. A., & Belsky, J. (2018). Attachment theory within a modern evolutionary framework. In J. Cassidy & P. R. Shaver (Eds.), *Handbook of attachment. Theory, research and clinical applications* (3rd ed., pp. 91–116). New York and London: Guilford.

Singer, T., & Kimbles, S. L. (Eds.). (2004a). *The cultural complex.* New York: Routledge.

Singer, T., & Kimbles, S. L. (2004b). Emerging theory of cultural complexes. In J. Cambray & L. Carter (Eds.), *AP: Contemporary perspectives in Jungian psychology.* Hove and New York: Brunner-Routledge.

Skar, P. (2004). Chaos and self-organization: Emergent patterns at critical life transitions. *Journal of AP, 49,* 245–264.

Smith, R. C. (1996). *The wounded Jung. Effects of Jung's relationships on his life and work.* Evanston: Northwestern University Press.

Solms, M. (2015). *The feeling brain: Selected papers on neuropsychoanalysis.* London: Karnac books.

Solms, M. (2016). Consciousness by surprise: A neuropsychoanalytic approach to the hard problem. In R. Poznanski (Ed.), *Biophysics of consciousness: A foundational approach.* New York: World Scientific.

Solms, M., & Panksepp, J. (2012). The "id" knows more then the "ego" admits: Neuropsychoanalytic and primal consciousness perspectives on the interface between affective and cognitive neuroscience. *Brain Sciences, 2*(2), 147–175.

Solomon, H. M. (1997). The developmental school. In P. Young-Eisendrath & T. Dawson (Eds.), *The Cambridge companion to Jung* (pp. 119–140). Cambridge: Cambridge University Press.

Sorenson, J. L., & Johannessen, C. L. (2006). Biological evidence for pre-Columbian transoceanic voyages. In V. Mair (Ed.), *Contact and exchange in the ancient world.* Honolulu: University of Hawaii Press.

Sotirova-Kohli, M. (2018). Experimental approaches to the study of the archetype. In C. Roesler (Ed.), *Research in analytical psychology.* London: Routledge.

Sotirova-Kohli, M., Roesler, C., Opwis, K., Smith, S., Rosen, D., & Djonov, V. (2013). Symbol/meaning paired-associate recall: An "archetypal memory" advantage? *Behavioral Science, 3*(4), 541–561.

Sotirova-Kohli, M., Rosen, D. H., Smith, S. M., Henderson, P., Taki-Reece, S. (2011). Empirical study of kanji as archetypal images: Understanding the collective unconscious as part of the Japanese language. *Journal of AP, 56*(1), 109–132.

Spelke, E. (2010). Innateness, choice and language. In J. Frank & J. Bricmont (Eds.), *Chomsky notebook*. New York: Columbia University Press.

Spencer, H. (1876). *The principles of sociology, three volumes*. London: Williams and Norgate.

Spillmann, B., & Strubel, R. (2010). *C.G. Jung: Zerrissen zwischen Mythos und Wirklichkeit. Über die Folgen persönlicher und kollektiver Spaltungen im tiefenpsychologischen Erbe*. Gießen: Psychosozial Verlag.

Stadler, M., & Kruse, P. (1990). The self-organisation perspective in cognition research. In H. Haken & M. Stadler (Eds.), *Synergetics of cognition*. Berlin: Springer.

Stein, R. L., & Stein, P. L. (2008). *The anthropology of religion, magic, and witchcraft* (2nd ed.). Boston: Pearson.

Stern, D. (1985). *The interpersonal world of the infant: A view from psychoanalysis and developmental psychology*. New York: Basic Books.

Stevens, A. (1983). *Archetype: A natural history of the self*. New York: William Morrow.

Stevens, A. (2003). *Archetype revisited: An updated natural history of the self*. Toronto: Inner City Books.

Stevens, A. (2006). The archetypes. In R. K. Papadopoulos (Ed.), *The handbook of Jungian psychology: Theory, practice and applications*. London: Routledge.

Stevens, A., Hogenson, G., & Ramos, D. (2003). Debate: Psychology and biology. In M. A. Mattoon (Ed.), *Cambridge 2001 – proceedings of the XV. IAAP international congress* (pp. 367–377). Einsiedeln: Daimon.

Stevens, A., & Price, J. (1996). *Evolutionary psychiatry*. London: Routledge.

Storch, A. (1930). *Wege zur Welt und Existenz des Geisteskranken (ways of access to the world and existence of the mentally ill)*. Stuttgart: Hippokrates.

Tacey, D. (1998). Twisting and turning with James Hillman: From anima to world soul, from academia to pop. In A. Casement (Ed.), *Post-Jungians today: Key papers in contemporary AP*. London: Routledge.

Talalay, L. E. (1993). *Deities, dolls, and devices*. Indianapolis: University of Indiana Press.

Tann, M. von der & Erlenmeyer, A. (Hg.) (1993). *C. G. Jung und der Nationalsozialismus. Texte und Daten*. Berlin: unveröffentlichtes Manuskript im Auftrag der DGAP.

Tattersall, I. (1998). *Becoming human. Evolution and human uniqueness*. San Diego, New York and London: Oxford University Press.

Taylor, T. (2011). Death. In T. Insoll (Ed.), *Oxford handbook of the archeology of ritual ad religion* (pp. 89–104). Oxford: Oxford University Press.

Thomas, J. (2011). Ritual and religion in the Neolithic. In T. Insoll (Ed.), *Oxford handbook of the archeology of ritual ad religion* (pp. 371–386). Oxford: Oxford University Press.

Tinbergen, N. (1951). *The study of instinct*. New York: Oxford University Press.

Tomasello, M. (2021). *Becoming human. A theory of ontogeny*. Cambridge: The Belkany Press of Harvard University Press.

Trachsel, M. (2008). *Ur- und Frühgeschichte. Quellen, Methoden, Ziele (prehistory. Sources, methods, aims)*. Zürich: Orell Füssli.

Trevi, M. (1992). Towards a critical approach to Jung. In R. K. Papadopoulos (Ed.), *Carl Gustav Jung: Critical assessments* (Vol. I., pp. 356–375). Hove: Psychology Press.

Turner, V. (1974). *Dramas, fields and metaphors: Symbolic action in human society*. Ithaca and London: Cornell University Press.

Turner, V. (1991). *The ritual process. Structure and antistructure*. Ithaca: Cornell University Press.

Tylor, E. B. (1871). *Primitive culture: Researches into the development of mythology, philosophy, religion, art, and custom* (2 vols.). London: Murray.

Üther, H.-J. (2011). *The types of international folktales*. Helsinki, Finland: Academia Scientiarum Fennica.

Van Binsbergen, W. M. J. (2007). Transcontinental mythological patterns in prehistory. *Cosmos, 23*, 29–80.

Van Eewynk, J. R. (1991). Archetypes: The strange attractors of the psyche. *Journal of AP, 36*(1), 1–25.

Van Eewynk, J. R. (1997). *Archetypes and strange attractors: The chaotic world of symbols*. Toronto: Inner City Books.

Van Gennep, A. (1909). *Les Rites de Passage*. Paris: Nourry.

Van Meurs, J. (1990). A survey of Jungian literary criticism in English. In K. Barnaby & P. D'Acierno (Eds.), *C. G. Jung and the humanities. Toward a hermeneutics of culture* (pp. 238–250). Princeton: Princeton University Press.

Van Schaik, C., & Michel, K. (2020). *Die Wahrheit über Eva. Die Erfindung der Ungleichheit von Frauen und Männern*. Hamburg: Rowohlt.

Vaughn, B. E., & Bost, K. K. (2018). Attachment and temperaments intersecting developmental projects and interacting developmental contexts throughout infancy and childhood. In J. Cassidy & P. R. Shaver (Eds.), *Handbook of attachment. Theory, research and clinical applications* (3rd ed., pp. 202–222). New York and London: Guilford.

Verhoeven, M. (2011). The many dimensions of ritual. In T. Insoll (Ed.), *Oxford handbook of the archeology of ritual ad religion* (pp. 115–132). Oxford: Oxford University Press.

Von Franz, M.-L. (1970). *The problem of the puer aeternus*. New York: Spring Publications.

Von Franz, M.-L. (1980). The hypothesis of the collective unconscious. In W. H. Kennedy (Ed.), *Projection and re-collection in Jungian psychology* (pp. 77–95). La Salle: Open Court.

Walach, H., Schmidt, S., & Jonas, W. B. (Eds.) (2011). *Neuroscience, consciousness and spirituality*. New York: Springer.

Walch, G. M. (2005). Ursprungsgeschichte des Bewußtseins von Erich Neumann. In Österreichische Gesellschaft für Analytische Psychologie (Ed.), *Zur Utopie einer neuen Ethik. 100 Jahre Erich Neumann. Kongressband* (pp. 162–181). Wien: Baiculescu and Mandelbaum.

Walker, R. S., Hill, K. R., Flinn, M. V., & Ellsworth, R. M. (2011). Evolutionary history of hunter-gatherer marriage practices. *PLoS One, 6*(4). e19066.

Weiss, K. M. (2018). The tales genes tell (or not): A century of exploration. *American Journal of Physical Anthropology, 165*(4), 741–753.

Westen, D., & Morrison, K. (2001). A multidimensional meta-analysis of treatments for depression, panic, and generalized anxiety disorder. *Journal of Consulting and Clinical Psychology, 69*, 875–899.

Wharton, B. (1985). Show me another reality! The need for a containing ego. *Journal of AP, 30*(3), 273–295.

Wheelwright, J. (1984). In conversation with Joseph Wheelwright. Interview by David Serbin. *Psychological Perspectives, 15*(2), 149–167.

Whitehead, A. N. (1916). The organization of thought. *Science, 44*(1134), 409–419.

Wilson, E. O. (1975). *Sociobiology: The new synthesis*. Cambridge, MA: Harvard University Press.

Wilson, E. O. (2012). *The social conquest of earth*. New York: Liveright.

Winnicott, D. W. (1964). Review of memories, dreams, reflections by C.G. Jung. *International Journal of Psychoanalysis, 45*, 450–455.

Withley, D. S. (2011). Rock art, religion, and ritual. In T. Insoll (Ed.), *Oxford handbook of the archeology of ritual ad religion* (pp. 307–328). Oxford: Oxford University Press.

Witzel, M. (2012). *The origins of the world's mythologies*. Oxford: Oxford University Press.

Wlodarski, R., Manning, J., & Dunbar, R. I. M. (2015). Stay or stray? Evidence for alternative mating strategy phenotypes in both men and women. *Biology Letters*, *11*(2).

Wolfradt, U. (2021). Psyche im kulturellen Spannungsfeld zwischen Universalismus und Relativismus. *Psychosozial*, *44*(3), 10–23.

Wunn, I. (2005). *Die Religionen in vorgeschichtlicher Zeit (The religions in prehistoric times)*. Stuttgart: Kohlhammer.

Wunn, I. (2019). *Barbaren, Geister, Gotteskrieger. Die Evolution der Religionen entschlüsselt (The evolution of religions)*. Berlin: Springer.

Young, F. W. (1965). *Initiation ceremonies: A cross-cultural study of status dramatization*. Indianapolis: University of Indiana Press.

Young-Eisendrath, P., & Dawson, T. (Eds.). (1997). *The Cambridge companion to Jung*. Cambridge: Cambridge University Press.

Zabriskie, B. (1990). The feminine. Pre- and post-Jungian. In K. Barnaby & P. D'Acierno (Eds.), *C. G. Jung and the humanities. Toward a hermeneutics of culture* (pp. 267–278). Princeton: Princeton University Press.

Zietsch, B. P., Westberg, L., Santtila, P., & Jern, P. (2015). Genetic analysis of human extra-pair mating: Heritability, between-sex correlation, and receptor genes for vasopressin and exytocin. *Evolution and Human Behavior*, *36*(2), 130–136.

Zinkin, L. (1991). The Klein connection in the London school: The search for origins. *Journal of AP*, *36*, 37–62.

Zoja, L. (1989). *Drugs, addiction and initiation. The modern search for ritual*. Boston: Sigo Press.

Züchner, C. (2009). Rezension von (review of) Aujoulat. *Germania*, *87*(1), 277–279.

Index

Note: Page numbers in *italic* indicate a figure on the corresponding page.

For Product Safety Concerns and Information please contact our EU
representative GPSR@taylorandfrancis.com
Taylor & Francis Verlag GmbH, Kaufingerstraße 24, 80331 München, Germany